Journeys of Fear
Refugee Return and National Transformation in Guatemala

Understanding democracy, human rights, and development in the conflict-ridden societies of the third world is at the heart of *Journeys of Fear*, a stimulating collection of papers prepared by Canadian and Guatemalan scholars.

Edited and with contributions by Liisa North and Alan Simmons, this collection explores the participation of the oppressed and marginalised Guatemalan refugees, most of them indigenous Mayas who fled from the army's razed-earth campaign of the early 1980s, in government negotiations regarding the conditions for return. The essays adopt the refugees' language concerning return – defining it as a self-organized and participatory collective act that is very different from repatriation, a passive process often organized by others with the objective of reintegration into the status quo. Contributors examine the extent to which the organized returnees and other social organizations with similar objectives have been successful in transforming Guatemalan society, creating greater respect for political, social, and economic rights. They also consider the obstacles to democratization in a country just emerging from a history of oppressive dictatorships and a thirty-six-year-long civil war.

LIISA L. NORTH is professor of political science and a fellow of the Centre for Research on Latin America and the Caribbean at York University.

ALAN B. SIMMONS is associate professor of sociology and a fellow of the Centre for Research on Latin America and the Caribbean at York University.

© McGill-Queen's University Press 1999
ISBN 0-7735-1861-4 (cloth)
ISBN 0-7735-1862-2 (paper)

Legal deposit fourth quarter 1999
Bibliothèque nationale du Québec

Printed in Canada on acid-free paper

McGill-Queen's University Press acknowledges the financial support of the Government of Canada through the Book Publishing Industry Development Program (BPIDP) for its activities. We also acknowledge the support of the Canada Council for the Arts for its publishing program.

Canadian Cataloguing in Publication Data

Main entry under title:
   Journeys of fear: Refugee return and national
transformation in Guatemala
   Includes bibliographical references.
   ISBN 0-7735-1861-4 (bound)
   ISBN 0-7735-1862-2 (pbk.)
   1. Guatemala – Politics and government – 1985–
   2. Return migration – Guatemala. 3. Guatemala –
Economic conditions – 1985– 4. Guatemala –
Social conditions. 5. Mayas – Guatemala –
Government relations. I. North, Liisa, 1940–
   II. Simmons, Alan
   F1466.7.J68 1999   972.8105'3   C99-900745-9

Typeset in 10/12 Baskerville by Acappella

Journeys of Fear

Refugee Return and National Transformation in Guatemala

Edited by

LIISA L. NORTH
AND ALAN B. SIMMONS

McGill-Queen's University Press
Montreal & Kingston · London · Ithaca

To the memory of Myrna Mack
For her courageous work on behalf of the refugees
and displaced people of Guatemala

Contents

Tables and Maps xi

Preface xiii

1 Fear and Hope: Return and Transformation in Historical Perspective / 3
LIISA L. NORTH AND ALAN B. SIMMONS

PART ONE PERSPECTIVES ON THE NATIONAL POLITICAL-ECONOMIC SETTING

2 Reflections on the Problems of Democracy in Guatemala / 31
RENÉ POITEVIN

3 Land and Peace: Two Points of View / 40
GONZALO DE VILLA AND W. GEORGE LOVELL

PART TWO NEGOTIATING AND MONITORING THE PEACE: NATIONAL AND INTERNATIONAL DIMENSIONS

4 Paradigms of Negotiation and Democratization in Guatemala / 57
MARCO FONSECA

5 Maximizing the Benefits of UN Involvement in the Guatemala Peace Process / 74
STEPHEN BARANYI

viii Contents

PART THREE LAND, LABOUR, AND MIGRATION

6 "Somos de la Tierra": Land and the Guatemalan Refugee Return / 95
BRIAN EGAN

7 Migration and the Displaced in Guatemala City in the Context of a Flawed National Transformation / 112
GISELA GELLERT

8 Exodus and Return with a Changing Migration System / 130
MANUEL ANGEL CASTILLO

PART FOUR IDENTITY AND COMMUNITY: GENDER, ETHNICITY, AND PLACE

9 The Unexpected Consequences of Violence: Rethinking Gender Roles and Ethnicity / 155
M. GABRIELA TORRES

10 To Whom Shall the Nation Belong? The Gender and Ethnic Dimension of Refugee Return and the Struggle for Peace in Guatemala / 176
ALISON CROSBY

11 Democratization and Popular Women's Organizations / 196
CATHY BLACKLOCK

12 Guatemalan Refugees and Returnees: Place and Maya Identity / 213
CATHERINE NOLIN HANLON

PART FIVE NGO NETWORKS AND GOVERNMENTAL ASSISTANCE

13 Theorizing Accompaniment / 237
BARRY LEVITT

14 Canadian Foreign Aid as Support for Human Rights and Democratization in Guatemala / 255
VIVIANA PATRONI AND JIM GRONAU

15 Concluding Reflections: Refugee Return, National Transformation, and Neoliberal Restructuring / 272
LIISA L. NORTH AND ALAN B. SIMMONS

Appendix: Acronyms 301
Bibliography 307
Contributors 333

Tables and Maps

TABLES

1 Internally Displaced People and Refugees, 1982/83 and 1990 / 17

2 Collective Refugee Returns Organized by the CCPP, 1993–July 1997 / 20

3 Official Guatemalan Census Returns, 1888–1994 / 51

4 Destination of Collective Returns, 1993–95 / 224

5 Distribution of CIDA-Financed Projects, by Sector / 262

6 Distribution of CIDA-Financed Projects, by Type of Organization / 262

MAPS

Settlements of the Ixcán Region, 1993 / 216

Refugee relocation to Campeche and Quintana Roo / 219

Location of refugee camps/settlements and returnee areas / 222

Preface

We dedicate this volume to the memory of Myrna Mack, a courageous Guatemalan social scientist who was assassinated in 1986, at a period in her life when her research and action on behalf of victims of human rights violations and genocide in her country was receiving widespread recognition. Her research sought to document the abuses and identify those responsible in the hope that this would open space for the construction of a new Guatemalan nation where human rights would be guaranteed, democracy would flourish, and peace would prevail. A decade after her death – and partly as a result of Mack's efforts and those of other pioneering human rights researchers in Guatemala – the situation has changed in the direction of her hopes. Continuing human rights abuses in Guatemala require the retention of rights as a central focus of research and action. Yet at this point we are also able to give attention to new research on the return of refugees and on the prospects for the ongoing fragile transition toward peace and democracy. These themes are the focus of the present volume. We hope that the process leading to the preparation of this volume has reflected the cooperative and forward-looking spirit of Myrna Mack's work.

The papers emerged as part of a joint project among several institutions, namely the Centre for Research on Latin America and the Caribbean (CERLAC) and the Centre for Refugee Studies (CRS), both at York University, the Guatemalan branch of the Latin American Faculty of Social Sciences (FLACSO-Guatemala), and the Association for the Advancement of Social Sciences in Guatemala (AVANCSO).

Myrna Mack was a founding member of AVANCSO, an organization that has been a leader in research on human rights and national transformation in Guatemala over the many years before and after her death.

Many of the researchers whose work appears in this volume come from the four centres just identified, and the former directors of both AVANCSO and FLACSO-Guatemala, Gonzalo de Villa and René Poiteven, contributed a statement and a chapter, respectively. Others come from a number of universities and research institutions with close ties to each other. Several of the authors are scholars who have recently completed their training. Their papers are based on graduate theses and dissertations, in several cases completed within the time frame and activities of the project (from 1993 to mid-1996). Other authors are well-established scholars. While the researchers involved cover a range of different backgrounds and interests, their collected work in this volume reflects a common hypothesis of "guarded optimism" regarding the direction of developments affecting human rights, peace, and democracy in Guatemala. This hypothesis (explained further in chapter 1) has two sides: a cautious one stressing the potential continuity of patterns of injustice, violence, corruption, and human rights abuses and another, more hopeful side pointing to changes within and outside Guatemala that may lead to an enduring transformation to peace and democratization.

The editors and all participants associated with this volume are indebted to the four research centres (AVANCSO, CERLAC, CRS, and FLACSO-Guatemala) that provided support. We also acknowledge with gratitude the grants from various sources that supported the travel and work of the researchers, specifically the Canadian International Development Agency (CIDA) (through the CRS), the Social Sciences and Humanities Research Council of Canada (SSHRCC), and York University (Small Grants Program). Finally, we wish to thank the CERLAC Secretariat for its generous assistance in the many tasks involved in the preparation of the manuscript for publication.

The preparation of the various chapters benefited from two workshops, one in 1994 and another in 1995, that brought together the authors and a number of other people with particular expertise and interest in the themes. The editors wish to thank all who participated in these useful exchanges, particularly Jim Handy, Frances Arbour, and José Herrán Lima, who served as outstanding commentators on, and supportive critics of, the work in progress; Victoria Foote and Virginia Smith at York University and especially Ron Curtis at McGill-Queen's for their editorial work on the volume; Brian Egan and Alison Crosby for their assistance in the organization of the workshops and their administrative backup in the management of this complex project, in addition to their intellectual contributions; Angus van Harten and Miguel Cifuents for always remembering to bring back publications from Guatemala; Gabriela Torres and Pablo Andrade for their assistance in the final stages of revisions; and Liddy Gomes, administrative assistant of CERLAC, who always responded cheerfully to our thousand and one requests for help. Finally, it should be noted that Alison Crosby, Liisa North, and Alan Simmons translated the chapters by Fonseca, Gellert, Poitevin, and de Villa from the Spanish.

Journeys of Fear

1 Fear and Hope: Return and Transformation in Historical Perspective

LIISA L. NORTH
AND ALAN B. SIMMONS

Guatemala's civil war was the most devastating of Central America's bloody conflicts of the last quarter of the twentieth century. At least 100,000 people were killed over the period of intense violence from the late 1970s through the early 1980s. In the same period, some 160,000 to 365,000 Guatemalans fled from war and massacres to find refuge in neighbouring countries. Most went to Mexico, but others went to adjacent countries of Central America; still many others went to the United States, and thousands went further to Canada. In addition to those who fled from the country in the early 1980s, more than a million people were forced out of their home communities and scattered throughout Guatemala when the army tried to crush rebellion with "scorched-earth" tactics. It was the country's indigenous people who took the brunt of the repression and made up the overwhelming majority of the displaced.

Guatemala's war also proved itself the most difficult to resolve. UN mediation culminated in peace accords and military demobilization in Nicaragua and El Salvador in the early 1990s, yet the peace process in Guatemala was much slower. Initial steps toward political dialogue followed upon the installation of an elected, civilian-led government in 1986, but subsequent progress in negotiations was fitful. The United Nations was not even invited to mediate until January 1994. A peace accord between the government (and military forces) and the armed insurgents was negotiated over several years and finally signed in December 1996.

Refugees gradually began to return as the peace process evolved. At first the numbers were very small, since those returning were still largely viewed as enemies by the army. Following the signature of accords between the Permanent Commissions of Guatemalan Refugees in Mexico (known by the acronym CCPP) and the government of Guatemala in October 1992, the numbers returning increased, yet the return remained troubled by continuing human rights abuses and scarce evidence of deeper transformations that would assure political freedoms, personal security, economic well-being, and respect for indigenous cultures.

The present volume addresses two intertwined issues. One is the carefully organized collective refugee return led by the CCPP, a difficult and contradictory process. The other is the transformation of political and human rights practices in Guatemala – a process that is at an early stage and even more problematic. Both issues can be interpreted from a hopeful perspective in which the refugee return and future national transformation go hand in hand, reinforcing one another. Yet both also have a deeply troubling and worrisome side in which the refugee return is partial, hesitant, and distorted by a continuation of deep-seated racism, class inequality, militarism, and authoritarian-elitist political practices.

Roughly half of the chapters in this volume deal with the ways in which the CCPP-organized refugee return from camps in Mexico reinforced other progressive forces for national transformation. The remaining chapters focus on dynamics of national transformation (or the lack of them) that shape the return and resettlement. In preparing their chapters, all authors worked from a broadly shared perspective regarding the nature of "return" and "transformation" and from a similarly shared understanding of the circumstances in Guatemala leading up to the civil war and the evolution of the peace process. This introductory chapter summarizes the main shared perspectives and understandings of Guatemala's recent history in order to provide background to the other chapters. The first section of the chapter clarifies the concepts of "return" and "transformation," noting how they provide linkages between chapters covering diverse topics. The second section provides a summary of the social, political, and economic context of the civil war and peace process. The third is an overview of refugee flight and return, and the fourth offers some observations concerning potential transformations in political power relations. We conclude the volume with a chapter that reviews the principal findings of the works included here and presents issues for future research on refugee return, migration, and national transformation in comparative Central American perspective and with reference to neo-liberal restructuring.

THE MEANING OF "RETURN" AND "TRANSFORMATION"

Guatemala's history – from the Spanish conquest and colonization through the civil war that ended formally on 29 December 1996 – has revolved around a repressive state based on the exclusionary control of the political process by a narrow elite, on violent repression of dissent, and on a racist exploitation of Maya peoples (still the majority of the national population). The terrible human rights abuses of the late 1970s and early 1980s, including the army's genocidal campaigns, are but extreme moments in that history. The inheritance of systematic political repression, social inequality, corruption of the legal process, racism, and human rights abuse will not be easily overcome. Thus it was not surprising that the peace process, including the refugee return, was deeply troubled by violence and repression. A culture of fear continued to prevail in Guatemala (Gelijeses 1988). Yet an erratic movement toward peace, democracy, and improved human rights continued, and it appeared to gather momentum during the course of the peace negotiations that brought the country's thirty-six-year-long civil war to an end in December 1996.

In analyzing the collectively organized return of mostly indigenous refugees from Mexico and the highly erratic pattern of improvement in respect for human rights, we are struck by a major contradiction. On the one hand, recent developments suggest a potential for progressive political and social change. On the other hand, reactionary forces that could easily reverse the gains that have been made are still very powerful. Both progressive and regressive tendencies are grounded in a broader matrix of historical change – inside and outside Guatemala. Efforts to analyze the correlation of forces involved requires new analytic perspectives and vocabulary. Identifying and developing useful new concepts is thus an underlying objective of this book. The following comments are intended to provide an overview of the perspectives underlying this collection of work.

Our approach draws attention to the understanding of refugee return and national transformation from the vantage point of changing power relations and their implications for peace, democracy, and human rights. The volume has been titled *Journeys of Fear* in order to draw attention to issues of power and politics in a society branded by a culture of fear. If the collection of papers in this book had been based on a more conventional framework and understanding of the processes involved, it might have been titled *Refugee Repatriation and Integration*. We, however, argue that in Guatemala – and most likely elsewhere – the concepts of repatriation and integration are based on an analytical standpoint and assumptions about power and social process that fit poorly with the reality of the situation. Furthermore, our approach to the power issue gives priority to the views, aspirations, and actions of the refugees and others who work "at the base" in civil society to build peace, democracy, and human rights. These views, aspirations, and actions are analyzed with reference to a specific sphere (refugee return) and its broader context (national transformation). The main concepts may be clarified as follows.

Refugee Return The return of Guatemalan refugees from Mexico is not simply a "repatriation" organized from above by the United Nations and other international actors. Although the UN High Commissioner for Refugees (UNHCR) did play an important role and about half of those who returned from Mexico did so as *individuals,* the CCPP-organized *collective return* was a political process generated at the base by the refugees themselves, supported by international, nongovernmental refugee assistance agencies. It involved people who went back to their home villages or other chosen sites in highly visible organized groups only after certain guarantees had been obtained from the Guatemalan government. From the perspective of those involved in organizing and negotiating the collective return, "repatriation" referred to people who left for Guatemala as anonymous individuals and families and who, upon arrival in their home communities, were frequently forced into the misnamed Civil Self-Defense Patrols (PACs) and "model villages" set up and controlled by the country's armed forces (Manz 1994, 191–211; Taylor 1998).

The emphasis on the political vision and organization of the refugees (examined in the articles by Nolin Hanlon and Torres) and the role of nongovernmental organizations (the focus of Levitt's work) is not intended to play down the importance of nation states and international agencies in establishing conditions for repatriation (as Baranyi's contribution to this volume makes clear). In the Guatemalan case, actions at the base and among states were interdependent. One approach would have been ineffective without the other, since the bottom-up and top-down processes were closely linked and mutually reinforcing. However, it was the bottom-up organization of the refugees in the Mexican camps, their success in negotiating the conditions of their return with the Guatemalan government and military, and their visibility in broader social and political processes that was particularly relevant for national transformation.

National transformation The objective of the refugees organized into the CCPP was not "integration" into the status quo ante. Rather, it was the transformation of Guatemalan society. The returnees wished to reintegrate, but into a new Guatemala where peace, democracy, and human rights would be enjoyed by all (as Crosby relates in her chapter). Related to this, refugee women involved in the return, as well as other women directly affected by the violence, had acquired a new view of women's political roles (examined here in chapters by Blacklock and Torres); refugee youths who had lived most of their lives outside Guatemala were influenced by other values and traditions that they took home; and returning indigenous people in general, who previously saw themselves primarily as members of distinct social groups (each speaking a different language), came to see themselves as Mayas, a political-cultural change pregnant with significant implications for national transformation in Guatemala.

The refugees' goal of national transformation largely coincided with the agenda of other progressive organizations in Guatemala and with the objectives of international governmental and nongovernmental organizations concerned with democracy, development, and human rights. But how are such progressive efforts faring in general? This is a very large question. Several chapters in this volume deal with selected dimensions of the matter. Fonseca examines the nature of the peace negotiations between the Guatemalan government and the revolutionary forces to see whether the narrow, closed, elitist, and militaristic discourse of the past yielded to a more participatory discourse giving greater attention to compromise and incorporation rather than crushing and eliminating the enemy. Baranyi assesses the role of the United Nations in the peace process, while Patroni and Gronau examine the role of Canadian foreign aid in addressing problems of inequality and underdevelopment.

Return and transformation Most refugees returned to Guatemala only after years of negotiations that culminated in accords that provided certain guarantees of respect for their civil and political rights. In effect, the refugees defined the fundamental conditions of their return. In light of the fact that returnees had achieved high levels of organization and acquired new skills and capacities in exile, their political role and their alliances with other progressive actors contributed to the likelihood that the return, under the terms of internationally monitored and negotiated guarantees, could contribute to fundamental and lasting transformations in Guatemala. The refugee return is a concrete matter of concern and support among various official and nongovernmental international agencies committed to, and involved in promoting, peace and development in Central America.

The return, consequently, supports a broader transformation of which it forms a part, a transformation whose basic difficulties are addressed here by Poitevin, de Villa, and Lovell from different perspectives. The basic point made by these authors, as well as by Gellert and Castillo in their respective papers on the internally displaced and on broader migration patterns, is that some features of national transformation were and still are extremely superficial – more apparent than real.[1] Deep problems of class inequality, racism, and authoritarian political practices remain, despite some evident progress on the human rights front. How these progressive trends and reactionary forces balance out is an extremely complex question.

THE HISTORICAL CONTEXT OF THE RETURN

Recent political developments provide the basis for hope that Guatemala has turned a corner in its history. A fragile peace has been taking hold. Democratic political space opened after 1986 under elected civilian-led governments. Massive, violent human rights abuses have declined since the terror of the early 1980s, although daily violence and repression have by no means been eliminated. By mid-1996, several of the accords that led to the final settlement of the civil war at the end of that year had been signed by the government and the insurgent forces of the Guatemalan National Revolutionary Unity (URNG), and some aspects of those accords were already being implemented under the supervision of the United Nations Mission in Guatemala (MINUGUA), established in late 1994.

These positive developments were clearly encouraging, but read in the context of Guatemalan history they constituted, at best, the basis for "guarded optimism." Such an optimistic view can be based on two arguments. First, the extremely repressive and racist politics of the 1954–86 period arose under particular international and historical conditions, some of which no longer exist, while others are changing. Second, progressive developments since 1986 have been deeply influenced by new forces around the world and within Guatemala. To provide a basis for evaluating the elements of the historical matrix that have changed as well as those that have not, we examine the post–World War 2 history of efforts to expand democratic practices and human rights in Guatemala. This is a history with a positive moment – "the democratic spring" – that was followed by an epoch of unprecedented repression, punctuated by moments of controlled political liberalization.

The Democratic Spring, 1944–54 The tortuous path of the peace negotiations in Guatemala and the resulting accords cannot be understood without reference to a post–World War 2 struggle between reformist and reactionary forces. Of particular relevance are the events of the "democratic spring," which were recent enough to mark directly the memories and perspectives of contemporary Guatemalans. Indeed, the current accords may be usefully viewed as steps toward recapturing earlier gains after a lapse of some four decades.

In 1944 a coalition of the country's progressive and nationalist middle class groups and junior military officers overturned the last in the long line of dictators who had ruled Guatemala since its independence. During the following decade, two popularly elected presidents – Juan José Arévalo (1945–50) and Jacobo Arbenz (1950–54) – led the country. Significant progress was made toward the constitution of a democratic system, with freedom of the press and room for the entire political spectrum, from the country's small communist party to its traditional right. Ambitious social programs were launched, among them an expansion of the educational system and national literacy campaigns. Forced labour, which in various guises had been the fate of the country's indigenous peoples since the Spanish conquest, was abolished, and a labour code was enacted that guaranteed collective bargaining rights through unions of the workers' choosing. Steps were taken to promote industrialization and agricultural diversification and attempts made to regulate foreign companies in the national interest.[2]

These initiatives were not universally welcomed. It was the agrarian reform law of 1952, however, and the inclusion in his government of members of the then recently established communist party, the Partido Guatemalteco del Trabajo (PGT), that propelled president Arbenz on a collision course with the agro-export oligarchy and the United States, then caught in the grips of Cold War paranoia. Though the law was designed to enlarge the internal market for the growth of a modern capitalist industrial economy, its strongly redistributive goals, along with the organization of agricultural workers and the Indian peasantry, threatened both the landlord class and the operations of U.S.-based corporations, among them the United Fruit Company (Handy 1994). United Fruit's holdings included telecommunications, railway lines, port facilities, and a shipping fleet, in addition to banana plantations – all affected, in one way or another, by the new labour, agrarian, and other legislation.

In mid-1954 the reformists – accused by the United States of turning Guatemala into a totalitarian, communist tyranny – were overthrown by a "liberation army." Headed by a former military officer who had conspired against Arévalo and organized by the Central Intelligence Agency (CIA), the army invaded Guatemala from neighbouring Honduras, following months of training in Nicaragua

(Schlesinger and Kinzer 1982). There, another U.S. protégé, Anastasio Somoza, had consolidated the "family dynasty" that was to rule the country until the Sandinista revolutionaries' victory in 1979.

To be sure, the U.S.-sponsored "liberators" could not have succeeded without support from disaffected sectors of the military and middle class, the country's then very conservative Catholic church, and its landed elite. For the latter, the agrarian reform and the political organization of the indigenous peasantry represented a cataclysmic reversal of fortune: not only a loss of economic power but the collapse of the traditional social order based on the landlords' life-and-death control of the country's indigenous majority. The fact that "serfs were becoming citizens" was intolerable in a culture in which "civilized Guatemalans had always understood the occasional need to kill an Indian" (Gleijeses 1991, 381, 13; Smith 1990). Nevertheless, Washington's role was pivotal in the events of 1954, and it remained so in subsequent years as Guatemala's armed forces came to be favoured by U.S. military assistance and training programs.

Rolling-back Reforms and Rising Inequality, post-1954 In the months following Arbenz's overthrow, the reforms of the previous years were rolled back. Castillo Armas' government repealed universal suffrage and became the first in a long line of increasingly oppressive military dictatorships. The labour confederations, political parties, and peasant associations that had prospered during the "democratic spring" were outlawed. The repression in the countryside was particularly brutal as "hundreds of peasants and rural organizers were killed" (Handy 1994, 194). By the end of 1956, few of the more than one hundred thousand rural families that had benefited from agrarian reform remained on their lands. Power was restored to its traditional holders – the landed oligarchy and its domestic and foreign business allies backed by the military – all the more intransigent as a result of the recent threats to their status. The Orwellian character of the counter revolution's aftermath is captured by Jim Handy: "In Liberation Guatemala, the government dissolved all the political parties and called it democracy, attacked workers and called it social justice, oversaw the killing of thousands because they had dreamed of a different Guatemala and called it peace, and forced tens of thousands of peasants and rural workers from the land they had so recently torn from the estates of landlords and called it agrarian reform" (Handy 1994, 202). Postliberation governments retained the industrial and agricultural diversification and modernization programs of the "democratic spring" but stripped them of their redistributive and nationalist content. Instead of promoting the expansion of national markets through agrarian reform, increased wages, social programs, and regulatory legislation, the subsequent military regimes sought to attract foreign capital and oriented Guatemala's economy towards export expansion and diversification – agricultural commodities for the world market and manufactured products for the Central American Common Market (CACM).

Economic growth and diversification were impressive from the late 1950s until the mid-1970s, when world market trends turned against Guatemala's economy – an economy that was at the time "highly dependent" on tariff protection (against imports), on subsidies and trade agreements with other Central American countries (for exports), and on international corporations (much of manufacturing, for example, was largely assembly of components produced elsewhere, while agro-exports were controlled by large international firms). Modernization was reflected in increasing literacy rates and in the spread of communication systems and transportation networks. Growth and modernization were exclusionary, however: society became increasingly polarized and large sectors of the population were marginalized. Industrial growth was not accompanied by equivalent expansion of industrial employment: it barely inched up from 11.5 to 12 percent of the labour force between 1950 and 1979 (Keen and Wasserman 1984, 440). Large plantations continued to swallow up the properties of Indian communities and smallholders, who, in increasing numbers, were forced into miserably paid migrant labour. Minimum industrial wages declined by 25 percent between 1965 and 1979, while agricultural wages fell by 21 percent between 1970 and 1980 (Gorostiaga and Marchetti 1988, table 6.8, 126). By the early 1980s, over half the rural population and almost 20 percent of the urban population were unable to meet their basic nutritional needs (UN-ECLAC 1984, table 5, 62).

Since popular needs were not addressed, and their organized expression was prohibited, cycles of rebellion and state terror dominated the country's post-1954 political life. From 1966 to 1968, guerrilla forces organized by dissident junior officers, who were infuriated by government corruption and the use of Guatemalan territory to train Cuban exiles for the Bay of Pigs invasion, were suppressed in the midst of generalized repression that took the lives of thousands of civilian noncombatants. The temporary elimination of the guerrilla was accomplished with substantial U.S. assistance, and it was accompanied by the organization of paramilitary groups that prefigured the infamous death squads of later years.

In the early 1970s terror was relaxed and popular organizations emerged once again – unions, student associations, agricultural and artisan cooperatives that incorporated indigenous peoples, and religious study groups or Christian Base Communities inspired by the liberation theology that was transforming the Catholic church's pastoral work. In 1976 urban unions established the National Committee for Labor Unity, the first unified labour front since the Arbenz years. The founding of the Peasant Unity Committee (CUC) in 1978 signalled the political daring of agricultural labourers and indigenous peasants. Augmented by alliances with professional service societies and moderate political parties, the popular movements of the 1970s attracted a broader social base than their precursors of the "democratic spring," not to mention the frail efforts of the early 1960s. By the late 1970s, however, a sector of the popular movement's leadership had abandoned open political struggle and opted for guerrilla war.

The popular organizational advances, the increasingly militant demands for reform, and the actions of the guerrilla – combined with the fears sparked in military and elite circles by the Sandinistas' 1979 overthrow of the Somoza dynasty in Nicaragua and by the escalating civil war in neighbouring El Salvador – brought yet another cycle of repression (Davis 1988). It began in the mid-1970s, but the worst of the violence came in 1981–83 (see, for example, Falla 1994). Even before the country's three guerrilla organizations, two of them composed largely of indigenous peoples, had unified into the URNG in 1982,[3] the military had apparently decided on scorched-earth tactics to regain total control in the countryside. The indigenous Western Highlands took the brunt of counterinsurgency operations. Military attacks on villages were so savage and brutal that Guatemala became an international pariah.[4]

The toll of the carnage of those years has been variously estimated, but with at least 440 villages razed to the ground (according to the army's count), the loss of life certainly climbed over one hundred thousand. Between 1981 and early 1983, 1 to 1.5 million mostly rural indigenous people became "internally displaced"; some two hundred thousand from the country's western regions trekked across the border to take refuge in Mexico; in several highland departments, 80 percent of the population fled at least temporarily. Most of the internally displaced – about 70 percent – returned (Sollis 1996a, 5), but most did so to "model villages" where the armed forces controlled just about all aspects of life through their monopoly on reconstruction and development programs as well as through the Civil Self-Defense Patrols (PACs), which, as has been mentioned, returnees were frequently forced to join. A significant minority fled to urban centres or remained in mobile Communities of Population in Resistance (CPRs) within the country or in exile in southern Mexico, where they were to organize themselves into Permanent Commissions (CCPP) to negotiate the terms of their return to Guatemala.

Progressive Developments and Continuing Problems since 1986 With the URNG in retreat, although not defeated, the military opted for holding elections to break the country's international isolation and make civilian politicians share responsibility for economic reconstruction. The inauguration of Christian Democratic president Vinicio Cerezo in 1986 led to a gradual political opening that was sustained under his successors, despite periodic setbacks and waves of repression. The military insisted that the negotiations with insurgent forces envisioned in the regional peace accord signed in Esquipulas by Central America's heads of state in mid-1987 did not apply to Guatemala's civil war. Nevertheless, a hesitant process of dialogue was initiated during Cerezo's presidency.

The dialogue began under the auspices of the National Reconciliation Commission (CNR), which was created to comply with the Esquipulas peace accords, and it culminated in the Oslo understanding of March 1990. There, the CNR and the URNG agreed that the guerrilla forces would meet – with a representative of the UN secretary-general acting as observer – first with the country's political parties, then with representatives of "social sectors," and eventually with the government and the armed forces. The latter were finally convinced in 1991 to participate in this process (Jonas 1996; Aguilera Peralta 1994; Aguilera Peralta and Ponciano 1994), which Fonseca examines in this volume.

Three years later, in January 1994, the United Nations was invited to take on responsibilities for mediation and observation of compliance with all agreements that might be signed. Even before the UN secretary-general's office began to mediate the terms for ending the civil war, however, the UN High Commissioner for Refugees (UNHCR) had become deeply involved in negotiations to permit the collective return of the mostly indigenous refugees from southern Mexico (see below). The negotiation agenda between the URNG and the Guatemalan government included all those issues that had remained unaddressed since 1954: democratization, respect for human rights and indigenous rights, socioeconomic reforms, and demilitarization among them.

The obstacles on the path to a viable peace and sustainable future development appeared overwhelming. Indeed, as the political system began to open up in the mid-1980s, those obstacles were in many respects more daunting than ever. The human and material toll of the civil war complicated the possibilities of addressing the socioeconomic and political grievances and demands engendered by four decades of exclusionary modernization and growth. Although civilians ruled, society had been militarized and the armed forces exercised effective power in many policy areas, and especially in the countryside, where two hundred thousand peasants still remained subject to service in the PACs in early 1996.[5] Human rights violators in the armed forces and police enjoyed virtual impunity (protection from prosecution), which, of course, meant that the judicial system was corrupted and inoperative. Political and civic organizations were crippled by a "culture of fear" – the harvest of the "violence, torture and death . . . [that had become] the final arbiters of Guatemalan society" (Gleijeses 1988, 1, 4). Thus the party system was weak, corrupt, and incoherent – plagued by personalism and opportunism – while the urban working classes and the peasantry had yet to recover the organizational levels they had achieved in the mid-1970s. Poitevin's contribution to this volume speaks eloquently to the political challenges the peace process faced.

In the socioeconomic realm, acute poverty and social polarization had increased in the course of economic crisis and counterinsurgency operations. Between 1980 and 1990, according to the UN Economic Commission for Latin America, the proportion of the population living in extreme poverty grew from 58 to 62 percent in the cities and from 66 to 85 percent in the countryside; according to World Bank data, between 1979–81 and 1989, the top 10 percent of the population increased its share of national income from 40.8 to 46.6 percent, while the share of the poorest 10 percent dropped from 5.5 to 2.1 percent (Vilas 1996a, 469, 471). With regard to the economic policy framework of the 1990s, several contributors to this volume (Gronau and Patroni among them) draw attention to the negative implications of the prevailing neoliberal model on the possibilities of consolidating peace in Guatemala through the resolution of the fundamental problems that led to the civil war. As elsewhere in Central America, the structural adjustment policies (SAPs) endorsed by international financial institutions (IFIs) and donor governments involved cuts in government subsidies and spending on education and health, the liberalization of trade and financial markets, the privatization of public enterprises, and general deregulation to attract foreign investment and promote export production.

The doubtful compatibility between SAPs, the peace agreements, and the creation of conditions for long-term peace and democratization was illustrated by the fact that, as of 1996, those economic policies had involved, among other things, the reduction of the education budget, despite a 45 percent illiteracy rate among the population over 15, and cuts in health spending, although 68 percent of children suffered from malnutrition. Meanwhile, public income from taxes, despite supposedly "progressive" tax reform, actually dropped below its 1980 level (Flores 1996, 3-5).[6] The *maquilas* (light manufacturing assembly plants) established by foreign corporations in new export processing zones did provide some employment but not enough to make a real dent in the numbers of unemployed.

Perhaps most troubling of all, although Guatemala's peace accords addressed some land issues, comprehensive agrarian reform was not contemplated (see Lovell's observations). It was rejected by government negotiators and multilateral organizations, since they, in accord with neoliberal ideology, eschew proposals that bring "property rights" into question. But land conflicts were inescapable as long as 90 percent of Guatemala's largely indigenous rural population lived below the poverty line and 2.9 percent of estates occupied 68 percent of agricultural land, as in the early 1980s. In 1996 there were 388 land conflicts of various types taking place in 15 of the country's 22 departments (Sandoval Villeda 1997). Meanwhile, the promised growth impacts of SAPs were slow in materializing: in 1994 Guatemala's per capita gross domestic product (GDP) still stood 14.7 percent below its 1980 level (Larrea 1996, 4).[7] In this context, while refugees were returning, ever larger numbers of people emigrated north, especially to the United States, in search of a livelihood; the families and communities they left behind became increasingly dependent on the remittances of money they sent home (see Castillo's chapter).

In mid-1996 foreign observers involved in monitoring the peace process in Guatemala would state in private that the country's fundamental political and social problems derived from the fact that, despite elections, it continued to be ruled by the military and CACIF, the Chamber of Agricultural, Commercial, Industrial, and Financial Associations, which is the umbrella organization of the business classes. With the implementation of adjustment policies, CACIF members, retired officers, and foreign investors were likely to reinforce their power through privatization and liberalization measures: it was the politically and economically powerful who were positioned to purchase public enterprises. But the possibilities of reforming an intimidated and ineffective judicial system, improving respect for human rights, addressing historically structured inequalities, and advancing genuine democratization were slim if adjustment policies reinforced the power of the traditionally powerful, who had always resisted even modest reform, enjoyed impunity, and concentrated an extraordinary amount of the country's wealth in their hands.

Most disturbingly, the basic contours of the "new" economic model bore a striking resemblance to the failed and conflict-inducing policies pursued by Guatemala's elites in the past.[8] A reliance on export promotion and fickle world markets, on foreign investment, and on private initiative rather than public authority – along with minimal spending on social and educational programs (now in the name of fiscal responsibility) – had characterized Guatemala since the conversion of the country into a coffee and banana export economy in the latter half of the nineteenth century. If the contributors to this volume are correct in their belief that social and economic democratization is necessary for sustaining political democratization in Guatemala, then major changes are required in the current economic policy framework.

REFUGEE FLIGHT AND RETURN

Of the hundreds of thousands of Guatemalans who fled into exile, some 52,000 settled in refugee camps in southern Mexico, initially in the state of Chiapas. (The numbers involved and the location of the camps are discussed in Nolin Hanlon's contribution to this volume.) Perhaps twice as many remained dispersed throughout Mexico. Others made their way to the United States and Canada (see table 1), and still others (no estimates available) went as far as Europe. While the Guatemalans in the Mexican camps were only a fraction of all those dislocated by violence, they became the most organized. The exiles who stayed in refugee camps soon discovered that the camps offered them greater visibility and links to international agencies and nongovernmental organizations (NGOs). These links provided important opportunities for them to mobilize support for policies and programs leading to their eventual return to Guatemala.

As pointed out earlier, the camp residents were mostly indigenous peoples who shared a commitment to return to Guatemala, but to a Guatemala where their quest for land, human rights, and democracy would be respected. The visible presence of the refugees was a tangible reminder to others – foreign governments, international agencies, and various international humanitarian and refugee assistance groups – of the unresolved developmental and political problems in their country of origin. With support from the UNHCR, various governments, and international NGOs, the refugees created permanent commissions (CCPP) in 1987. These commissions served both as a vehicle for negotiating the terms of their return and as the

Table 1
Internally Displaced People and Refugees, 1981/83 and 1990

	1982/83	1990
Internally displaced	1,300,000–1,500,000	100,000
Refugees		
Honduras	1,000	450
Mexico	200,000	40,500
Costa Rica	500	
United States		100,000–200,000
Belize		6,000
Canada		7,326

Source: Sollis (1996a, 7). Data on Canada refers to 1987 (Egan and Simmons 1994, 5).

voice of Guatemalan refugees in the peace negotiations. The refugees' achievements and demands represented, in a concrete and highly visible way, the broader struggle for peace.

In Chiapas the refugees were met by a largely sympathetic Maya population with a common indigenous background. Thus the refugees were generally well-received, and many integrated successfully into local communities (Earle 1988). A hostile Mexican army, however, initially forced many back to Guatemala. It was pressure from Mexican civil organizations, including the Catholic church in Chiapas, that obliged the government to allow the establishment of refugee camps along the Mexico-Guatemala frontier.

Cross-border raids by the Guatemalan army were common during this early period, pushing many refugees further into Mexico. Then, beginning in 1984, the Mexican government moved some twenty thousand refugees (almost half the total in the area) to camps in the nearby states of Campeche and Quintana Roo, ostensibly to protect them from raids carried out by the Guatemalan army (Earle 1988). In Campeche and Quintana Roo, the refugees – particularly women and younger people – were more isolated but also subject to different cultural influences, as discussed in Torres' study.

In general, the Guatemalan refugees in Mexico enjoyed a certain amount of freedom to travel and work, and they provided an important source of labour for small and large farmers alike. The Mexican government, however, did not welcome their presence and continued to favour their repatriation. About six thousand refugees did return in the years following a military-initiated repatriation program of 1984. Certain changes in regional and national political conditions were required, however, before large numbers would consider going back. These changes included the following:

- The signing of the regional peace accord (Esquipulas II) on 8 August 1987 by the presidents of Costa Rica, El Salvador, Guatemala, Honduras, and Nicaragua. The accord linked peace and development efforts with the resolution of the region-wide refugee crisis.
- The formation of the CCPP, also in 1987. Established under international auspices, the CCPP began planning a mass return, to take place as soon as promised improvements of conditions in Guatemala were in place. Discussions with the government of Guatemala concerning return moved slowly, however, until the Plan of Action of the International Conference on Central American Refugees (CIREFCA) had been adopted.
- The adoption of the CIREFCA regional Plan of Action in May 1989. The plan, which emerged from CIREFCA's first meeting, was sponsored by the Central American presidents and the United Nations. It established conditions for the return of refugees throughout the region and, among other things, committed the region's governments to respect the rights of refugees and to recognize the legitimate role of NGOs (Weiss Fagen 1993, 32).
- The accord signed in October 1992 by the CCPP and the Guatemalan government. The accord recognized certain basic rights of the refugees upon their return. It also specified that groups of refugees, organized by the CCPP and aided by the UNHCR and various nongovernmental refugee assistance organizations, could visit Guatemala to meet with state officials to verify that local conditions and the lands they were to be granted by the government would meet their needs. The dialogue between the government and the CCPPs strengthened the role of the refugees in the peace process, in large part, because it "allowed the refugees an opportunity to acquire a new negotiating capacity" (García 1996, 318).

Although human rights protection and economic conditions in Guatemala remained uncertain, about three thousand refugees had *returned* in collective movements by the end of 1993 and another four thousand by the end of 1994. In her contribution to this volume, Nolin Hanlon provides a detailed account of the patterns, locations, and difficulties of return through May 1995, a year during which the numbers involved increased dramatically to about seven thousand persons; the majority were destined for Huehuetenango and Quiché, but many headed to other departments. Altogether, by mid-1997, some eighteen thousand refugees had returned in collective movements (see table 2). Between 1984 and mid-1997, the UNHCR recorded a more or less equivalent number of individual returns, mostly from Mexico but also from other countries (COINDE, in *Acción Concertada* 6, no. 19, 1994, 12).

Refugee return – collective and individual – faced highly volatile circumstances in Guatemala. Thus, while UNHCR projections had predicted a rise in numbers to twelve thousand returnees in 1996, events in late 1995 (discussed below) heightened fear among potential returnees and consequently, only about four thousand did go back (Reding 1997, 62), the majority of them in collective form. The same UNHCR report indicated that, of the thirty-four thousand still in camps in Mexico, 70 percent wanted to return, while commenting that the "main obstacle" to the fulfilment of this wish was "lack of security in Guatemala."

But in addition to volatile circumstances in Guatemala, refugees faced uncertain circumstances in Mexico. In combination, these factors constantly reshaped attitudes regarding return. First, security was indeed the main worry. The refugees were well informed about continuing human rights abuses in Guatemala and about acts of violence perpetrated against refugees who had returned. Second, they had received information from previous returnees about the problems of regaining land, the focus of Egan's contribution to this volume. In many cases, the Guatemalan government had been slow to live up to promises of providing credit for land purchases. The refugees also knew that small farmers who had moved to farm the lands in the communities abandoned by the refugees were sometimes hostile to the refugee return. Third, many refugees had established important ties in Mexico, and children born in Mexico had no lived experience in Guatemala. In varying degrees, the refugees had also developed a lifestyle in Mexico that made that country feel increasingly like home, even though they did not have any right to continued residence there. While the government of Mexico had given the refugees a place of asylum, this right was officially viewed as temporary and subject to termination – until August 1996, when the Mexican government decided that remaining refugees could apply for residency (Reding 1997, 65).

In light of the various uncertainties affecting their decisions, refugees gave different answers regarding their plans to return, depending on when and how the question was asked. For example, in contrast to a UNHCR survey reporting that 70 percent of refugees wished to return, a survey by the Mexican Commission for Aid to Refugees (COMAR) found that the majority would stay in Mexico if allowed to do so. In the latter survey, more than two-thirds (73 percent) of refugees polled in Campeche indicated that they would remain in Mexico if allowed, while the proportion in Quintana Roo was

Table 2
Collective Refugee Returns Organized by the CCPP, 1933–July 1997

Year	Communities	Department	Families	People
1993	Victoria and Veracruz	Quiché	767	3,747
1994	Chaculá Xmán and Fray Bartolmé Ixcán Grande, and others	Huehuetenango Alta Verapaz Quiché	892	4,123
1995	Ixcán Grande, and others Momolac and Chancolin Frey Bartolome La Lupita El Quetzal La Providencia	Quiché Huehuetenango Alta Verapaz Suchitepéquez Petén Escuintla	1,544	7,018
1996	La Lupita Entre Ríos, and others	Suchitepéquez Petén, and others	623	2,685
1997 (to July)	Xoc Iac, and others	Huehuetenango, and others	145	566
Total			3,971	18,139

Source: Reunion 2, no. 2, February/March 1996, 4; COINDE, in Acción Concertada 6, no. 19, 1997, 12.

55 percent (*Reunion* 2, no. 6, February-March 1996, 4). The key factor explaining the differences in poll results had to do with assumptions concerning security of residence in Mexico and the security situation in Guatemala. With a Guatemalan army massacre of returned refugees in late 1995 (discussed below) and the possibility of residency in Mexico as of August 1996, the return numbers dwindled.

In sum, key developments affecting refugee return involved issues of security and the rule of law, access to land in Guatemala, and the possibilities of continued residence in Mexico.

Security The following events, the Xamán massacre of October 1995 prominent among them, illustrate the contradictory process of transformation in Guatemala and the issues that refugees faced upon return. As Human Rights Watch/Americas reported in its investigation of the massacre,

On October 5, 1995, twenty-six soldiers opened fire on at least 200 unarmed Guatemalan men, women, and children in Aurora 8 de Octubre, Xamán, in the municipality of Chisec, Alta Verapaz department, killing eleven villagers and wounding more than thirty. Ninety of the 256 families (1,356 people) in the community had returned to Guatemala from Mexican refugee camps exactly one year before the massacre, where they were joined by 116 families from Victoria 20 de enero and other Ixcán settlements, and fifty local families. At the time of the massacre, the community was preparing to celebrate its first anniversary in Xamán. Approximately 2,000 refugees scheduled to return in late 1995 temporarily suspended their plans in response to the massacre (Human Rights Watch/Americas 1996, 8).

The army initially claimed that the soldiers had acted in self-defense against hostile and armed villagers, but the presence of MINUGUA, the UN observation mission, and the UNHCR in the country ensured a rapid on-site investigation that contradicted the army's version. The villagers, it turned out, had no weapons. The changing political climate in the country was reflected, nevertheless, in the tragedy's aftermath: the defense minister was forced to resign and Ramiro de León Carpio (president at the time of the massacre) "accepted institutional responsibility for the killings, pledged to bring those responsible to justice, and to compensate the victims and their families" (Human Rights Watch/Americas 1996, 10A).

Just one day before the Xamán massacre, returnees in the village of El Quetzal, Petén department, reported that their community had been raked by bullets and rockets from a helicopter gun ship. The attack destroyed a section of the road linking the town to the region's main commercial centre. The refugees claimed that this was the government's response to their demand that the road be improved (*Cerigua*, no. 38, October 5, 1995).

Some attacks on returnees were perpetrated by unknown parties. In mid-December 1995, an assassin killed the seventeen-year-old son of CCPP leader Sebastián Chen Tut and injured another returnee, the brother of CCPP leader Ricardo Curtz. Other events over the following days and weeks followed a similar tragic pattern. Two returnee children were killed when gunmen opened fire on a group of former refugees near Cantabal in the Ixcán. The offices of the CCPP in Guatemala City were broken into, and money and documents were stolen. (*Reunion* 2, no. 5, December 1995–January 1996, 1).

Alvaro Arzú, inaugurated president in January 1996, did "cast new life" into the peace process that had become "moribund" under his predecessor (H. Clegg, *San Francisco Chronicle*, 14 May 1996, 10). He had campaigned on a platform that promised reforms to end impunity for human rights violators in the armed forces. During 1996 progress was made in that area: a few days after his inauguration, Arzú sacked thirteen of the country's twenty-three army generals, along with many colonels (Anderson 1996, 17); on 11 June three high-ranking officers were indicted by a military court for the 1990 murder of AVANCSO researcher, anthropologist Myrna Mack (*Cerigua*, no. 24, 20 June 1996); on 12 June, Congress eliminated military trials for members of the armed forces accused of common crimes, "a great step forward" for human rights, according to the head of MINUGUA (*Cerigua*, no. 24, 20 June 1996).

The extent of such legal reforms and the way they might be applied remained to be seen, however, since other signals emitted by the Arzú government were disquieting. For example, after a year-long campaign, the government succeeded in pressuring the UN Human Rights Commission (UNHRC) to remove its representative, Monica Pinto, from Guatemala in 1997. Pinto, who was mandated to speak out on individual cases and to issue detailed reports, was so effective in this role that the government wanted her replaced by a permanent advisor to the state who could address only general policy issues and hence would not be able to address, and disseminate views on, specific cases. In the context of mounting pressure from other countries (including Cuba, India, Indonesia, and Pakistan) who were uncomfortable with close international monitoring of their human rights, the UNHRC bowed to Guatemala's demands (*Reunion* 2, no. 6, February–March 1996, 1; *Libertas* 7, no. 1, summer 1997, 8). It was feared that the UNHRC's role, and even MINUGUA's capacity, would be diminished as a consequence.

In effect, Guatemala continued to suffer from systematic human rights abuses, perpetrated with impunity. Widespread violence persisted in the form of almost daily killings and kidnappings. Abductions to terrorize and torture reporters and others speaking on behalf of human rights reforms were all too frequent.[9] But it was the assassination of Bishop Juan Gerardi on 26 April 1998 that drew international attention to Guatemala once again. Bishop Gerardi had been a leading figure in the interdiocesan Recuperation of Historical Memory (REMHI) Project, which had collected fifty-five thousand testimonies concerning human rights violations and identified the army as responsible for 90 percent of the abuses investigated. Just before his assassination, the bishop had presented the REMHI report, which could potentially be used for launching civil suits against violators (Amnesty International 1998)

Although the peace accords between the Guatemalan government and the URNG included establishment of the Historical Clarification Commission, that commission was mandated only to report what had happened; it could not identify those responsible. Moreover, just before the signing of final accords in 1996, the Guatemalan Congress had passed a Law of National Reconciliation, which granted amnesty to both the military and the URNG for abuses committed during the civil war. In this context, where, in the words of Bishop Gerardi, "anyone who works for human rights in this country runs the risk of death" (*Miami Herald*, 4 May 1998), it was clear that CCPP leaders and returning refugees represented but one of several high-profile targets that were perceived as potentially subversive and dangerous.

The continuing violations of human rights and security of person challenged the assumption that Guatemala and the areas of refugee return were safe, given the presence of MINUGUA monitoring. The still-disappointing results of the UN mission's work are discussed by Baranyi in his contribution to this volume. Yet, as noted above, some of the reactions to abuses showed evidence of precarious but positive changes.

Land A critical issue – addressed from contrasting perspectives by de Villa, Lovell, Nolin Hanlon, and Egan in their contributions to this volume – is the possibility of access to land. Under the terms of the accords governing collective returns, the government was to provide credit for the purchase of land in sufficient quantity. Representatives of the CCPP, who made advance trips to prospective settlement sites to make contact with government officials regarding land acquisition, reported that the process was very slow, that promised credits to purchase lands did not always materialize, and that the lands allocated were often insufficient or not adequately serviced by roads and other infrastructure.

In the summer of 1995, one group of returnees staged a fifteen-day hunger strike in front of the National Palace in Guatemala City to attract attention to the fact that for three years the government had failed to provide credit to buy the lands that their community of ninety-four families had been promised (*Cerigua*, no. 32, 17 August 1995). An indication of the refugees' insertion into a broader social movement was the arrival of other groups to support the strikers, including the National Council of Displaced Guatemalans and the National Coordinator of Guatemalan Widows (CONAVIGUA) (*Cerigua*, no. 33, 31 August 1995). Eventually, the National Peace Fund, a government agency, approved 5 million quetzals in revolving community credits, and the government agreed to provide an additional 3 million quetzals to meet the price demanded by the owner. A few years earlier such a positive resolution to the conflict would not have happened. Nevertheless, complaints concerning government violations of the agreements negotiated with the refugees were still frequent in 1998 (see, for example, *La Nación*, 18 June 1998).

An additional problem was the quite frequent hostility of small farmers resident on the lands the returnees had previously occupied and hoped to occupy on returning. That hostility, however, was not necessarily spontaneous. Human rights organizations confirmed that local political bosses linked to the PACs and backed by the military often manipulated the new residents and instigated violence against returnees (Americas Watch 1996, 13–30).

The possibilities of remaining in Mexico Until August 1996 the Mexican government resisted granting residency status to the Guatemalans in the camps in southern Mexico. When that policy changed – and in light of the lack of security, exemplified by the Xamán massacre and the problems of access to land faced by those who had returned – it appears that most Guatemalan refugees in Mexico decided not to risk going back home. Thus, as noted earlier, only just over four thousand persons, instead of the expected twelve thousand, returned to Guatemala in the course of 1996.

In total, about thirty-five thousand refugees had returned as of mid-1997, about half of them collectively under CCPP auspices (COINDE, in *Acción Concertada* 6, no. 19, 1997, 12). While the collective return process and national transformation are the focus of the works included in this volume, it should not be forgotten that, according to Guatemalan government figures, persons internally displaced by the civil war numbered about one million (Sollis 1996a, 7; Reding 1997, 67). About these people, as Gellert notes in her contribution, little is known, since they have tried to make themselves "invisible" in Guatemala's cities and towns. It was the conditions of these internally displaced that Myrna Mack was attempting to research when she was viciously murdered in 1986.

CHANGING POWER RELATIONS?

The problems and conflicts reviewed above may appear overwhelming. Yet they were being addressed in a situation that differed significantly from what prevailed from the 1950s to the late 1980s. The differences – arising from developments within and outside Guatemala – sustained hopes of continued movement toward genuine democratization and sustainable peace with social progress.

Although the popular movement had not recovered the effervescence and dynamism of the mid-1970s, it had acquired new dimensions: the numbers and diversity of indigenous peoples' organizations were unprecedented in the country's history (Bastos and Camus n.d., 1995; Solares 1993; Warren 1998); women's and environmental concerns were finding organized expression for the first time (see Blacklock's and Egan's chapters); human rights organizations occupied centre stage in political debates; and a great number of nongovernmental organizations that dealt with issues ranging from health and popular education to entrepreneurial training had sprung up. Meanwhile, one old popular organization, the Peasant Unity Committee (CUC), survived the ethnocidal repression of the early 1980s, albeit in a weakened state. Both old and new organizations were linked by a renewed commitment to human rights and democracy. Moreover, a pragmatic "modern" sector of the elite more disposed to accepting moderate social reform may have emerged alongside the more recalcitrant sectors. Furthermore, the Catholic church hierarchy took on a leadership role in the promotion of dialogue and reconciliation as well as respect for human rights, in addition to the clarification of continuing and past abuses through the REMHI Project.

Perhaps the most remarkable of the new forces on the sociopolitical stage was the indigenous-Maya movement, which, in fact, overlapped with other types of old and new organizations. Although the seeds of some Maya organizations – especially those that focus on educational and cultural activities – can be found as far back as the 1960s, most of them emerged out of the crucible of repression and displacement in the 1980s. The CUC, founded in 1978, represented indigenous peasants and *ladino* (that is, non-indian) agricultural workers; CONAVIGUA, founded in 1988, was composed mostly of indigenous women and focused on human rights and women's issues; the Grupo de Apoyo Mutuo (GAM), founded in 1984 and well-known internationally as the representative of the families of the disappeared, in fact, was also largely made up of indigenous women; and the CCPP, of course, represented mostly indigenous refugees (Bastos and Camus n.d., 119–21, and passim). The increased organizational capacity and high international profile of the indigenous movement was opening up spaces for the eventual participation of the Mayas as full citizens of Guatemala.

At the same time that these internal transformations were taking place, Guatemala found itself in a dramatically changed global, hemispheric, and regional context. With the end of the Cold War, the United States abandoned its dogged resistance to the peace and negotiation processes that culminated in the Central American regional peace accord of 1987. The new U.S. posture also yielded space for an active UN role in the Western Hemisphere for the first time in that international organization's history. Along with the United Nations, other international actors entered the scene: from

Western Europe and also Canada came humanitarian and development assistance programs, often delivered through NGOs (see Patroni and Gronau's contribution to this volume). From both Europe and Latin America came diplomatic support for the UN-led conflict mediation and peace accord supervision missions in Central America.

Meanwhile, with the dissolution of national security states in South America, the Organization of American States (OAS) revitalized its charter commitment to democracy: a Unit for the Promotion of Democracy was established in 1990; the General Assembly adopted the Santiago Commitment to Democracy and the Renewal of the Inter-American System in 1991; and another 1991 resolution empowered the organization's secretary-general to convene the Permanent Council to take action in case of any "irregular interruption of the democratic institutional process" in a member state (North, Shamsie, and Wright 1995, 29–40). Thus in May 1993, when Cerezo's successor, president Jorge Serrano, attempted to seize dictatorial powers with the support of the military, both the OAS and U.S. reactions were immediate, forceful, and coherent. They provided significant assistance in the restoration of the formal democratic order by supporting the efforts of local civic organizations to maintain political spaces open for democratization (Poitevin 1993).

The contrast with the events and circumstances surrounding the overthrow of Arbenz could not have been more striking. In 1954 the United States called on friendly Central American dictators for assistance, cowed the OAS into silence, and prevented the UN Security Council from considering Guatemala's complaints against the impending U.S.-orchestrated "liberation." The contemporary democracies of the Caribbean–Central America region may be, as critics charge, both "shallow" and "fragile." But even "shallow" democratization represented progress in Guatemala where, for decades, "murder [was] the government's preferred method of controlling those citizens who encourage reform and democracy" (Schöultz 1988, 183).

NOTES

1 A similar point is made by Daniel Wilkinson (1995–96) in his recent analysis of Guatemala's tortuous path to change.
2 For an in-depth treatment of the Arévalo and Arbenz presidencies and their conflicts with the United States, see the book *Shattered Hope* (Gleijeses 1991).
3 When the Central Committee of the Partido Guatemalteco del Trabajo (PGT) joined the URNG in 1989, it became the fourth member of the coalition.

27 Historical Perspective

4 For an analysis of the guerrillas' strategies and the government's counterinsurgency campaign, see Gabriel Aguilera Peralta's "The Hidden War" (Aguilera Peralta 1988).
5 Those numbers, nevertheless, represented great improvement: only four years earlier, half a million peasants were serving in the PACS; that number, in turn, represented a reduction from 700,000 in the early 1980s (Americas Watch 1986, 2).
6 Flores is citing statistics collected by the UN Economic Commission for Latin America and the Caribbean (UN-ECLAC), where she works.
7 From data derived from UN-ECLAC (1995), *Statistical Yearbook for Latin America and the Caribbean.*
8 Pettis makes the same point with regard to Latin America in general (1996, 2–7).
9 The day-to-day violence was evident in the constant flow of news items reproduced by *Central America NewsPak.*

PART ONE

*Perspectives on the National
Political-Economic Setting*

2 Reflections on the Problems of Democracy in Guatemala

RENÉ POITEVIN

As the twentieth century draws to a close, Latin America finds itself at a difficult crossroads marked by problematic transitions to democracy. Continuing political violence and increasing levels of social violence, profound cultural transformations, and the dislocations provoked by neoliberal adjustment policies are among the problems they face. Unfortunately, the social sciences – and sociology, in particular – have not shed much light on these region-wide problems. Indeed, sociologists have failed to generate any sort of meaningfully objective works that can be used to interpret events in this part of the world. Instead, the political ideologies of the left produced biased analysis. Subsequently, the work and interpretations of sociologists were discredited because the fear induced by repression led to conformism and cooptation. Consequently, the social sciences have failed to come to terms, in any genuinely insightful way, with the social processes that surround us; nor have the social sciences provided any interpretations of political and social events that could be described as adequate to the task of responding to the gravity of the problems that face us (among others, Weffort 1994).

Given this state of affairs, it might be argued that any attempt to deal with the problems of democracy in general terms entails the double risk of either engaging in overgeneralization of little practical value or offering impressive-sounding, but ultimately meaningless, discourse. Clearly, this is not the time for sweeping generalizations, but that should not prevent us from using what has been, after all, the principal instrument of the discipline I am discussing: reflective thought. The best approach is to reflect on lived experience and attempt to understand it; that is, to try to make sense of the seemingly inextricably tangled processes that assault us every day.

Here, I intend to examine the political process called democracy within the Guatemalan context. That, in turn, means dealing with some of Guatemala's multiple problems and the conflicts that are tearing it apart. It also involves addressing that country's particular historical processes.

A Question of Perspective The first quandary in this undertaking involves how to analyze democratic processes in a society where democratic principles, for the most part, do not exist in either political or civil society. Some analysts would even argue that it is pointless to delve into these kinds of questions when there are so many concrete and pressing problems that deserve our attention. Others would say that it is simply a matter of the existence or nonexistence of democracy, arguing that the conditions necessary for democratic development barely exist in Guatemala. These positions, however, lead to totally negative discourse, without meaning or purpose.

The truth is that if we focus on the problem of democratization from the perspective of all that is lacking, we may despair; undoubtedly, the road to democracy will take a long time to build. Nevertheless, we must reflect on this *problematique*. The construction of democracy in Guatemala is necessarily a long-term project, since it involves something more than change in the formalities of a political regime. First and foremost, we have to address the urgent need for recognition of, and respect for, human rights. Secondly, we must address the possibility of providing the majority of the population with the minimum material means necessary for meeting basic physical needs (68 percent of Guatemalan children suffer from malnutrition, according to UNICEF) so that they can enjoy a productive and socially useful life. One need not be guilty of economic determinism to argue that minimum social standards are a necessary foundation for the creation of citizens who, as members of their communities and society at large, can experience the personal and political liberties that permit effective participation in the construction of the political regime (Gálvez 1995; Rojas Bolaños 1995).

It cannot be denied that Guatemala is a society that has yet to overcome its social pathologies. As I write this in mid-1996, the civil war remains to be settled and its traumas are omnipresent, ranging from the problems of refugee return to the culture of fear that permeates all social relations. As well, Guatemala is one of the most poverty-stricken countries in the Western Hemisphere, in both economic and social terms. Guatemala ranked 103rd out of 160 countries on the UN Human Development Index in 1991 (UNDP 1991).[1] Poverty, as measured in studies conducted by the Latin American Faculty of Social Sciences, affects almost 89 percent of the population (FLACSO 1992). Health, education, housing, and employment indices have been deteriorating as unemployment reaches 40.5 percent (CEPAL 1992).

The inability of various governments to address these problems is clearly apparent. As a result, Guatemalan society has become more economically polarized than ever. Only construction, basic services, transportation, and the financial services sectors have experienced growth. And it is worth pointing out that much of the activity in these sectors is sustained by the massive inflow of dollars derived from drug trafficking.

Yet some spaces for democratization have been created, albeit erratically and in bits and pieces. The country now faces the real and critical possibility of either opening and expanding these fragile democratic spaces even further or of descending into new forms of violence that would risk adding Guatemala to the list of "failed states" that have been plunged into chaos.

The Problem of Social Actors Guatemalan society's principal problem arises from the combined presence and activity of diverse social actors who function at different levels. The configuration and character of these actors is linked to the diversity of Guatemalan society, especially to the sharp contrasts between the young and the old, between modernity and the archaic (García Canclini 1995). The different characteristics of all these actors are evidently tied to their respective "times" and the way in which those times are perceived. Varying perspectives, in turn, become the basis for social action.

The result of this phenomenon, first of all, is the heterogeneity that prevails within any one cluster of social actors. For example, within the indigenous communities, there are local *caciques* (political bosses) and *principales* (elders).[2] At the other end of the social spectrum, there are those who make up the new financial and industrial groups, which cannot simply be equated with the traditional coffee export oligarchy. In any case, the future of the nation as envisioned by both old and new elites has little in common with that envisioned by the traditional authorities within the indigenous communities. The latter, moreover, are involved in conflicts with "modern" community leaders of various types.

The differences in the configuration and formation of social actors are typically based on material interests. In addition to material interests, however – most notably in the case of indigenous communities – the possibility of political participation and leadership may also derive from prestige based on extra-economic principles, that is, from the provision of services to the community. In this way, prestige is converted into political legitimation, a conversion that may take place through practices rooted in custom. Or it may occur through the new indianist ideology that also appeals to tradition.

For others, however, legitimacy is a secondary matter, since the motivation for participation derives from an awareness of class interests. In this case, the relevant actors are highly conscious of the need to maintain the existing power structure; the political legitimation of one's actions is of secondary concern. This is typically the case of the landlord (Hunter 1995, 22) who can employ private violence in addition to relying on the state's military and police forces to act in his interests.[3]

Naturally, such a heterogeneity of unequal social subjects results in a great diversity of (often opposed) demands. At one extreme of the political spectrum, among those who historically have been excluded, the critical issue is access to participation; at the other extreme, the central issue is maintaining power, which is even perceived as a matter of survival. It is, in short, the Guatemalan version of time-immemorial social and political struggles.

All this has repercussions for the difficulties that the peace process encounters and, in more profound terms, for the near impossibility of arriving at political agreements that would permit governability, not to mention the consolidation of a national project. Perhaps what needs to be emphasized here is that this struggle is a veritable war of position (in the Gramscian sense). All discussion in Guatemala is politicized, and it is politicized in all spheres of society. All disagreements convert themselves into matters of politics; there are no agreements without political implications, except perhaps in the interpersonal realm, and not necessarily even there. (Judicial/legal issues or understandings between politicians or between leaders of one or another sector or of a corporation are obviously political.)

But as others, such as Millán Valenzuela (1995), have pointed out, there is no political core, no state power that acts as the locus of politics as conceived in terms of general social interests. Or perhaps the state is simply too weak or delegitimized to function as a stabilizing core for society. This situation, of course, is related to the fact that the real nucleus of power in Guatemala has been comprised of three principal actors: the army, the business class, and the political class, with the latter sometimes acting as the connecting nexus between the other two, while at other times serving merely as a transmission belt.

Under these circumstances, the relationship between the political and the economic becomes so entwined that it is possible to state that the political, in its own right, disappears and is replaced by economic interests.

There is, moreover, as pointed out so often, a power vacuum: there is no leadership or organizational coherence within Guatemalan society, which produces an impression of chaos, a general lack of direction within the social body. This is a critical issue. Without broadly based social organizations or recognized leaders, there is no one to provide orientation to a social and political movement that points in different directions: to ethnic participation and the promotion of social policies; economic liberalism and privatization; the struggle against corruption; the struggle to ensure respect for human rights, and so on.

In the case of Guatemala, as we await the future implementation of a peace accord, the disarticulation of civil society is evident in the weakness of both the social fabric and the state. Yet most of the agreements signed to date by the government and the Guatemalan National Revolutionary Union (URNG), as well as those yet to be negotiated, will require organized social actors in order to be implemented. In this regard, some advances have taken place: for example, the Maya have been allowed to participate in the Assembly of Civil Society (Bastos and Camus 1995; for a discussion of the Assembly of Civil Society, see Fonseca's chapter). But in light of the scope of the task and the nature of the challenges, much remains to be done.

As if all this were not problematic enough, the political arena, understood in its narrowest sense, no longer makes sense. First, the power that is supposed to direct political action is overly diffuse, as discussed above. Second, precisely because the political has permeated all of society, all activities that are traditionally political, along with institutions such as political parties, which perform a mediating role, have lost their general social goals and have come to be regarded as activities that serve only private or narrow group interests. Politics, when it is mired in corruption and violence – as it has been in Guatemala – does not serve society. It is an understatement to say that corruption and violence cannot solve social problems. The result of all this is the disenchantment and frustration manifest in very high levels of electoral abstention and in the condemnation of political activity as useless.

Yet another consequence of the hollowness of the political arena is that the constituent members of the traditional power structure – the armed forces and the business classes in the case of Guatemala – can limit themselves to their traditional practice of co-opting potential opposition through pay-offs of various kinds. This capacity to co-opt the less powerful demonstrates that there is no organized counterbalance of any significant consequence to the pursuit of the political interests of those who wield power within Guatemalan society. There are no healthy and strong political parties that are able to formulate and sustain policy platforms that attract broadly based social support.

It is also worth mentioning that the anti-statist, anti-intellectual, pragmatic (and so on) teachings of neoliberalism bear a sizable share of the responsibility for this sad state of affairs. Because the market is posited as the only regulator of society, neoliberalism both inspires and imposes a state of unrest and resignation. In part it does so because it prescribes that state power should not provide direction to society (a prescription that neoliberals translate into actual policy in a selective fashion and, it should be said, in a hypocritical way at that). More importantly, neoliberalism's prescriptions drain politics of all meaning or goals, since all struggles for power will be in vain, given the disappearance of the state as the centre of power or as an instrument of change. The resulting disillusionment is of such proportions that it can turn into desperation. Hostage to the laws of the market and to the forces of capitalist development, the individual is relativized. Liberty and free will become good intentions; social movements or collective subjects, in tune with idealistic philosophies that locate principles of order outside society, become illusions – creations of the imagination (Brunner 1992).

Undoubtedly, the above analysis is only one way of interpreting a very complex phenomenon. While there are no unilinear or unidimensional explanations, my analysis provides one viable way of visualizing the particular disenchantment with politics that is so characteristic of Guatemala, and indeed of Latin America, today.

In addition to facing the problems of backwardness and heterogeneity already discussed at some length, Guatemala suffers from its own specific problems as a society that has been subjected to centuries of repression and violence, especially during the last few decades. The weakness of social actors, the aftermath of a civil society so shattered and manipulated that there are few historical parallels, is such that we are faced with a panorama of cracks and chasms rather than milestones or paths to be recovered or followed. The culture of fear persists. It inhibits political participation and the organization of civil society. Fear, originating from the trauma of past and present repression, expresses itself in the belief that any form of political activity is to be avoided, since it is dangerous and even despicable, thanks to the immoral behaviour of the majority of the political class. The pathology of terror has made politics opaque and secretive; the public is confused by appearances, and duplicity has become the norm.

All this is further complicated by the fact that, during the past few decades, Guatemala, like other Latin American countries, has sheltered a multitude of nongovernmental organizations (NGOs). The NGOs have been taking on some of the tasks of civil society, tasks having to do with both development and the participatory organization of social movements. The problem with this phenomenon is that the NGOs are, in effect, replacing the state by carrying out the tasks that the latter either does not or cannot take on. Moreover, the NGOs have become substitutes for social actors, since they, despite good intentions in some cases, assume the responsibilities of those actors. This happens most frequently in the case of the very heterogenous range of foreign NGOs that sponsor projects from diverse philosophical perspectives. As a result, inappropriate dynamics are introduced into the societies that are the object of their work.

In any case, a substitution for social actors and the state has taken place, and this has generated a concrete social dynamic that must be evaluated. Yet after almost thirty years of NGO activity in Guatemala, an evaluation of their impact and role remains to be done.

In addition to their weakness and heterogeneity, another problem related to social actors arises from their functional inconsistency over time and a lack of coherence in their demands. Furthermore, the same people systematically appear in leadership positions in diverse organizations, even ideologically opposed ones. Honourable exceptions aside, there is the case of the guerrilla of yesterday who is a member of the army's intelligence services today, or the case of the union leader who becomes the candidate of a right-wing party, the intellectual of the left who suddenly assumes a very conservative position. In addition to the ethical problems this type of behaviour raises, we are compelled also to consider the pervasiveness of ideological incoherence and a widespread lack of education. Education and coherent proposals are, of course, the responsibility of leaders but, in the final analysis, deficiencies in these realms result from the insufficient development of social actors.

The Problem of Space The problem of space arises from the problematic relationship between the central state and political development at the local level – the latter being conceived of as a relatively autonomous space. Relatively autonomous, because it is necessary to situate the local within the broader society, a point that may be obvious but is often forgotten. The local, that is, the community, or its equivalent, is often studied as if it were completely autonomous, as if it were a microcosm in itself, specific in its totality; what is forgotten is that the local is necessarily influenced by the larger society of which it forms a part.

This lack of contextualization tends to appear in studies of local power. Frequently, the analyst invokes the hypothesis that everything local is original, democratic, representative, and, in one way or another, pure. The local – the small community – is perceived as a space uncontaminated by the Western civilization that has spoiled all the good features of what could have been an ideal society. But it is necessary, first of all, to keep in mind that primitive societies, or non-Western societies as the case may be, have not been shaped by democratic practices, although there are some exceptions. Rather, they have been subjected to authoritarian and despotic forms of domination of various types.

Second, the local communities that we find in the rural areas of Guatemala have at no time corresponded to the idealized models. Rather, we are dealing with communities that are very heterogenous, that have come under multiple influences, and that represent very complex processes of historical evolution. (In *Sajcabajá*, an exhaustive and exemplary piece of research, Piel (1989) demonstrates how the impact of distinct historical periods is reflected in local spaces, how the broader society determines the local, rather than the other way around).

Third, the authoritarian models of domination that have prevailed in Guatemalan society tend to be reproduced at the local level, sometimes with their own variants and characteristics. The local never escapes from the general influences of the broader society.

Finally, we find ourselves in a situation in which the many years of repression not only have profoundly transformed the social fabric but have privileged a counterinsurgency vision of the local problematic. This is the antithesis of a vision based on empowering social actors for a democratic process. In addition, there is yet another view of the local that fixes its attention only on the decentralization of the state and is based entirely on administrative considerations.

In sum, there is no local democracy; it remains to be created as the foundation for a broader democracy. In any case, the local is not a model to be imitated but, rather, one that has to be changed. A recent study of local communities completed by FLACSO concluded, albeit in a preliminary fashion, that they are rife with internal struggles – sometimes opaque, sometimes transparent – in which the traditional and the modern are pitted against each other. These struggles are present among the social actors as well as in social practices, which are never free of contradictions. (For example, young people wear tennis shoes and jeans but sometimes combine them with traditional clothing such as red scarves.) In the case of power relations – the antagonism between traditional authorities (the *ancianos*) and the authorities and leaders who have emerged from community improvement committees (and, in a few cases, among the mayors) – the traditional is being eroded.

The desire of the young to emigrate to the United States contrasts with the traditionalist discourse of other young people who are reaffirming their identities, their languages, and their indianness in a more intellectual fashion. The rejection of the Spanish language by Indian intellectuals who speak their native language and the adoption of English as the lingua franca, are but elements of a pastiche modernity as well as a reflection of the profound ways in which indigenous communities are being torn apart. All this allows us to affirm that some features of cultural and racial identity are in tune with the culturalist and minority movements characteristic of postmodernity.

Faced with this picture – to which further complications can be added by considering the presence of the returnees in some communities, especially in the department of Huehuetenango – we see enormous diversity, a heterogeneity that appears to point towards a fragmented multiform society. It is a society in which the different elements fail to cohere in a way that allows for the construction of democracy to be visualized as the responsibility of all society's members. But it is precisely the construction of democracy that is one of the few cohesive elements that might permit Guatemala to confront its immediate future in a viable fashion.

Democracy is uncertainty, but it is uncertainty with liberty, political spaces, institutions, and real possibilities for participation. It is uncertainty about the future but certainty about change and security, and confidence in being able to attain other possibilities.

NOTES

1 In 1997 Guatemala ranked 117th out of 175 countries on the UN Human Development Index (UNDP 1997; note added by the editors).
2 "The traditional control of Indian communities was in the hands of a group of men known as *principales* (elders) who achieved their position by ascending through the ranks of the civil-religious hierarchy [of each community] and who often used their positions to gain control of land or Indian labor" (Arias 1990, 232; note added by the editors).
3 None of these social actors is fully aware of the implications for power relations of the demands that they make.

3 Land and Peace: Two Points of View

GONZALO DE VILLA
AND W. GEORGE LOVELL

ALTERNATIVE STRATEGIES FOR RURAL
DEVELOPMENT
Gonzalo de Villa

The land question in Guatemala is very complex. I begin by noting the great disparity in land ownership. A small elite of wealthy landowners is in possession of most of the land under cultivation, while the majority of farmers and rural people own very little land and are correspondingly poor or even extremely poor. This enormous gap in land ownership can be explained in historical terms; its origins are well understood to be the outcome of an imperialist conquest and settlement. Clearly the distribution of land is unjust and is the source of poverty and suffering. Yet the solution may not revolve around the correction of historical injustice by redistributing land. Although poverty in rural areas must be addressed, various factors must be taken into account in establishing what should be done and what new perspectives must be developed.

Since the origins of unequal land tenure include an accumulation of wrongs over a long history, it is natural to think that the solution to this question lies first and most directly in redistributing land. Many people think in these terms, but in my view they are wrong. I maintain that the question of land cannot be taken out of context from the social, political, and economic transformation that Guatemala is currently undergoing. Those who wish to give priority to changing land ownership should take into account that any redistribution of land would be very difficult to accomplish in contemporary Guatemala. Resistance from land-owning elites would undermine new reform efforts, just as it destroyed earlier ones (see the introductory chapter to this volume). In fact, the current political-economic context suggests other alternatives.

Guatemala's future development will necessarily involve a reduction in the importance of agriculture and farm employment within the national economy. As in the case of other countries that have become wealthier over time, future economic growth in Guatemala will necessarily mean that the size of the work force in agriculture will decline. Diverse contemporary and historical authors within different analytic frameworks (from Marxism to neoclassical economics) have pointed out how agricultural employment becomes less important in the course of economic transformation. In the process of economic growth, farm workers made redundant by rural mechanization are necessarily reallocated to other economic activities. For this reason, the basic challenge that Guatemala faces today with regard to both rural and national development is less one of how to change land ownership patterns and more one of devising alternative policies to ensure economic growth and a reduction in poverty.

What alternatives can we offer to that very large number of peasants who have historically depended on agriculture, who are being expelled from rural communities today, and who will continue to be expelled in coming years? This is the fundamental challenge. It is not simply or even necessarily a question of whether or not land can be found for all those peasants without land. Rather, it is a question of finding various alternatives for them, so that their children will have a better future. Posed in these terms, the problem must be resolved in ways that go beyond land redistribution. In fact, large-scale land redistribution would be an inappropriate priority. It could be entirely counterproductive. It would open a false hope to people and distract the peasantry and the rural work force from examining alternatives. It would open once again the destructive social and political conflicts of the civil war and undermine other promising development alternatives.

Economic development policies in Guatemala must focus on options for generating new wealth over the longer term. Such policies will require increased utilization of modern technology in both urban industry and rural production. Particular attention must be given to sustainability – that is, to adopting measures that will protect the environment and improve, rather than degrade, agricultural lands. Achieving those goals will require a wide range of complementary measures. In the following sections I will examine several rural development policies that can contribute to an overall national development strategy.

Increasing the Productivity of Small Farms Agriculture in Guatemala is characterized by very low productivity per hectare of land under cultivation. Low land productivity, in turn, reflects low levels of investment in productive technology. For example, in 1985–87 only about 4.1 percent of all arable and permanently cropped land (A&P land) was irrigated in Guatemala, while 21.9 percent of such land in Costa Rica was under irrigation (Bilsborrow and Georas 1992, table 3). Similarly, fertilizer use per unit of A&P land in Guatemala was about one-third of that in Costa Rica. The overall figures hide the fact that irrigation and fertilizer use in Guatemala are almost entirely concentrated on large agro-export farms.

Agriculture in Guatemala thus must go through a series of transformations that involve the intensification of land use and technological investments to generate higher incomes. Consequently, agrarian issues will have to be addressed from an entrepreneurial point of view. This is the case not only for large-scale producers but also for the small farmers who will continue to work as cultivators. Irrigation and fertilizers are capital intensive – that is, they require investments that small farmers are likely to adopt gradually, with external support, as their productivity and income rise. It is therefore also important to pursue policies to increase farm productivity through the introduction of new crops, new farming methods, and new markets. It has been demonstrated that small farmers in Guatemala can benefit from extension programs that introduce new farming methods and technologies for increasing the yields of traditional crops and encourage experimentation with new crops and techniques through farmer-to-farmer communication (Krishna and Bunch 1997). It has also been shown that Guatemalan peasants will shift away from an exclusive focus on traditional crops such as corn and beans when new export markets for fruit and vegetables are opened to them (Wing 1998). The new crops lead to the intensification of land use and to greater use of available labour in farm families. Similar findings have been reported in other countries in Central America as well as in parts of South America.

Protecting and Improving Land Quality Land is and will be a scarce resource. Its value must be allowed to grow to ensure that it will be looked after and serve the nation in the future. What will the next generation do if it inherits a useless desert? We have to encourage responsible land use for long-term development. This will require investment in the care of land and in its use for farming and production. It will also require efforts to educate the public so that they will abandon misconceptions about the nature and extent of Guatemala's land resources.

Guatemala faces very serious problems of land fragmentation (in which each peasant farmer is left with increasingly small plots of land), the over exploitation of agricultural lands, and the extension of agriculture into ecologically fragile zones that cannot sustain production under current use patterns. These trends arise from a productive system that favours short-term solutions over longer-term sustainable development investments. The result is deforestation and degradation of agricultural lands.

The United Nations Food and Agricultural Organization (FAO) estimates that Guatemala had (circa 1990) about 1.8 million hectares of A&P lands (Bilsborrow and Georas 1992, table 2). The total amount of such land in Guatemala has tended to increase over time as new lands have been brought into production. Over the period between the 1964 and 1970 agricultural censuses, for example, agricultural land in Guatemala grew by about 1.2 percent per year, or about 20 percent in total over the entire period (Stupps and Bilsborrow 1989; Bilsborrow and DeLargy 1991). About three-quarters of newly opened farmlands were concentrated in the largest size groups (holdings of 45 hectares or more) and were located in the Petén, an ecologically fragile, semitropical forest region in the north of the country. Much of the remaining new agricultural lands were opened in the highlands, on steep slopes, on the western rainshed, and in arid southeastern areas, which are considered inappropriate for crops because of poor rainfall and infertile soils. All this was associated with the elimination of most of the remaining highland tree cover and serious deforestation of the watersheds flowing to the Pacific. The expansion of agricultural lands in Guatemala has already gone far beyond limits that make sense for long-term development.

The notion of unused land is a mythical theme in Guatemala. To be sure, there are underutilized lands, namely lands that could be better utilized than they are today. If we introduce an element of ecology to our vision of land, we will realize that what we are often identifying as unused land is actually uncultivated because it cannot be farmed. In Guatemala, much land that should not be farmed because it is ecologically fragile is actually under cultivation. This happens when poor farmers have no other way to grow food or survive. Yet it results in soil erosion and sterility. This fact further shapes policy options and priorities. The question of unused land must be addressed realistically. I do not believe that there is much high-quality land that remains uncultivated in Guatemala.

The state has in the past held large tracts of land, and over time it has granted or sold (often at undervalued prices) much of its original holdings. Still, the state remains the owner of very considerable tracts. For the most part, however, these lands consist of strategic forest reserves and hydraulic basins that should not be farmed. Consequently, the solution for peasants without land cannot be easily found in the land resources held by the state. At most, some specific groups could benefit from the careful distribution of selected parcels of state land. But this distribution will not resolve the problems of the landless more generally, since the land that could be distributed from state holdings is simply not sufficient to respond to the large numbers of people who need an alternative source of income.

In sum, sustainable rural development will require an end to the extension of agriculture into ecologically fragile areas, coupled with more intensive use of existing agricultural lands, the introduction of new crops, and the utilization of farming techniques that protect and improve the quality and productivity of lands under cultivation. These efforts will lead to an increased demand for skilled farmers and agricultural workers. Overall labour demand in rural areas may increase somewhat, but not to levels that will come even close to absorbing the very large numbers of unemployed and underemployed workers in rural areas.

Investing in Human Capital Rural workers who cannot be absorbed into agricultural production will necessarily have to develop new skills that will allow them to find employment in towns and cities. In some cases, the new skills will be in areas that contribute directly to agricultural development, such as the repair of farm machinery, distribution of fertilizer, transportation and marketing of new crops, and so on. In other cases, the skills will contribute to expanding urban services and industry.

Of course, the land question in Guatemala is not purely economic – it is also cultural. Land has had a particular significance in Maya culture and for peasant farmers more generally. Both economic and cultural dimensions of land must be taken into account in future action. As a national resource and a reference point for national culture, the land issue is of concern to all Guatemalans and not only to the owners of land or to those who work it. It is a vital issue to urban and rural residents, Indians and *ladinos*. We must therefore examine land in terms of new cultural visions, as well as economic considerations. Land is not only a handful of earth, a farm, or an estate; it is also a landscape and, finally, the *patria*, a homeland. It is the territory that defines social relationships and that transcends possession, ownership, and use.

Transforming the vision of rural Guatemalans from one focused on the question of land to one focused on the acquisition of technology and skills will not be easy, but experience indicates that it is possible. Many people who define themselves as "peasants without land" do so for two reasons. Obviously, they have little or no land. Less obviously, they have no alternative to working on land that they do not own in order to survive. Consider a contrasting case where the vision is different. There are huge housing shortages in Guatemala City, and the poor live in shacks and crowded dwellings, but those affected do not perceive that their major need is land for farming. People move to and live in Guatemala City because they have shifted their vision toward ways of work and survival that do not involve possession of a piece of land. No one in the capital is demanding farmland. Their view has changed. They no longer equate work with land.

An attack on unemployment and poverty must be organized on many fronts. The overall strategy must include strong programs to increase rural education, improve health, and reduce human fertility in rural areas. The fact of poverty is most evident in material shortages and inequalities, as well as in the suffering that these shortages lead to. Yet it is also apparent in less evident ways, such as in ignorance and lack of education and work skills. Poverty becomes a vicious cycle when the poor lack the education and training necessary to pull together resources to overcome poverty. In such circumstances, the poor person is in a prison, trapped in poverty, and passes the poverty on to the children. The next generation then suffers from a perspective and future as limited as that inherited by the previous one.

I do not wish to suggest that the poor should in any way be blamed for finding themselves in a poverty trap, since this trap is imposed on them by a lack of alternatives. Rather, I wish to draw attention to the urgent need to open alternatives by encouraging a new vision of the future, greatly expanded educational opportunities, and the introduction of technology into the rural areas that directly benefits poor people and involves them in the search for, and application of, new productive techniques.

Indigenous people suffer most from land scarcity. Their communities, for the most part, are based on the cultivation of tiny plots – *minifundios* – in land-scarce and ecologically fragile regions. Yet their cultural values have made land into something extremely necessary, impossible to do without. There is great pressure on the lands in the western region of Guatemala where native people are concentrated. Land poverty in these regions is linked to poverty in all respects, and to the attendant consequences of poverty in ignorance and suffering. One obvious path out of this situation is to provide educational opportunity to these communities. Education must be central to confronting poverty and overcoming it. It will eventually boost the possibilities of new productive alternatives and new jobs.

Human Fertility Demographic issues should also be brought into future priorities. The very high birth rates and rapid population growth in rural Guatemala add to other challenges to overcoming national poverty. Human fertility in Guatemala is very high, particularly in rural areas, and this constitutes an additional challenge for quickly reducing poverty. Women in Guatemala give birth to more than five children each, on average. Women in Costa Rica, by contrast, give birth to about three children each (Bilsborrow and Georas 1992, table 1). This overall difference between Guatemala and Costa Rica hides the fact that Guatemalan women in larger urban areas have relatively low fertility, similar to the levels of Costa Rica. Women in rural Guatemala have particularly high fertility. Many of their children die due to poverty, malnutrition, poor sanitation, and inadequate health services. Yet those who survive contribute to a high level of natural population growth in rural areas and hence also to rising numbers of young workers who cannot find jobs in agriculture and must find employment in town and cities. Several well-known economic development models argue that urban wages will rise more slowly in the process of industrialization if rural population growth and rural-urban migration are at high levels (Lewis 1954; Fei and Ranis 1964).

Improved nutrition and maternal-child health must be a priority if rural population growth is to be reduced. When children risk death due to poverty, malnutrition, and poor sanitation, peasants will want to have many children to ensure that some survive. Under such circumstances, women do not space the births of these children and, tragically, this places them and their surviving children at risk of malnutrition and poor health. The solution to these interlinked problems is to provide a mix of health, nutrition, and family planning services targeted directly at poor families (Zurayk, Younis, and Khattab 1994). However, experience in other countries indicates that health programs work much better when they are implemented alongside other progressive policies.

The best way to bring down high birth rates is through massive investment in education. When people have the opportunity to obtain an education and to have more choice in their future lives, fertility will decline on its own. This outcome can be expected because there is a direct correlation between higher levels of schooling and fewer children. In contrast, less schooling means more children are born; this is the case around the world (Bongaarts 1982; Cleland and Rodríguez 1988) and in Latin America as well (Chackiel and Schkolnik 1997).

The proposals outlined above are intended to broaden and reorient the debate on strategic priorities for addressing poverty, inequality, and development in Guatemala. They are intentionally future-oriented and seek alternative solutions to the injustices, poverty, and underdevelopment arising from historical patterns of extremely unequal land tenure. These proposals are, in my view, priorities. But they will not by themselves lead to development. Other complementary strategies will be required. If land redistribution were possible in Guatemala, I would count it as an important complementary measure, given evidence on the favourable impact it has had in the economic development of other countries (Griffin 1989, 235–6). However, in light of the violence and paralysis of all progressive change that would likely arise from any effort to implement a meaningful redistribution of land, I believe that it is better to give priority to alternative measures. These have contributed to economic development elsewhere and should do so in Guatemala as well.

LAND REFORM AND RURAL DEVELOPMENT
W. George Lovell

As with most issues affecting economic, social, and political life in Guatemala, those pertaining to an understanding of land and landholding are best seen in historical perspective.

For a country whose present-day problems are so clearly rooted in events and circumstances of the past, it is disconcerting to hear historical origins alluded to but not engaged with in an informed, sophisticated fashion when the question of land in Guatemala arises. Worse still is to see them tackled in a cavalier manner that, in the end, serves only to perpetuate inaccuracy and misconception. Inaccuracy and misconception, alas, abound when it comes to serious contemplation of land issues in Guatemala, despite the fact that solid, scholarly work is available to clarify the admittedly difficult business of determining what actually happened to deprive so many of so much.

Gonzalo de Villa rightly observes that issues related to land in Guatemala are "very complex" and "involve an accumulation of wrongs." Inequality, he notes, is the most obvious feature of the relationship between those who own land and those who work it. In Guatemala official government statistics indicate that 90 percent of the total number of farms account for 16 percent of total farm area, while 2 percent of the total number of farms occupy 65 percent of total farm area. The best land is used to grow coffee, cotton, bananas, and sugar cane for export, not to feed malnourished local populations. Recent UN statistics indicate that 85 percent of Guatemalans live in poverty, 70 percent of them in a state of deprivation described as extreme. Only 15 percent are considered to live well. They live well not only because they enjoy the fruits of the land but also because lenient taxation laws and rampant tax evasion mean that their contribution to state revenues, in percentage terms, is among the lowest in Latin America.

This, in turn, means that the money any government has at its disposal for social spending – on, say, health and education – is also among the lowest, in percentage terms, in Latin America (Lovell 1995). Furthermore, plantation owners are notorious for not paying their workers the legally set minimum wage, which is at best a survival wage. More often than not, however, survival wages are, in truth, starvation wages. Guatemala thus defies the logic of that age-old saying, "You can't have your cake and eat it." In Guatemala, plantation owners not only have their cake and eat it *once* – they get to eat it *twice more*, by (1) nonpayment or minuscule payment of taxes and (2) paying their workers less than, under law, they are supposed to. These are not mere assertions. They are, sadly, well-documented facts.

A study by the Inter-American Development Bank (IADB), looking at such diverse countries as Argentina, Bolivia, Brazil, Chile, Colombia, Mexico, Peru, and Venezuela, indicates that inequality results in slow or negative per capita growth of a country's gross domestic product (Birdsall and Sabot 1994). This poor economic performance throughout Latin America is in marked contrast to the experience of a similarly diverse set of countries in East Asia, where narrower gaps between the rich and the poor, while apparent, do not impede or indeed retard economic growth nearly so much. The IADB study also indicates that inequality has a negative impact in the Latin American setting on educational opportunities, fertility rates, and the incidence of child labour.

Though not singled out in the IDB study, Guatemala fits the general Latin American pattern regrettably well. De Villa states that the "enormous gap in land ownership can be explained in historical terms" and that "its origins are well understood." While I concur with the former statement, I cannot agree with the latter, for I believe that the nuances of the origins of land inequalities are *not* well understood at all, even among specialists, to say nothing about popular beliefs and imaginings. Let us first, then, try to set the record straight before discussing some of De Villa's "alternative strategies" for rural development.

There can be no doubt: during the colonial period Maya communities in Guatemala lost land to Spanish intruders, especially in highly prized pockets around the capital city of Santiago, today Antigua, and in expanses suitable for the cultivation of cacao in the sixteenth and seventeenth centuries and for the production of indigo and cochineal dyes in the eighteenth and early nineteenth centuries (MacLeod 1973; Pinto Soria 1989). Cattle and sheep ranches, as well as properties specializing in growing wheat, also appeared on the scene, geared to the requirements of a Spanish, not a Maya, socioeconomic agenda (Joba 1984; Luján Muñoz 1988; Lutz 1994).

Far more striking than Spanish acquisition of land, however, is the extent to which Maya communities held on to it and fostered a sense of identity around it. They achieved this through active recourse to an imperial legal system they realized could be manipulated to their advantage and by adhering to certain ancient geographical preferences. Despite sustained attempts to redesign where and how they lived and farmed, a good many Indians remained intimately tied to ancestral land in remote, mountainous areas not the least amenable to Spanish entrepreneurial ambitions (Bertrand 1987; Hill and Monaghan 1987; Lovell 1992; Lovell and Swezey 1990). For the Spaniards, control of Maya labour was considered a higher priority than control of Maya land, particularly in the wake of the demographic collapse that native peoples experienced as a consequence of European intrusion (Kramer 1994; Kramer, Lovell, and Lutz 1991; Lovell 1993; Lovell and Lutz 1994; Sherman 1979). That the native estate was plundered, therefore, is hardly remarkable; that the colonial era drew to a close with large tracts of it still intact perhaps is (Luján Muñoz 1993, 1994; Lutz and Lovell 1990).

Not until 1871, half a century after independence had been attained, did erosion of the native estate, coupled with assaults on native labour, begin to alter age-old ways of living with the land, as President Justo Rufino Barrios embarked on the Liberal project of modernizing Guatemala (Cambranes 1985; Woodward 1993). Land was transformed from a cultural resource into an economic one, spun from community into commodity, by Liberal desires to capitalize on Guatemala's untapped potential as a producer of coffee for the world market. The Pacific piedmont and the Verapaz highlands, in particular, offered ideal growing conditions (King 1974; Carmack 1983, 1995). Both these regions had been relatively untouched by the search for a successful cash crop during colonial times, which had seen cacao, cochineal, and indigo experience short-lived cycles of boom and bust. Investment by domestic and foreign capital resulted in coffee emerging as Guatemala's principal export crop, a position it has maintained in the national economy from the time of President Barrios until today (Burns 1986; Smith 1978, 1984).

Organized on a *finca*, or plantation, basis, coffee production demands intensive labour input, mostly at harvest time. What suits the requirements of coffee planters best, therefore, is a seasonal work force, one that provides labour when needed and that can be dispensed with when not. Outright coercion in the form of a draft known as *mandamiento*, authorized by President Barrios in 1876, reinforced the long-standing practice of legalized debt peonage, which endured well into the twentieth century in Guatemala, when it was eventually replaced by a vagrancy law requiring individuals holding less than a stipulated amount of land to work part of each year as wage labourers for others (Jones 1940; McCreery 1994; Whetten 1961). During colonial times, Spaniards controlled Maya labour, but not necessarily Maya land. Turning Guatemala into a coffee republic during the national period meant that an enterprising *ladino* elite needed to control both (Williams 1994).

By the 1940s the need to coerce labour to work land commercially began to diminish, an inevitable consequence of population increase. Between 1944 and 1954 serious efforts were made to address land issues in Guatemala. However, it was also during this "democratic decade" that population began to spiral upwards at unprecedented rates (Handy 1994; Early 1982). The "land question" in Guatemala, De Villa recognizes, is related not only to arrangements for the procurement of labour but also, very importantly to "demographic issues."

Guatemalan censuses are notoriously problematical. Even allowing for significant margins of error, however, official government returns (table 3) demonstrate that the country's political woes are fueled by population increase as well as by social and economic inequality (Lovell 1985, 1990; Lovell and Lutz 1994). While the national population doubled in size between 1880 and 1950, it took less than thirty years to double in size again, topping six million in 1981. Such accelerated population growth would challenge the governability of any country; in the case of Guatemala, where land inequalities have ethnic as well as class dimensions, it contributes directly to political

Table 3
Official Guatemalan Census Returns, 1888–1994

Year	Total Population
1880	1,224,602
1893	1,501,145
1921	2,004,900
1940	2,400,000
1950	2,790,868
1964	4,287,997
1973	5,160,221
1994	9,433,293

turmoil and exerts enormous pressure on natural resources and human resolve (Stoll 1990, 1993).

De Villa believes that "any redistribution of land would be very difficult to accomplish in contemporary Guatemala," pointing out that opposition "from land-owning elites would undermine new reform efforts, just as it destroyed earlier ones." Neither does he see a solution in "the land resources held by the state," for these are "simply not sufficient" to satisfy a fraction of the need. What, then, might be done to improve the abject lot of most Guatemalans, especially in the countryside?

A successful attack on poverty begins for De Villa in the classroom. Getting landowners to pay taxes on their properties so that a responsible government can build schools, and train teachers to teach in them, is a crucial first step. Instructing landowners of the need to pay their workers, if not a decent, liveable wage then at least the legally decreed daily minimum, which in Guatemala, it does no harm to reiterate, is barely enough to survive, would be another. Access even to the rudiments of education and fair treatment in the labour market are basic human rights currently denied Guatemala's impoverished majority.

De Villa makes the sobering point that in the years ahead "the size of the work force in agriculture will decline." If he is correct in his assertion, and IADB thinking (Birdsall and Sabot 1994) suggests that he is, the implications are harrowing in the extreme. One consequence would surely be an increased exodus of "transmigrants" leaving to live and work in the United States and Canada, where perhaps as many as one million Guatemalans presently have residential and occupational ties (Burns 1993; Hagan 1994; Jonas 1995; Vlach 1992; Wright 1993a). Indeed, Castillo's chapter in this volume suggests that such an exodus has already begun. Canadians need to be much more aware of this population movement and of its implications for our already multicultural society. NAFTA has made Guatemala – geographically as much as socially, economically, and politically – Canada's next-door neighbour. Whatever happens in Guatemala now happens a little closer to home.

Canadian development assistance, in conjunction with that of other countries and institutions like the World Bank and the IDB, could, and certainly should, be channeled into the "intensification of land use and technological investments" in Guatemalan agricultural production, whether on a large commercial estate or in a small subsistence plot. But no matter how hard we try to imagine solutions "from an entrepreneurial point of view," sooner or later we must confront the reality that in Guatemala a few have lots, while many have next to nothing. Changing that reality will not be easy, but unless some kind of land reform becomes part of the political agenda, Guatemala's woes will not only continue but will continue to worsen. Programs of land reform, especially when implemented alongside programs of rural industrialization and infrastructure improvement, have resulted in people remaining economically active in the countryside, thereby reducing outmigration and increasing rural incomes. Both Taiwan and China are cases in point (see, for example, UNDP 1996, 94–5). I thus disagree with de Villa that "large-scale land redistribution would be an inappropriate priority." To my mind it would be a most appropriate priority, if undertaken properly, not just talked about in the abstract. However, in this regard, as with so much in Guatemala, the "firm and lasting" peace accord signed on 29 December 1996 promises much but seems certain to deliver very little. What is it, indeed, that this accord and others that preceded it hope to accomplish on the land question?

Two agreements contain articles pertaining to land issues: the first is an Agreement on the Identity and Rights of Indigenous Peoples, signed on 31 March 1994, the second an Agreement on Social and Economic Issues and the Agrarian Situation, signed on 6 May 1996. Article 28 in the latter document reads as follows:

Land is central to the problems of rural development. From the conquest to the present, historic events, often tragic, have left deep traces in ethnic, social, and economic relations concerning property and land use. These have led to a situation of concentration of resources which contrasts with the poverty of the majority and hinders the development of Guatemala as a whole. It is essential to redress and overcome this legacy.

The agreement on the "agrarian situation" commits the government of Guatemala, among other initiatives, to the following courses of action:

1. Establish a land trust fund "for the acquisition of land through government funding," in order to "enable tenant farmers who either do not have land or have insufficient land to acquire land through long-term transactions at commercial or favorable interest rates with little or no down payment."
2. Encourage conditions "that will enable small and medium-scale farmers to have access to credit."
3. Promote "legal reform" in the land administration and land registry systems.
4. Put into place procedures "for the settlement of disputes relating to land."
5. Provide "advice and legal assistance to small farmers and agricultural workers with a view to the full exercise of their rights."
6. Take measures to "ensure that labor legislation is effectively applied in rural areas," in order to curb abuses, including the adoption of "sanctions against offenders."
7. Ensure that "by the year 2000, the tax burden, measured as a ratio of gross domestic product, increases by at least 50% compared with the 1995 tax burden."
8. Address "the most serious issue relating to tax injustice and inequality, namely, evasion and fraud, especially on the part of those who should be the largest contributors," on whom the government pledges to impose "exemplary penalties."

While these clauses are encouraging, one searches in vain for an agenda of genuine structural reform to tackle land inequalities. Status quo patterns of land ownership remain intact, which means that a privileged few will retain lots and the impoverished majority will be left, still, with next to nothing. The most one can hope for is that wealthy landowners will be content to hold on to what they have and finally comply with the principle of being responsible taxpayers and fair employers. This, in truth, would be a considerable advance. But is it enough? Guatemala is *not* a poor country. It is rich in resources, natural and human. Guatemala has been *made* a poor country because access to its resources, especially its land resources, is characterized by crippling structures of inequality. It makes strategic sense to proceed, as the government of President Alvaro Arzú has attempted to do, on matters pertaining to land taxation and remuneration of agricultural labour. The fundamental issue of unequal ownership of land, however, can be resolved only if it is actually addressed. If it is not, then the peace that has supposedly been signed into being in Guatemala may prove neither firm nor lasting.

PART TWO

Negotiating and Monitoring the Peace: National and International Dimensions

4 Paradigms of Negotiation and Democratization in Guatemala

MARCO FONSECA

The evolution of the negotiation process provides an important vantage point from which one can analyse the tortuous path democratization has taken in Guatemala. Two fundamentally opposed paradigms of negotiation can be identified: an elitist "strategic paradigm" sustained by the political-military forces and a democratic "discursive paradigm" advanced by sectors of civil society.

For the purposes of this paper, negotiations are considered strategic when they are conducted according to the logic and force of political-military power that the contending parties bring to the negotiation table. Such negotiations are fundamentally antidemocratic and elitist, and they derive from Guatemala's political history of oligarchic rule and culture. In contrast, the discursive paradigm represents a new way of negotiating in Guatemala, still in its early stages. Its defining characteristic, following the work of Jurgen Habermas (1995), is the establishment of a real communication community in which the dynamics of argumentation concerning public issues are sustained by democratic norms of participation and argument, where the "structure of ... communication rules out all external and internal coercion other than the force of the better argument and thereby also neutralizes all motives other than that of the cooperative search for truth" (88–9). According to the logic of the discursive paradigm, then, no proposal of national or constitutional import is agreed upon or considered generally acceptable without first being discussed within a framework of extensive and open participation. Unlike the strategic paradigm, the discursive paradigm has as its goal genuine consensus arrived at by all relevant parties. This type of consensus has as its ideal not merely a balance of strategic interests but mutual forms of understanding.

Although Guatemala hardly provides a historical case in which all the elements of the discursive paradigm are in place, the peace process does provide examples of various social actors attempting to implement elements of such a democratizing paradigm for the first time in the country's history (Trudeau 1993). Such attempts began in 1989, when the Great National Dialogue was launched by the elected civilian government of Vinicio Cerezo Arévalo (1986–90).[1] A second stage in the evolution of the paradigm was provided by the Oslo Process in 1990, in which the Guatemalan National Revolutionary Unity (URNG) engaged in consultations with various sectors of civil society. Finally, a third stage was reached with the establishment of the Assembly of Civil Society (ASC) in 1994.[2]

The emergent discursive practices and the new vocabulary of human rights in Guatemala's political debates, rather than the specific elements of the peace agreements, may indeed become the most important legacies of the past years of negotiations. Listed below is, first, a chronology of key events that took place during Guatemala's long and difficult peace negotiation process up to mid-1995, a process to which even the historically excluded Maya people were eventually able to make proposals through the ASC (Bastos and Camus 1995). In the following sections, I discuss those events, first with reference to ways in which the strategic negotiation paradigm manifested itself and then with reference to the new discursive practices that gradually emerged.

THE CHRONOLOGY OF THE PEACE PROCESS

7 August 1987. The Central American governments sign the Procedure for the Establishment of a Firm and Lasting Peace in Central America (Esquipulas II).

6 October 1987. A National Reconciliation Commission (CNR) is created to comply with the Esquipulas II agreement, which stipulated that such commissions be established in all the Central American countries in order, among other things, to supervise implementation of provisions for democratization included in the agreement.[3]

7 October 1987. The government and the URNG hold talks in Madrid, Spain.

October 1988. The CNR invokes the National Dialogue to advance the stalled peace process.

20 February 1989. The Great National Dialogue (GND) is initiated by President Cerezo. It was to involve eighty-four delegates from forty-seven organizations representing almost all social sectors. However, the most powerful organizations did not participate: the CACIF (the umbrella organization of agricultural, commercial, industrial, and financial businesses), UNAGRO (the association of landowners), certain ultra-right-wing parties, the army, and the URNG.

February 1990. President Cerezo agrees to establish a dialogue with the URNG, under CNR moderation, without the precondition that the guerrilla forces lay down their arms.

30 March 1990. The CNR and the URNG sign the Basic Agreement for Seeking Peace (the Oslo Agreement) in Norway.

28 May–1 June 1990. The Oslo process, which was to last through October, begins with meetings between the URNG and representatives of nine political parties. Those meetings culminate in the signing of the San Lorenzo de El Escorial Agreement in Spain.

30 August–1 September 1990. A delegation from the CACIF and the URNG meet in Ottawa and make separate declarations.

24–26 September 1990. The religious sector and the URNG meet in Quito, Ecuador and agree on the Quito Declaration.

23–25 October 1990. The labour union and grassroots organizations meet with the URNG in Metepec, Puebla, Mexico and issue the Metepec Declaration.

27–28 October 1990. Small and medium-sized entrepreneurs, cooperative leaders, academics, and intellectuals meet with the URNG in Atlixco, Puebla, Mexico and issue the Atlixco Declaration.

14 April 1991. President Jorge Serrano Elias (inaugurated in January) presents his Initiative for Total National Peace.

24–25 April 1991. The government and the URNG initiate bilateral meetings in Mexico. Monseñor Rodolfo Quezada Toruño, head of the CNR, serves as moderator in the presence of a UN observer. They sign the Agreement on the Procedure for Seeking Peace through Political Means, or the Mexico Agreement, which includes the General Agenda for Negotiations.

25 July 1991. The government and the URNG sign the Framework Agreement on Democratization for the Search for Peace through Political Means, or the Querétaro Agreement, in Mexico.

15 May 1992. The URNG presents its proposal – Guatemala, a Just and Democratic Peace: Content of the Negotiations – to the CNR. The Coordinator of Civil Sectors (CSC) is established about the same time.

11 June 1992. The CSC issues a declaration stating that its participation is essential to the negotiation process on the future of the country. The Civil Coordinator for Peace (COCIPAZ) is established.

8 August 1992. The government and the URNG sign the Agreement on the Civil Self-Defence Patrols in Mexico as part of the discussion of human rights.

8 October 1992. The agreement on refugee return is signed between the Guatemalan government and the Permanent Commissions (CCPP).

19 January 1993. President Serrano Elias presents his Proposal for the Speedy Signing of a Firm and Lasting Peace in Guatemala.

25 May 1993–3 June 1993. President Serrano Elias attempts to assume dictatorial powers through an *auto-golpe* (presidential suspension of constitutional guarantees) and the broadly based National Organization for Consensus (INC) emerges in opposition.

6 June 1993–8 July 1993. Congress elects the human rights ombudsman, Ramiro de León Carpio, as president; de León Carpio dissolves the CNR, presents his Proposal for the Reinitiation of the Peace Process, and seeks the mediation of the Organization of American States (OAS) and the United Nations.

12 August 1993. The INC proposes that civil sectors be included in the negotiation of substantive issues, such as human rights.

21 September 1993. Monseñor Quezada Toruño presents his Preliminary Project for Reinitiating the Peace Negotiations, proposing that civil sectors be included in the negotiation of substantive issues such as human rights in general and the rights of the native peoples in particular, socioeconomic issues and the agrarian situation, and other issues.

4 October 1993. The government officially presents its National Plan for Peace, suggesting the formation of a Permanent Forum for

Peace that would include civil sectors, but the URNG rejects the plan on 13 October.

10 January 1994. The government and the URNG sign the Framework Agreement for the Reinitiation of the Negotiation Process; the United Nations is brought in as mediator (in contrast to its previous observer role).

29 March 1994. The government and the URNG sign the Comprehensive Accord on Human Rights in Mexico City and agree on a schedule for continuing negotiations.

17 May 1994. The ASC is formally set up.

17 June 1994. The government and the URNG sign the Accord for the Resettlement of Populations Uprooted by the Armed Conflict, in Oslo, Norway.

23 June 1994. The government and the URNG sign the Accord on the Establishment of a Commission to Clarify Human Rights Violations and Acts of Violence That Have Caused the Guatemalan People to Suffer, in Oslo, Norway.

8 July 1994. The ASC puts forward a revised version of a proposal submitted to the ASC by the Coordinator of Guatemalan Maya Organizations (COPMAGUA) entitled The Identity and Rights of Indigenous Peoples.[4]

19 September 1994. The United Nations authorizes the establishment of an observer Mission in Guatemala called MINUGUA (see, for example, Baranyi 1995 and his chapter in this volume).

5–9 December 1994. The ASC presents its proposal on Reforms to the Constitution and to the Electoral Regime, concluding its discussion of substantive issues.

31 March 1995. The government and the URNG sign the Accord on the Rights and Identity of Indigenous Peoples.

July 1995. The New Guatemala Democratic Front (FDNG) is founded to participate in the November elections.[5]

THE PARADIGM OF STRATEGIC NEGOTIATIONS

Neither the Great National Dialogue (GND), nor the Oslo-process consultations of March–October 1990 were adopted as models by the government or the URNG when they began bilateral negotiations in Querétaro, Mexico, in July 1991. In fact, the bilateral negotiations marked the end of the multiparty, multidimensional process for discussing the terms of peace. Instead, the negotiations were monopolized by the two parties, carried out in secret and away from public scrutiny, and conducted along the lines of political-military rationality – as a war game that guided their communicative actions. Strategic bilateral bargaining rendered subordinate the earlier discursive experimentation of the GDN and the Oslo process, through manoeuvres that were normatively guided either by the revolutionary vanguardism of the URNG or the nationalism of the government/army.

No doubt the complexity of the issues that had to be negotiated, in addition to the fact that the negotiations were attempting to end a war that had lasted more than thirty years, necessarily made for slow progress (Jonas 1996). The mediating role of, first, the National Reconciliation Commission (CNR), which was established to comply with the Esquipulas II accord of mid-1987 and, later, of the United Nations, would be very difficult. Setbacks were inevitable. Nevertheless, the strategic bilateral negotiations can be understood as essentially antidemocratic in character. Such a perspective reveals the sources of setbacks and demonstrates the inability of civil society, until rather late in the process, to carve out a space for itself in the negotiation process.

In accordance with the Mexico Agreement of 26 April 1991, the negotiations between the government/military and the URNG were private and discrete in nature. This institutionalization of secrecy indicated two things: first, it was a violation of the democratic norms that both parties had agreed to respect in the El Escorial Agreement of June 1990; second, it maintained an antidemocratic and elitist form of negotiation. The Framework Agreement of 10 January 1994, whose terms brought in the United Nations as a mediator, reiterated the same rules of procedure already enshrined in the Mexico Agreement: that negotiations should continue "in strictest confidence" in order to maintain "an environment of trust and serenity." Characteristic of such a closed process were the military actions that continued to punctuate the negotiations – even during moments of ceasefire – until early 1996.

The secrecy that permeated the bilateral negotiations negated the putative democratizing goals of the negotiations. Secrecy may have been essential to the parties in order to shield the process from "distractions" such as the demands from the popular sectors. Such pressures could have transformed – even derailed – the negotiating agenda set up by the government/military and the URNG. Many in the public sector were interested in knowing how the parties at the negotiating table were using their interests – or perhaps sacrificing those interests – as bargaining chips. The secrecy that enshrouded the negotiations meant that neither the government nor the URNG needed to account for its actions before a popular tribunal. For this reason, the adoption of secrecy as a negotiating method was open to the charge that it represented the continuity of the oligarchic tradition.

The "meetings" with political parties and with popular, religious, business, and other sectors during the Oslo process were consultations on "ways to resolve national problems"; they did not involve negotiations. Indeed, with the ratification of the Oslo Agreement, the country's political parties immediately gave up any pretence of functioning as mediators between the social sectors that supported them and those involved in the negotiation process. For example, in the El Escorial Agreement of June 1990, the political parties called on the URNG to give "an impulse to the incorporation of all forces, social and political sectors," in any negotiations. However, for all practical purposes the civil sectors and the political parties themselves were excluded from what was supposed to be a democratic discourse of inclusion and participation.

The Quito Declaration, signed by the URNG and Guatemala's religious sectors in September 1990, called for the "participation of all political and social forces and sectors" in negotiations. Nevertheless, the Quito statement failed to stipulate exactly what form that participation should take. Although the religious leaders emphasized the importance of the Great National Dialogue of 1989 as a model in searching for solutions through "rational consensus and a social pact," the Oslo Agreement, *in principle*, excluded the model of negotiation established by the Great National Dialogue. As will be seen, the religious leaders did not resolve this contradiction between models until Bishop Quezada Toruño offered his peace proposal in September 1993.

Even the popular and union sectors declared themselves in favour of the strategic process. Following the line of the Oslo Agreement, these Sectors of Metepec – so called because of their meeting with the URNG in Metepec, Mexico, during the Oslo Process – called on "the active participation and contribution of all Guatemalans." Paradoxically, they supported the idea of a process that, *in principle*, impeded their own active participation. The Sectors of Matepec, which formed the CSC, did not change their position until June 1992, when they presented a statement declaring the necessity of their participation in the bilateral negotiation process.

In that statement, the civil sectors openly criticized the government and the URNG, arguing that direct civil participation in the negotiations represented a "national demand." Nevertheless, the civil sectors would not be active participants in the negotiation process until after the crisis provoked by the *auto-golpe* of President Serrano Elias on 25 May 1993 and the formation of the INC on 3 June of the same year; it was joined by the Multisectorial Social Forum, which included the CSC. The proposal that emerged from the INC represented a challenge to the secrecy of the negotiations and their monopolization by the government/military and the URNG.

Despite all this, following the renewal of negotiations with the signing of the Framework Agreement of January 1994, the URNG and the government decided to maintain the strategic bilateral model established in Oslo and Mexico. In clear opposition to the demands of civil sectors and Quezada Toruño, the parties declared in the Framework Agreement that they would continue negotiations "in strictest confidence," arguing that only by proceeding in this way would they be able to ensure "an environment of trust and serenity." Similarly, they agreed that "any public information concerning [the development of the bilateral negotiations] would be provided by the Representative of the Secretary General of the United Nations." Nevertheless, even this agreement was carefully qualified. The information that would be shared with civil sectors would in no way violate the "reservation required for the work of the bilateral table."

To be sure, the Framework Agreement established the ASC, with Monseñor Quezada Toruño as its head. No doubt that initiative was a significant concession to the demands of civil sectors and the project of the Monseñor. The creation of the ASC was unprecedented. However, it must be noted that the design of the ASC retained very little of what the civil sectors and Quezada Toruño had proposed earlier. Although the ASC represented an opportunity for civilian organizations to have a say on the substantive themes of the negotiating table – a key demand of civil sectors and Quezada Toruño, the ASC would not and could not aspire to influence the general course of the negotiations or their outcome. Still, one could argue that the parties to the bilateral negotiations failed to evaluate the consequences the creation of the ASC would have on the peace process as a whole. In short order, the ASC trespassed – at times without intending to – the parameters assigned to it by the Framework Agreement, above all the restriction to merely discuss the "substantive agenda" of the bilateral negotiations and to transmit, via the moderator, its "recommendations" to the bilateral parties. Soon, the ASC found itself at the centre of an entirely different agenda for peace and a different approach to negotiating that agenda.

As for the negotiating agenda that the Framework Agreement reestablished, the strategic unity of substantive (for example, human rights and socioeconomic issues) and operational (for example, a cease-fire, guerrilla demobilization, and overall demilitarization) themes was maintained. As Bishop Quezada Toruño rightly observed, "experience demonstrates that it is not viable to treat the substantive and operational themes simultaneously," since this would guarantee not only the maintenance of secrecy but also the perpetuation of the exclusionary nature of the negotiations. After all, if civilians are not allowed to discuss properly military matters and if these matters are thought to be necessarily linked to questions of human rights and socioeconomic conditions, then the participation of civilian organizations is fundamentally limited *in principle*.

Undoubtedly, there were many reasons for celebrating the renewal of negotiations in January 1994. But it must be recognized that this renewal represented the continuation of a negotiating paradigm that was being vigorously criticized by broad sectors of civil society in Guatemala.

THE DISCURSIVE PARADIGM OF NEGOTIATIONS

All practical discourse oriented toward the recognition and understanding of demands coming from conflicting, sometimes antagonizing, parties requires what some philosophers, such as Habermas, have called a bridging principle, that is to say, an approach to argumentation that fulfils at least two requirements: First, a broad participatory process must be engaged in. This process should be oriented toward the production of consensus through democratic and discursive means so that the agreements that emerge from such processes may acquire a normative, binding character. Second, practical discourse must facilitate the translation of consensus into common knowledge and understanding (Habermas 1995, 62–8). These common understandings can then serve as the normative framework of daily interaction and mutual recognition on the part of social actors from the bottom to the top.

These two critical requirements of practical discourse "exclude as invalid any norm that could not meet with the qualified assent of all who are or might be affected by it." This is so because, at least theoretically, the "bridging principle, which makes consensus possible, ensures that only those norms are accepted as valid that express a general will" and that can be expressed as "universal laws" (Habermas 1995, 63). Only those norms can be truly democratic, or "valid," that "can claim to ... meet (or could meet) with the approval of all affected" (66).

Needless to say, the satisfaction of these conditions imposes rigorous demands on the participants. These demands centre on the famous Kantian categorical imperative, now reformulated by Habermas as follows: "Rather than ascribing as valid to all others any maxim that I can will to be a universal law, I must submit my maxim to all others for purposes of discursively testing its claim to universality. The emphasis shifts from what each can will without contradiction to be a general law, to what all can will in agreement to be a universal norm" (1995, 67, citing T. McCarthy). In spite of the practical rigour of these principles, it is possible to use them to examine the Guatemalan peace process and to contribute some ideas to clarify their complexity and fluidity.

A general objection to using this perspective can be raised to the effect that Guatemala's public sphere did not offer "objective conditions" that permit the organization of practical discourse of the kind mentioned above. No doubt the country's public sphere is saturated by oligarchic and authoritarian symbolism and lacks institutions that can serve as the basis for a deliberative process conducted principally through argumentation. Nevertheless, spaces have opened up for discursive practices in the search for solutions to the country's profound social conflicts.

I have already emphasized the closed strategic character of the bilateral negotiations. Nevertheless, the peace process – from the days of Contadora through Esquipulas and the bilateral negotiations – opened up possibilities for transformation in the public sphere, including the development of a political vocabulary centred on human rights and pointing toward democratic and discursive practices. The clearest example of this reorientation of the Guatemalan public sphere was provided by the short history of the ASC.

Already in February 1988 the Guatemalan Episcopal Conference asked the government of Cerezo to organize a National Dialogue that would involve "all sectors, including the guerrillas" (Inforpress Centroamericana 1995, 25). Nevertheless, it was not until 20 February 1989 that the CNR received authorization from the government to initiate the dialogue and, with it, what can be identified as the first discursive experiment of national dimensions in the history of Guatemala. Although the dialogue gradually lost momentum, becoming an irrelevant mechanism by the end of 1989, it set a precedent for the ASC.

It was during the Oslo process of 1990 that the social sectors that would later become the "blocs" of the ASC were constituted. But it was the initiation of bilateral negotiations in 1990 that, given their closed and exclusive character, provided an even greater impetus to the demands of civil sectors, demands that began to exceed the limits these sectors had imposed upon themselves during the Oslo process. Beginning in 1991 the government and the URNG found themselves under pressure from civil sectors that wanted to discuss possible mechanisms of information sharing and participation in the negotiations. Thus, in spite of their public opposition to the direct participation of civil sectors in the negotiations, already in February 1992 the government and the URNG began to consider – albeit behind closed doors – the pressures emanating from civil sectors (Inforpress Centroamericana 1995, 93).

In May 1992 one of the "blocs" that was to later form part of the ASC was already being formed. In fact, various social and religious groupings – among them the Catholic Church, human rights organizations like the Runujel Junam Council of Ethnic Communities (CERJ) and the Mutual Support Group (GAM), as well as the Unity of Union and Popular Action (UASP) – expressed themselves publicly for the first time as constitutive parts of what they called the CSC. Other sectors joined in the Coordinator of Civil Institutions for Participation and Information in the Peace Process (CIC). These were the same popular organizations that had formed the Metepec Sector during the Oslo process (Inforpress Centroamericana 1995, 100).

The rise of the CSC was certainly noticed by the parties to the negotiations. The URNG presented a new proposal to the CNR entitled, Guatemala, a Just and Democratic Peace: The Contents of the Negotiations. It contained two critical points. First, "the URNG reiterates its willingness to discuss immediately, upon completing the agreement on human rights, a restructuring of the negotiations" in order to "consider the participation of the civil society forces and sectors," but only in the capacity of observers at plenary sessions. Second, the URNG made it clear that civil sectors could in no way aspire to convert the negotiations between the government and the URNG into a "meeting of multitudes for discussion and agreement." The revolutionaries warned that, in any case, the "principle of discretion ought to be reviewed appropriately in order to determine what ought to remain confidential and what, by its very nature and repercussions, ought to be in the public domain." In sum, the document of the revolutionary leadership left no doubt about the continued exclusion of civil sectors from the negotiations. At the same time, to protect its interests in the event of greater future civilian participation, the URNG gave itself and the government great latitude for defining "what ought to remain confidential" (Inforpress Centroamericana 1995, 122).

In June 1992 another of the blocs that would later form part of the ASC publicly spoke out. This second bloc, the Civil Coordinator for Peace (COCIPAZ), was made up of organizations that had also participated in the Oslo process, such as the Sector of Atlixco, composed of small and medium-sized entrepreneurs, cooperative leaders, academics, and intellectuals. Immediately after establishing its public presence, both COCIPAZ and the CSC, in coordination with each other, presented separate proposals to the CNR. These proposals demanded the direct participation of these blocs in the negotiating process (Inforpress Centroamericana 1995, 101). With these proposals the emerging blocs of the ASC were beginning to elaborate what would later become a relatively sophisticated critique of the bilateral negotiations. It was clear in June 1992 that the statements of the URNG in response to civilian demands for participation had not been well received by the civil sectors.

As the political pressure from the civil blocs increased, they made their clearest and most energetic intervention in favour of direct and egalitarian participation in the negotiations. In their "Statement of Civil Sectors Concerning the Necessity of Participation in the Negotiating Process on the Future of the Country," the civil blocs announced their vision of the evolution of the negotiations and how they might be improved. They argued that "as the negotiation process between the parties began to unfold, technical and political elements were introduced that affected and made impossible the concretization of a participatory dimension to the peace process." Moreover, "the secrecy [of the negotiations] and lack of participation of civil sectors directly threaten such a dimension, which is essential to the construction of a truly democratic project" (*Pronunciamiento de los Sectores Civiles* 1992).

Along with a sophisticated critique of the negotiation process, the statement issued by the civil blocs reminded the government and the URNG that, already in December 1991, the blocs had sent an open letter to the conciliator, as they then referred to Bishop Quezada Toruño, and the parties, but they had "never received a direct and official reply." (Nor had a reply been given to a petition that the Maya sector had presented to the bilateral parties in February 1992. The

Maya had demanded participation, at least during the discussion on the theme of the Rights and Identity of Indigenous Peoples (COMG 1995, 15–16).) The conclusions of the civil blocs concerning the negotiations speak for themselves:

If Oslo gave a participatory character to the search for peace; if El Escorial spoke directly about the participation of all sectors in the definition of changes; if Quito, Metepec, and Atlixco reiterated such concepts and developed them to the point of proposing the celebration of a representative and participating Constituent National Assembly; if the Plan for Total Peace of President Serrano recognized and endorsed the previous Accords; and if the URNG manifested in its Global Proposal the need for the participation of civil sectors in reflections and contributions to the themes; this signifies that the necessity of the participation of civil society is a *national clamour* (Inforpress Centroamericana 1995, 142; emphasis in the original).

The continued silence of the government and the URNG concerning the civil sectors' proposals meant that the latter would continue to loudly criticize the negotiation process. In August 1992, taking advantage of a closed-door bilateral meeting in Mexico, six representatives of the civil sectors went to Mexico and publicly demanded direct civilian participation. As usual, the government and the URNG responded that the participation of civil sectors could be considered only *after* the signature of the accord on human rights, reiterating the URNG's May statement. In the meantime, however, negotiations on the human rights accord had no clear end in sight.

Clearly, a process as complicated as the Guatemalan peace process was bound to suffer from contradictions and ambiguities. And in spite of what could be considered a unanimous critique of their exclusion from the negotiations, civil sectors exhibited contradictions among themselves on this crucial matter. For example, the six delegates of the CIC, who had been present at the August meeting in Mexico, stated, in a press release dated August 5 "that the negotiations [are taking] place between the two fundamental parties – the government of the republic and the URNG – which have confronted each other in armed conflict; as a consequence, our participation would not be comparable, nor do we form another party to the conflict, but we can contribute to the search for solutions" (Inforpress Centroamericana 1995, 108).

It is possible that strong pressure was exerted on some of the CIC delegates to make them soften their position in accordance with the perspective shared by the government and the URNG. However, other sectors that had also signed the June statement maintained their original position.

In spite of the contradictions among the civil sectors, on the whole they continued to demand their inclusion in the negotiations (Inforpress Centroamericana 1995, 109, 112–13). But that pressure, and the negotiations themselves, were temporarily suspended by the so-called *Serranazo* – the attempted *auto-golpe* – of May 1993. Paradoxically, Serrano Elias' attempt to establish dictatorial rule led to a series of events that significantly deepened the transformation of Guatemala's public sphere (Poitevin 1993). In August 1993 opposition political parties had organized themselves into the Multisectoral Social Forum; during the coup attempt various civil society sectors, including the CACIF, had already established the INC to oppose the *auto-golpe* and to offer proposals for reviving the negotiations.

The INC reintroduced the possibility of negotiating substantive and operational issues separately and incorporating representatives of civil society into the negotiation of the substantive issues (Inforpress Centroamericana 1995, 199). In this fashion, then, the INC reiterated the proposal that had been made a year earlier in the statement presented by the civil sectors. Briefly, the INC proposal called for a radical restructuring of the negotiation process *before*, rather than *after*, the signing of the Comprehensive Accord on Human Rights, as proposed by the government and the URNG.

Remarkably, the INC proposal became the conceptual basis for the National Plan for Peace accepted by President Carpio on 30 September 1993. The INC proposal also served as the basis for the much more radical proposal presented the same month by Monseñor Quezada Toruño, entitled Preliminary Project for Renewing the Peace Negotiations (*ibid.* 1995, 201).

The principle goal of Quezada Toruño's proposal was the resolution of "a problem that had dragged along, without solution, from the previous phase" of the negotiations, from Oslo to Querétaro. That was the problem of secrecy. Its second objective was the dissolution of the fabricated idea that substantive issues (for example, human rights) and operational issues (for example, guerrilla demobilization and overall demilitarization) needed to be considered simultaneously and only bilaterally. According to Quezada Toruño, the simultaneous consideration of these issues infused a political-military logic into the negotiating agenda that resulted not only in frequent "deadlocks" but also in the continuing exclusion of civilian organizations from the negotiations. A third objective -which grows logically out of Quezada Toruño's critique of the process – was to obtain a commitment from the URNG and the government to desist from offensive military operations during the negotiations. Quezada Toruño, in effect, attempted to untie the Gordian knot that had kept the various issues being negotiated tied together in such a way that civil sectors were excluded. Once again, however, the bishop's proposal failed to receive the kind of attention that he and the civil sectors would have liked.

It was not until the signing of the Framework Agreement in Mexico City at the beginning of 1994 that the government and the URNG took into account some isolated elements from the various proposals concerning the participation of civil sectors. As a result of this emerging need for civilian participation, the ASC was created.

In the Framework Agreement, the government and the URNG recognized "the contribution of those sectors that ... participated in the meetings of El Escorial, Ottawa, Quito, Metepec, and Atlixco with the URNG," and they recognized how they "provided a stimulus to the negotiation process in Guatemala." What the agreement did not mention was the history of more than two years of political struggle by civil sectors for their direct inclusion in the negotiations *before* the signing of *any* agreement. Far from satisfying these demands, the parties decided to grant the ASC the role of "discussing" the substantive issues and of formulating "consensus positions" outside the direct negotiations. Further, the consensus positions of the ASC would not have a binding character and would be oriented only toward "facilitating understanding between the parties" without, under any circumstances, "slowing down the bilateral negotiation process." Finally, the two parties reserved for themselves the right to approve or reject the consensus positions of the ASC, while "if for any reasons, [the ASC] were not to approve a bilateral agreement, that agreement would still maintain its force." Therefore, it remained clear that the ASC – and the discursive practices among its members – would remain subordinate to the political-military logic of the two parties.

In spite of all this, the structure, functioning, and dynamics of the ASC were to be modelled, more or less, on the Quezada Toruño proposal, which, in turn, was based on the experience of the Great National Dialogue. Not only did the four blocs that had been constituted during the Oslo process participate in the assembly, but civil society organizations such as the COPMAGUA also participated (Bastos and Camus 1995). In total, ten civil sectors constituted the ASC, each one with five regular representatives and five substitutes, which brought up the number of delegates at each plenary session to at least fifty.

The work of the ASC took place in meetings under the direction of five working commissions, each one responsible for discussing one of the five substantive issues on which consensus documents were to be produced (Padilla 1995, 60). Therefore, despite its subordinate position in the peace process, the ASC succeeded in its own deliberations, to a certain extent, in implementing democratic principles and arguments in its own deliberations beyond what had been prescribed to it in the Framework Agreement (see FUNDAPAZD 1994). Needless to say, this emerging discursive paradigm of negotiations had a tremendous impact on the Guatemalan public sphere.

The first formal task of the assembly – the elaboration of consensus proposals on the substantive issues of the negotiations – was completed on 14 October 1994. At the end of 1995 the ASC found itself occupied with its second formal task of receiving and giving its opinion on the agreements signed by the parties, and it was also already debating the role that it would play in the remainder of the negotiation process and after the signing of a final peace agreement.

CONCLUSION

The peace negotiation process lasted several years. Without a doubt, much was accomplished. For fundamentally strategic reasons, the two parties found themselves in a negotiation process without precedent in the history of Guatemala. Beyond the agreements signed, a critical legacy of the peace process was the ensemble of discursive practices and democratic forms of conflict resolution. The future transformation of the public sphere in Guatemala will depend, to a great extent, on the consolidation, deepening, and eventual institutionalization of these discursive practices and their normative and procedural underpinnings.

Democratic practice guides participation, argument, and the securing of agreements among sectors of civil society, rather than the agreements themselves. It is democratic practice that can sustain a firm and lasting peace beyond the termination of internal armed conflict and the peace negotiations. If these practices are converted into regulating principles for the elaboration of state policy, then it will be possible to say that Guatemala is on the threshold of a functioning and participatory democracy.

NOTES

1 Among the many works on the limits of democracy in Guatemala, see Centro de Estudios de Guatemala (1994), *La democracia de las armas*, as

well as Aguilera Peralta (1995a); on the military and demilitarization, see Mejía Molina (1995).

2 The ASC was formally the result of the Framework Accord signed between the Government of Guatemala and the URNG guerrillas in January of 1994. However, as I attempt to show in this essay, all of the particular "sectors" that eventually composed the ASC were formed during the Oslo process of discussions between the guerrillas and various sectors of Guatemalan civilian society. These discussions preceded the bilateral negotiations between the government and the guerrillas initiated in 1991.

3 All citations from the specific agreements to which this paper refers are drawn directly from the texts of those agreements; they have been printed in a variety of sources, such as Inforpress Centroamericana (1995). The various steps in the negotiation process are discussed in IRIPAZ (1991), Aguilera Peralta (1994; 1995b), and Aguilera Peralta and Ponciano (1994). UN mediation is discussed in Padilla (1995) and one UN evaluation of the situation can be found in MINUGUA (1995).

4 The Accord on the Rights and Identity of Indigenous Peoples was signed 31 March 1995. The subsequent agreements signed were the Accord on Socioeconomic Aspects and the Agrarian Situation (6 May 1996); the Accord on Strengthening Civil Power and the Role of the Army in a Democratic Society (19 September 1996); the Definitive Cease-Fire Accord (6 December 1996); the Accord on Constitutional and Electoral Systems Reform (7 December 1996); the Accord on the Incorporation of the URNG into Society (12 December 1996); the Passage of the Law of National Reconciliation (18 December 1996); and the Accord on a Firm and Lasting Peace (29 December 1996). (Note added by the editors.)

5 See Fundación Myrna Mack (1995) for a critical perspective on the FDNG, revealing the authoritarian tendencies within it.

5 Maximizing the Benefits of UN Involvement in the Guatemalan Peace Process

STEPHEN BARANYI

In my last report on the activities of MINUGUA, I reiterated my conviction that the presence of the Mission could be an important factor in improving the human rights situation in Guatemala and in enhancing the prospect for an early end to the armed confrontation. MINUGUA's second report confirms that the full deployment of the Mission throughout the country since February 1995 and its verification and institution-building activities are already having a positive impact in promoting human rights and the rule of law.
  Boutros Boutros-Ghali, UN Secretary-General, New York, August 1995[1]

Impunity is the swamp that swallows everything in this country. We have created a large opening for expression. But we haven't had an effect yet on the daily lives of the victims.
  Leonardo Franco, MINUGUA Director, Guatemala, March 1996

Today, with MINUGUA here, the Army has its hands tied a bit. But what will happen when MINUGUA leaves?
  Anonymous human rights promoter, Colotenango, April 1996

These statements, fleeting interpretations of reality by individuals who were located in different institutional and geographic settings but were all part of the peace process in Guatemala, reflect the complex, paradoxical, and protean character of this process and of the role of the United Nations in that context. They provoke questions that may make some of us uncomfortable. If the on-site presence of the UN verification mission had not, by mid-1996, had a significant impact on the daily lives of the victims, if it had not led to a diminution of human rights violations or made a dent in the wall of impunity, then was MINUGUA reaching the goals set out in its mandate? Could it be that MINUGUA and broader UN involvement helped lay the foundations for resettlement, reconciliation, and reconstruction even though the human rights situation remained quite worrisome? How do we explain the contributions and the limitations of the UN's role in the peace process? What could different sectors (Guatemalans from distinct sectors, as well as the international community) do to make better use of the UN's unique presence in the future?

In an attempt to provide tentative answers to these questions, this paper presents four arguments concerning the role of the UN in the peace process to mid-1996:

1 The UN's contribution to the peace process was crucial and generally quite positive.
2 Still, its role was limited in certain respects, particularly with regard to its impact on the practices of Guatemalans who were involved, as perpetrators or prosecutors, in the country's human rights tragedy. Moreover, concerns endure about the future role of the UN and other international bodies in the peace process.
3 The limitations of the UN's role were partly due to dynamics within the UN system. Yet the constraints on UN performance also stemmed from exogenous factors, namely, certain tendencies in the international system and in Guatemalan society.
4 As such, the ability of the UN to contribute more to peacebuilding in the future depends partly on steps it could take but also on a greater coherence of strategies by more powerful international entities (the International Monetary Fund (IMF), the multilateral development banks, and the governments of the United States and the European Union) and especially on more cooperative strategies by Guatemalans themselves. International nongovernmental organizations (INGOs) can help foster the convergence of these sectors' strategies to make better use of the UN's historically unique presence in Guatemala – before and after the signing of a final accord.

This chapter does not present a detailed analysis of the UN's work, since this has been done elsewhere (Baranyi 1995, 1996; Jonas 1996). Nor does it attempt to theorize the UN's role: for now, I have left the linkages between this case and relevant debates in social theory buried in the subtext. The purpose of this chapter is simply to provide elements for reflection and constructive dialogue between interested sectors on strategic options.[2]

UN CONTRIBUTIONS

There were many UN agencies with important programmes in Guatemala, but those most actively involved in the peace process were the Department of Political Affairs (DPA), MINUGUA, and the UN Development Programme (UNDP). The role of the DPA grew out of the UN's long involvement as an observer in the peace talks that had been mediated by Monseñor Quezada Toruño. In January 1994 the government and the National Revolutionary Unity of Guatemala (URNG) signed a Framework Accord, which upgraded the UN's status to that of moderator, or lead mediator, in the negotiations.

DPA officials did not play the role of innocent bystanders in the negotiation of the Framework Accord. Indeed, officials in the Americas Division of the DPA were influential in getting the parties back to the table to discuss a more sensible framework than the one that had been proposed by the government in the autumn of 1993. DPA officials also backed the URNG proposals that the UN be brought in as the mediator and verifier of the process and that an Assembly of Civil Society be created to articulate the views of civil society, which, in turn, would be reflected in the negotiations. After the signing of the Framework Accord, the DPA created a Guatemala unit to provide support for the moderator and to house the small team that would accompany the development of an on-site verification mission.

The Calenderization Accord, signed in March 1994, envisaged that the talks would come to a conclusion with the signing of a final accord by the end of 1994. Measured against that initial timeline, UN mediation was not very successful. Yet if UN peacemaking is assessed against the benchmark of progress towards the signing of accords that could lead to major changes in Guatemalan society, and therefore to the consolidation of lasting peace, mediation by DPA officials was impressive. By mid-1996, UN peacemaking had helped the parties reach the following five substantive agreements:

1 The Comprehensive Accord on Human Rights, also signed in March 1994, under which the Government in particular, but also the URNG, committed itself to immediately taking steps to curtail human rights violations, end impunity, and strengthen the institutions responsible for protecting human rights, including non-governmental organizations (NGOs). The Accord on Human Rights also called for the deployment of an on-site UN mission to verify and facilitate compliance.

2 The Accord for the Resettlement of Populations Uprooted by the Armed Conflict, signed in June 1994, laid out a framework for the return of refugees and the resettlement of returnees and internally displaced persons in Guatemala. The agreement also authorized the immediate establishment of a technical commission including representatives of the government and of uprooted peoples to plan the full implementation of the accord.

3 The Accord on the Establishment of a Commission to Clarify Human Rights Violations and Acts of Violence That Have Caused the Guatemalan People to Suffer was also signed in June 1994. It authorized the creation of a commission after the signing of a final accord with a mandate to identify those institutions responsible for the grave human rights violations committed during the war, since the early 1960s.

4 The Accord on the Rights and Identity of Indigenous Peoples, signed in March 1995, contained provisions for constitutional, legislative, policy, and organizational changes that could help end discrimination and guarantee indigenous peoples the capacity to exercise their civil, political, economic, social, and cultural rights. Under this agreement, the UN was given a mandate to immediately verify compliance with those human rights provisions that did not require constitutional reforms in order to be put into practice.

5 The Accord on Socioeconomic Aspects and the Agrarian Situation, signed in May 1996, contained provisions for changes to the system of land tenure, labour-capital relations, and the administration of fiscal policy, as well as provisions for changes to social services, and for making equity, transparency, and participation a priority, in each instance. Although the bulk of this agreement would also go into effect only after the Final Accord was signed, the UN was given a mandate to verify that the Government was taking steps to prepare the ground for its eventual full implementation.

None of these accords are perfect but most were well-received by key sectors inside Guatemala. Given the renewed momentum of the talks generated by the election (in January 1996) and the first steps of the Arzú Government, it was already then believed that agreement could be reached on the remaining items by the end of 1996. Though hardly the only force behind progress at the negotiating table, the DPA played a crucial role in forging the accords signed by the parties during the 1994–96 period.[3]

The DPA was also responsible for overseeing the development of the UN Mission for the Verification of Human Rights in Guatemala. Shortly after the signing of the Accord on Human Rights, UN secretary-general Boutros-Ghali dispatched a preliminary mission to Guatemala to begin planning the deployment of a field operation; the group was led by Leonardo Franco and was composed of UN officials and other external advisors with considerable experience in Guatemala or in the area of UN verification. The preliminary mission consulted widely with government officials, the Church, human rights organizations, independent analysts, and the diplomatic community; on that basis, it produced a report with sound proposals for the gradual deployment, training, and operations of an on-site mission.

On 19 September 1994 the UN General Assembly adopted resolution 48/267, authorizing the establishment of MINUGUA. The next day, Leonardo Franco and a small team of UN officials flew to Guatemala to establish a preparatory office; during the following weeks, they negotiated their political space inside Guatemala, made the necessary logistical arrangements, and laid the basis for the recruitment and training of almost four hundred staff by early 1995.

On 21 November 1994 MINUGUA officially opened its doors and began to receive complaints of violations. By February 1995 it had established and staffed a network of eight regional offices and five subregional offices across the country. During the first year several institutional strengthening projects were initiated with the attorney general's office, the national police, the judiciary, the Human Rights Counsel (PDH), and other governmental agencies, and with national human rights NGOs.[4] A decentralized multimedia campaign to disseminate the Human Rights Accord was carried out. By 1996 staff performance had been enhanced in most areas, including verification methodology and programming approaches for institutional strengthening. A campaign to disseminate the Indigenous Accord was launched, and steps were taken to develop the capacity to verify compliance with this agreement; this included preparing a verification manual, training staff in its use, and developing relations with the complex network of organizations representing indigenous peoples in Guatemala.

By April 1996 the international community had spent over U.S.$35 million on MINUGUA. What had MINUGUA produced in return? First, through its quarterly reports to the UN General Assembly, its regular press releases, and the public declarations of its senior officials, the mission had produced a detailed, comprehensive, and authoritative record of the grave human rights situation in Guatemala. It had rigorously documented the persistence of serious violations of the rights to life, personal integrity, individual liberty, and due legal process; as well, it had documented and explained the institutional underpinnings of these violations and of impunity. It had reported on violations of the Accord on Human Rights by the URNG and especially by the government, while also reporting on the positive steps taken by both parties in this regard. Finally, MINUGUA had reported on the government's compliance with its obligations under the Indigenous Accord.

In some ways, this information was not new: the Office of the Human Rights Counsel (PDH), the Human Rights Office of the Archbishop (ODHA), and national human rights NGOs such as the Guatemalan Human Rights Commission (CDHG) had all produced exhaustive human rights reports for years; these had been echoed and supplemented by the reports put out by the independent expert of the UN Commission on Human Rights, by the UN's thematic rapporteurs, and by international NGOs like Amnesty International and Human Rights Watch. Some of these reports had included constructive recommendations for institutional reforms to put an end to systematic violations and impunity.

What MINUGUA contributed to this broad human rights monitoring effort were reports based on the in-depth investigation of cases by a network of over two hundred professional observers deployed across the country. The mission's pronouncements were authoritative because its mandate resulted from a peace accord signed by both parties and because it was able to maintain their confidence in the impartiality of its reports. In addition, MINUGUA's recommendations for institutional reforms were more detailed than those of other bodies. Though not strictly binding on the parties, they were nevertheless influential, due to MINUGUA's mandate, its on-site advocacy capacity, and the fact that certain international donors hinted that future funding would be linked to compliance with the mission's recommendations. Finally, MINUGUA took the lead in developing the capacity to report on compliance with the Indigenous Accord; its first reports on this score made a useful, if modest, contribution to the debate on indigenous peoples' rights.

There is also a sense that MINUGUA increased the space for human rights promotion and political organization. In rural areas, local human rights promoters felt somewhat safer with a MINUGUA office in the area and with MINUGUA observers visiting even quite remote communities regularly; they were no longer alone with the Voluntary Civil Self-Defense Committees (CVDCs, or PACs) and the local army detachment. At the national level, analysts believe that without the mission's field presence, popular organizations would not have participated in the elections in November 1995 and January 1996 under the New Guatemala Democratic Front (FDNG) banner; few believe that without extensive UN involvement, the URNG would have encouraged this development. MINUGUA's declarations on impunity prompted discussions of issues that were previously off limits in the public sphere. The mission's presence and its verification work had a positive impact on the peace process by helping to build confidence in the process, at least within the government and the URNG.

It is doubtful that MINUGUA would have been able to establish such an effective presence in Guatemala so quickly had it not been for the prior experience and assistance of officials from the UNDP and the offices of the UN High Commissioner for Refugees (UNHCR). The link with the UNDP was particularly important in the area of institutional strengthening, given the agency's contacts and its experience in the areas of project design and delivery and resource mobilization. MINUGUA coordinated its strategy in this domain with the UNDP through the joint unit established in January 1995.

Beyond this, however, the UNDP played a strategic role in pressing its own agenda. Based on its conception of sustainable human development, and especially on its experience in the Salvadoran peace process, the UNDP believed that for peacebuilding to be successful and sustainable, it must be firmly anchored in national commitments and capacities. The international community's role, from the UNDP's viewpoint, was to coordinate the leverage it had during the peace process to foster a national consensus on compliance with the peace accords, on the adequate national financing of implementation, and on the application of complementary policy measures in areas such as tax reform, fiscal policy, and social services. The problem in El Salvador was that while the UN was negotiating the peace accords with the government and the Farabundo Marti National Liberation Front (FMLN), the international financial institutions (the IMF, the World Bank and the Inter-American Development Bank) were negotiating a national reconstruction programme with the government that included economic policies that were at odds with the peace accords. This conclusion was shared by the DPA officials who had negotiated the accords; together, the UNDP and the DPA were determined to avoid a repeat of the Salvadoran saga (de Soto and del Castillo 1994).

Applying these lessons to Guatemala involved two advocacy challenges. First, the international community needed to be convinced they should harmonize the signals being sent to Guatemalans; second, the government and the Chamber of Agricultural, Commercial, Industrial, and Financial Associations (CACIF), representing big business, had to be persuaded that without compliance, adequate national financing, and complementary policy measures, the international community would not invest in the peace process and, therefore, lasting peace would, quite simply, not be built.

The UNDP and the DPA applied pressure at both levels by lobbying donors during the Informal Donors Meeting in June 1994 and by launching a serious economic policy dialogue with the government in August of the same year. In early 1995 the UN began involving the multilateral development banks as advisors in the negotiations on the Indigenous Peoples Accord. This practice continued during the negotiations on the Socioeconomic Accord, thus providing further opportunities for coordinating international approaches. In May 1995 the UNDP published *Adjustment towards Peace* – a critical study of the economic aspects of the Salvadoran peace process – which added weight to its advocacy of policy harmonization (Boyce et al. 1995). The first public success in this effort came during the Informal Donors Meeting in June 1995. It is worth quoting at length from the closing statement made by a senior World Bank official on that occasion:

The representatives welcomed the structural reforms being undertaken by the Government of Guatemala ... and urged that the authorities persevere in their implementation. Of critical importance is the effort to increase public savings through the strengthening of tax receipts so as to finance increased public investment, especially in health and education, aimed at the rural areas and indigenous peoples ... No adequate development effort will be possible in the absence of a reinvigorated commitment by all sectors to equitable social and economic development. On the expenditure side there was wide agreement on the need and scope for reducing defense outlays ... donors also believe that agrarian policy is a major issue requiring urgent national attention.

The donors welcomed the Government's efforts to strengthen democratic institutions in Guatemala. Greater participation of NGOs, observance of human rights and free democratic elections will be a necessary condition for sustainable development and increased support from the international community. (World Bank 1995)[5]

The joint advocacy campaign by the Forum of Guatemalan NGOs (endorsed by the Assembly of Civil Society, or ASC) and a group of U.S. NGOs operating under the umbrella of the Latin America Working Group (LAWG) certainly influenced this final statement (Ruthrauff 1996; see also Sollis 1996b). But these NGOs would not have had much impact if the UNDP and the DPA had not already negotiated their economic policy priorities onto the agendas of traditionally more orthodox donors. The codification of these ideas in the Accord on Socioeconomic Aspects and the Agrarian Situation, in 1996, confirmed the emergence of this new policy consensus.

LIMITATIONS

Some critics of the peace process suggest that the failure to reach a final accord by the original deadline of December 1994, the second deadline of September 1995, or even by mid-1996 reflected the weakness of UN mediation. There is no doubt these delays put an inordinate amount of pressure on UN officials and especially on MINUGUA, which has felt quite exposed, given its limited mandate. Yet this author shares the view of many Guatemalans – forcefully expressed by the Catholic Church and the ASC (particularly the latter's Maya sector) during the breakdown in the talks in mid-1994 and again during the early 1995 rescheduling episode – that the problem resided in the original deadlines and not in UN mediation or the inflexibility of the parties.

What was most important to these sectors was the signing of *acuerdos consecuentes*, namely, agreements that provided frameworks for truly resolving the conflict. The delays experienced since 1994 have, in this sense, provided time for negotiating serious agreements on complex and highly controversial issues; they have also provided time for building the confidence of key sectors, particularly the URNG, the army, and the business elite, in the viability of the peace process. Delays in signing key agreements did not, therefore, necessarily amount to a failure of UN mediation.

The fundamental limitation of the UN's impact was its inability to help close the gap between the accords and their implementation on the ground. This was particularly apparent with regard to the Accord on Human Rights, which had not led to a reduction of grave human rights violations by mid-1996. In its fourth report MINUGUA observed that from November 1994 to December 1995 it had verified the occurrence of 420 cases of human rights violations affecting a total of 3,161 victims. Of these cases of proven violations, 270 were violations of the rights to life, integrity, and liberty. The institutional identity of the perpetrators was also clear 24.5 percent of the violations were attributed to national police personnel, seventeen percent to the army, seventeen percent to the PACs, and 5.4 percent to the URNG (MINUGUA 1996, para. 132).

According to MINUGUA, impunity was the foundation of these ongoing human rights violations. Impunity persisted because the National Police and the attorney general's office (Ministerio Público) did not properly investigate allegations of violations; if they did investigate crimes for which security forces' personnel or their strategic allies were presumed to be responsible, they were likely to receive threats or other more drastic deterrents against law enforcement. Moreover, even if they did investigate properly, the courts would simply not prosecute or sentence those guilty of abuses. There was much truth in MINUGUA's assertion that these institutional failures were due to the confluence of two factors: a lack of political will and massive administrative-technical deficiencies. Hence the honest admission by Leonardo Franco, quoted at the outset, that MINUGUA had not yet made a major difference in the daily lives of the victims. The mission, the UN Commission on Human Rights, and other human rights bodies continued to express alarm at this condition of persistent violations and pervasive impunity.

It would be incorrect to blame the United Nations for this situation. Yet it is fair to observe that MINUGUA's human rights verification did not have an appreciable impact on the human rights situation per se. The same can be said for the UN's institutional strengthening projects. The mission and the UNDP could point to the impressive, quantifiable outputs of their activities in this area: Most public prosecutors received training on the application of the new Code of Criminal Procedure through UN seminars; UN consultants accompanied prosecutors in processing over two hundred cases; UN advisors seconded to the national police carried out an evaluation of its investigative capacity; a comprehensive assessment of the capacity-building requirements of human rights NGOs was completed, and so on. Yet these activities did not lead to substantial improvements in the defense of human rights by governmental institutions, as noted by MINUGUA itself (1996, paras. 143–4; Aldana 1996). Anybody familiar with Guatemalan history or with the difficulties of promoting good governance in the South could have predicted that real reform would take time, but MINUGUA and the UNDP set themselves up for some criticism by dubbing their interventions "rapid-impact projects" and by not transparently setting out meaningful criteria for assessing these initiatives.[6]

There were also difficulties with regard to the Accord on the Identity and Rights of Indigenous Peoples. Demetrio Cojti, a respected Maya intellectual, cogently argued that compared to the government and even the Maya sector, MINUGUA had taken the most significant steps to implement this agreement by March 1996. Nonetheless, it is also true that MINUGUA's activities did not have much of an impact on the actual situation of indigenous peoples in Guatemala. During the first year after the accord was signed, the mission admitted less than six complaints of violations under this agreement. Even fewer were thoroughly investigated and corroborated, this in a country where discrimination is pervasive and endemic. More fundamentally, with the important exception of the ratification of ILO (International

Labor Organization) Convention 169 on Indigenous and Tribal Peoples by the Guatemalan Congress in March 1996, MINUGUA's efforts did not spur significant compliance initiatives by the government (Cojti 1996).

MINUGUA's performance should be evaluated against its mandate to promote and verify the implementation of the Accord on Human Rights and of certain provisions of the Indigenous Accord, thereby building the confidence required to bring the peace negotiations to a successful conclusion. On the basis of these criteria, one could say that MINUGUA performed well with regard to verification, though better on the Human Rights Accord than on the Indigenous Accord. As for the promotion of compliance, even the former director of MINUGUA recognized that MINUGUA's activities did not have a major impact on compliance with critical provisions of said accords (Franco 1996). Yet overall, MINUGUA's work did have a positive impact on the peace process.

But this assessment excludes an analysis of other aspects of MINUGUA's performance that could yield important insights for the future. Two phenomena are relevant in this connection. The first was MINUGUA's decision to interpret its verification mandate narrowly, on the basis of the definition of "priority rights" set out in the Accord on Human Rights. This decision seemed justifiable. Textually, it rested on a defensible interpretation of the accord; operationally, MINUGUA's verification resources were already quite stretched; strategically, it was predicated on an argument about the danger of encompassing economic rights before the political parameters for taking these on had been agreed upon in the peace negotiations. Yet one cost of adhering to this narrow interpretation was that it held the mission back from engaging in the vital issues of land disputes and labour rights. This, too, must be signaled as a limitation in UN verification.

Another area in which the UN's contribution was unnecessarily limited concerned the verification of the Resettlement Accord. By the mid-1990s, the only provisions of that agreement that had gone into effect were those pertaining to the establishment and functioning of the Technical Commission. The Resettlement Accord was signed in June 1994; it took six months for the government to accept the representatives proposed by uprooted peoples' organizations and another six months for the commission to reach the necessary procedural agreements. In June 1995, the government presented seventeen projects for the implementation of the accord to the international community at the Informal Donors Meeting. None of these projects had been formally consulted with the Technical Commission, in clear violation of the Resettlement Accord. Influential donors such as the European Commission allocated funds for some of these projects despite this lack of consultation with beneficiaries, further undermining the consultative mechanism created under the accord. Although MINUGUA was present at the meeting, it did not express concern about these developments, on the grounds that it had no mandate to verify compliance with the Resettlement Accord. Again, this position reflected a narrow interpretation of responsibilities that was inconsistent with the UN's overall verification mandate as set out in the 1994 Framework Accord (Quiñonez 1996).

It is in their connection to the wider debate on the future of UN verification that these tendencies gain significance. In March 1996 the longstanding conflict between the United Nations and the United States over UN financing came to a head when the secretary-general threatened to wind down MINUGUA and the UN Civilian Mission in Haiti (MICIVIH), two priority missions for Washington, unless the United States paid its dues to the regular budget. A temporary solution for funding those missions was found, but uncertainties about the future generated worries about the possibilities of financing an expansion of MINUGUA's mandate to cover the verification of other agreements after a final accord was signed (WOLA 1996).

Against this backdrop, agencies whose budgets were not as vulnerable began manoeuvring to acquire their own verification mandates. Some UNDP officials used MINUGUA's lack of expertise in the socioeconomic realm to explore the possibility of playing a role in monitoring the Accord on Socioeconomic Aspects, while certain UNHCR officials suggested that their agency could verify the Resettlement Accord.

Some observers believed that the government backed these bids in order to weaken the prospects for rigorous verification by MINUGUA; indeed, broadening the ambit of UNDP and UNHCR involvement could have been convenient, since those agencies were more closely bound to the state – given that they were in Guatemala only at the behest of the government and not at the invitation of both the government and the URNG, in contrast to MINUGUA – and had no record of impartial verification of peace accords. In May 1996 a spokesman for the UN secretary-general temporarily squelched the verification turf war by stating that after a final accord was signed, "MINUGUA would expand its activities to cover verification of all agreements reached" (Secretariado de la ONU 1996). Yet the mission's ability to hold onto its verification monopoly in a context of severe financial pressures would depend on its ability to show that it had the capacity to verify compliance beyond the limited sphere of "priority rights."

UNDERSTANDING THE DYNAMICS OF UN INVOLVEMENT

The limitations of the UN's ability to promote compliance with the accords were partly due to certain tendencies within the UN itself. MINUGUA's insistence on a narrow definition of its verification mandate was rooted in the legitimate operational and strategic concerns noted above; yet it was also due to the lack of experience within the UN human rights system in the verification of rights that lie outside the civil and political realm. This absence of well-defined methodological guidelines for verifying economic, social, and cultural rights dogged efforts to respond to labour and land conflicts and to monitor compliance with the Indigenous Accord. The difficulties of embarking on new terrain were reinforced by the great aversion to risk-taking inside the UN. Despite its boldness on many fronts, MINUGUA was unable to escape this aspect of the organization's culture.

Moreover, despite the experimentation with institutional strengthening projects in El Salvador and the prior experience of the UNHCR with quick-impact resettlement projects, MINUGUA had to develop its own methodology for designing, administering, and evaluating institutional strengthening activities. The partnership with the UNDP through the Joint Unit helped in this regard, but despite a degree of cooperation, the UNDP later appeared to minimize MINUGUA's role in an area that it viewed as its preserve. Complicating matters further, the UN Centre for Human Rights was pulled into this conflict. In early 1996 the government requested that the UN Commission on Human Rights reduce the monitoring mandate of the independent expert, Mónica Pinto, in exchange for the development of institutional strengthening projects by the centre, under its mandate to provide technical and advisory services to Guatemala in the field of human rights. Such rivalries are endemic to the UN, but they were aggravated by the financial crisis as each agency struggled to protect its area of distinctive competence and take on new tasks in order to attract increasingly scarce financial resources. Unless this issue is resolved through a rational division of labour based on true competence, there is tremendous potential for duplication and for a weakening of the UN's capacity to promote the profound institutional reforms required in Guatemala.

These intra-UN dynamics are important. However, the constraints on UN performance also stemmed from exogenous factors. At the international level, the first relevant factor was the impasse created by the insistence of the U.S. Congress in reducing U.S. contributions to the UN's regular budget and linking payments to cuts in the UN's expenditures. The decision by the secretary-general to use MINUGUA and MICIVIH as levers to soften the American position was perhaps somewhat cynical, yet it did highlight the fact that it was in the U.S. interest to find a rational solution to the financial crisis – soon. In the meantime, it is imperative for other large contributors, like the European Union, to ensure that the work of these missions is not jeopardized and that planning can proceed for the necessary expansion of MINUGUA in the phase after the final accord. Until the international community sends a clear signal on this score, Guatemalans like the rural human rights promoter cited at the outset (or uprooted peoples representatives and even military personnel) will lack sufficient incentives to take the risks required for lasting reforms, given the possibility of a premature UN withdrawal.

The second major international constraint was the UN's structural weakness vis-à-vis the IMF, the multilateral development banks, and large donors like the European Union and USAID, and the fragility of these more powerful institutions' commitment to "peace conditionality" in practice, that is, to making international assistance dependent on the implementation of the peace accords. Together, the DPA and the UNDP made impressive headway in persuading larger donors and lenders about the need to harmonize peace processes and economic strategies, at least in Guatemala. As a result, it became commonplace to speak of linking international cooperation to adequate national financing and compliance with the peace accords, consulting with beneficiaries, reducing military expenditures, and targeting assistance at the most marginalized sectors of society, such as indigenous peoples. Yet the UNDP is a rather small player; it did not, given its resource limitations, have much leverage vis-à-vis large donors, and especially the IMF. Off the record, officials in these organizations scoffed at the UNDP's "pretense" of coordinating international cooperation efforts. In practice, despite the rhetoric of collaboration, large donors tended to follow their own logic in their cooperation programs and wider policies.

Let us take the European Union as an example, since the EU (the European Commission plus fifteen member states) was the largest provider of grant funding to Guatemala (compared to the multilateral development banks, which lend money) and is expected to be the largest donor in the reconstruction phase. We have already seen how the EU decided to provide funding for resettlement projects without adequately consulting with the Technical Commission established under the Resettlement Accord. The European Commission's draft "Strategy for Medium-Term Aid to Guatemala," tabled in November 1995, suggests that this was not an isolated incident:

indeed, despite its many positive aspects, the draft was silent on issues like the coordination of international cooperation efforts, peace conditionality, consultation with beneficiaries, and other themes that were highlighted at the 1995 Donors Meeting.

In May 1996 in response to a joint advocacy campaign by the ASC and the Copenhagen Initiative for Central America (CIFCA, a network of twenty-three European NGOs), Holland, Sweden, and the United Kingdom called on the commission to revise the strategy to address these lacunae. To its credit, the commission took these concerns on board and a substantively revised strategy was adopted by the intergovernmental Asia–Latin America Committee in June 1996. The commission's flexibility demonstrated that dialogue between the EU, European NGOs, and Guatemalan civil society organizations could have a constructive impact on policy, yet the fact that the European Commission had to be lobbied on principles that it had agreed to in other contexts reminds us of the ongoing difficulties of attaining the hallowed goal of policy consistency in practice (European Commission 1995, 1996).

These international factors converged with profound national constraints. The most significant was the ambivalence of Guatemalan elites regarding the extent to which reforms were required to obtain URNG demobilization, stability, growth, and international legitimacy. The Arzú cabinet included individuals with reformist credentials, yet the government's attempt to get large-scale international support for changes to the National Police prior to an agreement on this issue in the peace talks, its attempts to reduce international human rights monitoring in the 1996 session of the UN Commission on Human Rights, and its blatant disregard for the ASC suggests that it had some difficulties putting its "progressive" rhetoric into practice.

Similarly, while the new High Command publicly expressed its commitment to the peace process and a reorientation of the army's role, persistent human rights violations involving army personnel, and the impossibility of bringing senior army officials to justice for their crimes, indicated that this institution remained divided over how far to go in the quest for peace. This does not bode well for the work and ultimate impact of the Clarification Commission, which is supposed to begin its investigations into past human rights violations after a final accord is signed. Finally, although the mainstream of the corporate sector represented by CACIF publicly backed the peace process (since mid-1995), it was ambivalent about key issues such as increasing taxes. Some big business interests, particularly the fraction of the agrarian sector represented by the National Agricultural Council (CONAGRO), remained fundamentally opposed to the on-site

UN presence and to the implementation of peace accords signed with the URNG.

The situation on the other side of the political balance was also worrisome. The political-military weakness of the URNG was widely asserted, although the guerrillas' ability to get the army to negotiate without preconditions and extract rather significant concessions from the state and the business elite in the peace process indicates that their weakness may have been somewhat exaggerated. The ability of the ASC – which includes sectors ranging from Maya organizations through representatives of uprooted peoples to political parties and research centres – to negotiate and channel serious proposals into the official peace talks in 1994 caught many people by surprise.

What was less surprising was that since Monseñor Quezada Toruño withdrew from his position as president of the Assembly in January 1995, the ASC had to contend with a number of problems. Some of its more visionary members tried to build the Assembly's capacity for policy dialogue in order to ensure that the ASC, and through it the less powerful sectors of civil society, had a role to play in the verification and implementation of the peace accords. The role of the Forum of Guatemalan NGOs in developing serious proposals and gaining the support of the assembly, before lobbying the government and international community prior to the 1995 Informal Donors Meeting, highlighted the political potential of the ASC (Ruthrauff 1996). Yet the divergent perceptions and uneven development of different sectors, combined with the hostility of the government and the ambivalence of the international community, posed enormous obstacles to the survival of the ASC as a novel mechanism for articulating popular and middle-sector views to the largely interelite peace talks.

Still, it is important to remember that the ASC was not the only such mechanism. Several accords included provisions for consultative bodies with representatives of beneficiary sectors. Organizations representing uprooted peoples were involved in the work of the Technical Commission established under the Resettlement Accord. Maya organizations prepared themselves to assume the responsibilities that they may take on in the bipartite commissions envisaged by the Indigenous Accord. The Accord on Socioeconomic Aspects provides for even broader consultative processes in which organizations representing peasants, co-ops, women, and so on, could participate. Yet judging from the low level of cooperation between MINUGUA and most of these sectors – in the area of institutional strengthening and at a political level – it seemed that popular organizations and most NGOs still have a long way to go before being able to take advantage of these new spaces.

STRATEGIC OPTIONS

Although by mid-1996 the UN had already made a significant contribution to the Guatemalan peace process and therefore set the stage for safe and voluntary returns and resettlement, the realization of the full potential of UN involvement, before and after the signing of a final accord, depends on key sectors making compromises and co-operating in ways that may defy traditional behavioural patterns. The UN will have to maintain the independence and rigor of MINUGUA's verification practices while broadening MINUGUA's scope to encompass the rights covered by the Indigenous Accord and its new responsibilities under the Socioeconomic Accord. In the area of institutional strengthening, MINUGUA and the UNDP should agree on a rational division of labour while working together to further develop the strategic focus and transparency of their common programme. Both should place greater emphasis on strengthening civil society. Finally, the DPA and the UNDP should continue to promote the national and international consensus required to effectively articulate short-term institutional strengthening projects devoted to peacebuilding programmes and to complementary policy measures.

The international community will also have to protect the UN's distinctive contribution to the peace process from the financial crisis that is being aggravated by U.S. policy, in particular. This community should actively contribute to laying the groundwork for the timely implementation of the peace accords as well as of complementary policy measures. This should include forward planning to harmonize donor strategies at the level of diplomacy and of cooperation in the field. It should also include well-targeted project support to strengthen the ability of historically marginalised sectors to fully participate in the operationalization of the accords and the construction of peace. The role of international NGOs as bridge-builders between states and beneficiaries in the International Conference on Refugees in Central America (CIREFCA) process suggests that INGOs could again play an important role in this regard (Sollis 1996). The initial efforts (and successes) of U.S. and European NGOs in providing advocacy training and support to Guatemalan counterparts and in coordinating their transnational advocacy efforts, indicates that at least some INGOs are strategically seizing the moment.

Above all, it is up to Guatemalans to take advantage of an opportunity that may never recur to implement the reforms required – with rare international support – to widen the political space, address historic injustices, and build social institutions for the future. As Rachel McCleary has noted: "The peace process ... has required patience and stamina from all parts – the United Nations, the Group of Friends, the successive governments of Guatemala – but most important, the Guatemalan people. Global events are overtaking the process, and the moment has come for Guatemalans to move decisively forward" (1996, 92). This will demand imagination and compromise from all key sectors. From the economic elite, it will require paying its share of taxes, abiding by the rule of law, and developing economic activities that do not depend on the repression of wage demands and political opposition to maintain international competitiveness. From the professional sectors, including the military, the police, the judiciary, the upper reaches of public administration, and legislators, it will require creativity in demilitarizing and rebuilding public institutions to increase their accountability and effectiveness in the delivery of services, root out corruption, and develop the rule of law in practice. From the popular sectors, including uprooted peoples, and especially the Maya, this process will require the deepening of their strategic vision, the rapid development of organizational capacity, as well as the broadening of both organic representation and unity. And if those responsible do sincerely recognize their responsibilities and ask for forgiveness, building peace might even include pardoning the atrocities and injustices committed in the name of stability or revolution. Only then will true reconciliation be possible.

NOTES

1 MINUGUA is the Mission of the United Nations for the Verification of Human Rights and Compliance with the Commitments in the Global Accord on Human Rights in Guatemala, in short, the UN Mission in Guatemala.
2 This chapter is based on document research as well as interviews in Brussels, New York, and Washington. In Guatemala, field research was conducted in the departments of Huehuetenango, Quetzaltenango, Quiché, Sololá, and in the capital. The list of interviews provided in Baranyi (1996) indicates the range of sources consulted. I would like to thank the Social Sciences and Humanities Research Council of Canada for the post-doctoral fellowship that made this research possible.
3 See Jonas (1996) for a similar conclusion. It is worth noting that the Clarification Commission Accord provoked a backlash by organizations like the Mutual Support Group (GAM) and the National Coordinator of Widows of Guatemala (CONAVIGUA), which represent victims of human rights abuses and their families; this was one of the factors that pro-

duced the breakdown in the peace talks during the summer of 1994. The Socioeconomic Accord was received poorly by the National Coordinator of Indigenous Peasants (CONIC), the Peasant Unity Committee (CUC), and other organizations representing landless peasants, but this did not have the same adverse impact on the negotiations.

4 "Institutional strengthening" is a UN code word for the reform of dysfunctional organizations and the creation of new organizations responsible for making the rule of law effective. For example, in 1995–96 MINUGUA and the UNDP funded projects to train public prosecutors in the use of the new Code of Criminal Procedure, train officials of the judiciary in the provision of legal services in Maya languages, and assess the capacity-building needs of human rights NGOs.

5 The interest of the World Bank and other large donors in equity and civil society participation is not limited to Guatemala (Banco Mundial 1995, 19–26; Michel 1996, 21–53).

6 Off the record, some MINUGUA staff expressed the view that some governmental institutions, especially the police, are "unreformable."

PART THREE

Land, Labour, and Migration

6 "Somos de la Tierra": Land and the Guatemalan Refugee Return

BRIAN EGAN

In her treatment of the Guatemala refugee crisis, *Refugees of a Hidden War*, Beatriz Manz noted that access to land is one of the key factors within which that country's refugee problem must be considered (1988a, 30). Indeed, the land issue has been of central importance to the country's many political and economic struggles. This issue has deep historical roots, starting with the Spanish conquest of Mesoamerica in the sixteenth century. Throughout the colonial period the Spanish sought to amass wealth through the exploitation of Indian (Maya) land and labour to produce exotic crops for export. During the coffee boom of the late nineteenth century, this form of exploitation was codified as a strategy of national economic development, thus legitimating the concentration of lands into the hands of Spanish landowners – a process that involved the confiscation of communal and Indian lands by fiat and force.

Throughout the twentieth century, the agro-export economy developed a succession of cash crops – bananas, sugar, cotton, and cattle – that led to further concentration of land ownership. By the 1970s the process of land concentration had proceeded to the point where the distribution of land in Guatemala was considered to be more unequal than in any other nation in Latin America (USAID 1982, 83). Agricultural census data from this period (1979) indicate that 65 percent of the country's farmland was controlled by just 2 percent of the farmers. On the other side of the land divide were some 288,000 farming families trying to eke out an existence on just over 4 percent of the land base – these farms all being under 1.4

hectares in size, far too small to support a family. The absence of any kind of serious land-reform program meant that this pattern of land distribution remained skewed during both the violence of the 1980s and the return of the refugees in the late 1980s and the first half of the 1990s.

To a large extent, Guatemala is still a rural country with an economy heavily reliant on agriculture. According to figures provided by the United Nations Development Program (UNDP), in 1993 60 percent of Guatemalans lived in rural areas, and agriculture accounted for 25 percent of the country's GDP and 50 percent of all employment (UNDP 1994, 180). Land and farming are especially important to the indigenous population for, as Manz notes, in Guatemala, "land is central to Indian life and culture." In Guatemala, land is also central to economic exploitation, conflict, and the struggle for justice.

The land issue was closely linked to Guatemala's refugee crisis for several reasons. For one, the inequitable distribution of land was central to the political conflict that produced large numbers of Guatemalan refugees in the 1980s. For another, the vast majority of the Guatemalans who sought refuge in Mexico during the 1980s were small farmers of Maya descent: for these returning refugees (returnees), gaining access to productive land was a critical factor in satisfying their economic needs. As will be discussed later, the issue of land for the refugees was intimately linked with human rights issues, militarization, and the attitudes of Guatemalans towards the returnees.[1]

This chapter examines the issue of land in Guatemala and its relation to the refugee return process. More specifically, it focuses on the problems returnees had in securing access to farmland in the Ixcán and the Petén, two of the areas that were hardest hit by the violence of the 1980s and that generated the largest number of refugees (Manz 1988a, 255).[2] Both of these areas saw large-scale and organized returns of refugees during the first half of the 1990s. This chapter reviews the process of colonization of these areas, the exodus during the counterinsurgency period, and the resettlement of these areas by new colonists. These events set up the difficult conditions faced by refugees who wished to return to the Ixcán and the Petén areas to reclaim old lands or gain access to new lands.

I have based my findings on observations, interviews, and documents collected during three separate trips to Guatemala – in May and June 1993, November through December 1994, and January and February 1995. During the first trip I visited the Ixcán and the return community of Victoria 20 de Enero in my role as accompanier (human rights observer) with Project Accompaniment, a Canadian NGO working with the Guatemalan refugees. The latter two trips were part of my field work for my masters thesis through the Faculty of Environmental Studies and the Centre for Refugee Studies at York University. The bulk of the field work during these trips took place in the Petén.

REGIONS OF FLIGHT: THE IXCÁN AND PETÉN

Occupying 1,575 km^2 of the northern lowland portion of the department of Quiché, the Ixcán was largely uninhabited rainforest until the 1960s. Colonization of the area began in 1966, organized by Maryknoll priests from Huehuetenango, with the support of Guatemala's National Institute for Agrarian Transformation (INTA). The first colonists of the area were indigenous people from the western highlands, mainly Mam and Q'anjob'al from the department of Huehuetenango. Each family was granted 17.5 hectares of land upon arrival in the region. Life was hard for these pioneers; clearing the dense forest to create farms and communities was backbreaking work. Even so, for many it was a big improvement over life in the highlands, for after the forest was cleared the land produced well (AVANCSO 1992, 35).

In 1970 the colonists formed the Ixcán Grande cooperative, which included five settlements in the area – Mayalán, Xalbal, Pueblo Nuevo, Los Angeles, and Cuarto Pueblo – and some 8,098 hectares of state and privately purchased (by the Catholic Church) land lying between the Xalbal and Ixcán Rivers. The Ixcán Grande cooperative officially became owner of the land in 1974. The population of the area grew quickly, and by 1970 INTA estimated that there were some five thousand people living in the Ixcán. By the mid-1970s, the communities in the area were thriving (AVANCSO 1992, 88).

A few years later (beginning in the 1970s), the area to the east of the Ixcán Grande cooperative began to be colonized. This was the Playa Grande colonization project, sponsored by INTA and supported with funds from the United States Agency for International Development (USAID). The Playa Grande project was carried out with the help of Spanish priests from the diocese of Santa Cruz del Quiché (Manz 1988a, 127).[3] Most of those who colonized this area were Q'eqchi' and Poqomchi' from the nearby departments of Alta and Baja Verapaz. Many poor *ladinos*, mainly from the south coast, also took part in this colonization project. By 1984 approximately two thousand families had been resettled in the Playa Grande area (Dennis, Elbow, and Heller 1988, 71). The Ixcán Grande and Playa Grande formed part of the larger process of colonization of the Northern Transverse Strip (or FTN). By 1985, the population of the FTN had reached sixty thousand (Colchester 1991, 182).[4]

The relative prosperity enjoyed by the colonists in the Ixcán proved to be short-lived. By the mid-1970s the region began to be affected by the conflict that was sweeping the nation. In the early 1970s, the Guatemalan Army of the Poor (EGP), one of Guatemala's insurgent guerrilla groups, became established in the Ixcán and sought support among the local population. As the insurgents became increasingly active during the late 1970s and early 1980s, the Guatemalan army entered the area, and the colonists found themselves in the middle of the conflict. During this period the army tried to discourage and punish community support for the insurgents by abducting, torturing, and killing community leaders (Falla 1992, 10). In 1981 the army adopted more horrific measures including the slaughter of all inhabitants – men, women, and children – in a number of villages. By 1982, most of the communities in the Ixcán Grande area had been abandoned, the residents having fled deep into the jungle or to Mexico.[5] The situation was similar in the Playa Grande area, where some one thousand to fifteen hundred residents were killed, three entire communities were destroyed (and all residents killed), and hundreds of families displaced into the jungle or to Mexico (Dennis, Elbow, and Heller 1988, 74).

Many villages in the Ixcán remained abandoned for years. Beginning in 1984 the army began to repopulate the area, starting with the community of Xalbal. Lands that had been abandoned by the initial colonists, who had fled to Mexico or into the jungle, were distributed to newcomers. They received lands on the condition that they comply with military authorities. The military directed the rebuilding of destroyed villages on a military model, with houses clustered together in a grid pattern to monitor and enforce control of the residents. There was little opportunity for cooperative work or community organizing in these villages.[6] Refugees and others who had been displaced and who returned to the Ixcán during this period were taken by the military to development poles near the Playa Grande military base, where they were completely dependent on the army for food. For those who stayed behind, for newcomers to the area, and for those who returned, the immediate post-conflict period was extremely difficult. All had to partake in Civil Patrols (PACs) and were forced to provide free labour for military construction projects. Human rights abuses by the military continued and the PACs became a new source of community control and repression.

Like the Ixcán, much of the Petén was uninhabited prior to the 1960s. This vast (36,000 km^2) northern lowland region, comprising one-third of Guatemala's land area, had long been viewed as a prime area for colonization. In 1959 the government created the National Enterprise for the Promotion and Economic Development of the Petén (FYDEP), an agency to oversee the colonization and development of the region. During the first decade of its existence, FYDEP sponsored few colonization efforts. In the late 1960s however, rumours that the Mexican government was planning to build a dam on the Usumacinta River that would flood parts of the west Petén spurred the Guatemalan government to accelerate colonization of the area along the river in order to assert Guatemala's sovereignty over the area. Between 1969 and 1973 approximately six hundred peasant colonists were settled in sixteen cooperatives along the banks of the Usumacinta River and its main tributaries. The size and number of these cooperatives grew steadily throughout the 1970s.

These settlements were extremely isolated and depended almost exclusively on river travel, not always a convenient or safe mode of transportation. They received little in the way of state (FYDEP) support. However, many did receive significant support from other outside organizations, such as the Catholic Church. For example, Centro Campesino, located on the bank of the Usumacinta in the far northwest corner of the Petén, was supported by Belgian priests and community workers. Thanks to the hard work of the colonists and this kind of outside support, Centro Campesino achieved a high state of development by the late 1970s – by the end of this decade the community had expanded to over seven hundred people and had electricity, vehicles, boats, and many animals, and it produced a food surplus that was sold at local markets (CEIDEC 1990, 128). La Técnica Agropecuaria, located not far upstream from Centro Campesino, was also a well-established and highly successful cooperative by the late 1970s, as was El Arbolito, located further south along the river (FEDECOAG 1993, 52).

Of all the communities in the Petén, the cooperatives along the Usumacinta were hardest hit by the violence of the 1980s. The conflict in the Petén developed along similar lines to the conflict that took place in the Ixcán. Insurgents belonging to the Rebel Armed Forces (FAR) established themselves in the west Petén in the 1970s and began to develop a popular base among the cooperatives. In response, the army began counterinsurgency operations in the area. During 1980 and 1981 the conflict was mostly restricted to fighting between the army and guerrillas. It was not long, however, before community leaders and civilians suspected of guerrilla collaboration were targeted by the military. The army quickly became less discriminate – in 1982 there were four massacres in the Petén, with a total of 228 people killed. All but 8 of these victims came from the western district of La Libertad, where the cooperatives were located (FEDECOAG 1993, 19).

As in the Ixcán, the violence spurred thousands to flee their communities for fear they would be the next victims of the army. In May 1981 some five hundred people fled into Mexico from the communities of Puerto Rico, El Mango, and Las Cruces. Since this was one of the very first large-scale movements of Guatemalans across the border due to political violence, there was considerable confusion over why the people had fled. Government officials maintained they were simply economic (agricultural) migrants who went to Mexico every year to find work. The people themselves told a different story to the Mexican press, maintaining they had fled from military patrols (FEDECOAG 1993, 20). Shortly after this, many people from the cooperatives along the Usumacinta began crossing the river into Mexico. By July of the same year, the Mexican authorities reported that close to three thousand Guatemalans had sought refuge on the Mexican side of the river. Two weeks later, Guatemala's ambassador to Mexico announced that another seventeen hundred refugees had crossed into Mexico from the Petén. Many also fled into the nearby jungle, where they set up semipermanent Communities of Population in Resistance (the CPRs of the Petén) or to Santa Elena and San Benito, the major urban centres of the department (CEIDEC 1990, 119).[7] Most of those who fled to Mexico and into the jungle came from the cooperatives along the river. Seven of these cooperatives were completely abandoned – El Arbolito, Centro Campesino, La Técnica Agropecuaria, La Lucha, Las Flores, La Nueva Felicidad, and Bonanza – while others were only partially abandoned. Several of the communities were destroyed by the army, all the houses burnt, and the animals slaughtered. Some who stayed behind and some of the few who did return from Mexico or the jungles were resettled by the army into a development pole established at Laguna Perdida (CEIDEC 1990, 120). Out of fear for their lives, most of the displaced refused to return to their communities for many years. In the meantime the military encouraged others to take over their lands. Apparently this counterinsurgency tactic was less successful in the Petén than it was in the Ixcán due to the continued presence of guerrillas in the Petén who strongly opposed this resettlement.

REPATRIATION AND RETURN

Once in Mexico, many of the refugees eventually found their way into refugee camps under the auspices of the United Nations High

Commissioner for Refugees (UNHCR) and the Mexican refugee agency (COMAR). A larger number of refugees lived outside the camps and therefore were not officially recognized as refugees by the UNHCR. Some made their way north to the United States, Europe, or Canada. While life in exile was safer than staying in Guatemala, it was anything but easy. The refugees' access to land and work (at a decent wage) in Mexico was very limited. They also had little freedom of movement. Most refugees longed to return home and, once the violence in Guatemala abated, they began to organize their return.[8] They selected leaders (the Permanent Commissions of Guatemalan Refugees in Mexico, or CCPP), formed support groups for women and youth, and built an organizational structure around promoters in various fields (for example, health, education, human rights, communication) (see also Torres contribution to this volume).

In considering the movement of Guatemalan refugees back into their homeland, it is important to recognize the distinction made between the concepts of "return" and "repatriation." The CCPP stressed that a "return" should be completely voluntary, organized by the refugees themselves, and carried out in a collective manner, with large groups of families returning together. They contrasted this with a "repatriation," which was associated with the government-sponsored program managed by COMAR, CEAR (the Guatemalan Refugee Agency), and the UNHCR. Under the government program, refugees were repatriated – that is, they were the subjects of government action and were less than full participants in the process. Under the government program, usually only one or a few families repatriated in a group.

The repatriation of Guatemalan refugees under the government program began in 1984, facilitated by the UNHCR and COMAR. However, only a relatively small number of refugees repatriated prior to 1987 due to continued political instability in Guatemala. The election of a civilian government in 1986 increased prospects for a resolution of the refugee crisis, especially since the new president, Vinicio Cerezo Arévalo, made repatriation of the refugees a priority. In 1986, the government created a new special commission (the above-mentioned CEAR) to provide support to repatriates. The rate of repatriation accelerated, and by 1990 over six thousand refugees had repatriated under the government program (AVANCSO 1992, 56).

In the Ixcán, the first large-scale (government-sponsored) repatriation occurred in 1987, when twenty-six families were returned to the Ixcán Grande area. These families faced considerable hardship upon their return to the area and had to be temporarily settled in Centro Veracruz. When the refugees tried to return to their old cooperatives, they were treated with suspicion and hostility by local residents, most of whom were relative newcomers and who had been resettled into the area by the army. Many of these newcomers viewed the returnees as subversives and guerrilla sympathizers, something the army encouraged them to believe. Many feared that the returnees would bring renewed military attention (and repression). Some feared that the returnees would reclaim land that they had been cultivating over the last few years.

There was good reason for the newcomers to be preoccupied with this last concern. It was extremely important to the returnees to regain access to the lands they had involuntarily abandoned – this issue was the biggest potential source of conflict with the new residents in the area. In some cases, the land had remained abandoned and so could be recovered without conflict. Often, however, their lands had been taken over by new colonists. In this case, a solution had to be worked out. Ideally, the returnees could return to the community and take over their old piece of land, and the newcomer would assume a different parcel within the community (if one was available), or vice versa. Those who returned first were often at an advantage, since there were still abandoned lands and these sorts of trade-offs were possible. The conflict over land was exacerbated by institutional conflict. For example, CEAR supported returning disputed land to the original owner, while the army and INTA opposed this arrangement.[9]

In the Petén there was also a movement of displaced people back to their communities during the late 1980s. After the election of the Cerezo government, some former cooperative members began to return to their communities on the Usumacinta under the government repatriation program. For instance, some families returned to El Arbolito in 1987. However, many of those families fled again following incidents of violence, and by the early 1990s only seven of the original member families of the cooperative returned. There was also a slow process of return to La Técnica, but by 1991 only one-quarter of the original families had repatriated to this community (FEDECOAG 1993, 52). Few refugees repatriated under the government program: in 1992, only sixty-three people returned to the region under the program. As in the Ixcán, fear kept most refugees in exile. The CCPP also tried to discourage participation in government repatriation schemes. As well, there were indications that CEAR itself discouraged returns to the Petén, citing concern that the return of large numbers of refugees would damage the region's fragile ecology (30).

While the government repatriation program limped along, the CCPP began negotiating with the Cerezo government over conditions for a larger-scale return of refugees. In October of 1992, after five years of negotiation, the CCPP and the Guatemalan government signed an accord that was to pave the way for the return. The accord contained agreements on several points designed to provide the refugees with the security they needed to begin their return. Among these was an agreement that the returning refugees had the right of access to land (CCPP 1993). The section relating to land was of great importance to the refugees (as Nolin Hanlon's chapter in this volume also emphasizes). The vast majority of returning refugees were small farmers for whom gaining access to land was crucial to their economic well-being. The accords recognized that as far as the question of access to land was concerned, there were three broad categories of refugees. The first category included all the refugees who owned private land. The second included those who had had access to land through their membership in an agricultural cooperative. The third category was for all those refugees who had no access to land at all. The accord stipulated in some detail how, in each of these cases, the returning refugees could gain or regain access to land in Guatemala. In cases where a refugee's private or cooperative land had been settled by newcomers, the accord allowed for either the removal of the new settler or the provision of other lands to the returnee (CCPP 1993).

OBSTACLES TO THE RETURN

While the various agreements, including the section pertaining to land, looked promising on paper, it remained to be seen how they would be implemented. Nevertheless, the signing of the accords was a major breakthrough and set the stage for the first return, which took place in January of 1993 when close to twenty-five hundred refugees returned to establish a settlement on a parcel of land known as Polígono 14 (later named Victoria 20 de Enero), located in an isolated section of the Ixcán.[10] The returnees began the hard work of clearing the dense forest and establishing houses and fields. From the outset the community suffered from health problems, a lack of adequate food, poor access, and concerns about their security.[11] Despite these difficult conditions, the spirits and expectations of the returnees were high and the community enjoyed significant support from Guatemalan and international relief agencies (Egan's field notes 1993).

After this first return, it was thought that the process of return would accelerate greatly – the CCPP predicted that fifteen thousand refugees would go back to Guatemala in 1993 alone. This expectation was not to be realized however, since the return process proceeded very slowly. Only one other return took place during 1993, when thirteen hundred refugees went back to the Ixcán. By October of 1994 only seven thousand refugees had returned in five collective returns. The slow pace of the return was due in large part to concerns about the security of the returnees.[12] Another crucial obstacle to the return had to do with securing land for the returnees. Problems with securing access to land for returnees falls into two general categories: the first category involved returnees attempting to regain their land and standing within cooperatives, and the second concerned finding and purchasing land for refugees without land.

The problems faced by refugees wishing to return to their former positions and lands within cooperative communities applied to both those returning to the Petén and those returning to the Ixcán. In both areas the returnees were often met with open hostility and distrust on the part of local military authorities and other residents. One instance of the degree of hostility that the returnees faced occurred in the community of Xalbal. Located on the banks of the Xalbal River, this village was the most important centre in the Ixcán prior to the counterinsurgency period. After massacres in Xalbal and neighbouring communities, the entire population of Xalbal abandoned the village in March of 1982. The military began to repopulate the village in 1984 – bringing in newcomers from different parts of the country (Manz 1988a, 55).

As part of the Ixcán Grande cooperative, the community of Xalbal had established legal title to the land – title that had been recognized by the Guatemalan government as equivalent to private land ownership. As members of the cooperative, the former residents of Xalbal who fled to Mexico and who later wanted to return had legal title to their old lands. While the Guatemalan constitution recognizes that "voluntary abandonment" of land can be grounds for forfeiting land rights, fleeing in fear for one's life can hardly be considered voluntary abandonment (Manz 1988a, 143). Despite their strong case, the refugees who wished to rejoin the community of Xalbal and regain their old lands faced strong opposition from the new residents of the village. In September of 1994 the returnees petitioned for the return of 111 parcels of land that they claimed as their former lands. The current occupants refused the request, saying that they had been living on the land for the last ten years. Similar conflicts occurred in several other communities within the Ixcán Grande cooperative. In an effort to end the conflict, in September of 1994 the General Assembly of the Ixcán Grande cooperative decided to establish a time limit for members of the Ixcán Grande cooperative who were in

Mexico to return and claim their places within the cooperative. Those who did not return by December of 1995 would lose their position and lands within the Ixcán Grande cooperative. Returnees seeking to return to their old cooperatives and lands in the Petén experienced similar problems.

While former cooperative members were struggling to regain their lands, those returnees who had no property at all were having difficulties finding and purchasing suitable land. Complicating matters for those without land was the need to find very large tracts of land (often several thousand hectares) as the refugees returned in large groups (for example, a single group could exceed two hundred families or a thousand people). Ecological factors also necessitated the purchase of large tracts of land. The land in the northern lowland areas of Guatemala, such as in the Ixcán and Petén, is not well suited to conventional agricultural techniques and was usually farmed using methods (swidden agriculture) that use long fallow periods. This required each farmer to make use of a relatively large tract of land over the cycle of cultivation and fallow. Anywhere from 7.5 to 45 hectares of land was needed to support one farming family in these areas.[13]

Looking for tracts of land of this size automatically restricted the options open to the returnees. They could either purchase vacant state-owned lands (of which there were few) or large tracts of privately owned land. This, in turn, brought up a second problem: the cost of purchasing the land. Reports circulated of rampant price speculation by large landowners who knew the returnees were looking only for large parcels of land.[14] It was a bitter irony that some of these large landowners, many of whom gained control of the land through less than legal or honourable means during the process of colonization and counterinsurgency, later made a fortune by selling the land back to people displaced by the conflict.[15]

Once a suitable piece of land had been found and a price agreed upon, further difficulties often awaited the returnees. Purchase of these lands was dependent on the refugees receiving land purchase credits from the Guatemalan government, which had received international financial assistance to purchase lands for the returnees. These funds were supposed to be made available to the returnees from two sources: FONAPAZ (Fondo para la Paz) and FONATIERRA (Fondo Nacional de Tierra). Before these agencies would release credits to the refugee group returning, however, the return and the land purchase had to be approved by CEAR, INTA, and any other government agency that might be involved with the return or the specific piece of land in question. Wading through the tangle of bureaucracy was often a lengthy and frustrating experience for the refugees. From the very first return, when the people planning to return simply packed their things and walked out of the camps in Mexico heading for the Guatemalan border, almost all groups of returnees experienced delays in their plans to return for some reason or other, many of them relating to getting their land credits approved or to CEAR granting approval for the return. On numerous occasions the refugees charged the Guatemalan government (and more specifically CEAR) with obstructing their plans to return. They also accused the government of misappropriation of funds provided by international donors for the return and resettlement process.

One of the most controversial returns centred around approximately 255 families who migrated as a group back to the finca (estate) El Quetzal in the Petén. Roughly eighty percent of the land they wished to return to lay within the Sierra del Lacandon National Park, one of the core areas of the Maya Biosphere Reserve. The finca El Quetzal had been founded and partly settled in the 1970s by a cooperative made up of a group of indigenous people from the western highlands. The few families that had settled on the land fled the area in the early 1980s during the counterinsurgency period. This land was identified as a suitable destination for returning refugees in 1993, and the CCPP negotiated a purchase agreement with the owners in 1994.

The next step for this group of returnees was to secure the credits needed to make the purchase and obtain government approval to settle on the land. The refugees soon ran into trouble with CONAP, Guatemala's National Council of Protected Areas, which is responsible for safeguarding national parks and other protected areas. According to the law that created the reserve, human settlements within any of the core areas were deemed illegal, and CONAP refused to approve any settlement at El Quetzal (Interview with Milton Cabrera, 2 November 1994, in Guatemala City). The refugees argued that because the finca existed prior to the creation of the biosphere reserve (the reserve was legally established in 1990) and because the ownership of private land was protected under the constitution, they (as new owners of the property) had full rights to settle on and develop the land. They also provided the government and CONAP with a plan for management of the land that they maintained would protect the ecology of the area.

There followed a long process of negotiation and consultation between the refugees and various government agencies, the main players being CONAP, CEAR, and INTA. While INTA and CEAR eventually supported the return to El Quetzal, CONAP did not. Lacking CONAP's approval, the returnees found themselves in a difficult position. Without CONAP's approval, none of the other Guatemalan government agencies nor the UNHCR would release the funds or land credits the refugees needed in order to return to their land. As a result, the return was postponed several times. After months of negotiation the refugees became frustrated and began to press more forcefully for a resolution. A group of refugees occupied CONAP offices in June of 1994. In December of 1994, their patience exhausted, the refugees took matters into their own hands and organized a self-financed work brigade to go to the site and begin preparations for the return. Shortly afterward, government opposition collapsed and the return was permitted in early 1995.

CONCLUSION: "SOMOS DE LA TIERRA"

Gaining access to land, either their old lands or new land, was one of the major reasons Guatemalan refugees wished to return to their country of origin. Most of the Guatemalan refugees were of indigenous origin and had strong economic and cultural ties to the land and to an agrarian way of life. As one of the returnees noted: "There [in Mexico] we had better living conditions because we had schools, clinics, electricity, there were NGOs helping us, there were many things, but it's not the same, because here [in Guatemala] we know that the work we do is for ourselves; we know that improvements we make to the land are for ourselves because we won't have to leave them, they are ours. Here there is hope that we can do something" (FEDECOAG 1993, 52). There was also the sense among many of the refugees of belonging to the land and the land belonging to them: "We are of the land because the land belongs to us; in Mexico the land was not ours, for this reason we always felt like strangers, like parasites, we felt lessened." For these people, the return was truly a return to home, land, and a better life: "Just by knowing the land is ours, it gives us confidence and we work harder, we care for the land and we're going to defend it, when necessary, because it is our life" (53).

The struggle to gain access to land was only part of the larger struggle of the return. Even when the returnees acquired adequate land, many difficulties befell them in their efforts to develop their communities. Most seriously, they had to establish themselves within a highly militarized setting where they were viewed by the military as subversives and as guerrilla supporters. They also found themselves in conflict with those who had stayed behind and endured the violence, and especially those who moved into the area (the Ixcán and Petén) and settled on lands that had been "abandoned" by the refugees when they fled to Mexico. The returnees tried to downplay this conflict, arguing that their aims and objectives were based not only on developing their own communities but also on extending the benefits of this development to neighbouring communities and the region as a whole, trying to build unity with other *campesinos*, rather than foster divisions. In fact, the refugees maintained that their efforts presented an opportunity to create a viable means of rural, community development in Guatemala.

This was perhaps the greatest promise of the return, the possibility of creating a rural development alternative, a new model for rural communities outside the bounds of military control. While these return communities were only a very small part of rural Guatemala, the promise was that they could have a wide influence, that they could spark a resurgent rural development movement similar to the one that flourished prior to the repression of the 1980s. The return created alternatives in the countryside and allowed for more democratic and participatory forms of community development. One can look at return communities as small islands of resistance in the sea of militarization that was rural Guatemala. Within the Ixcán and west Petén, the return communities were relatively large, well organized, and based on relatively democratic principles. Return communities refused to participate in PACs something most other rural communities did not dare to do. The return communities thus became positive symbols for other rural Guatemalans.

While these communities challenged the status quo, the returnees still faced enormous difficulties. The most serious short-term threat was a hostile and powerful military structure. In the longer term, obstacles concerning economic and ecological sustainability also stood in their way. Finally, as the returnees themselves reiterated, the return was just part of the larger struggle for peace, justice, and democracy in Guatemala. The success of this larger struggle will determine the long-term success of the return itself.

NOTES

1 The land issue is also linked to environmental issues. Large groups of returning refugees settled in ecologically sensitive areas, and concerns were expressed by environmentalists and others about the impact of these settlements on the local ecosystems. At the same time, given the general unsuitability of these areas to conventional agriculture, there were also concerns about the long-term sustainability of the return communities.

2 Manz notes that the Ixcán generated the largest number of refugees, with the second largest number coming from the West Petén.
3 The Playa Grande colonization area is also known as Ixcán Chiquito or the Zona Reyna.
4 The FTN is a wide belt of low-lying land covering the northern portions of the departments of Huehuetenango, Quiché, and Alta Verapaz. Colonization of the FTN proceeded rapidly during the 1960s, 1970s, and 1980s due to a combination of state-sponsored settlement schemes and spontaneous migration. Land inequity in southern Guatemala generated large numbers of landless and land-poor people in the highlands. According to Jonas (1991, 79), by the late 1970s 90 percent of the highland population lacked sufficient land to meet their basic needs. Another 400,000 rural people were completely without land at all (Dunkerley 1988, 473). These people were attracted to the area by the prospect of owning their own land. The colonization schemes also benefited the state and their allies in the landed elite, for they served as a painless substitute for a much-needed land reform program. As Jones (1990, 102) noted, "in Guatemala, a decision has quite clearly been taken to substitute colonization of new lands for land reform." This is not to say that colonization resulted in a more equitable distribution of land in colonized areas. The FTN became the site of intense land speculation as powerful interests scooped up huge parcels of land. The area gained the nickname "Land of the Generals" as huge tracts were parcelled out to the military and other government supporters – General Lucas Garcia alone acquired more than 32,000 hectares in the area (Jones 1990, 106).
5 Falla (1992) provides an account of the repression in the Ixcán, including the massacre of over 300 people at Cuarto Pueblo in March of 1982. The report by AVANCSO (1992) is also an excellent overview of the period of colonization and repression in the area.
6 Manz (1988a, 138) quotes original settlers who lived through this period of reorganization and militarization: "There is no cooperation, there is no trust among us. We don't know each other now ... We would like the refugees in Mexico to come back so we can be a community again."
7 According to one report, the town of San Benito (adjacent to Santa Elena and Flores) received many victims of the violence – some 1,000 refugees, including many orphans, took up residence there (CEIDEC 1990, 119). As for the CPRs, there were an estimated 1,000 people living in five separate CPR villages in the jungles of Petén in the early 1980s (Bernstein 1995).
8 The decision to return was not an easy one for the refugees. Despite the difficulties of living in the camps, they did have access to schools, health

clinics, and other services provided by the Mexican government and international NGOs. After weighing all the pros and cons of staying in Mexico or returning to Guatemala, many decided to return. Perhaps as much as anything, the decision to return was based on the hope for a better life. As one former refugee (who had already returned to Guatemala) put it, "There [in Mexico], we work only to survive, whereas here ... well here we also work to survive, but we also have hope; there was no hope there" (FEDECOAG 1993, 52).

9 The situation was somewhat different in the Ixcán Grande area than it was in Playa Grande. In the Ixcán Grande area, former residents were members of the cooperative and thus had legal title to their lands within the community. In the Playa Grande area, no such legal title existed, and when the colonization was set up there was a clause that stipulated that abandoned lands would revert to state ownership. In such cases, returnees had no right to the lands they had abandoned and were thus made to seek other lands.

10 Of the 510 families that returned to Victoria 20 de enero, 86 were former members of the Ixcán Grande cooperative. The remainder either had title to other lands or were without land (CHRLA 1993b).

11 Because the settlement was in a zone of active conflict between the army and insurgents, the entire surrounding area was heavily militarized. Throughout 1993 it was common for army helicopters to pass over the settlement at night, and explosions and machine-gun fire in the direction the helicopters were headed was commonly heard. The returnees also found unexploded mines on their land and a field of marijuana. On several occasions army patrols passed near the village, in direct contradiction to the accords (CHRLA 1993a; CHRLA 1993b).

12 These concerns were heightened by the coup of May 1993 and by a number of specific conflicts that returnees to the Ixcán were experiencing – for example, due to the heavy military presence in the area and the hostility of other colonists in the area (*Reunion* 2, no. 2, June–July 1995, 1).

13 There is some disagreement over how much land was needed to support a family farming in these areas. For example, the return community of Victoria 20 de Enero has over 4,500 hectares of land. The returnees to this community maintained that each family needed 18 hectares of land to be self-sufficient. INTA, on the other hand, claimed that each family would require only 7.5 hectares. Even larger tracts of land are needed in the Petén, where soil conditions are more difficult. Schwartz (1990, 286–8) reports that each farming family in the Petén required anywhere from 21 to 45 hectares of land. The 225 families who planned to return to one part of the Petén, to the finca El Quetzal, purchased a piece of land over 6,000 hectares in size (almost 27 hectares per family).

14 The cost of the land at Victoria 20 de Enero was relatively modest, some 1.36 million Quetzales (approximately U.S.$250,000), because it was public land. Private land purchases were much more expensive: the finca El Quetzal, for example, cost around U.S.$450,000, an astronomical sum for poverty-stricken returnees.
15 Perhaps the most blatant case of this cruel twist of fate came in late 1994 when one group of returnees purchased three estates owned by General Romeo Lucas Garcia, one of the architects of the counterinsurgency campaign.

7 Migration and the Displaced in Guatemala City in the Context of a Flawed National Transformation

GISELA GELLERT

There is no doubt that Guatemala has undergone a major transformation since the mid-1980s. Yet the changes that have taken place have been largely limited to two areas: the return to formal democracy with rather low levels of public participation, manifested in low voter turnout among other things, and the adoption of neoliberal macroeconomic policies of the kind in vogue all over Latin America. Little else has changed. Racism, the marginalization of the Maya peoples and peasants in general, and weak state structures (characterized by inefficient taxation, low levels of support for social programmes in comparison to military and other expenditures, and so on) have remained largely as they have been historically. In addition, long-standing patterns of extreme poverty and social inequality have worsened, as have human settlement and environmental problems related to deepening poverty: slum housing has spread in the cities and land erosion in the countryside.

It is important to note that Guatemala stands out among the majority of other Latin American countries with regard to extreme and multiple expressions of inequality, manifested especially in the subordination and marginalization of the Maya peoples, who form the numerical majority of the population and remain both rural and desperately poor. The Maya were the most tragically affected by the country's civil war – the longest and most violent of Central America's recent civil wars. One can therefore understand why the various agreements that form the December 1996 peace accord include a major focus on rural development intended to benefit the most disadvantaged peasants and agricultural workers. However, as I will argue in this chapter, over the 1980s and 1990s large numbers of Maya and other peasants moved to Guatemala City and secondary urban centres in an effort to escape rural violence and extreme poverty. The precarious situation of these displaced and culturally uprooted people in the urban areas has been largely ignored.

The circumstances of desperately poor displaced people in Guatemala City can be understood only with reference to a much broader analysis of the complex web of development issues and policy priorities facing the nation as a whole. While the peace accords constituted an important part of the policy package required to address this web, they will have to be supplemented by additional measures. Policies that address the needs of returning refugees with respect to land and infrastructure are very important and absolutely necessary, but they may turn out to be ineffective in the absence of other policies to address the progressive deterioration in socio-economic conditions in rural areas and the prevailing patterns of marginalization, discrimination, and exclusion, which are on par with those of earlier historical periods. Refugees who seek to resettle in the northern regions of the country face the same poor prospects as others who have moved to those regions, unless they can adopt farming strategies suitable for the area's fragile soils and are able to overcome the lack of economic infrastructure and basic social services. Those returning to the western highlands and southern coast face the very difficult employment prospects that confront all those who live there. The help that refugees receive from "accompaniers" and from resettlement programmes (see Levitt's chapter) is only temporary and does not solve the broader problems in the places where they hope to develop their futures. And, last but not least, the problems of displaced people in the cities cannot be understood without reference to the broader national picture and, in particular, the current crisis in the rural areas and the lack of opportunities for displaced people to return to their places of origin, even though this return is what is anticipated in the peace accords.

The situation of rural peoples who were displaced and find themselves in Guatemala City and other urban centres is every bit as bad as and, in some instances, perhaps even worse than that of returning refugees and others in rural areas. Moreover, as I have said, the problems of displaced and poor migrants in the cities have not been recognized, although they too are victims of the armed struggle and the related collapse of rural communities. In fact, the displaced people in the cities are almost invisible. They struggle to survive under circumstances in which they remain unnamed, marginal, and misunderstood, in the peace accords and other policy documents alike. This chapter addresses their plight from the perspective of the transformations that are taking place in the nation as a whole. It also draws attention to the new migration patterns that arose in the 1980s (of which the movement of the displaced peoples forms a part), the multiple causes of the new population movements, and the policy implications that arise from research in this area.

THE CONTEXT OF THE CURRENT TRANSITION

As the peace accords were about to be signed, the end of the armed conflict was anticipated with enthusiasm and hope by some, with scepticism and indifference by others, and with disapproval by still others. These reactions reflected not only the gamut of positions, involvements, and interests in the conflict but also the prevailing marginalization of significant sectors of the population with respect to national political processes. A 1992 United Nations Development Program study (UNDP) revealed that out of every one hundred Guatemalans, only three bought newspapers, sixteen had a radio, and six owned a television set. Marginalization, however, was not only the result of lack of access to communications but also a consequence of the fact that little information concerning the peace process was disseminated. The contents of the partial accords that were signed (prior to the final accord at the end of 1996) were disseminated and discussed only among those sectors of society that were directly connected to this political negotiation process.

Despite some enthusiasm, feelings of concern prevailed among those sectors that were committed to building a better future for the country – concern that, although the war was ending, the real "battle for Guatemala" was just beginning, a battle that would be long and with an uncertain outcome. The sense of encouragement stemmed from the fact that throughout the peace process dialogue had been achieved and previously unmentionable topics were discussed. That is, certain spaces were opened up, and a favourable climate was being created for constructing a new social project by peaceful means (see Fonseca's chapter). In particular, the Maya sector emerged on the political scene to claim its social, cultural, and participatory rights. There were many reasons for concern, however. The character of the social, economic, and political status quo that had led to three decades of armed conflict remained to be changed. Moreover, the prevailing social and economic conditions – the starting point for constructing a "new Guatemala" – were deteriorating. Without entering into details, the deterioration in the general quality of life was obvious, given the lack of basic services, infrastructure, and housing and the increasing insecurity, violence, and environmental degradation.

Responses to social and environmental deterioration in Guatemala were weak because the political system was weak. The country continued to suffer from crises in the realms of institutional order and governance. The move towards democracy proclaimed by the last of the de facto military governments in the mid-1980s was limited to the election of civilian governments: no real change took place in the actual structures of power within the centralized and authoritarian state. The governments elected after 1985 increasingly lost credibility due to the seriously flawed performance of all governmental branches – executive, legislative, and judicial. High levels of corruption, together with constant conflict arising from personal and partisan interests, culminated in the coup attempt of May 1993 and provoked an enormous loss of confidence in the political system. The high levels of abstention in recent elections were just one of the indicators of alienation.

In addition, the development programmes of post-1985 governments did not produce the promised results. A decade after the formal creation of a system of urban and rural development councils, no significant effects could be observed at the regional or national levels. Moreover, the corresponding system of regionalization of development efforts, although decreed during the first days of Cerezo Arévalo's presidency (1986–90), was actually the progeny of the last de facto military government: it was dictated by strategic considerations, and it did not correspond to any recognized form of regional planning. In 1996 the central government's development program was being pursued through a dozen "social funds" were financed mainly by resources and loans from the international community.

In sum, Guatemala continued to function within the logic of paternalistic traditions that executed "public works" (building roads, bridges, schools, and so on) without any real development policy and without any of the necessary social reconstruction. But this was not all. Alongside the economic and political crises and deteriorating social conditions, the nation suffered an accelerated breakdown of social structures with the spread of common violence and the establishment of the so-called violent economy (drug trafficking, smuggling, kidnappings, and organized robberies).

The preceding observations provide a glimpse of the discouraging scenario that formed the starting point from which Guatemala would finally begin to work towards participatory, representative democracy and a sustainable development that could improve the quality of life without further depleting the ecosystem. It is clear that future advances toward democracy and development will depend on multiple and complex developments within the international, regional, and national spheres. The determining factors – the perspectives, positions, motivations, attitudes, and agreements among groups with diverging interests – are constantly evolving, difficult to grasp, and can result in contradictory outcomes. The possibility of "negative future scenarios" must be given serious consideration in light of the extremely unfavourable conditions that prevail in Guatemala and the opposition to progressive change on the part of traditional elites and certain new powerful interest groups.

Addressing the many challenges outlined above will require an expansion of knowledge, new skills in policy formulation, and a considerable improvement in managerial capacity. Even in comparison with the other less developed countries of Central America, Guatemala is a "country without information." Most of the data used in social analysis and policy formulation are projections or estimates generated by various national and international organizations on the basis of scattered and incomplete statistics. The measures of social and economic conditions in different parts of the country are of uncertain reliability – indeed, at times they vary widely and are even contradictory. The last reliable census dates back to 1973. The most recent census (1994) is widely considered to be flawed, but it is nevertheless used extensively because it is the only recent source available to answer many of the questions at the national level.

Reform of the state administrative system has been repeatedly postponed, despite the fact that for decades it has demonstrated its incapacity to deal with national problems. To be sure, the period since the mid-1980s has involved a significant "move towards democracy" and a great deal of planning and dissemination of laws and the creation of new institutions.[1] But many, if not most, of those laws were not respected, and the new institutions lacked executive or implementing capacity; in effect, they were as dysfunctional and inflexible as the old institutions. The plans and strategies that were formulated were unsuccessful because they did not take into account the social and political structures, mentalities, and perspectives generated in the course of Guatemala's prior history. Effective planning, after all, requires a gradual learning and adjustment process involving openings, changes, and practical mechanisms that are defined through an analysis of both the causal factors that have generated the problems to be confronted and the factors that have obstructed effective and efficient local, regional, and national development planning and promotion in the past.

Various factors explain why many laws and decrees exist only on paper. One major factor is the obsolete, deficient, and incompetent character of the judicial system; another is the traditional culture of impunity that envelops the interests of the powerful.

In sum, the need for a broad, integrated national perspective on the multiple challenges to development in Guatemala must be emphasized. In order both to understand the current challenge and to identify the most promising solutions, research should be concerned not only with specific narrow problems – the focus of many studies – but also with broad national and regional trends and challenges. At the same time, it will be necessary to overcome the current breach between scholarly and policy decision making, so that the findings from research are taken into account in policy decisions and programme implementation.

MIGRATION IN GUATEMALA: AN OVERVIEW OF THE SITUATION

Population growth and decline in the different regions of Guatemala is deeply shaped by migration. Migration, in turn, is closely linked to social and economic change. Consequently, an improved understanding of migration patterns can be used as the starting point for understanding the context and challenges of national development. Migration arises from a combination of social, economic, and political forces and it has a direct impact on development and environmental conditions in the regions of origin and destination. Large numbers of people have been moving in Guatemala during the past two decades, and their mobility has had profound impacts.

Migration is a well-established survival strategy for the rural population of Guatemala. The agricultural lands available for each family in areas characterized by *minifundia* (very small fragmented holdings) simply do not produce enough to sustain the people who live in these areas; consequently, the residents have turned to migration in search of a livelihood. Two traditional patterns of migration emerged over the period extending from the late nineteenth century up to the 1980s. These were, first, the movement toward the southern coast dating from the latter part of the nineteenth century when export agriculture expanded in this zone (see, for example, Samper 1993) and, second, a movement toward Guatemala City beginning in the 1950s, in response to opportunities created by industrial development policies and the growth of the urban service sector (Ordoñez Yaquián 1995). Both of these traditional movements involved a mix of permanent migration and circular mobility for seasonal or short-term work.

Until the end of the 1970s these two migration patterns operated within a certain balance or equilibrium between new jobs available in the areas of migrant destinations and the lack of work in the areas of migrant origin or migrant expulsion. However, this equilibrium started to break down at an accelerating rate in the 1980s as a result of two changes. On the one hand, the numbers of workers without jobs in the areas of outmigration, particularly in the highlands and the eastern regions, increased noticeably because of a deepening crisis in *minifundio* production and the lack of any other sources of employment. On the other hand, no other region or economic sector in the country was able to provide opportunities for those seeking employment or self-employment, most of whom were unskilled rural workers. In fact, over the 1980s, both the southern coast and Guatemala City lost their capacity to absorb migrants.

A dramatic change took place in the southern coast, which became an area of migrant expulsion, due in part to a decline in the market for some of the traditional products grown in the region. The shift to migrant expulsion also arose because "the large export-farms used their economic advantage in a labour-surplus context to adopt policies that progressively reduced the size of their permanent labour force by replacing them with seasonal (temporary) workers" (Castillo 1993, 16).

Over the same period, the labour market in the metropolitan region surrounding and including Guatemala City collapsed, and immigration there decelerated rapidly, in sharp contrast with the explosive inflows of migrants in the 1950s. A clear indicator of the stagnation in rural-urban migration in the 1980s is the fact that the proportion of the economically active population (EAP) in agriculture scarcely shifted: according to census data, it was 54 percent in 1981 and only slightly less, at 53 percent, in 1994. In contrast, between 1950 and 1981, the EAP in agriculture had dropped from 68 to 54 percent.

The clear rupture with previous migration patterns that took place in the 1980s was the result of two interacting trends: the crisis in production and employment and the escalation of armed conflict and generalized political violence. Three new migration patterns emerged in this new situation. Two of these involved – for the first time in Guatemala's history – massive movements to destinations outside the country. The new migration patterns were

- emigration of refugees and the internal displacement of people, both in response to the armed conflict;
- migration toward unsettled "frontier" areas, particularly those in the north of the country, motivated by a search for land;
- migration of individuals seeking employment, particularly to the United States but also to southwestern Mexico.

These new patterns of movement were all survival strategies for families facing either a direct, violent threat to their lives or extreme poverty, or both. At the same time, their departure drained human resources from their home communities and made them even less viable places to live for those who remained behind. In sum, the new patterns of migration were highly interdependent. Migration as a flight from violence later became an economic necessity, not only for those who left for the United States, Canada, and other foreign destinations but also for the internally displaced who had fled to urban centres. The migration that was provoked by violence obliged many *campesinos*, and especially indigenous Mayas, to cross the border and, for the first time, expose themselves to previously unknown experiences. In turn, those experiences may have facilitated the subsequent migration of other members of their families and communities to foreign countries.

It bears emphasis that these recent migratory movements were massive and, in the case of migration for access to land and work, they are still increasing. While the flows of refugees and displaced persons declined over time in the late 1980s and early 1990s, movements in search of places for economic survival within and outside Guatemala increased at the same time.

With respect to refugees and displaced people, it is estimated that more than one million Guatemalans either fled the country or were forced to move within the country as a result of violence. "Seventy percent of these people returned to their previous places of residence following the amnesty decreed by the de facto government of General Rios Montt. This meant that there were still about 250,000 displaced people within Guatemala during 1983–85 and a similar number of refugees outside the country" (AVANCSO 1997; see also Lopez Rivera 1997).

Internal migrants and returning refugees who moved to the sparsely settled Petén and to northern Alta Verapaz had an enormous impact on population growth in these areas. Between 1973 and 1994 the population of Guatemala as a whole grew by 62 percent, but the population of the Petén increased by 251 percent.[2] *Municipios* where migrants settled in the Petén doubled in size several times over. La

Libertad was ten times larger in 1994 than it had been in 1973, growing by 1,090 percent: rapid growth was also notable in Sayaxché (467 percent), Santa Ana (414 percent), San Benito (346 percent), and San Andrés (320 percent). Meanwhile, the *municipio* of Chisec in Alta Verapaz (on the border with the *municipio* of Sayaxché in the Petén) grew by 460 percent between 1993 and 1994 (Gellert 1997b, 75–6).

Perhaps the best indicator of emigration from the country is provided by the numbers of Guatemalans living in the United States: between 1980 and 1990, they increased from 63,073 to 235,739, according to u.s. Census data (Castillo and Palma 1996, 151). These numbers may, however, be underestimates. The government of Guatemala estimated that there were 1,570,000 Guatemalans living in the United States in 1998 (*Prensa Libre*, 18 September 1998, citing Guatemala's ambassador in Washington). That number corresponded to about 18 percent of the 8,331,874 persons resident in Guatemala in 1994. Given that the average household in the country has 5.2 members, including adults and children (INE 1996), the number is also equivalent to having one person from each household resident in the United States. Bank of Guatemala data indicate that remittances from the United States to Guatemala rose from u.s.$64 million in 1989 to u.s.$417 million in 1995 (Gellert 1997b, 73). Consequently, migrant remittances are the second most important source (after coffee exports) of foreign exchange. This said, only a part of the money remitted home by migrants passes through the Bank of Guatemala (Gellert 1997a).

The new patterns of migration described above were generated in addition to the armed conflict, by the failure during the period from the 1950s to the 1970s of the economic development model based on agricultural exports and import-substitution industrialization and the absence of a new economic model that could generate increased production and employment (Alavarado 1988). Moreover, the civil war and economic collapse took place in a nation whose population was still largely rural (65 percent in 1973), very poor, and growing quickly. In contrast to the trend toward increased urbanization in virtually every other less urbanized country in the world, the proportion of Guatemala's urban population did not change between 1973 and 1994. It was 35 percent in both these census years: this stability clearly contrasts with the rapid urbanization of the 1950s and 1960s (Alvarado 1988). Moreover, of those living in urban areas in 1994, 44 percent were living in the Guatemala City metropolitan area. This is not to say that the cities and the metropolitan area did not grow between 1973 and 1994 but to emphasize that the urban growth that did take place was principally the result of fertility and natural increase in the towns and cities and that, because rural populations were also growing in this period, the urban proportion remained stable.

In the period 1973 to 1994 the population of Guatemala grew by 2.9 percent per year, the highest population growth in Central America, reflecting very high fertility, particularly in rural areas. The total fertility rate for the country as a whole between 1990 and 1994 was between 5.1 (the figure provided by the Ministry of Public Health) and 5.4 children per woman (the figure cited by APROFAM 1994). The particularly high fertility in rural areas and the stagnation in rural-urban migration explains why the rural population grew by 65 percent between 1973 and 1994 while the urban population grew by 55 percent.[3] When one considers that Guatemala (in a tie with Brazil) has the most unequal distribution of land in Latin America, it is easy to understand why very rapid population growth in the 1980s created increasing demographic and environmental pressures, including a serious deterioration in the quality of farm lands in *minifundia* areas (Bilsborrow and DeLargy 1991).

Related to the problems described above is the fact that Guatemala has very low levels of literacy, schooling, and labour-force skills. Investment in human capital, according to UN-ECLAC, is the lowest in Latin America.[4] Total expenditure on social services amounted to only U.S.$21.40 per person in 1990, and this had fallen to U.S.$20.90 in 1995, when total social expenditure came to 2.4 percent of GDP. In 1997, according to SEGEPLAN, total public expenditure on education (1.6 percent of GDP) and in health (1 percent of GDP) was the lowest in the region.[5] Similarly, in 1997 only 27 percent of EAP was affiliated with the Guatemalan Institute of Social Security, signifying that only this percentage had a formal (officially recognized) job. Moreover, due to low wages, few workers could afford private health care and educational services. In 1997, 1.6 million poor households (families) had average monthly incomes of just Q358.84 (U.S.$60). This was only about one-third of the Q1,062 that was necessary to purchase a minimum food basket for the average household (*La Hora*, 17 July 1997, citing data provided by SEGEPLAN and INE).

Labour migration to destinations outside the country and the migration of individuals and families in search of land inside Guatemala are the principal survival strategies for rural people. They are as important for survival as the pursuit of multiple informal-sector jobs in the commercial sectors of the rural and urban areas.[6] Nevertheless, all these survival strategies are highly susceptible to failure. The migrants and their families live in a permanently precarious state, threatened by unstable patterns of production, environmental degradation, lack of social security, and lack of legal protection when they migrate without proper documentation to other countries or when they occupy land without legal title.

Despite the importance of migration to understanding development problems, academic institutions in Guatemala have not payed much attention to the topic. Nor is there a state agency that focuses specifically on migration and issues faced by migrants. The lack of up-to-date information is apparent, for example, in the recent document that was supposed to form the basis for preparing a strategic plan for land use (SEGEPLAN/GTZ 1995). In that document the evaluation of migration was limited to a few general observations on interdepartmental movements that took up barely two pages. Moreover, those observations were based on out-of-date figures from 1950 and 1981. Among the major institutions, only the Church has given any priority to the issues.[7] For these reasons, significant segments of the population are involved in a territorial movement that began two decades ago, but no organization has much qualitative or quantitative data on its nature, impact, and patterns.

Here it is necessary to reiterate one of the central preoccupations of this chapter: while it is possible to explore certain aspects and particular features of migration through field research, it is necessary to have access to information that only a national census can provide, in order to obtain a comprehensive picture of the situation. In light of the peace process and the "reconstruction" of the country, the execution of the tenth national population census and the fifth national housing census, proposed for 1992, was a matter of national urgency. As noted earlier, the last reliable census that contained detailed information was carried out in 1973. Although a national census was conducted in 1981, its results were disputed; consequently, only "general characteristics" were published for the municipal level. That census did not provide data even on such basic indicators as place of birth, which would have permitted an analysis of internal migration flows. A new census, nevertheless, was postponed several times due to the "disappearance" of funds reserved for the project. When that census was finally conducted in April 1994, its contents and form were the subject of much preparatory work and debate.[8] This led to a more precise definition of the different variables (most importantly, concerning indigenous populations), as well as the introduction of new categories, such as international migration.

When the first (preliminary and definitive) results of the 1994 census came out, there was widespread surprise: Guatemala's population was much smaller than had been estimated.[9] The census indicated 8,331,874 inhabitants, while projections calculated for 1994 had come to 10,322,109 (General Statistical Office 1985). There is consequently much uncertainty about whether or not it is possible to work with the 1994 census figures. According to postcensus studies undertaken with international technical assistance by the National Statistical Institute (INE), the rate of omission was 11.8 percent (10.6 percent in urban areas and 12.8 in rural areas), a figure that is quite normal for the region. In spite of this finding, however, the census results were rejected outright by Guatemala's public sector institutions. Above all, they were rejected at the political level because a smaller population implies fewer "benefits" – for example, a reduction in the number of deputies to be elected to the national congress.

An extreme illustration of statistical inconsistencies concerns the number of people living in the metropolitan area of the capital city. The municipality of Guatemala City produced and published the following figures as part of its urban planning project Metropolis 2010: the population of the metropolitan zone, that is, all the municipalities surrounding the capital combined, was set at 2.8 million in 1995, and it was predicted to rise to 5,411,000 by the year 2010.[10] Guatemala City itself (that is, the capital city area) was predicted to reach the 3 million mark by the year 2010 (*Prensa Libre*, 2 June 1996. The 1994 national census found only 823,301 inhabitants in the capital and 1.5 million in the metropolitan zone. In other words, the discrepancies in the figures are great: the municipality of Guatemala City claims to have double the number of people found by the national census in the capital and the metropolitan area!

While the 1994 census identified a decrease in migration toward the Guatemala City Metropolitan Area (GCMA), other data showed a significant increase in poverty and marginality (below-standard housing, lack of access to water, sewerage, and so on) over the previous decade, much of it concentrated among migrants who had arrived during 1975–85 (MUNI 1986). In 1986 there were 130 "precarious settlements" or "marginal zones" (basically, shanty-town housing with no services) identified within the GCMA. By 1991 this number had increased to 222. A few years later some 337 urban areas, or barrios, in the city met poverty criteria in certain respects (SEGEPLAN/UNICEF 1993; COINAP/UNICEF 1997). The poorest 161 of the precarious settlements contained 38,650 families, or roughly one-quarter million people. Fifty of these terribly poor settlements existed prior to 1991, while 111 were formed in the five years between 1992 and 1997. Virtually all (93 percent) of the land on which they sat was taken by "invasion," that is to say, by spontaneous occupation by people too poor to buy the property. Poor families looking for a place to live identify vacant lands within the city (lots, hillsides, ravines) and then move in as squatters, building shelters and shacks out of whatever scrap materials they can find. Such settlements would be typical of the places where some 45,000 persons displaced by violence came to live in Guatemala City during the civil war (Bastos and Camus 1994).

THE DISPLACED IN GUATEMALA CITY: A DIAGNOSIS

The institutionalized political violence that became ascendant towards the end of the 1970s and the beginning of the 1980s has been well documented from different perspectives. The social causes of the violence have not been as fully studied, however. The subject has been addressed as a whole in general terms, but little research has been done on specific elements. The best-documented aspect has been the approximately 100,000 people who took refuge in other countries, Mexico in particular, in the early 1980s. There were much larger numbers of people, however, who were not able to leave the country, although they had to leave their home communities. These are the "internally displaced," or simply, "the displaced" (Bastos and Camus 1994).

The problem of the displaced is a very difficult subject for analysis because of the variation in their situation from one settlement to another. It contrast to the abundant research on the groups of organized refugees, there are few studies of the displaced. The Association for the Advancement of the Social Sciences in Guatemala (AVANCSO) took some early steps in this area, and its publications identify two different categories of the internally displaced (AVANCSO 1990, 1992). First, there are *the displaced in the mountains,* that is, those who fled mainly during the period from 1980 to 1982 to the mountains and jungles near their places of origin. The Communities of Populations in Resistance (CPRs) are an example. Second, there are *the dispersed displaced,* who fled to two areas in particular – the capital city and the southern coast.

An analysis of the dispersed displaced is particularly difficult because they are scattered, hidden, and anonymous among the urban and rural poor. Among the victims of the repression and violence, they are probably the most frequently forgotten. As "dispersed peoples" who have not been recognized as victims with rights, they do not identify themselves (nor do others identify them) as a collectivity with particular needs arising from their forced relocation, poverty, and uprooted cultural situation (Bastos and Camus 1994). In consequence, the large number of displaced persons who moved to urban areas have remained out of sight and are inadequately portrayed within the social sciences, nongovernmental organizations, the international community, and the state agencies that could offer them protection and assistance.

What is known about the displaced people in Guatemala City comes primarily from two studies: Bastos and Camus (1994) and AVANCSO (1997). Both provide information based on interviews with a small number of cases (thirty families and fifty-eight persons, respectively). The families and individuals form part of a much larger population of displaced people who are dispersed widely among the poor and marginal settlements scattered through the city. Given these settlement patterns, these studies based on small samples did not attempt to be representative; rather, they focused on deepening an understanding of particular features of their situation. Above all, the two studies sought to show how violence and forced flight left enduring scars that extended far beyond their immediately devastating effect.

While the results of the two studies are different in some important respects, they both point to similar conclusions and policy priorities. These priorities include

1 Recognition of the fact that internally displaced peoples face particular challenges;
2 Support for efforts to facilitate their return to their home communities when the displaced people themselves still wish to return and when of those have who stayed behind would like them to do so (in some cases, the displaced are not welcomed back, as explained below);
3 Respect for people's decisions to remain as "internal refugees" in Guatemala City when a return home is neither desirable nor possible, and the provision of assistance to help them overcome their precarious, vulnerable, and marginal situation.

Action along the lines identified will require collaboration among state agencies and nongovernmental organizations at all levels – local, national, and international – that have a commitment to addressing poverty. While the need for urgent action has been recognized since the publication of the Bastos and Camus report (1994), the plight of the displaced in urban areas has been ignored to date, a fact that was confirmed in June 1998 at an internal, or working, meeting of the Commission for Historical Clarification (Comisión para el Esclarecimiento Histórico) which was established in the peace agreements. In consequence, the conclusions reached by Bastos and Camus are as valid in 1998, two years after the general peace accord was signed, as they were when the study was published.

Bastos and Camus found that displaced families live in extreme poverty, in conditions that are even worse than those of the indigenous urban community in general. Since they had been in the city for a decade at the time of the interviews, poverty is so prevalent that it can only be attributed to their lack of adaptation to urban life. Aside from the fact that they were peasants, illiterates, and, for the most part, speakers of indigenous languages, they were unable to adapt to urban life because of a general "loss of will," or demoralization.

With the birth of a second generation in the capital, strong contradictions have emerged in the family system: the urban young people and children have grown up in families strongly identified as "dispersed," but they have also been more influenced than their parents by city life. Various social pressures impinge on these young people, and it is hard to know what the future holds for them.

Refugees, as individuals, are commonly prevented from returning to their communities of origin because their houses have been destroyed and their lands – if they still own them – are uncultivated or worked by others. Nor do they have the means to start from scratch again. Social relations and ties with the abandoned communities have changed, not only as a direct result of the violence but also as a consequence of the imposition of a new system of social control and the rise of new local power elites, above all, through the PACs. Restructured power elites have managed to instill in the people who remained a negative perception of those who have left. (In these cases, opposition to the process of reintegration is coming from former neighbours, a very difficult problem to solve.) This destruction of old social relations is one of the most important effects that the institutionalized violence has had and will continue to have.

Given the barriers to return, displaced families in the city have to confront the fact that – for lack of other options – they are likely to remain where they are now (an option that becomes more likely with each passing year), rather than return to their place of origin which raises yet another problem with respect to reintegration. This possibility has not been considered within the context of reintegration policies: the Accord for the Resettlement of Populations Displaced by Armed Conflict signed by the government and the Guatemalan National Revolutionary Unity (URNG) in June 1994 does not recognize the particular option of permanent residence in the city. That accord refers only to return. Moreover, it does not take into consideration the city as a site of resettlement and refers to the "areas of resettlement" as "predominantly rural."

To ensure the satisfactory integration of this group of displaced people into the urban world, the same terms of reintegration that have been agreed upon with reference to the rest of the displaced population must apply. This requires at least three conditions that have yet to be met.

First, there is an urgent need to provide aid to improve living conditions. In order for the displaced to become the subjects of aid programs, however, they need to identify themselves as displaced. Second, there is a need to overcome the conditions that have led the displaced to maintain their anonymity – that is, it is necessary to change the image of the displaced as "subversive" (which has stuck to them in their urban environment) and the stigma that goes with such a label.[11] Third, the social fabric in the communities of origin must be repaired, and the displaced must be allowed to freely establish ties with those communities. While military control, whether direct or through the civil patrols, does not permit the displaced to return and may force them to decide to remain in the city, demilitarization would permit them to reestablish contact through visits, possibly to work in their corn fields, and eventually to establish double residences. If the conditions making this possible are created, the displaced in the cities of Guatemala will be able to reclaim one of the significant features of the life of Guatemala's indigenous urban peoples, a fundamental characteristic of their ethnicity today: they would join the thousands of Maya who live in the city and, when they can, return to their homes to visit families and participate in community events.

A traditional institutional practice in Guatemala is to take a technocratic approach to social problems that require urgent solutions, without trying to gain a better understanding of the various actors and subjects involved: the conditions in which they actually live, as well as their perspectives, motivations, and ways of making choices. Consequently, even in the best of circumstances, certain specific problems are effectively addressed, but in a way that does not contribute to the resolution of the underlying social problems. For example, the need to address the situation of the displaced or the urban poor is recognized, but little is known about the numbers of people involved and even less about the situations that affect, characterize, or differentiate them as part of a conflict-ridden and multifaceted society with respect to ethnic, political, and social divisions.

The importance of research on scattered populations of internally displaced people does not rest simply on its capacity to provide significant data in this respect – that is, data for the formulation and implementation of policies that can effectively contribute to social peace. Such studies, which are only a starting point, would also be significant for recovering certain elements of Guatemala's immediate history, so that the suffering that parts of the population, particularly the Maya, have endured and continue to endure as direct victims of political repression, would be known, acknowledged, and not forgotten.

NOTES

1 Some institutions have already been revoked, such as the new Ministry of Rural Development and various presidential "secretariats."
2 The population of Guatemala City Metropolitan Area increased by 62 percent between 1973 and 1994, a rate of growth similar to that of the nation as a whole.
3 For purposes of comparison, the rural population of neighbouring El Salvador grew by only 16 percent, and its urban population increased by 82 percent over the same period.
4 UN-ECLAC defines investment in human capital as investment that favours the intellectual and physical growth of individuals and, therefore, growth in productive capacity over the medium and long term.
5 For in-depth analysis of health, education, and other social indicators, including comparisons with other Latin American countries, based on UN-ECLAC and other data, see Sistema de las Naciones Unidas en Guatemala (1998).
6 Aware of this problem, FLACSO-Guatemala inaugurated a series of studies on migration (Gellert 1997a). Some of the initial conclusions from that research are summarized in this chapter.
7 The Guatemalan Episcopal Conference issued, in a National Migrant Day pastoral message on 3 September 1995, the "Pastoral Letter on Human Mobility." It deals with the situation of refugees, the displaced, returned refugees, emigrants, the deported, and migrant agricultural workers. Other similar initiatives may have escaped notice, but that, in itself, would be another indicator of the lack of information resulting from the fragmented and uncoordinated nature of Guatemalan institutions.
8 Support was provided by international organizations such as the UN Population Fund, the Interamerican Development Bank (IDB), the UN Latin American Demographic Centre (UN-CELADE), and the UN Economic Commission for Latin America and the Caribbean (UN-ECLAC), among others (they also helped with the compilation and analysis of data).

9 The first definitive figures from the "General Characteristics" were published by the INE in March 1996. The publication of more information, including data concerning national and international migrations trends, is still unsure, however.
10 This prediction was publicized in the 2 June 1996 issue of the newspaper *Prensa Libre*, which said, "By the year 2010 the metropolitan area will contain more than five million inhabitants."
11 The following example provides an illustration of this stigma on the refugees and displaced in the eyes of the power elites and security forces: Minister of Defense Enriquez Morales, during a press conference that he held to announce his resignation (resulting from the October 1995 massacre in the community Aurora 8 de Octubre) stated that "the 28,000 refugees who have returned to the country are acting as a shield for the guerrillas." During an interview conducted by a television news team with the arrested second lieutenant of the military patrol responsible for the massacre, the accused answered in the affirmative when asked whether there were guerrillas among the returned.

8 Exodus and Return within a Changing Migration System

MANUEL ANGEL CASTILLO

Guatemala is increasingly affected by international migration and by accelerated rural-urban migration, but these are relatively recent developments. Both these migration trends have multiple and overlapping causes, including the civil war and violence of the past two decades, transformations in national and hemispheric economic development patterns that affect employment and income-earning opportunities; and the incorporation of Guatemalans into the evolving inter-American migration system (Castillo 1994a). The purpose of this paper is to place the ongoing refugee return in the context of these broader migration trends and the forces that influence them. The paper draws attention to emerging hypotheses on the links between migration and development problems in Guatemala, and on related policy questions.

THE HISTORICAL CONTEXT

Historically, most migration in Guatemala has been confined within its national boundaries. The country has a long history of temporary and seasonal movements of workers from peasant farming areas in the highlands to export agriculture zones, that is, to the fertile coastal and lower hillside lands (CSUCA 1978a, b; Schmid 1967; Figueroa 1976). Harvests of agricultural export crops – principally, coffee, sugar cane, cotton, cardamom, and tobacco – are highly dependent on the timely and sufficient availability of seasonal workers. Although seasonal employment generally offers only low wages, it provides an important income supplement that allows peasants to return home with some savings that contribute to the survival of their home communities.

Recent research on the internal migration system is very limited, but it is generally understood that, overall, the seasonal flow of workers from the highlands to the lowlands continues to operate as in the past. With regard to specific civil-war-induced changes in farm employment and migration patterns, one can only speculate on the basis of general information. It seems likely that traditional flows of labour from highland source communities were reduced, simply as a consequence of the enormous decline in the population of these communities as people fled from them during the war. Meanwhile, many former residents of highland communities settled permanently in lowland areas near the plantations where they were employed. The extent to which such resettlement was encouraged by the plantation owners themselves is not known.

Other features of the internal migration system have also evolved considerably over the recent past. In addition to the peasants who moved permanently to coastal areas, many other peasants moved to cities, inducing broad transformations in social relations and in the distribution of the population between urban and rural areas. Beginning in the 1950s increased investment in export agriculture led to the dislocation of many peasants and small farmers, while investment in urban industry and commerce attracted internal migration to urban areas, particularly to Guatemala City, where most of the amenities, sources of industrial and commercial employment, and public services were located (Alvarado Constenla 1983, 1984; Gellert 1992; Velásquez Carrera 1989, 1993). Some of the migrants found wage employment in the new urban enterprises; others (perhaps a majority) survived through diverse "informal" economic activities – casual work, scavenging, and so on (Bastos and Camus 1994; Pérez Sainz, Camus, and Bastos 1992). All these migration trends accelerated with the civil war and the crisis in employment opportunities (CEPAL 1980a, b).

At the same time, seasonal patterns of internal migration from the highlands to the lowlands evolved in tandem with similar movements toward the south of Mexico. Since the middle of the nineteenth century, peasants from Guatemala's western highlands have crossed the Mexican border on a seasonal basis to work mainly for the coffee plantations located in the nearby Soconusco region in the state of Chiapas (Castillo 1990). Although this seasonal movement of workers from Guatemala to Mexico was well established by the 1890s and continued over the first half of the twentieth century, it intensified during the 1950s (Castillo 1995a; Mosquera Aguilar 1990). How Guatemalan seasonal workers came to replace large numbers of Mexican seasonal workers since the 1950s has been the subject of some debate (Castillo 1995b), but it is clear that the harvest of agro-exports in the Soconusco region became highly dependent on Guatemalan migrant labour (Ordóñez 1990, 1993).

VIOLENCE AND REFUGEE FLIGHT: A TURNING POINT

Historically established migration patterns changed suddenly toward the end of the 1970s as political conflict and a general crisis – political and socioeconomic – increasingly affected all aspects of social life, not only in Guatemala but also in the neighbouring Central American countries. Violence and economic crisis combined to provoke enormous population displacements within Guatemala and a great exodus of refugees and international emigrants. Within the country, rural-urban migration increased dramatically, with Guatemala City remaining, as before, the principal destination (AVANCSO 1991); large numbers also fled to the forests and mountains to escape the armed confrontations and the harassment of military forces. Since then, peasants' migration and settlement patterns have been driven by their need to find safe havens and opportunities for survival, however precarious and limited (see among others, Falla 1994; Jonas 1991; Lovell 1995; Manz 1988a).

The most intense combat and the most merciless army operations were concentrated in the western highlands and the northern forests. The Guatemalan military's scorched-earth operations were carried out overwhelmingly in these areas. These regions also suffered most from the organization and operation of so-called Civil Self-defence Patrols (PACs) controlled by the army (Carmack 1988). All these factors contributed to large-scale population displacements and an enormous transformation of settlement patterns in these areas, with spill-over effects in other areas. The social and demographic map of the country began to change and the capital city grew rapidly with the inflow of large numbers of rural emigrants (AVANCSO 1991; Bastos and Camus 1994; see also Gellert's contribution to this volume).

One of the most remarkable features of the migratory response to war, violence, and military repression was the massive movement of rural people to destinations outside the country. Although some of those who were displaced moved east into the neighbouring countries of Honduras and Belize, the largest number sought refuge across the northwestern border in adjacent regions of Mexico. In spite of international and local assistance, many, if not most, of the refugees faced major problems. Those who settled in recognized "camps" in Mexico (some 46,000 by the mid-1980s) were better assisted in relative terms.[1] In contrast, the so-called dispersed refugees, who appear to have been larger in number, but not known with precision, had to survive on their own, with some assistance from local Mexican peasants in rural areas and through informal social support networks in cities. Eventually they were assisted also by nongvernmental organizations (NGOs), with ties to Catholic bishops and the Church as a whole (Castillo and Palma 1994; CNDH 1995; O'Dogherty n.d.; Salvadó 1988).

From the mid-1980s through the mid-1990s, the "return" process dominated the refugees' lives. The internationally mediated accord established between organized refugees and the Guatemalan government provided formal guarantees for the security of the returnees, but the implementation of the accord was uneven and the return process was fraught with uncertainty. In that context, international NGO accompaniment programs (see Levitt's chapter) were very helpful in ensuring the fulfillment of the negotiated security guarantees. Thus, despite the risks almost half the 46,000 refugees in Mexican "camps" had returned by the end of 1996. The Mexican Commission for Aid to Refugees (COMAR) identified a total of 29,930 officially recorded collective and individual or family returns in the 1984–95 period (INM 1996). Meanwhile, the Mexico office of the UN High Commissioner for Refugees (UNHCR) identified 31,891 refugees still living in camps in Campeche, Chiapas, and Quintana Roo at the end of December 1995 (Castillo and Venet 1996).[2] Nearly all of the relatively small number of refugees in Honduras returned. By contrast, most refugees in Belize apparently decided to remain there (Lungo and Castillo 1996). In sum, in the mid-1990s there were still large numbers of refugees abroad, including people who wished to return, as well as people who wanted to stay put. Both groups faced many challenges and uncertain futures (Castillo 1995b).

UNDOCUMENTED INTERNATIONAL
EMIGRATION: A NEW TURNING POINT?

According to U.S. and Mexican census data and immigration records, few Guatemalans and other Central Americans moved north from Guatemala prior to the period of rising violence and refugee flight. By the mid-1980s, however, there were signs of large-scale arrivals of Guatemalans in Mexico and the United States (see INS; Castillo 1995b).[3] Between 1980 and 1990, U.S. national censuses recorded a

12.8 percent intercensus growth rate in the number of Guatemalan-born individuals residing in the United States. This increase was surpassed only by the increase in the number of Salvadoreans, the highest among Central Americans – namely, 15.9 percent (CEPAL/FNUAP/CELADE 1993).[4] According to Warren (cited in Fix and Passel 1994, table 2, 24), of the total undocumented population living in the United States in October 1992, Guatemalans were estimated to number 121,000 (4 percent), fewer than Salvadoreans (9 percent). Mexicans (31 percent), of course, constituted the largest single contingent of undocumented immigrants (Fix et al. 1994, table 2, 24; see also Gellert's chapter in this volume).

By the 1990s undocumented transmigration from Central America had become a major issue not only for the Mexican but also for the U.S. government. At mid-decade the U.S. Immigration and Naturalization Services (INS) reported that the numbers of deportations of undocumented migrants remained at high levels as the United States deported 41,819 individuals (from all countries) in fiscal year (FY) 1995 and 50,064 in FY 1996. Mexicans were the most numerous deportees – 29,726 in 1995 and 35,428 in 1996; the number of Central Americans deported during those two years came to 5,836 and 7,636 respectively. The list was headed by Hondurans (1,875 and 2,693), followed by Guatemalans (1,783 and 2,360) and Salvadorans (1,654 and 1,980).[5] Meanwhile, the data available on detentions and deportations of undocumented Central American transmigrants by Mexican authorities (see INM 1996) indicate that the highest proportion corresponded to Guatemalans. It is likely that during the 1980s high proportions of detained undocumented migrants were Nicaraguans and Salvadorans; however, their percentages diminished in the 1990s, while the Guatemalan average rose to 49 percent of all – not just Central American – undocumented migrants deported by Mexican authorities during 1990–95 and January–May 1996 (Castillo 1996, 21).

Meanwhile, because of its geographic location Guatemala turned into the funnel for all Central Americans entering Mexico, either to stay or with the intention of entering the United States. Nationals from other Central and South American countries passed through Guatemala, usually stopping en route to make contacts and arrangements to continue their trip. While their stay was temporary, it could last for some time, depending on how long it took to resolve difficulties and reach agreements with traffickers or others who might assist or guide them.

Transit through Guatemala and Mexico was not an easy process; for instance, South Americans who arrived at the international airport in Guatemala City suffered assaults, rapes, and other harassment during their temporary stay in the city or in transit to the north. Even after repeated attempts, some were unable to cross the border from Guatemala into Mexico, while the path through Mexico was also full of dangers. The use of clandestine routes through jungles and over mountains created risks of injury or death from natural causes or, the greatest hazard, from attacks by criminals and police or military units (Frelick 1991; CNDH 1995).

The lack of systematic research on migration from and through Guatemala to Mexico and further north makes it impossible to state anything definitive about that phenomenon. Yet recent ethnographic field research, often of a preliminary nature, does cast some light on the matter and points to hypotheses for future study. It seems that a significant increase has taken place in Guatemalan rural and urban emigration to the United States.[6] It also seems that males have continued to predominate in this movement, but that the presence of single women has increased significantly. There is evidence of some migration of mothers with children as well as of children traveling alone. While the migration stream appears to be dominated by individuals of urban background, field observations suggest that rural emigration is not only growing but also spreading, touching more communities than ever before.[7]

Little is known about the integration of these rural migrants into the communities to which they move. The very low average levels of schooling and the high illiteracy rates of the Guatemalans (and Central Americans in general, with the exception of Costa Ricans) was likely to slow down the integration of many into the foreign urban areas where social and cultural patterns diverged from those of their own backgrounds. In addition, a high proportion of rural Guatemalans do not speak Spanish, the national language of Mexico and the language of daily use in the large Hispanic-origin communities where migrants settled in North America. Clearly, rural Guatemalan emigrants faced more obstacles to immigration and integration abroad than their urban counterparts. Yet, sporadic field results and interviews suggest that Indian populations had generated highly developed strategies to overcome the barriers they faced. It seems that they may even have enjoyed certain advantages vis-à-vis their more urbanized fellows who spoke only Spanish. For instance, Mexican migration authorities and people in general could easily mistake them for Indian people from Chiapas or Oaxaca, a resemblance that may have helped them succeed in undocumented migration through Mexico. In the United States, rural Guatemalan migrants succeeded in finding employment in a broad spectrum of agricultural or related jobs. There is a long list of crops – more than thirty different fruits and vegetables – that temporary rural migrants from Guatemala's northwestern communities harvest in the United States. In addition, they found employment in occasional and less precisely defined occupations in industry and services.

MIGRATION AND REFUGEE POLICIES IN RECEIVING COUNTRIES

Since Central American emigration was not a major issue before the late 1970s, earlier minor flows from the region to Mexico and the United States were not given any special consideration in the receiving countries. U.S. immigration policy was far more concerned with Mexican immigration. Meanwhile, Mexican preoccupation with international migration also focused on the movements of its citizens back and forth across the U.S. border, even though Mexico was increasingly playing the role of a receiving as well as a transit country for Central American migrants.

In the early 1980s rapidly rising flows from Central America northward led to a shift in policy in the main receiving countries. In this context, Guatemalan refuge/asylum claimants joined the tide of Salvadoreans and Nicaraguans who had previously appealed to the United States for protection; however, treatment of these populations was and is selective, in accordance with U.S. foreign policy interests.[8] Nicaraguan opponents of the Sandinista regime were warmly received and protected by U.S. authorities, while people fleeing persecution by the "friendly" Salvadoran regime faced strong restrictions on access to refugee/asylum status. Guatemalans shared the Salvadoreans' fate even though the international community was fully aware of the extent of human rights violations in both their countries of origin (Castillo and Palma 1994, 49–50). During the 1990s, Salvadoreans in the United States were in serious jeopardy, as American authorities frequently announced their intention not to extend temporary residence permits, given the UN-mediated end of the country's civil war in 1992, as well as the ongoing process of democratization.[9] To what extent this might be a precedent for Guatemalans residing in the United States remains to be seen.

The other destination countries of Guatemalan refugees adopted more open policies. Governments of third countries of asylum could more easily apply selective procedures to admit people willing to settle in faraway places like Australia, New Zealand, Norway, Sweden, and Canada. Their refugee admission policies, however, although originally based on humanitarian grounds and on legitimate criteria such as fear of persecution, appeared to be moving dangerously toward enforcing nonentry practices and selective procedures that matched the potential refugees' profile to general immigration admission policy criteria (Castillo and Hathaway 1996).[10]

Mexico initially resisted the large new inflows from Central America. Although Mexico's official policy provided protection to political asylum seekers when large numbers of Central Americans began to arrive in the 1980s, the legal provisions in force could not be rigorously interpreted as applicable to them, since they could not prove individual political persecution in the strict sense. As a consequence, few or none of the refugees were granted official asylum in Mexico.[11] A large percentage of newcomers were allowed to stay, however, and they received special assistance from Mexican authorities (in conjunction with assistance from the UNHCR and various national and international NGOs).[12] In any case, the lack of official receptivity did not stop refugee flows to Mexico. As a large Spanish-speaking country, that is relatively stable politically, with a culture similar to that of Central America, Mexico was the logical place of first refuge and a likely place of settlement for Central Americans urgently seeking a safe haven. Moreover, in the early 1980s, in the era before the economic crisis of the 1990s, Mexico was relatively prosperous. Another positive feature for some refugees was the Mexican government's active role in the search for peace in Central America.

Mexico's contradictory features as a destination for Central American refugees led to a situation in which refugees in the country were not always secure, protected, or well cared for. Refugees in organized camps fared the best, but even they suffered because their status was ambiguous: they were de facto refugees only, without official recognition of this status. Their children born in Mexico were still foreigners according to Mexican policy. Access to employment and productive land was limited and controlled. Moreover, refugees were subject to the whims of a bureaucratic aid administration that they did not understand and could not readily influence.

In 1990 diverse pressures from Mexican NGOs and international organizations finally led Mexico to modify its General Law of Population and to define a refugee as explicitly different from a person in asylum.[13] Nevertheless, strictly speaking the status of refugee was never granted, although the concept was formally adopted and enabling legislation was passed in 1992. By that time discussions with the Guatemalan government had led to the accord concerning the refugee return process, and this dramatically reduced pressure for full application of the new law to Guatemalans who had not received any legal recognition of refugee status prior to changes in the law.

However, Mexican authorities did start a program to facilitate the stay of those refugees unwilling to return. Some of them – especially those residing in Campeche – obtained Mexican nationality, which allowed them to move freely and accede to property and credits. Others, such as the majority of those who had settled in Chiapas, obtained residence permits that also improved their situation with regard to freedom of movement and employment. Moreover, a lengthier time of residence favoured the later granting of Mexican nationality.

Overall, although there is no concrete evidence concerning the matter, it seems that the beginning of the organized and collective return process in 1993 at least momentarily lessened the need of the refugees who still remained in Mexico to secure legal status.[14] Around the same time, they had received news of planned reductions in international assistance to the refugee camps. Thus both the accord with the Guatemalan government and the news of declining international support for the camps contributed to speeding up returns, which began as organized movements in 1993.

The return process became more complex when conflict erupted in Chiapas between armed guerrillas and the Mexican army in January 1994. Chiapas became, first, a zone of social and political confrontation and then a region under army occupation, although political negotiations also took place at the same time (Castillo 1994b). Political conflict and military control in the area, which threatened the refugee camps in addition to Mexican communities, thus became an additional source of pressure for return to Guatemala (Yaschine 1995).

CONTINUED MIGRATION DESPITE DEMOCRATIZATION

Among the many underlying causes of the conflict in Guatemala, the absence of democracy was a key factor. Channels of political expression for peasants and indigenous communities were persistently and systematically closed and repressed over most of the country's history, with particular intensity at certain moments such as the early 1980s. The intolerance of any opposition and the impunity of civil and military authorities from prosecution for corruption and human rights abuses were probably the most blatant features of Guatemala's authoritarian political model.

The armed forces were central players in the enforcement of severe constraints on democratic processes. In the latter half of the 1980s, in response to pressure for change from diverse sectors (including both armed revolutionary groups and other actors in civil society), the army announced a "return to the institutional system," that is, to a constitutional democracy.[15] Although the proposed political model was not specified very precisely, the general shift in direction was crucial: it led first to the democratic elections of 1986 and the installation of a civilian president and then to a draft peace accord and agreements for the return of refugees. The transition toward an imprecisely defined democratic model was not smooth. Consequently, human rights violations, repression, and widespread insecurity related to high levels of violent crime and kidnappings were major matters of concern not only for returnees but for all Guatemalans (PDH 1996).

The increasingly important dialogue and negotiation between the Guatemalan National Revolutionary Unity (URNG) and government commissions, which included top army officials, were key elements in the progress toward peace and democracy. Although some analysts have criticized the development of closed conversations between the parties (as does Fonseca in his contribution to this volume), it is understandable that certain aspects of the negotiations would require some degree of secrecy to protect and guarantee confidence. The dialogue, moreover, allowed and even promoted open discussion concerning the future of the country by diverse groups. Perhaps the most articulate expression of popular views occurred in the Assembly of Civil Society, which brought together various groups and institutions that previously had little political voice. Moreover, some of the proposals aired in the assembly entered into the political accords, a promising development in light of the country's history.

The major element considered by all those who became involved in the discussions concerning peace, democratization, and refugee return referred to the concept of development. How would development be defined in the social, economic, and political models to be adopted? Peace and democracy could not be attained by political measures alone. Outstanding questions of access to land, employment, and income had to be resolved. For most of Latin America the 1980s was the "lost development decade," during which national per capita income fell by 10 percent or more in many countries, but in Central America the economic crisis had begun already in the 1970s. Thus, economic recovery and the improved well-being of the poor were necessarily integral to a sustainable peace.

Indeed, the impoverishment of large sectors of the population – the growth in the numbers of people living in poverty and extreme poverty, particularly in the rural areas (INE/FNUAP 1991) – was both a cause and a consequence of the civil war. Peasants and indigenous communities as well as the urban poor suffered the worst consequences of the economic decline, which fueled political, social, and cultural conflicts. Thus, it was hoped that democratization would lead not only to the peaceful resolution of conflicts but also to economic recovery and new opportunities for all. This hope, however, remained to be fulfilled.

In sum, even as the peace process moved forward and refugees returned, Guatemalans continued to leave their country in large and increasing numbers. Their exodus had important impacts on the communities they left behind.

Migration research has frequently sought to confirm that the poorest sectors of society are the most likely to move during phases of rapid economic transformation and development, and that finding applies to short-distance moves as well as to more expensive long-distance moves.[16] However, the recent history of the Central American countries constitutes a radically distinctive migration context leading to atypical migration outcomes. This is particularly evident in the case of Guatemala.

Over the past two decades, population mobility within and from Guatemala has not been restricted to any specific social class, although the poor must have been displaced in disproportionate numbers. Highland peasants and other peasants were displaced to wage-labour zones, to new frontier settlements and to urban areas. They were also displaced to work and settle outside the country, becoming increasingly involved in transmigrant communities in Mexico and the United States. The migrants who found work in developed countries became a source of increasing remittances of money and goods to family and home communities in Guatemala. This is one of the positive consequences of outmigration: families, economies, and societies in general obtain a material profit from the successful incorporation of their members in wealthier economies abroad. In this way the emigrants serve as escape valves for the failures of the development model in two respects: they reduce the number of workers looking for employment and demanding services at home, and they provide income-support to family members who do not migrate.

The only available global study on remittances sent home by Central Americans, mostly from the United States (CEPAL 1991a), ranked the Guatemalan economy second (after El Salvador's) in the hierarchy of major recipients of external resources from migration over the period 1982 to 1989. This represented a change from Guatemala's leading position in 1980–81. From 1980 to 1989 estimates of family remittances more than doubled in Guatemala (from $U.S. 107.6 million to U.S.248.1 million), multiplied by five in Nicaragua (from $U.S.11.0 milltion to U.S.59.8 million), and went up by a factor of ten in El Salvador (from $U.S.73.8 million to U.S.759.4 million) (CEPAL 1991a, table 2, 62). [By 1994, according to the Bank of Guatemala, remittances had increased to $U.S.302 million, continuing their upward climb in 1995 to $U.S.416.5 million and to U.S.306.9 million during the first ten months of 1996 (Pensabenne 1997, 8).][17]

Several indexes have been used to demonstrate the increasing importance of remittances in Central American countries. For example, the value of remittances has been compared to the value of coffee export earnings, whose historical significance in the national economies of the region's countries is well known: according to 1989 estimates, remittances equalled 66 percent of the value of coffee exports in Guatemala and Nicaragua and added up to triple their value in El Salvador. Data extrapolated from studies conducted in selected localities to compare national cases have yielded figures even higher than the official ones: CEPAL estimated that total family remittances to the region in 1989 came to $U.S.707 million (under a low-emigration hypothesis) and to $U.S.1,070.1 million (under a high-emigration hypothesis) (CEPAL 1991b, table 4, 56).

In the absence of other global studies, the only references to the importance of remittances are periodic statements by government spokespersons reported in newspapers and based on ill-explained estimates by the region's central bank authorities who have asserted that by mid-1995 remittances could have added up to $U.S.550 to $U.S.600 million per year. This figure is well under CEPAL's low-emigration hypothesis calculus for 1989 (CEPAL 1991b, table 4, 56). Meanwhile, no systematic research has been conducted on effects on individuals, families, and communities, beyond the limited survey carried out by CEPAL.[18]

While the families and communities from which emigrants departed were conscious of the short-term benefits of migration, they were not fully aware of and concerned about the long-term effects of sustained emigration. As of 1996, neither village leaders nor authorities had yet reported clear concerns about increased family disintegration linked to emigration processes, changes in consumptions patterns that will be difficult to sustain without continued emigration and high flows of remittances, and increasing disregard for social traditions that have sustained their communities through past crises. Recent interviews with officials, scholars, and some NGO staff indicated that the effects of emigration were often invisible among broader social processes and were lost to observers because of their focus on increasing poverty as an explanatory factor (Lungo and Castillo 1996).

By the 1990s authorities argued that political persecution and violence were no longer as important as in the past in poor peoples' emigration decisions. Rather, community leaders reported that general social, political, and economic insecurity, combined with the absence or scarcity of social and economic opportunities, combined to sustain a large, and perhaps rising, outflow of Guatemalans, even as some former emigrants (and many officially recognized refugees) were returning.[19]

The processes of migration and return were replete with contradictory currents. Increasingly, faraway places were becoming the principal destinations of emigrants, as they discarded alternative local or regional centres. Often, the migrants intended to return, but not all do return, at least not permanently. A recent study of Guatemalans and Salvadoreans in the Los Angeles area documented many of the contradictory feelings underlying the evolution of migrants' perceptions toward both the country of origin and the country of settlement. Its authors concluded that "plans at the time of arrival and current plans with respect to remaining in the United States or returning to El Salvador or Guatemala indicate a striking change" (Chinchilla and Hamilton 1996, 3). Meanwhile, periodic return visits and some permanent returns increased information about migration routes, destinations, employment possibilities, and so on, among those who had remained in Guatemala and expanded migrant networks, facilitating the increasing incorporation of Guatemalans into a hemispheric migration system.

CONCLUDING REMARKS

This paper has attempted to highlight the importance of the accelerated process of internal and international population displacements that affected Guatemala during the 1980s and 1990s. I conclude with reflections on the latest developments (through 1996) and likely upcoming issues in light of the trends examined. The issues are mainly framed to outline hypothetical scenarios and to pose questions concerning the need for political action.

The overall pattern of migration appears to have shifted in the opposite direction from the politically important refugee-return movement that began gradually after 1986 and accelerated after 1992. While refugees were returning, in general, to rural areas (not necessarily their original home communities) with permanent settlement in mind, Guatemala's rural peoples drifted in search of employment and survival to urban areas in general and Guatemala City, in particular. They also tended to emigrate, either permanently or for relatively long periods, less and less to Mexico (because of the reduction of opportunities created by the ongoing economic and political crisis there) and more frequently instead not only to the United States (which did remain the most frequent destination) but also to Canada and elsewhere.

The refugees and emigrants of the 1980s found themselves in diverse circumstances – some had returned to Guatemala and were in the process of reincorporation into national life; others were still in the planning or initial stages of return, while yet others remained abroad, weighing their options for permanent settlement where they lived (Chinchilla and Hamilton 1996). Each category of migrants had particular problems and needs for assistance, and future research should be developed to uncover the multiplicity of situations and the complexity of trends.

The arguments presented here suggest that the refugee problem is in no sense resolved but that it has reached a new stage. It therefore demands new types of responses. Thus, for example, one can anticipate an ongoing need for the continuous monitoring of return and, especially now, settlement in Guatemala to ensure that the returnees' human rights are fully protected. Since massacres and violations of the human rights of returnees have continued to take place, monitoring and preventive action are required. The officially decreed dismantling of PACS in 1996 improved the situation with regard to the constant harassment of returnees by the PACS which were formed, backed, armed, and manipulated by the army. However, some PACS resisted the implementation of the decree and insisted on their need to keep their weapons for "defensive purposes" in a climate of insecurity.

Moreover, the international community should be aware that peace and democracy have not been fully achieved and that the return of refugees will depend on major progress in these areas. Since the situation in Guatemala is still highly unstable, those promoting peace and development should recognize that new refugee movements (individual or collective) could emerge at any time, in reaction to gaps in, and the unevenness of, current measures to end violence and protect human rights.

Ongoing refugee concerns cannot be eradicated by government decree in either the receiving or the sending countries, nor can they be abolished by international organizations turning a blind eye to them. This means that national, regional, and international forums should keep on their agendas provisions to face likely new migration processes and measures to fully employ the legal provisions adopted and experience gained from past attention to displaced populations.

For instance, it is important that countries that subscribe to the UN Refugee Convention or those that have formally adopted the refugee definition proposed in the Declaración de Cartagena should apply the principles of those international agreements to populations fleeing their countries in a new context, which includes the belief that violence and human rights violations should not cause migration out of Guatemala any longer.[20]

Perhaps the most outstanding emerging outmigration trend involves the growing movement of people to the United States. Not only have the numbers of Guatemalans moving to U.S. destinations increased year by year, but it seems that the flow involves an expanding set of communities of origin in Guatemala. As of 1996 no statistics were available to describe the origin and profile of Guatemalan migrants to the United States, but various limited case studies have recorded the expansion of U.S.-bound movement from every region and locality, whether urban or rural. It seems that the movement involves individuals of diverse educational levels – illiterate individuals as well individuals with middle-level schooling could be found among undocumented Guatemalan immigrants detained and deported by U.S. and Mexican authorities.[21]

Current migration trends point to the emergence of a new pattern of population distribution in Guatemala. While available data do not permit a precise assessment of this pattern, it is clear that the major trends include more voluminous and complex international emigration and circulation and an intensified urbanization process. Unfortunately, 1994 census data do not provide as much clear information as one might expect about these processes, largely as a consequence of apparently uneven coverage and serious underregistration during the census operation. The total population recorded in the 1994 enumeration is far lower than projected (see Gellert's contribution to this volume). This could have resulted from a mix of factors, including underenumeration for logistical reasons, in addition to much higher than expected (or recorded) migration from the country in the 1980s.

Social, economic, and political instability – including rising levels of social violence and insecurity – continue to form part of the complex set of reasons promoting emigration from Guatemala. Young workers, who constitute a large and increasing proportion of the labour force, appear to be particularly mobile, and this trend is likely to intensify unless policies are devised to increase employment opportunities. Indeed, generating such opportunities should be a principal consideration in the plans and programs designed to assist the returnee communities; they come from a context in which self-organization and the search for sustainability are highly valued and promoted. The difficulties that have emerged in the course of resettlement (bad quality land, lack of productive resources or employment opportunities, and deficiencies in social services and infrastructure) and the harassment of local people may contribute to the compulsion that young people feel to migrate, leaving adults behind. The latter may not be willing to face another resettlement experience, whether in the national urban setting or, even worse, abroad.

New data also suggest that emigration is increasingly a family decision. The frequent detention by U.S. authorities of married Guatemalan couples or single mothers with children for undocumented immigration provides indirect evidence of a strong family dimension.[22] The magnitude of remittances from relatives already settled in the United States also leads to the hypothesis that migration is a family strategy based on information sharing and solidarity in social and kinship networks. In addition to the figures on remittances cited above, CEPAL's local surveys indicated that remittances were used primarily to satisfy basic needs: in most sample cases, more than 80 percent of remittances were devoted to consumption, and especially to food (CEPAL 1991a, tables 25–8, 81–4).

The migration landscape described above highlights a set of problems and challenges both for Guatemalan state authorities and for Guatemalan civil society as a whole. Current patterns of social and economic inequality will tend to encourage migration in search of better living conditions. Refugees and returnees form only a small proportion of the huge and dynamic mass of Guatemalan people on the move. Emigration, mainly to the United States, is leading to social transformations that include temporary solutions (economic survival) and apparently emerging problems (the breakdown of families and community). Guatemalan authorities do not seem to be paying adequate attention to the broader migration picture; they appear to be more concerned about the beneficial impact of remittances on macroeconomic indicators than about the impacts on individuals and communities. Nevertheless, preoccupations concerning an eventual massive return of Guatemalans living abroad have started to emerge among government officials and, especially, among civil sectors. They parallel the Salvadorean government's concerns and actions in anticipation of the U.S. government's likely suspension of temporary residence permits for Salvadoreans in response to the ongoing peace process.

More recently, increasing concern about the human rights situation of migrants has arisen in response to growing anti-immigration policies and attitudes. While the U.S. treatment of migrants remains the principal concern of Guatemalans, complaints have surfaced also about abuses by authorities, civil groups, and individuals in Mexico. Efforts in the latter case have resulted in some preliminary agreements in regional forums.[23] The human rights dimension of migration could become a major aspect of future undertakings of activists and advocates and an important matter for discussion and lobbying in open forums, governments agencies, and the legislatures of host and origin countries.

The governments of countries of origin should develop strong protection programs to gain legitimacy for their citizens who have fled and are still fleeing in search of opportunities not available at home. Protection means adequate, vigorous action to help migrants defend their rights under any circumstances, whether they are documented or undocumented residents in a foreign country. In their own country, measures are urgently required to generate conditions that facilitate the sustainable and durable resettlement of returnees and the generation of employment opportunities.

Meanwhile, it is obvious that accelerated internal and international migration trends cannot be reversed. Development plans, programs, and actions must take into account this ongoing phenomenon, as well as the consequences of past movements abroad that influence the migrants' countries of origin, communities, and families in diverse ways. This dynamic process is generating often-unnoticed effects on the social fabric that easily become invisible among the complex characteristics of the ongoing crisis in the Central American region. Among the cumulative consequences of several linked elements and processes at play is the formation of social networks that help defend migrants' rights and that also facilitate and encourage continued migration.

NOTES

1 The figure of 46,000 is an approximation; reported numbers varied with the periodical censuses by the UN High Commissioner for Refugees (UNHCR) and Mexican migration authorities; the numbers were affected also by the refugees' frequent nonregistered movements and by the demographic dynamics of the population.
2 The sum of returnees and those remaining does not match with the totals recorded at the beginning of the period under consideration because of the obvious and not quantified effects of fertility, mortality, and returns that were not officially recorded.

3 Statistics of detentions and deportations of undocumented immigrants by Mexican authorities show two turning points in the rise of volumes: the first in the 1980s, when arrests started to surpass ten thousand per year (13,184 in 1980); the second in the 1990s, when they reached the hundred thousand per year mark (126,440 in 1990) (Castillo 1996, 20, quoting several official sources).

4 The population born in Guatemala recorded by U.S. censuses was 63,073 and 225,739 respectively in 1980 and 1990, which means that that population almost quadrupled during the decade. In contrast, the Mexican-born population – the largest Latin American group residing in the United States – recorded an intercensus growth rate of 6.7 percent per year and only doubled in size. Although the censuses may register undocumented populations, their figures do not represent the total of both documented and undocumented resident populations (CEPAL/FNUAP/CELADE 1993).

5 The figures refer exclusively to deportations – that is, the formal removal of an alien from the United States when the presence of the alien is deemed inconsistent with the public welfare. Deportation is ordered by a judge (INS 1997, 169). The figures do not include "voluntary return under safeguards," which is the most frequent procedure followed by an alien who admits to illegal status and agrees to leave the United States without a hearing before an immigration judge. Voluntary departures were as high as 1,313,444 and 1,572,798 in the fiscal years referred to above. About 99 percent of aliens in this category are Mexicans who are returned across the southern border soon after their apprehension.

6 This preliminary research was conducted by Silvia Irene Palma and the author over the period 1991–96. The interview procedures involved open-ended discussions with small numbers of interviewees in villages that have experienced high levels of out-migration. Some interviews were conducted with groups of village leaders and spokespersons. The main objective was to generate hypotheses for future research (see Castillo and Palma 1992, 1994, and n21, below).

7 Analysis of an adjusted data base containing information of arrests and deportations by Mexican authorities over a twenty-one month period (1987–88) showed that undocumented Central American migrants of rural origin by then formed nearly one-third of the total (Castillo 1996, 15–16).

8 The influence of foreign policy criteria on admission rates has been and still is a constant in U.S. asylum/refugee policy. Ignatius comments that the "INS received over 133,000 asylum applications in the first eleven months of FY 1993. This compares with 103,000 applications filed last

year ... The top ten nationalities generated almost 70% of the claims filed with INS during 1993 ... The highest asylum approval rates were for applicants fleeing from communist or former communist countries ... Certain nationalities historically suffering discriminatory treatment under the previous process received asylum in a greater percentage than before. Previously ... the approval rate for Salvadorans, Guatemalans and Haitians, for example, was less than 3%, despite documentation of widespread human rights abuses and political violence. Under the new process in FY 1992 the approval rate for Guatemalans increased to 21%" (1993, 3–4).

Frelick asserts that "During 1994, 147,605 asylum applications were filed in the United States ... INS asylum officers granted 8,254 and denied 29,176, for a 22 percent approval rate. The highest number of applications continue to come from Central America, led by Guatemalans and Salvadorans ... The highest asylum approval rates were found among nationalities with fewer applicants ... By year's end, the asylum backlog had grown to 420,794. Guatemalans, with 126,496 pending asylum applications, represented about 30 percent of the total backlog" (1995, 187).

9 Fix and Passel write: "Salvadorans who were granted temporary protected status by the 1990 Immigration Act were since granted deferred enforced departure (DED). Although only 80,000 of the 200,000 or so Salvadorans who were given temporary protected status have actually registered for DED, the rest are considered protected because the Immigration and Naturalization Service (INS) will not take any action to deport them. Others with limited legal status include persons paroled in the United States individually on humanitarian grounds, asylum applicants, and those awaiting adjustment of status" (Fix and Passel 1994, 86n10).

10 Much of this shift in refugee policy deals with the association between the assumed temporary character of refuge and the frequently permanent stay in countries of settlement. As Frelick (1996, 16) asserts, "Since World War II, most Northern states have built a link between refugee protection and immigration. Persons recognized as refugees, usually, have been allowed to remain in host states on a permanent basis. However, even those societies more open to immigration, for example, the United States and Canada, have signalled their unwillingness to continue high levels of immigration generally, and their specific unwillingness to be open to the arrival of asylum seekers."

11 There are no data available regarding the number of individuals granted asylum during the period of the refugees' arrival. The difference between asylum and refuge in the Latin American tradition of international law – which contrasts with Anglo-Saxon law and tradition –

was established by default through the definition of asylum included in the conventions and treaties subscribed to by the region's governments since the first decades of the current century (Convención sobre Asilo 1928; Convención sobre Asilo Político 1933; Convención sobre Asilo Diplomático 1954; Convención sobre Asilo Territorial 1954). Actually, the principles of asylum in the Latin American tradition recognize and protect citizens of neighbouring countries who, because of their beliefs or political activities, suffer direct persecution that can be corroborated; they are then granted asylum through a diplomatic initiative. These principles differ from other concepts of refuge that may be less restrictive, such as the UN Convention.

The refugee phenomenon was barely recognized as different from asylum by some Latin American countries during the 1980s (Declaration of Cartagena 1984), when turmoil in the region gave way to mass movements of populations not directly involved in armed conflict. These movements became the basis of a regional definition of refugee similar to that adopted by the Organization of African Unity in 1969. The Declaration of Cartagena is a nonobliging instrument – with a definition of refugee broader than that of the UN Convention – which encourages but does not compel governments to grant protection to individuals and families who may not be able to prove direct persecution, but who could have been caught in the middle of a conflict. This was the case for most Guatemalans fleeing the country in search of a safe haven. For a discussion of these various definitions of refugee, see Zolberg, Suhrke, and Aguayo (1989), chap. 1, "Who is a refugee?"

12 In several contexts, but mainly in international forums, Mexican representatives frequently express their pride in their historical tradition of granting asylum to persons persecuted because of political activities or beliefs. There is an obligation for countries that subscribe to the Latin American Conventions on Asylum to grant asylum under the rulings established there. For a long time, the adherence to those instruments was an argument against subscribing to the UN Convention on Refugees; nevertheless, the limits of the restricted definition of asylum in Mexican law and Latin American conventions made them insufficient to face the region's emerging mass movements during the 1980s. Moreover, in recent decades asylum-granting has been a very restricted practice in Mexico, according to the author's observations and indirect information that has been obtained in the absence of official data (Castillo 1995b).

13 The changes addressed three sets of issues. One was the enforcement of sanctions on persons involved in either assisting foreign people to enter Mexico illegally or assisting Mexican nationals to go to a different country. Terms of imprisonment were increased and fines for offenders were updated on the basis of multiples of minimum wages (Art. 118).

Another set of issues was the incorporation of categories that made the entry and exit of individuals more flexible, to fit the requirements of foreign investment promoted by the government-approved integration process, that is, the North American Free Trade Agreement (NAFTA). There were also some other prescriptions specifying procedures and sanctions related to the conditions under which foreigners could remain in the country (arts. 6, 42, 47, 48, 56, 64, 66, 67, 106, 121). A third change referred exclusively to the definition of refugee (art. 42, sec. 6).

14 Still in 1996, four years later, Guatemalan refugees living in Mexico had not been granted refugee status. Mexican authorities subsequently shifted their policy toward the refugee population, announcing their decision to grant more stable legal status – that is, temporary work permits for those who wished to return, a move that would enable them to look for better jobs and to move more freely in the region. Permanent work permits for those wishing to stay in Mexico were promised, which could permit them to own property and, in the long run, request permanent residence and eventually naturalization.

15 This was the final stage of the "return to constitutionality" foreseen in the National Plan of Security and Development designed by the military leaders who headed the 1982 coup d'etat.

16 This has been a major controversial issue regarding Mexican emigration to the United States. Some surveys show that migrants do not belong to the poorest, the less-educated, and the unemployed sectors. One key argument in the discussion is peoples' diminishing capacity to afford the rising costs of migration in view of the economic crisis in Mexico since 1994 (Bustamante 1995).

17 The figures in the brackets were added by the editors.

18 The field survey comprised a sample of 672 low-income families that had settled in cities and semiurban areas in six departments. A total of 555 had migrant relatives and received remittances; the remainder had no migrant relatives and did not receive remittances at the time of the study (CEPAL 1991b, table 4, 56).

19 Leaders interviewed in the course of the fieldwork conducted by the author and Silvia Irene Palma in 1991–96 found it difficult to separate the impact of increasing insecurity from the lack of social opportunities, especially among young people who confronted more and more problems in obtaining employment and opportunities for personal development.

20 The 1995 Xaman massacre (discussed briefly in the introduction to this volume) should be considered a warning that new population displacements are possible.

21 As mentioned above, there are no sources that systematically record information concerning migration patterns as well as migrant character-

istics. In collaboration with Silvia Irene Palma, the author has conducted numerous interviews in conjunction with different research projects during the 1990s, both at detention points along the southern Mexican border and in migrant-origin communities in several regions of Guatemala. Interviewees have included migrants themselves, community leaders, and relatives of migrants. All of them agree about the increasing participation of a larger number of communities and diverse social sectors and about the more diverse sociodemographic profile of migrants, including the growing presence of female migrants. A unanimous observation is that most of them are of working age. There are no statistics that register variables such as the educational level of deported undocumented migrants, but the analysis of a limited sample of individuals deported by Mexican migration authorities in 1983–84 showed a broad spectrum of origins and previous employment. This sampling provided an indirect idea of their educational situation and capacities; however, the principal findings are mainly based on interviews conducted in the 1992–95 period.

22 Interviews conducted with both detained migrants and families of absentees confirm that, in most cases, migration decisions stemmed from family agreements. Moreover, in several cases migrants and relatives have reported that migration costs are provided by family contributions, as a sort of investment to win a new source of income: remittances are sent, first of all, to cover those expenses and, after that, to satisfy family needs.

23 These forums include the Regional Conference on Migration staged in Puebla, Mexico, in March 1996, which included participation by both North American and Central American governments and a prior declaration at the San José, Costa Rica, meeting of the presidents of Mexico and the Central American countries – that is, Tuxtla II – in February 1996. An announcement has also been made about another regional conference on the issue organized by the Central American Council of Human Rights Prosecutors and co-sponsored by the Inter-American Institute of Human Rights and the regional office of the UNHCR.

PART FOUR

*Identity and Community:
Gender, Ethnicity, and Place*

9 The Unexpected Consequences of Violence: Rethinking Gender Roles and Ethnicity

M. GABRIELA TORRES

The most prominent outward manifestation of the extreme violence of Guatemala's counterinsurgency policies was the exodus of thousands of Guatemalans to Mexico.[1] This paper will attempt to assess some of the effects of that extreme institutionalized violence and enforced exile upon indigenous refugee women in particular. The analysis is based on field research in the refugee camp of Quetzal Edzná, located in the Mexican state of Campeche. The research focused on the part of Quetzal Edzná's population that returned to the department of El Petén in Guatemala on 5 April 1995.

Interviews were carried out in Quetzal Edzná in October 1994 during a ten-day visit, the maximum amount of time that Mexican immigration authorities allowed.[2] During that time I lived with two refugee families and interviewed both women and men, formally and informally. Outside Quetzal Edzná, I also interviewed refugees returning to the Petén area from other refugee camps in Mexico and participated in the general assembly and gender workshops of the Vertiente Norte – one of the branches of the Permanent Commissions of Guatemalan Refugees in Mexico (CCPP) – where the April return to the El Quetzal agricultural cooperative was planned. It was located within the Biósfera Maya, an area designated as an ecological reserve by the Guatemalan government.

The basic instrument of inquiry was the biographical interview of selected refugee women. This method was chosen because of the ability of life stories to reveal the subject's conscious and unconscious perceptions of her surroundings, describe her society, and provide an account of the historical process to which she has been exposed. In this paper, life stories provide not only illustrations of the process of refuge but also indicators of broader processes of sociocultural change. In the words of refugee women it is not only possible to catch a glimpse of life as they see it, but it is also possible to ascertain how – through their way of "re-presenting," talking, and "re-membering" – events are ascribed with social significance (Stewart 1996 40, 64). To transmit the nuances and special quality of their voices, below, I provide the original statements in Spanish, a language only recently learned by the Maya women, in addition to translations into English.

The social effects of violence generated permanent changes in the social relations and ways of life of Guatemala's indigenous peoples. Although all groups affected by the violence experienced physical and social transformations to some extent, the refugees' experience gives us one of the most pronounced examples of the social aftermath of violence, due to the complete and potentially permanent physical removal of refugees from their cultures and lands of origin. As part of the effort to assess the complex, overarching effects of violence, this paper looks at the effects of refuge on ethnic and gender relations. Before turning to these specific types of changes, it is fitting to explore the general effects of the violent experience itself.

THE GENERAL IMPACT OF THE VIOLENT EXPERIENCE ON PERCPTIONS OF AUTHORITY

The experience of violence marked the starting point for the autonomous sociocultural reconstruction that was to take place in refugee communities. I begin here by providing a description of the general impact of the violent experience, as a necessary first step for the subsequent description and analysis of the restructuring of ethnic identities and the redefinition of gender relations.

Among the most significant effects of the extreme violence experienced by refugee populations was the way it prompted these communities to question the legitimacy of state authority. Until they experienced the indiscriminate violence that drove them to exile, respondents agreed that they had believed that state power could be used against them only for legitimate reasons. Whereas previous encounters with authority had often resulted in individual injustices, the violence of the 1980s was perceived to be repression aimed at destroying entire rural communities (Grupo de Apoyo 1993b). The blatant misuse of power made the refugee communities lose their trust in the legitimacy of state power.

In restructuring attitudes towards authority, the refugees' experience with violence also provided an incentive for greater community reliance on common ethnic identities and on the new communities created in exile. The genesis of real refugee communities began through a process defined as "reactive consciousness," which denotes a process of group ascription that initially relies heavily on external influences such as forced exile and confinement. Refugees formed communities explicitly because of their shared experience with violence and, more importantly, because they had resolved that they would not allow that kind of violence to engulf them again. Renate Siebert discusses reactive consciousness as a negative tradition based on the adage "Do not forget" (Passerini 1992, 166). For Siebert, actively keeping memories alive is a means for survivors to elaborate on the process of mourning and attain some form of release. Thus, by maintaining a negative tradition, first during the struggle of life in exile and then in the struggle of the collective return, refugees were going beyond simply confronting their past with their present; they were, in addition, beginning to resolve their violent experiences through concrete political action.

This apparent politicization of the psychological "healing" process is not restricted to refugee populations. Jennifer Schirmer, in "Seeking Truth and the Gendering of Consciousness" argues that both El Salvador's CoMadres and the National Coordinator of Guatemalan Widows (CONAVIGUA) have been based on the negative tradition of not forgetting the violence that made women widows. In recounting the transference of memories from mothers to daughters in the CoMadre organization, Schirmer notes that to pass on collective memory is to ensure that the past is not repeated (1993, 49). Evidently, popular organizations like CONAVIGUA and CoMadres, as well as refugee groups, have taken the negative tradition beyond the personal sphere and into the political sphere.

An example of politicizing negative traditions can be seen in a story told by Claudia. For her, the movement from violence to a refugee identity involved two steps: from violence to a search for survival and from physical survival to political action. In the excerpt that follows, Claudia documents the physical survival of her family. (The original Spanish-language versions of the refugee women's stories are given in the notes.)

I left Guatemala when I was very small because of the repression. The army came and they massacred all the people in my town. They burned all the houses and everything in people's houses. After that, we couldn't resist any more because all the houses were burnt. We had to leave. It was a very hard massacre – some people lost their parents, others lost their spouses or siblings. They tortured them or they cut them up with machetes. They cut the children into three pieces. This is our suffering. We had to leave because we couldn't stand it any more.[3]

Claudia recounted her experience with violence not only as a victim but also as an actor. Within this particular re-telling of her history/autobiography, she emphasizes the seeds of her new political participation in her defiant final statement: "we couldn't stand it any more." It is clear that Claudia was more than just a witness to the violence. In re-telling, she transforms a traumatic sentient experience into an almost physical embodiment of concrete political power that was later harnessed by the movement to form a refugee organization.

The violence of the early 1980s was not only responsible for radical changes in the environment, the perception of the world, and the way of life of refugee women (Grupo de Apoyo 1983a). For those interviewed, the experience with state-sponsored violence became an organizing or constitutive part of the refugee community. The shared experience of violence and the searing psychological and physical traumas of this experience were incorporated into the organizational rules and practices of the refugee community, and thus began a process of community genesis in which violence became the originating history needed to establish self-identification as a refugee. While the violence of the Guatemalan state was aimed at disorganizing, destabilizing, and destroying communities, refugees turned the destabilizing power of violence in on itself and utilized that experience as the constitutive principle for the founding of their new communities. The subversion of the intended power of state-sponsored violence was reiterated by each woman's re-telling of the past, in which the destruction intended by state violence was converted into a space for the development of political agency.

The creation of refugee communities grounded on a violent past was particularly relevant to the return process. By planning their return and thereby reacting to violence, the refugees planted the seeds of what can be called a culture of resistance. Returning communities were structured primarily to withstand further government incursions on the physical well-being of their members. Links were established with nongovernmental monitoring agencies, and continuous foreign accompaniment was ensured for the first year of El Quetzal's existence (UNHCR 1993b). Yet it was not only the practical planning and foresight with which refugees ensured their safe return to Guatemala that signaled the emergence of a culture of resistance; a cultural shift also occurred in the complex process of changing social relations that began in the refugee camps. In the following sections, I will briefly discuss changes in ethnic and gender identities that supported the birth of an organized and politicized refugee community.

REDEFINING ETHNICITY IN THE REFUGEE CAMPS

The redefinition of ethnic identity was a result of fundamental changes in the way of life that refuge entailed and of the multiethnic composition of the refugee camps.[4] This section attempts to explore how those redefinitions of ethnic identities evolved through a process of cultural transformation in which refugees embraced, rejected, or changed their previous cultural behaviour and outlook in order to come to terms with their new experiences.

The struggle over indigenous identity today is a continuation of the historical process of decolonization. In Guatemala's charged political landscape, where the right to define ethnic ascription is a politicized action, the refugees attempted to exert their legitimate right to define and represent their own ethnicity. The struggle to define refugee identity is an excellent example of Anna L. Tsing's concept of "negotiation from the margins." Unlike typical contemporary observes of resistance and protest, Tsing looks at marginality, taking into account its varied contextualizations, analyzing it as a "shared space" within which local groups demonstrate both their creativity and their degree of exclusion from the national (1993, 5). What is particularly resonant in Tsing's conceptualization for the case of Guatemalan refugees is the idea that the shared space of marginality, where refugees reside, does not merely denote a site of pure asymmetrical relationships. The marginal space is also a space of negotiation, contestation, and creativity where local groups, in their negotiation for power, choose to include and exclude externally imposed identifiers in order to better position themselves in national and international spheres (8).

In a continuous process of negotiating for power from the margins, refugee identity based on the past experience of violence and on the experience of exile is not static. Rather, it is a dynamic identity that responds to changing circumstances. And it is precisely the flexibility ingrained within that identity that may allow refugees to retain it upon their return to Guatemala. At the time that the fieldwork was conducted, it was clear that the power of the refugee identity was based on its demonstrated and potential capacity to orchestrate organized communal action.

Ethnicity first came into play as an overt political tool when the CCPP began participating in the Guatemalan peace process.[5] In order to open up a political space within this process, refugee representatives participated both as part of "ethnic" organizations and as an independent member organization of the Societal Sectors Arising from Violence.[6] In this process, ethnic ascription of the Maya label became an important response to government policies such as the creation of the Biósfera Maya, purportedly, an ecological reserve. (For a more detailed discussion of the conflict surrounding the return to El Quetzal, much of which lies within one of the core areas of the reserve, see Egan's chapter in this volume.) The creation of the Biósfera not only hindered the refugees' ability to acquire land for their subsistence but also challenged their authorship of Maya ethnicity. In the political struggle over the Biósfera Maya, the CCPP and the Guatemalan authorities were engaged in a conflict over what Richard Adams has identified as one of the most important determinants of ethnicity: territory.

In effect, the refugee situation placed the exiles in a constant struggle with Guatemalan authorities over who controlled the refugees' ethnic ascriptions. In the past the state had attempted to create and define ethnic identity and membership through government policy and national culture mandates that included the ways in which the country was represented in tourist brochures as an exotic Maya nation (Nelson 1996, 288). For the refugee leaders involved in organizing of the return to El Quetzal, the site of contestation between state-created identities of indigenous peoples and autonomously created indigenous identities was located in the terms under which the government had recently established the Biósfera Maya. Refugee leaders perceived a state that intended to define and control refugee ethnic ascription by limiting the access that refugees could have to the Biósfera. Thus, refugee representatives became active players in contesting the unfinished process in which indigenous people in Guatemala had lost their lands as they were "forcefully subordinated by conquest" (Adams 1991, 159).

The Biósfera Maya is purportedly, as just mentioned, an ecological reserve located in the lowland tropical jungle of the Petén and administered by the National Council of Protected Areas (CONAP). It was established after part of the area had already been proposed as a return site for refugees. The refugees' insistence on settling on their originally chosen site – located within the borders of the newly established ecological reserve – impeded their return to El Quetzal for more than a year. The CONAP refused permission until February 1995, arguing that the returnees would damage the ecological reserve. In the debates that ensued, it was clear that government agencies believed that *they* held a Maya ecological heritage in trust. By excluding returning refugees from the site, the state explicitly defined them as being outside the national construct of "Real Maya" ethnicity. In authoring their entitlement to the Biósfera Maya, refugee leaders negotiated for power in the margin through the double play suggested by Tsing. Refugees both demanded to be identified as Real Maya in national discourse and also rejected the power of the state to define ethnicity.

Amidst allegations of continued official support for the commercial deforestation of the ecological reserve, CONAP's restrictions on refugee resettlement were apparently more a tool of political manipulation than an environmental safeguard measure. It was ironic that the government aimed to protect the Biósfera Maya from Maya peoples. The refugees' rearticulation was made in the re-telling of the past in the Tikal Declaration. It reminded the authorities that it was not the refugees who were infringing on the Biósfera Maya, but rather it was the laws and practices of government authorities that were infringing on the populations that had historically maintained the area (CCPP 1995, 2). In returning to the Petén and overcoming government restrictions, the refugees gained control over who could determine their ethnic identity. In a politically effective fashion, Maya refugees claimed their historical right to their ancestors' lands.

In the Tikal Declaration, presented upon the first return of Guatemalan refugees to the Petén area, the refugees described the permanent, indigenous "refugee" identity in their own terms. As sons and daughters of Ixpiyacoc and Ixmucané, the refugees declared:

Those of us who survived that brutal violence, and so much injustice and cruelty, WE ARE HERE AGAIN. Our vision is firm and we carry with us the memories of all our history, of how we used to live, of how we were forced to flee, and of how we survived in exile. We have come back to plant in our lands, fertilized by the blood of so many martyrs, the seed of what will be the new dawn for Guatemala, the beloved country that has always lived in our hearts. (CCPP 1995, 1)[7]

Among the most noteworthy elements of this passage is the self-reliance on the idea of a Pan-Mayan community. Having lost much of their confidence in the state as a legitimate authority, many refugee communities took the power to legitimize authority into their own hands. The participation of refugee representatives in peace processes, return negotiations, and community planning empowered returnee communities as a whole and fueled ambitious plans of reintegration into the Guatemalan regions of return (UNHCR 1993a). The return was described in the slogan used in all the official letters and communiques of the CCPP: "Porque hoy más que nunca el retorno es lucha y no resignación" (Because now, more than ever, the return is a struggle and not an abdication). The slogan was evidence that the struggles they carried out as refugees would persist throughout the process of reinsertion in Guatemala.

The overall changes in ethnic self-ascription resulted from two related processes: the population's "cosmopolitization," or broadening of its worldview, and the arrangement of physical cohabitation of the refugee camps. Through the constraints of the camps' physical settlement, ethnicity was redefined by a process of cosmopolitization. The realization that there was a vast array of ethnic differences and similarities in Guatemala began for many refugees only when they became exiles. During this time the refugee population underwent a general process of redefining its world vision, which resulted from three factors: cohabitation with a multiplicity of ethnic groups, settlement within Mexican society, and the presence of nongovernmental organizations representing North American and European cultures. The cosmopolitization of the refugee communities moved the immediate individual and community references from the traditional family circle or regional area to the international community.

Upon arrival in Mexico, indigenous peasants from all parts of Guatemala were concentrated together in refugee camps situated in or near Mexican communities and run by international governmental and nongovernmental organizations. The life experiences that the refugees brought with them were diverse and combined with idiomatic and ethnic differences to create a context of multiethnic living to which the majority of indigenous peasants were not accustomed. The experience shared by the refugees was the exposure to violence and a common indigenous heritage.[8]

The process of redefining and representing their ethnicity as refugee communities is described by Claudia in the following passage, in which the political aims of an overt ethnic ascription are evident.

At the beginning it wasn't that easy because the camps are multiethnic. They are multiethnic because people are from different departments and different cultures. And how can you understand all of those people. So we had to begin to make friends, to get to know each other, and to understand each other. Also, the way that camps are organized is by groups. For example those who come from Ixtahuacán have their own group. Those that speak K'iche' also have their own group. In order to be able to understand all those people you have to understand what democracy is – public consultation. You have to begin to understand other languages.[9]

For Claudia, ethnicity is articulated, in essence, as part of the organizational problem faced in the refugee camps. For her, the organization that developed in the camps resulted in part from an understanding or a harmony that was established among ethnic groups. As they achieved relatively harmonious relations with each other, it seems that the refugee's ethnic divisions became blurred. While the specific ethnic origin of any one refugee was still impossible to overlook, it would seem that the ethnic harmony of camp life led to the establishment of an additional, more encompassing ethnic identity: the Maya.

The process of cosmopolitization also inadvertently resulted in a *castellanización* of the refugee population, a process that affected the refugees' conception of ethnicity. The concept of *castellanización* denotes a shift from the use of indigenous languages for everyday communication to the generalized use of Spanish. This process traditionally connotes a mechanism of ascription to national *mestizo* identities. In the case of the Guatemalan refugees in Mexico, *castellanización* simply meant the use of Spanish as a much-needed lingua franca that did not override the use of indigenous languages. In effect, the use of Spanish meant that one indigenous language was not privileged over another. Spanish was also chosen because it allowed refugees to function within the predominantly Spanish environment in Mexico. Thus, varied ethnic groups were incorporated into Spanish language systems in the refugee situation as a result of the necessity to facilitate communication among them. (Unlike much of the Andean region, Guatemala does not have one indigenous language that prevails over regional dialects, and ethnic divisions are usually accompanied by a linguistic separation.)

In general, refugees had a positive attitude towards learning Spanish as a means for multicultural communication. In the following paragraph Carla uses a common metaphor: learning Spanish represents the possibility of wider social-ethnic relations.

I came here without ever having studied anything. I came here without knowing one word in Spanish. What made us organize and what made us learn is the union with other languages. For example, we had never known of the Mams, the Q'anjob'al, or the Jacaltekos. We had never met other peoples. We are all indigenous. We all have different languages and we shouldn't, I think, live like it is in Guatemala, where you only live where your language lives. That is very strange for me because in refuge we have always lived integrated in groups. My people are K'eqchi but we are always in groups where there are no K'eqchis, only our three families. There are Mam, Q'anjob'al, Chuj, Kaqchikel, and Spanish speakers there. We have had many experiences.[10]

In this passage, it is possible to see the politicized rearticulation of a Pan-Mayan ethnicity that was later used by refugee leaders to negotiate for power in national circles. This re-definition of ethnicity was key to the construction of a broader culture of indigenous resistance. The experience with past violence and the overriding goal to avoid further physical threat in the future led refugees to re-present their ethnicity, their forms of social organization, and maintain a flexibility in their ascription of social significance to past and future events.

THE GOVERNMENT FATHER: THE MEETING OF GENDER AND ETHNIC RELATIONS

The loss of confidence in government authority creates an interesting metaphor where changing gender and ethnic relations converge. The father-child metaphor discussed below demonstrates just one of the areas where different social relations intersect and intertwine. In Marcela's re-telling of her experience with violence (see below), she "re-orders" the power of patriarchal authority. In this rearticulation, Marcela proposes a clear vision for new relations of authority that not only affect the political relationship between government and refugees but also destabilize the patriarchy of gender relations within indigenous society.

In the account that follows, Marcela uses a common father metaphor for the Guatemalan government. Her perception of the government as father, however, was radically changed by the unnecessary punishment of exile.

We realized that we couldn't meet because the government had us under its control. We lost our morale. The government said that it saw no reason for us to be doing things – you know, as if we were his children. He is the father of all Guatemalans, and we have to respect everything that he says. It made us feel like that. It dominated us a lot. It controlled us so that we couldn't do anything ... so that is why we didn't organize and we couldn't ask for our rights within the country. He did what he wanted with us. He even kicked us out and chased us out of the country. That is what we have thought. It is the same as when our parents fight with us and hit us and hurt us and kick us out of the house. That is what the government did when it kicked us out of the

165 Gender Roles and Ethnicity

country. Here we have begun to analyze how it was possible for the government to dominate us. The government is a person and we are also people. Now we believe that we can stand up and that is how the organization was born here.[11]

Two aspects of Marcela's new vision of authority are worth emphasizing. The first refers to the similarities between the traditional father-child relationship and the relationship between the Guatemalan government and the refugees. It was the father's abuse of power that enabled him to remain in command, but it also subsequently provoked the rebellion of his child. As a result of the process of estrangement, Marcela realizes that the government and the people who are governed should enjoy equal status: both are groups of individuals, and neither has inherently superior powers.

Second, Marcela's challenge to the government's paternal use of power and the dispersal of the patriarchal metaphor in her account, in addition to signifying a challenge to government abuse of power, can be taken further to suggest the beginning of a change in attitude towards familial relatoins. This can be seen in the last sentences, where she presents us with the metaphor of familial relationships – the government is the father and we are the children – and assumes that we can recognize and accept the existence of the normative codes that maintain the relationship. She does not challenge the inequality of the father-child relationship but she does use it to make the interviewer understand how the abuse of paternal power led to organized opposition. Marcela uses familial relations in which gender relations are played out as a preestablished category through which violent or unjust actions are normally explained or represented. Nowhere in her account does she question the normative status of the father-child relationship. Yet, she is led to describe the government as a parent without legitimacy. When the government exceeded the abuse norm, the illegitimacy of the government – and, by extension, of an abusive father – was made "real" to Marcela (Butler 1992, 15).

In essence, this re-telling disorders the notion of a masculine state authority and re-orders what counts as "legitimate" gender relations. Yet, Marcela's re-telling and re-ordering is not purely discursive; rather, it is imbued, in Butler's terms, with the constitutive power of a nascent set of social relations. For Butler, "power pervades the very conceptual apparatus that seeks to negotiate its terms, including the subject position of the critic" (1992, 6). From this perspective, Marcela's story can only be construed as part of a highly politicized process of reconstructing gender relations.

RETHINKING GENDER-ECONOMIC INFLUENCES

Material changes in the way of life in exile further fueled the conceptual re-thinking of gender relations. The most notable change in gender roles was the overturning of male predominance in the provision of family sustenance through the production of agricultural commodities for consumption and sale. Camp life, with little or no available arable land, made it very difficult for men to be able to continue working as agriculturalists in order to sustain their families. At the same time, women began to play a very important role as mediators between nongovernmental aid institutions and their communities. Material aid projects – such as health promotion, disease prevention, hygiene promotion, and cooking brigades – all utilized women's labour to distribute aid.

In a joint interview Doña Lucía and Doña Cristina explained their role as community cooks in the first refugee camps. As food was donated to the refugees, groups of women became responsible for its distribution and preparation. Thus, women exercised the only control over subsistence available to camp residents in the early refugee context.

Doña Lucía: That was how we began to meet with our other compañeras, because we had to cook for the children. To be able to do that I had to begin to meet with my compañeras, but because I wasn't used to speaking I would tremble, but I made an effort to talk to the compañeras. After that we formed another committee of women so that those compañeras could help me to deal with all the people, because I didn't feel capable of doing it on my own.
Doña Cristina: There were a lot of people. Each day there were four hundred people in the lunchroom and after that we came here.
Doña Lucía: They told us that we had to go to Campeche – here. Many people didn't want to come here. Then, we had to make a big dining room down there at the edge of the river in Pico de Oro so that the people that were arriving could be fed for two weeks. When the last people left they brought us here too.[12]

For Doña Lucía, it was this newly acquired responsibility that stimulated the formation of the first organizations of women and encouraged them to begin speaking in public. Through her account of the origins of women's participation, she also provides a good characterization of female leadership in the refugee situation. First, the participation of women responded directly to specific and immediate survival necessities. Second, women's participation followed traditionally accepted gender activities. Thus, it was not necessarily the way in which women participated in the household economy that changed; rather, it was women's work that gained influence when men were unable to provide subsistence within the constraints of refuge. Finally, women's leadership was not concentrated in one individual. Instead, a group of women together handled the management of basic needs projects, cooperating in ways without precedent in their communities of origin.

Women's work retained its importance throughout the first four to five years of the instability of the refugee situation and allowed women to gain confidence in their productive roles in the community. Even in the relocated camps, women's work continued to play a leading role in family subsistence. Female contributions to the household economy in the Campeche camp of Quetzal Edzná can be seen in three ways.

First, women added cash to the household by participating in income-supplementing projects. One such project was the communal raising of patio animals such as pigs, turkeys, rabbits, and chickens, which was encouraged by nongovernmental agencies that provided the start-up costs. A second activity involved sewing and design. Women received training, and as a result, they could sew pieces for sale within and outside the community, or they could choose to participate in piecework contracts awarded to refugee community workshops. In both cases the training allowed women to contribute much-needed cash income to the family. In the second type of project women received cash incomes directly, but, in the first example men usually sold the women's animals outside the refugee community and gave women only part of the profits. The economic participation of women in refugee organizations was deeply influenced by the presence of governmental and nongovernmental organizations. These organizations helped to determine not only the extent but also the character of women's participation.[13]

A third way that women contributed to the household economy was by hiring themselves out as domestic servants in the urban centres near the camp. Although women had not initially sought paid work outside the refugee camps, it seems that the number of domestic servants began to increase as men's earnings for unskilled labour fell far below the potential earnings of female domestic servants. Indeed, women could earn up to 50 percent more than unskilled males in mid-1994.[14]

While this relatively large difference between women's and men's incomes did not have notable effects on older people, it resulted in attitude changes among young refugee women. As young women realized their earning potential, they resisted early marriage and became more willing to remain independent and contribute to their family of birth. The concrete changes in women's and men's roles in production served to reinforce the discursive and conceptual changes in gender roles that were identified in the discussion of government authority. It is important to note that these material changes and the related cultural transformations occurred only as a result of the situation of refuge that, for the women interviewed, was still conceptually a direct result of the violent past. In re-membering their history and re-ordering their present, refugee women attributed even the improvements in their economic status and other changes in their lives in exile to the "opening of their eyes" provoked by violence.

POLITICAL PARTICIPATION – THE DISSOLUTION OF AUTHORITY

The nascent participation of women in the political organization of the refugee community was perceived by many of the women interviewed as a radical change in their societies, despite the fact that, by their own estimates, no more than 20 percent of the members of the female refugee population were active political participants. According to Catalina, it was cultural constraints that had limited women's participation in the past and continued to do so in the present.

I will tell you that both the cultural system and the ideological system in which we have lived has stopped women from participating freely. There are brakes. There are only a few spaces that women have been able to conquer. They are minimal spaces. In my case I have been here for many years. My compañero is very aware of this process, but I still have some limitations, and it is a big challenge for women themselves to conquer space in the very heart of their family so that they can then go out and demand their place in other organizations.[15]

Catalina rooted the impediments to women's participation in the heart of the family structure and, in particular, in her personal relationship with her husband. For Catalina, it was only through changes at home that women could even begin to conquer spaces in society as a whole. The interviewees' emphasis on the dependence of female participation on male approval refers to the dominant role that men continued to play within the refugee society. While Catalina identified male resistance to women's political participation, she also stressed that both men and women had to participate in changing their attitudes and perspectives to attain changes in gender relations. This is particularly noteworthy in the light of many feminist studies, especially those that try to analyze social phenomena by restricting their vision to the women's sphere (Moore 1988).

There was evidence of a process of gendered consciousness-building within the existing women's groups. The realization that social injustices had taken place in Guatemala had led some refugee women to look inward to their own personal situations and to question the social injustices in the gender relations they had grown up with.

In her "Seeking Truth and Gendering Consciousness," Schirmer details how the participation of Guatemalan women in the CONAVIGUA union of widows led to a rethinking of familial gender relations (Schirmer 1993, 63). For her, gendering consciousness occurs at the point where the state can no longer be trusted to set the laws and boundaries of behaviour (62). The process of gendering consciousness among the refugee women interviewed in Mexico parallels that found in Schirmer's case study of CONAVIGUA. As with the process of rethinking ethnicity discussed in the previous section, women began to question their prescribed gender roles when the experience of refuge forced a rethinking of their overall role in society, including the right and legitimacy of authority.

Indigenous women became politically active despite their difficulties with the Spanish language. (Eighty percent of the women leaders interviewed were of indigenous origin.) The process of *castellanización* clearly contributed to their growing participation in refugee political organizations. For some of the indigenous women interviewed, learning Spanish became a liberating action that allowed them to extend themselves beyond their immediate families and ethnic groups. Strikingly, the international representative of the CCPP for the Vertiente Norte was an indigenous woman who had not completed the third year of primary school. The high percentage of indigenous persons, particularly women, at high levels of responsibility was an important change that took place in the refugee camps, and it carried potentially profound implications for change in Guatemalan society.

In addition to encouraging the participation of indigenous women outside their immediate circles, speaking and understanding Spanish also gave women access to information and community supports that were previously denied to them. With knowledge of Spanish, women were able to access training programs offered by governmental and nongovernmental organizations. Additionally, women who wanted to become literate were able to access special programs sponsored by nongovernmental organizations in the camps.

The education and increased literacy in Spanish that were acquired by many refugees in exile through training programs is highlighted by Doña Olga as one of the most important factors leading towards an advancement in the situation of women.

In Guatemala the people grew, but all of them with the same ideas, and there was no stretching their thoughts so that you could begin to think about studying something. Here in Mexico things are different. Here there is studying and even the old ladies like it. When were there literacy classes for adults in Guatemala? There were none in Guatemala. That is the advance that people are taking with them. The women who came here and who were around thirty years old when they got here did not even know what their name was or what was the first letter of their name. Now these women are coordinators and they know how to sign their name and make notes. Here there has been an advance. And that is how others begin to do things, by seeing other compañeras do it too.[16]

For Doña Olga the period of exile changed not only women's situations but also women's self-perceptions. In this act of re-telling, Doña Olga presents a progress narrative in which women gradually gain their liberty through literacy. In exile Doña Olga saw women of all ages value education and use it to advance both their own persons and their society. Yet it is also evident that for Doña Olga the process of education was not solely responsible for the advancement of women's situations. For her it was the example that women gave to each other that generated the strength needed to participate.

The importance of education and Spanish literacy is reiterated in the passage that follows, where Catalina explains how the cultural structures that maintain male domination in Guatemalan society attain their goals by limiting women's educational opportunities.

I'll tell you that I wasn't able to study much. I could have had a scholarship from the Catholic Church, but I couldn't use it because my father didn't care. It is also the culture – our ideology tells us that education is useless for women, since they're only destined to be mothers. The situation with the man is different because he has to fulfill responsibilities towards the woman. There are those inequalities in the culture.[17]

For both Catalina and Doña Olga education is something that was culturally denied and not a necessary result of economic inequality. For Catalina, an indigenous woman, it was her culture's ideology that placed unfair limitations on women. Yet Catalina's narration concentrates on her personal experience, from which she derives a critical view of her own society. Thus, she does not blame her father alone for her lack of educational opportunities, but she blames her culture as well for endorsing values that deprecate women.

Actively remembering their recent past, refugee women re-told their experience with violence as a springboard to radical changes in the ways in which they viewed authority, the relationships between men and women, and their ethnic ascription. The act of witnessing violence seen in each re-collection of the past is not passive, and its social meaning has more to do with the construction of their present than with their past victim status. In each case, the women's discourse was produced "in a dialogue" that gains meaning "understood against the background of other concrete utterances on the same theme, a background made up of contradictory opinions, points of view and value judgments" (Bakhtin 1981, 279, 281). The dialogue in this case included, but was not exclusive to, the conversation with the interviewer, the violent past, current government policies, refugee organizations, ethnic tensions, and changing relations of production in exile. In each case explored, social significance was ascribed to these re-tellings in relation to or in dialogue with the invoked images or utterances – the past, the government – and was grounded in the situation of the re-telling, in this case with the white Guatemalan interviewer (see Stewart 1996, 155). The interviews demonstrate the transformative power of violence: not violence that begins and ends in the event of a massacre or a political assassination but violence in its full effects as it was embodied physically in scars, birth defects, and the like, and cognitively in the memory of an individual and her community.

CONCLUSION

Women's participation in community struggles began the gendering of their consciousness. That is, women became politically aware both as social actors and, subsequently, as female social actors. Throughout this paper, it has been possible to detail the process of gendering consciousness that began with the violence in Guatemala and was cemented in refuge. The process of change in gender relations was in many ways similar to changes that occurred in the refugee's self-perception of ethnicity. These similarities were not coincidental. Rather, both ethnicity and gender were affected by the overwhelming effects of Guatemala's "massacres in the jungle" (Falla 1994).[18]

State-sponsored violence attempted to disorganize, destabilize, and destroy communities, and while it was savagely successful in its aims, the violence of the 1980s also brought about some unexpected consequences. The violent past also created a space for agency. In refugee camps re-membering a violent past became an organizing principle of new communities. In their re-telling of the past, it is clear that refugee women were able to turn the intended effects of violence on their head by exerting their power to re-name and re-order the past and the present. Women were able to negotiate for power from the margins by harnessing the transformative power of their memory in order to affect their community's political goals in the process of return. Yet the re-ordering in which women engaged was not limited to state and politics; women also actively re-ordered the past to reform the way in which they were treated in their own indigenous society.

What is striking about the rethinking of gender and ethnicity is the increased empowerment of social actors. In gaining a political role in the refugee society, women felt that they had greater control over their lives through their improved technical and oratorical abilities. These perceived improvements represented radical departures from the refugee women's accounts of their original self-perceptions – "No eramos nada" (we were nothing) or "el pobre no vale nada" (the poor are worthless).

Whether these changes endure through return and resettlement in Guatemala remains to be seen. What is certain, however, is that the period of refuge did not serve to suffocate and subjugate the population. Rather, refuge provided the peasant population with an opportunity to become literate and learn both about their world and about themselves. The result of refuge was, in part, the opening of new sites of re-articulation of power and the effective empowerment of a new community. Guatemala's harvest of violence also harvested unexpected seeds of reform.

NOTES

1 The Guatemalan Human Rights Commission estimated that between 1981 and 1985, 337 massacres had taken place in nineteen of the twenty-two departments that make up Guatemala.
2 The author would like to acknowledge the guidance and supportive critiques of Blanca Muratorio, who supervised the MA thesis on which this chapter is based.
3 In Spanish: Yo salí de Guatemala cuando era chiquita. Salimos por la represión. El ejército llegó a masacrar a toda la gente de mi pueblo y quemaron todas las casas y todo lo que había en las casas de la gente. Entonces, ya no pudimos resistir más porque ya todas las casas estaban quemadas. Tuvimos que salir. Fue una masacre muy dura, pues. Algunos

perdieron a sus papas, otros a sus esposos o sus hermanos. Los torturaron o los amachetearon. Cortaron a los niños en tres pedazos. Esto es nuestro sufrimiento. Tuvimos que salir porque no podíamos aguantar.

4 "Multiethnic" refers to the varied ethnic origins of the refugees in Mexico, including both peoples of various Mayan ethnicities and peoples of mixed Spanish and indigenous origin.

5 The peace process began after the signing of a bilateral agreement in Madrid between the Guatemalan government and Guatemalan National Revolutionary Unity (URNG) representatives in 1987. Parallel to these negotiations, popular organizations began to play a role in restructuring Guatemalan society through direct or indirect participation in the National Commission for Reconciliation.

6 The Societal Sectors Arising from Violence is a union of popular organizations that began to work together in 1991. Previously, the refugee representatives formed part of the Commission of those Affected by Violence.

7 In Spanish: Los que sobrevivimos a tal brutal violencia, a tanta injusticia y crueldad, ESTAMOS AQUI DE NUEVO. Nuestra mirada es firme y llevamos las memorias de toda nuestra historia, de cómo vivíamos, cómo fuimos obligados a huir y cómo sobrevivimos en el exilio. Venimos para sembrar de nuevo en nuestras tierras, abonadas con la sangre de tantos mártires la semilla de lo que será un nuevo amanecer para nuestra Guatemala, para esta querida patria que ha vivido siempre en nuestros corazones.

8 A similar process took place in the aftermath of the 1930s Chaco War in Bolivia, which radically altered the worldview of the soldiers who had fought there. According to sociologist Silvia Rivera Cusicanqui (1986), the war had a nationalizing effect on the consciousness of the Bolivian population. In Guatemala the forced union of ethnic groups can also be expected to result in the radical rethinking of state-individual relations.

9 In Spanish: Al principio no fue tan fácil porque los campamentos son multiétnicos. Son multiétnicos o sea que son de diferentes departamentos y de diferentes culturas. Y que, cómo puedes tu entender a toda esa gente. Entonces se tuvo que entrar en un proceso de amistad, de conocer, de entender. Y también la otra forma organizativa de los campamentos es el de los grupos. Digamos que por ejemplo los de Ixtahuacán, ellos tienen su propio grupo. Los de habla K'iche' también tienen su propio grupo. Para poder entender a la gente tienes que aprender qué es la democracia – la consulta popular. Hay que pasar por un entendimiento de otros idiomas.

10 In Spanish: Entré sin ningún estudio, entré sin saber ni una palabra en castilla. Lo que nos hizo organizarnos, lo que nos hizo aprender es la unidad con otras lenguas. Por ejemplo nunca hemos conocido el Mam, el Q'anjob'al, nunca hemos conocido el Jacalteko, nunca hemos cono-

cido otras gentes. Pero somos indígenas todos. Tenemos lenguas todos y no debemos, siento yo, vivir como en Guatemala donde sólo existen por lenguas. Eso es muy extraño para mí porque yo en lo que he estado en el refugio siempre he estado integrada en grupos de mi gente K'eqchi. Siempre estoy en grupos donde no existen K'eqchis, solo nosotras tres familias. Mam, Q'anjob'al, Chuj, Kakchikeles, Castellaños allá. Hemos tenidos muchas experiencias.

11 In Spanish: Nos dimos cuenta que no podíamos reunirnos porque el gobierno nos tenía bajo su control. Nos desanimamos, pues. El gobierno decía, pues, que no tenía porqué vernos haciendo cosas – como éramos sus hijos. El es el papa de todos los que somos Guatemaltecos y todo lo que él dice lo tenemos que respetar. Así nos tuvo, pues. Nos dominó mucho. Nos controló para que no pudiéramos hacer nada ... por eso no nos organizamos y no pudimos reclamar nuestros derechos en el país y él nos hizo lo que quiso y hasta que nos hizo correr y nos sacó del país. Eso es lo que hemos pensado nosotros. Que es igual a que nuestros papas se peleen con nosotros y nos pegan y nos golpean y nos corren de la casa. Así nos hizo el gobierno nos sacó del país. Porque aquí empezábamos a analizar cómo era posible que el gobierno nos hubiera dominado. El gobierno es una persona y nosotros también lo somos. Nosotros ahora creemos que podemos levantarnos y así empezó a nacer la organización.

12 *Doña Lucía*: Así fue como nos empezamos a reunir con nuestras compañeras, porque tuvimos que hacer cocina para los niños. Para eso a mí me tocó empezar a reunirme con mis compañeras pero como yo no tenía esa costumbre yo temblaba pero le hacia lo posible de hablar ahí con las compañeras y en eso formamos otro comité ya de compañeras mujeres para que estas compañeras me ayudaran a lidear con la demás gente que sola yo no me sentía capaz.
Doña Cristina: Habían bastante gente. Diario pasaban cuatrocientas gentes al comedor. Después la venida para acá.
Doña Lucía: Ya nos dijeron que nos teníamos que ir para Campeche mucha gente no se quería venir para acá. Entonces ya nos tocó hacer un comedor aquí abajo en la orilla del río en Pico de Oro para que la gente que venía teníamos que darles de comer por dos semanas. Cuando salió la ultima gente ya nos sacaron para acá.

13 I mention only the main actors and their most prominent programs, but their influences deserve a more thorough analysis that cannot be carried out in this paper. The Mexican Commission to Aid Refugees (COMAR), was the most important governmental organization in the refugee camps throughout Mexico. COMAR is a Mexican government institution, based in Tuxtla Gutierrez, Chiapas, and it administered much of the United Nations aid program. COMAR implemented various programs, including the provision of agricultural credit, sewing and design work-

shops, and food payments to nonaccredited primary school instructors. In the states of Campeche and Chiapas, the Mexican Commission to Aid the Displaced (COMADEP), a nongovernmental umbrella organization, was one of the most influential groups. COMADEP was responsible for financing training workshops on women's and human rights issues, as well as training workshops in technical publishing for young refugees. A final, long-standing, and key organizational actor in the refugee context was the Catholic church, which provided materials for subsistence throughout the period of exile.

14 It was estimated by the interviewees that the monthly salary of a construction assistant, the most common job available to a unskilled male refugee, ranged from 100 to 120 new pesos in October 1994. After paying for food, shelter, and transportation while living in the city, the worker was left with a net income of approximately 60 new pesos. By contrast, female domestic servants earned between 90 and 100 new pesos, from which only minimal payments for transportation were necessary.

15 In Spanish: Yo te digo que en la cuestión cultural y en la cuestión ideológica y el sistema en que hemos vivido ha impedido que la mujer tenga una libertad para participar. Hay frenos. Son pocos los espacios conquistados por la mujer. Han sido mínimos. En mi caso yo tengo muchos años de estar aquí. Mi compañero es super claro de este proceso pero tengo ciertas limitaciones y es un reto de la propia mujer de conquistar sus espacios dentro del seno de la familia, a exigir su reconocimiento dentro de otros organismos.

16 In Spanish: En Guatemala ahí crecía el pueblo, pero en la misma idea todos y no había un estiramiento de pensamiento que alcanzara a pensar en algún estudio en algo. En cambio acá en México acá es diferente. Aquí hay estudio hasta las viejitas sí les gusta. Cuando en Guatemala había alfabetización para los adultos? Allá no había. Ese es un avance que la gente lleva. Las señoras que venían de allá que venían como de treinta años. No sabían ni cómo se llamaban ni cuál era la primera letra de su nombre. Ahora son mujeres que son coordinadoras que ya saben firmar y apuntar algo. Aquí ha habido un avance. Es como se agarran las cosas de ver como otras compañeras lo están haciendo.

17 In Spanish: Te diré que tampoco no tuve mucho estudio. Tuve oportunidad de tener beca de una iglesia Católica pero no tuve la oportunidad porque mi padre también no se preocupó. También la cultura – la ideología de decir a la mujer para qué le va servir la educación si sólo tiene destino de ser madre y el varón sí porque el tiene responsabilidades hacia la mujer. Esos desniveles que hay en la cultura.

18 "Massacres in the jungle," a phrase coined by Guatemalan anthropologist Ricardo Falla, who wrote a book of the same name, refers to a distinct period of heightened repression from 1975 to 1982.

10 To Whom Shall the Nation Belong? The Gender and Ethnic Dimensions of Refugee Return and Struggles for Peace in Guatemala

ALISON CROSBY

In the years since exile began for some women, conditions in their countries changed, allowing them to return to their homeland. They discovered the irreversible nature of the exile experience. Not only has their country changed, but they themselves are no longer who they were when they left. They learned that once one looked at one's home from outside, as a stranger, the past, whether in the self or in the land, cannot be recaptured.

Mahnaz Afkhami, *Women in Exile*

While the Guatemalan peace accords certainly signaled an end to civil war, they are only a starting point. The profound transformation of social and political organization needed to counteract and dismantle a culture of fear created by decades of militarized violence will require the construction of a new Guatemalan nation. Whose images of the new nation will be taken into account in such a construction? Or, as Susanne Jonas asks, "to whom shall the Guatemalan nation belong?" (1991, 225)

This paper addresses these questions through an exploratory analysis of contesting imaginings of nation in Guatemala, with a particular focus on exile, the very nature of which, I argue, challenges the discourse of belonging that is prominent within nationalist ideologies.[1] As Homi Bhabha contends, refugees are not "contained within the *Heim* of the national culture and its unisonant discourse, but are themselves the marks of a shifting boundary that alienates the frontiers of the modern nation" (1994, 164). I examine the experience of organization among Guatemalan refugees in exile in camps

177 Gender and Ethnic Dimensions of the Return

in Mexico, highlighting the gendered nature of this process. To what extent was a new imagined community, involving changing social relations of gender and ethnicity, developed in exile, and what will happen to such a construction as the refugees return to Guatemala? If, as Afkhami contends, the exile experience is one of irrevocable change, what are the implications of the interaction between "those who left" and "those who stayed" for new understandings of nation in Guatemala?

The objective is to offer a preliminary assessment of very recent developments by examining the relationship between particular counternarratives and a still dominant national narrative of the past that sought to obliterate contesting imaginings. Specific attention is paid to the events of 1994, based on documents collected and fieldwork carried out in that year. The perspective is partial because it arises from a study of particular interactions between returning refugee women, women within organized civil society, the wider popular movement, and certain elements of the international community. It is also selective in that most observations are based on interviews conducted during visits to Guatemala City and El Petén in Guatemala and Chiapas in Mexico over a period of two and half months.

There are three main sources of data for this chapter. The first, in addition to some key theoretical works, consists of studies that cover the historical background and developments up to the recent period. The second consists of several types of documents that were collected in the course of field research – newspaper articles, papers, newsletters, and journals in particular.[2] The third source of information comes from observations made during fieldwork and from the twenty-three informal interviews I conducted, which were open-ended and exploratory. The interviewees were key actors in refugee women's organizations, refugee groups, a government human rights institution, international organizations (such as the United Nations) involved with the return process, international nongvernmental organizations (NGOs), Guatemalan research institutions, and several Guatemalan and Mexican NGOs.

In the following section I seek to contextualize the exile experience historically by examining the inclusionary and exclusionary practices through which the boundaries of the Guatemalan nation have been constituted, with particular emphasis on the intertwining practices of class exploitation, ethnic oppression, and gender exclusion. I then focus on the gendered experience of exile as a transformation process, my source of data coming mainly from fieldwork. Then, again using field data, I examine the return process and the experiences of organized refugee women in particular. Finally, I argue that further research on the interaction of refugee women with those women "who stayed behind" can illuminate spaces for transformation within Guatemalan society in the context of a postwar era.

THE DYNAMICS OF INCLUSION AND EXCLUSION

This section provides a general background and some key references to the conceptual approach and historical perspective that informs my exploratory study of recent developments in Guatemala. A key objective is to outline the historical formation of the hegemonic nation that created the condition of exile. I consider the dynamics of inclusion and exclusion at work in constructing national boundaries and the nature of what Edward Said describes as "the perilous territory of not belonging" (1984, 51), looking in particular at the positioning of indigenous communities and women within this context. The marginalized are the constitutive "other" to the nation and can never be banished because their existence is necessary to the survival of dominant selfhoods.

The nation-state emerged in its absolutist form during the fifteenth and sixteenth centuries in Europe (Anderson 1979). It then evolved in the eighteenth and nineteenth centuries into the modern nation-state with the development of the concept of citizenship in terms of membership in the collectivity and in an administrative system backed by the rule of law. "[T]he specific character of indigenous encounters with nation-states is linked to the peculiarities of the state system that grew up in Europe and took root in the New World" (Urban and Sherzer 1991, 8). Khachig Tololyan (1991, 6) sums up the ability of the modern nation-state to both incorporate difference and develop the boundaries of citizenship: "In [the nation-state] differences are assimilated, destroyed or assigned to the ghettos, to enclaves demarcated by boundaries so sharp that they enable the nation to acknowledge the apparently singular and clearly fenced-off differences within itself, while simultaneously reaffirming the privileged homogeneity of the rest, as well as the difference between itself and what lies over its frontiers."

Guatemala's independence in 1821 and the formation of the modern nation-state should not be seen as a unilateral transition from the violence of conquest and colonization to the just and impartial rule of law. Rather, the primary practice of difference continued, with modification to its discourse and methods, either through the overt practice of segregation or through incorporation. As Díaz-Polanco (1992, 13) states with respect to the situation in

Latin America more generally: "The colonial regime took as its point of departure ethnic inequality, the nation formal equality under the law, but in both cases difference itself – self-determination for the Indian communities – was denied any recognition whatsoever. Later Liberals would even come to deny different ethnic groups the right to exist."

While the colonial state's goal was to obtain the labour of the Indian population by means of coercion, the purpose of the postcolonial nation-state was to "transform Indians into citizens" subject to the rule of law of the state and to "gain sovereignty simultaneously over their lands" (Urban and Sherzer 1991, 9). The nation-state requires a sense of nationalism on the part of its citizens, a sense of belonging to what Anderson (1983) calls the national "imagined community," that is, a system of cultural representation through which identification with an extended group of people is possible. However, as Rigoberta Menchú states in her testimonial account of her life and that of her people, *her* country is not the *ladino* nation-state: "We didn't even understand what our parents told us – that the *ladinos* had a government. That is, the President who had been in power all this time, was, for my parents, for all of us, President of the *ladino's* government. It wasn't the government of *our* country" (Menchú 1984, 26).

Carol Smith argues that the construction of difference between Indians and non-Indians over time has not been based on biological heritage but rather has depended on a "changing system of social classification, based on ideologies of 'race,' class, language and culture which have taken on different meanings over time" (1990, 3). Those conquest survivors who continued to identify themselves as Maya retained a core of beliefs and traditions. Indians also identified themselves as belonging to particular communities that, to a certain extent, corresponded to the *municipio* (municipality) rather than to the Guatemalan indigenous population as a whole.

To indigenous communities it is not identity but justice that is the most pressing concern. "Most Indians wish to retain their distinctive traditions, while taking a position of economic and political equality with others in a modern multicultural nation" (Smith 1990, 5; also see COCADI 1989). Indian intellectuals, however, came to see the question of non-Indian identity as crucial, an identity that they asserted cannot exist without an oppressed "other." They claimed that non-Indians could not accept the possibility of a modern nation being multicultural (Smith 1990, 5; see, for example, Cojtí Cuxil 1989).

In post-1954 Guatemala, the homogenization of the "nation" was achieved through extermination, difference being interpreted as resistance. Beatrice Manz (1994) argues that the counterinsurgency campaigns were fuelled by nationalism and anti-communism. "The subversives – in the military's mind not simply armed combatants but anyone who opposes the status quo – were portrayed as servants of a 'foreign ideology' capable of destroying the nation itself. Those who organized cooperatives ceased to be loyal patriotic Guatemalans and became linked to 'international communism.' Few countries saw the cold-war rationale inflated to such excess." (200) The double spectre of the "other" is described by Gleijeses: "The Bolshevik fiend and the savage Indian: two words, one threat" (1988, 3). The Guatemalan flag was raised and lowered on a daily basis by villagers in even the most remote rural areas to avoid the risk of association with international communism (Manz 1994, 200).

During this time the military was able to continue, accentuate, and finally complete a process begun at the time of conquest in 1542 – domination of the countryside and the shattering of any sense of village autonomy (Handy 1984, 254). By the time the dictatorship of General Ríos Montt was overthrown in August 1983, the military had successfully completed its project of national hegemony. In the army's own words, "the supreme expression of the state" could not construct a "national destiny" without first wielding "national power" (cited in Lovell 1995, 76).

Falla argues that the massacres that occurred during this time should be seen as "a new expression of the existing conflict between the corporate indigenous community and the ladino state" (1994, 184). However, Jonas argues that the class dimensions of the repression should not be ignored – the bourgeoisie must not be allowed to disappear from analysis. Over the centuries, the bourgeoisie sought a protector to maintain and expand its lands and property privileges, be it Spanish or home-grown dictators, United States marines, the CIA, or the army. And what of the nationalism of the bourgeoisie?

This upper class is proud of being Guatemalan, of Guatemala's past as the seat of the *Capitanía General de Centro América* in colonial days, and of Guatemala's traditional role as the strongest country of Central America since independence – strongest economically and militarily. It is proud of its country's beauty – of its volcanoes and its mountains, of its tropical birds and its Mayan ruins. And it is proud of itself ... It is not proud, however, of its countrymen. Its nationalism is warped. It loves an estate, not a nation. It loves a Guatemala which includes only a few thousand Guatemalans: for the rest – for the Indians and for those Ladinos who are not upper class – it feels no kinship. It feels contempt. (Gleijeses 1988, 23)

In the face of this contempt, thousands died during the late 1970s and early 1980s, with hundreds of thousands more fleeing to Mexico and beyond or being internally displaced. The counterinsurgency campaign generated pervasive and deep-rooted terror and fear among the population – a "culture of fear" that became an integral part of everyday life (Gleijeses 1988; Green 1994). A local militia, known as the civil patrol system (PACs), was established by the Guatemalan army as the cornerstone of its rural counterinsurgency program. The civil patrol system was particularly invasive, since it effectively inserted the enemy within the community.

For the most part, "the other" has been understood from the perspective of the *ladino* population as being Indian or Maya. There was, however, yet another dimension, a gendered dimension, to this particular dichotomy. Nations are often constructed symbolically through the iconography of familial and domestic space (McClintock 1993, 63), which of course varies cross-culturally and historically. While sovereignty can be conceived of as masculine, the nation is feminine. Women are often represented as symbols of that feminized nation. Because of their reproductive capacity, women are seen as transmitters of group values and traditions and as agents of socialization of the young. When group identity becomes intensified, women are elevated to the status of symbol of the community, becoming iconic representations responsible for the reproduction of the group. Nevertheless, according to Anne McClintock, "no nationalism in the world has ever granted women and men the same privileged access to the resources of the nation-state." Access to the nation-state has often been through marriage to a male citizen. In this way, women have been "subsumed only symbolically into the national body politic," thus merely becoming "the limits of national differences between men" (1991, 105).

Cynthia Enloe argues that the women who are most directly affected by militarized violence and war, and who have much to contribute to peace processes, are precisely those who are denied the means to disseminate their views and opinions: "Societies in the grip of foreign or civil war and those dominated by militarized regimes have not been receptive to women's need to have their ideas taken seriously. Indeed, women who question their own subordination are often perceived as threats to national security" (Enloe 1993, 38). With a rigidly defined sexual division of labour restricting them to the private sphere, women in Guatemalan society have mostly remained outside the public sphere of the political activities of the nation. Rigoberta Menchú and other indigenous women argue that they suffer doubly as a result of ethnicized and genderized oppression: "It has been difficult for me as an indigenous woman to find the confidence to speak publicly, particularly since we were raised to believe that the only role for women is to maintain a household and bear children. If you broke with this role, you were seen as abandoning tradition and you would lose the respect of the people" (Menchú 1993, introduction).

It is important to keep in mind the class-based nature of women's iconic status with respect to the nation – the feminine image of the nation is a very particular one, linked closely to middle-class and colonial ideologies. Subaltern women's labour most often forms the material rather than ideological basis of the nation (Spivak 1992), but the specific roles of women are maintained by this dominant ideology. In her analysis of the identity of Guatemalan communities in Mexico, Nash finds that an important component of a "fictive or imagined representation of a distinct ethnic identity is the gender specialization in responsibility for adhering to custom." But she also argues that "this stereotype of women as culturally conservative carriers of tradition has been attacked in feminist revisions of Latin American history" and has shown that "this stereotyping falsifies female participation in the labour force over time" (1995, 14–15). Thus she argues that the imagined representation of identity fails to illuminate the reality of women's lived experience, which is ever-changing and dynamic. Around the world women are in demand in the workforce – both as labour for transnational corporations and as workers selling so-called traditional handicrafts to global consumers. Their lived experience belies their perceived symbolic status within the community.

The construction of the "other" has been integral to the formation of the modern Guatemalan nation. Historically, indigenous communities, women, and the poor have formed the markers of difference, perceived as threats to the "national" interest, whether through segregation under colonialism or the violent homogenizing practices of recent counterinsurgency campaigns. The extreme violence employed in the reinforcement of the hegemonic nation pushed the boundaries of difference to the very frontier of the nation and beyond. However, there is a continuous relationship between hegemonic ideologies of nation and counter-strategies of resistance. The boundaries of difference are also spaces of contestation. As Stepputat argues, "power working through the organization and representation of space produces resistance and new political subjectivities as well" (1997, 4). In the following section, I examine how indigenous communities in exile, particularly refugee women, have mounted a challenge to the dominant national narrative of the country's controlling forces through their experience of organization.

COUNTER-NARRATIVES

Counter-narratives of the nation that continually evoke and erase its totalizing boundaries – both actual and conceptual – disturb those ideological manoeuvres through which "imagined communities" are given essentialist identities. (Bhabha 1994, 149)

The scorched-earth offensives resulted in new organized forms of community, in particular the Communities of Population in Resistance (CPRs), and the refugees in Mexico who organized under the umbrella of the Permanent Commissions of Guatemalan Refugees in Mexico (CCPP). As Falla notes, "these communities have continued to resist and distrust the army and the Guatemalan state." He goes on to say, however, that "their vision has also widened as a result of the level of confrontation, the mixture of tongues and ethnic groups, and their contact with different government and non-governmental forces. Their situation has transcended the interests of the local indigenous community, and has a national relevance beyond that of independent communities in conflict with the state" (1994, 187). I argue that such processes of transformation in consciousness and organization can provide spaces for contesting imaginings of nation.

Guatemalan refugees in Mexico were considered "subversive" by the Guatemalan state and military. On the one hand, they have been portrayed as mere pawns of the insurgency, while on the other hand they have been perceived as an organized threat to the homogeneous construction of the nation. In this section, I consider the counter-narratives that were constructed by organized refugees, particularly women, in Mexico.

In his essay *The Mind of Winter: Reflections on Life in Exile*, Edward Said describes exile as "an unhealable rift forced between the human being and a native place, the self and its true home" (1984, 49). However, the experience of exile can also result in the remaking of self. Refuge cannot be simply equated with victimization: the struggle for recovery occupies a central place in the lives of many refugees. In Guatemala, Maya Indians identified particularly with their own community and ethnic group, rather than with the indigenous population as a whole. The composition of the Guatemalan refugee population in Mexico, however, was heterogeneous, not just in ethnicity, language, and religion but also in political views.

What the refugees did have in common was that they were peasants and they shared a common experience of having fled the army's violence. Moreover, they had been labelled by the Guatemalan military as subversives. When faced with difficult conditions in refugee camps, the common goal of survival created a sense of unity among refugees. In exile, according to one refugee woman, "indigenous identity has become more generic" (Mamá Maquín 1994), and, as Stepputat (1994) found, refugees began to identify themselves as Guatemalans, whereas previously, to say you were "Guatemalan" meant you were from Guatemala City. The construction of an "imagined community" (which was not necessarily homogeneous or harmonious) among refugees from different ethnic groups, in turn, created a space for organization.[3]

Most of the women who had fled to southern Mexico were indigenous peasants who were often illiterate and spoke only indigenous languages. In Guatemala, the refugee women said, they were often dismissed by the military as *vientras que producen guerilleros* (guerilla-producing wombs) (Mamá Maquín 1994, 14). When first arriving in Mexico, because they were unable to communicate in Spanish, women were isolated and had little contact with the United Nations High Commission for Refugees (UNHCR), the Mexican authorities, the international community, or local solidarity groups. According to the women themselves, refugee women were subordinated at all levels of the refugee community, and this was reflected in the way that aid and development projects were carried out. Many of the women could not leave their houses without permission from their husbands. Women who were heads of households (10 percent of the total number of families) suffered additional discrimination for assuming a traditionally male role. Until l989 women mostly organized for the production of *artesanía* (handicrafts).

In the camps in Campeche and Quintana Roo, exposure to different cultural influences resulted in a perceived loss of indigenous identity. Women in particular expressed concern over this loss. As the keepers of the culture, Maya women became increasingly worried and upset about young people "going away from the culture." In Mexico young people were presented with different opportunities and greater possibilities. Many found work in tourist resort towns such as Cancún. Some women felt that it was important to return to Guatemala so as not to lose the young people. Parents listed drug addiction and social disintegration as the most troubling problems affecting their children. In the space of one generation, a culture and a way of life was seen to be rapidly disappearing. Many of the women stopped wearing their traditional costumes or *traje*, often for work-related reasons, since their employers did not want to get into trouble with Mexican immigration. The *traje* was in many ways the external symbol of communal identity, a symbol of cohesion. It marked the divisions between different ethnic groups. Since colonial times each ethnic group, and consequently almost every municipality, had its own *traje* (often used to control the movements of the indigenous population). When the *traje* was no longer worn, women felt that community identification was lost (Mamá Maquín 1994; Crosby fieldnotes 1994).

Maya women felt it was their duty to maintain the traditions of the community. Displacement and exile resulted in the breakdown of both community systems and familial structures. Without the social system that had formerly acted as a safety net, many women said that the pressures of exile often led to an increase in violence against women.

However, changing relations within the community and family also resulted in identity transformation. The loss of previous forms of "traditional" social cohesion and the mixing of different ethnic groups, customs, and identities generated a search for new forms of community and the opening up of new spaces. More and more women began to participate in the daily running of the camps, as well as preparing for organized, collective returns. Women cited "learning to deal with their husbands" as a particular challenge while living in exile. This process in itself contributed to changing relations between men and women within the family system.

A second arena for women's organization was through the UNHCR workshop series Rights of Women and Children. Until then, the concept that women had rights was an alien one. UNHCR, the European Community, and local Mexican NGOs also began to provide training in such areas as reproductive health, nutrition, and administration, as well as workshops on women's rights.

Third and finally, the formation of the CCPP provided an organizational umbrella for other related groups to begin to organize. In 1987 the CCPP were elected by the refugees themselves to begin negotiations for a safe, dignified, and collective return. Two of the first eight elected representatives of the CCPP were women (Arbour 1994).

The process of becoming organized placed many additional burdens on the women. In addition to their traditional responsibilities within the family, the women had to contribute to the family economy through wage labour. For women in the camps, a typical work day lasted from 5 a.m. until 9 or 10 p.m. (Mamá Maquín 1994). In order to cope, the women sought time-saving measures such as cooperative, mechanized tortilla making and cooperative child care. These measures allowed the women to participate more fully in political, organizational, productive, and other important activities (Arbour 1994). Many women also learned to speak Spanish, thus enhancing their ability to communicate.

The first Guatemalan refugee women's organization to emerge publicly was Mamá Maquín, founded on 25 May 1990.[4] The name honours the memory of a Q'eqchi' woman assassinated by the Guatemalan military in a 1978 massacre of indigenous peasants seeking land rights. Mamá Maquín came to represent about eight thousand refugee women from eight different indigenous groups who lived in the Mexican refugee camps located in the states of Chiapas, Quintana Roo, and Campeche. Mamá Maquín defined itself as being part of the Guatemalan popular movement. It identified its biggest challenge as enabling refugee women to participate on equal terms within the community power structures and decision-making processes. Two areas of particular concern were improving women's economic situation and providing more training for women. "One of our biggest objectives is to train ourselves, in order to develop a knowledge of new things, and in particular our rights as women, and how to defend those rights. Above all, we want to be in control of our own futures" (Mamá Maquín 1994, 58).

In its first year, Mamá Maquín carried out a survey of refugee women in the camps that sought to obtain general information concerning their situation. The objective was to determine the extent of women's participation within their communities and thus find ways to involve women in self-sufficiency projects being carried out by the Mexican Commission for Aid to Refugees (COMAR) (Mamá Maquín 1994). The women within Mamá Maquín learned a great deal from the survey experience, having discovered the differences and similarities in women's problems within the various refugee communities. Not surprisingly, they also encountered opposition within certain communities. Sometimes the men would want to respond for the women: "They don't know how to talk; I'll answer your questions" (quoted in Mamá Maquín 1994, 61). The results of the survey conveyed the needs of refugee women, thereby allowing Mamá Maquín to design its work specifically around those needs, and they were published (in conjunction with a local Mexican women's organization) as a journal entitled *De Refugiadas a Retornadas: Memorial de Experiencias Organizativas de las Mujeres Refugiadas en Chiapas* (1994).[5] The most pressing desire expressed by the refugee women Mamá Maquín talked to was to return. Mamá Maquín became a major player in the negotiated process of return alongside the CCPP. Preparing women for the return became one of the organization's principle activities in Mexico.

The "remaking process" in exile had a particular impact on women, affecting their relationships with men, their families, and communities (see Torres' chapter in this volume). In many ways, the exile experience violates the particular ways in which men and women define themselves and each other. I began this chapter with a quote from Afkhami in which she describes how women (from such diverse countries as Afghanistan, Chile, and El Salvador) returning to their country of origin discovered "the irreversible nature of the exile experience. Not only has their country changed, but they themselves are no longer who they were when they left" (1994, 16). Despite (or even *because* of?) the many difficulties encountered by refugee women in Mexico, they became an organizational force to be reckoned with. Women's rights were brought to the forefront of the public political space of the refugee community. Mamá Maquín described the returning women as being "different": they had higher self-esteem, more spaces in which to organize, and "more strength and hope for the future" (1994, 78). Given the strength and depth of the change process, returning to the country of origin is necessarily very difficult for men, women, and children, as the exile experience is in many ways an "unhealable rift," as Said described it. Exile provided a space outside the nation from which to develop contesting imaginings. What happens to that process on return to the nation, where the boundaries of difference are internalized? In the following section I will explore the implications of return for the gendered contestations of imagining constructed in Mexico.

RETURN: STRUGGLE, NOT RESIGNATION

The refugee return was described by one member of the international diplomatic community as "peculiar" because it took place in the midst of ongoing conflict within Guatemala (Crosby fieldnotes, 1994). The slogan of the return became "return is struggle, not resignation" (Stepputat 1994, 15). The negotiation of the return process was an extremely politicized struggle between the government and the CCPP. The attitude of the Guatemalan authorities, to some extent, had shifted since the period of extreme violence in the 1980s, but many still considered the refugees to be subversives in disguise. The returnees themselves had deeply ingrained antistate attitudes: "Their imaginations and practices are informed by their experiences with state-terror and more than a decade of life in refugee camps."

One area where several returns occurred was the Ixcán, a conflictive area in the northwestern part of the country where the war had become an integral part of people's lives. The guerilla movement, the URNG (Guatemalan National Revolutionary Unity), maintained a presence until the ceasefire in 1996. Mamá Maquín played a vital role in the first and second organized returns to the Ixcán, which took place in January 1993 and January 1994. The group represented 670 women returnees to the first return community, Victoria 20 de enero, located in Quiché province. Four members of the leadership also returned to that area.

Upon returning, Mamá Maquín identified four main organizational objectives: to extend the organization to the surrounding communities, to strengthen women's participation within the community, to integrate into the popular movement, and finally, to establish relationships with the Communities of Population in Resistance (CPRs) (Mamá Maquín, Plan de Trabajo). Moreover, in the camps in Quintana Roo and Campeche women had had access to piped water, *molinos* (corn mills), and tortilla makers. In Mexico they had schools and clinics; they had come into contact with a system of government that provided at least some services for the people. Consequently, upon their return the women saw the need for schools and clinics as fundamental.

According to both refugee groups and international organizations, the women encountered many problems upon their return. As previously discussed, new conditions and shifting relations in the camps created spaces in which women could organize. But more traditional structures where roles for women and men were more rigidly defined awaited them in their return communities. Although the return communities were intent on reestablishing the organizational structures they built in Mexico, the refugee men began to reassert their traditional roles and authority through contact with Guatemalan society.

At its inception, the return process seemed to have had the effect of weakening rather than strengthening the power and vision of women's organizing. The main purpose of organizing in Mexico was to prepare women for the return. Once they were back, though, there were difficulties in meeting the stated objectives for return, since they had not been prepared for the reintegration process. An additional issue concerned women's rights with respect to cooperatives and land. The accords signed between the government and the CCPP allowed for one plot of land for each family, registered in the name of the head of household (almost always the man). For returning women, this land-titling practice was just one of the many problems they faced that related to traditional views of women's social position.

The return community of Victoria 20 de enero organized itself as a cooperative. The social structures in the cooperative gave overwhelming power to the central organizing committee (*junta direc-*

tiva), and any projects that women's organizations wanted to undertake had to be cleared with that committee. The community had difficulty dealing with issues of power and organization. To complicate matters, the tradition of not admitting to problems within the community was ingrained. Should women fight to change the social arrangements within the cooperative? Or, as one woman NGO worker asked, "should the women inscribe themselves as separate members of the cooperative, thus splitting the conception of the family?" (Crosby fieldnotes 1994). However, with the second return (to Chacula) women's needs were not only recognized, but steps were taken to establish women's position on a more equal footing. The structures were not so hierarchical; efforts were made to get women into the central committee. Nonetheless, when women did become involved in the central committee, they felt torn between their duties on the committee and their loyalty to their organization.

It became apparent early on that the central issue for the women returnees revolved around a delicate balancing act: how to respect the communal structures of the return communities while at the same time increasing women's participation in community life. Upon their return, the communities built houses, established food cooperatives, and so on, while women's organizing was not regarded as a priority.

As the return process continued, things did not get any easier for women, particularly those who were organized. In 1998 refugee women were still seen to be losing ground in return communities. According to one refugee woman leader, "Many of the men, the leaders, leave the women out. They don't take women into account anymore" (Roberts 1998, 1). In early 1997 Mamá Maquín's office in Victoria 20 de enero was robbed by men from that same community. Shortly thereafter, a Mamá Maquín house in Pueblo Nuevo, Ixcán, was destroyed and some contents burned by community members led by the *junta directiva*. The justification for the attack was that Mamá Maquín was affiliated with former guerillas, but more clearly, the actions seemed to signify a reassertion of control over community decision-making structures. The *junta directiva* "declared it illegal for any group to meet in the community without its permission." In June 1998 several members of Mamá Maquín were attacked on their way home from the organization's annual assembly by men armed with grenades, guns, and machetes. The assailants made it clear that they knew that the women were members of Mamá Maquín. During the assembly itself male leaders from the committee intimidated the women during the election of the new coordinating committee. The attacks have not just been directed against Mamá Maquín. In June

1998 in Nuevo México, Escuintla, two milk cows belonging to a successful cheese-making project run by the refugee women's organization Madre Tierra were killed. These cows were the best milkers, and the action was seen as an attack against the organization.

A member of the outgoing coordinating committee of Mamá Maquín sees the objective of this concerted campaign against organized refugee women as being "to demoralize the women in Mamá Maquín. It affects our work and it limits participation" (Roberts 1998). She goes on to say that according to their male colleagues, "a woman who is active, who works, is no good any more as a wife; that she can't set up a house. In all the organizations, it's the widows, young women, and single women who participate most."

Roman Krzanic is critical of the assumption that the refugees form a homogenous community: "There is a common perception that the experience of Guatemalan refugees in terms of communal persecution, resisting a common enemy (generally the government and the military), the shared experience of refuge in Mexico, and ethnicity have created a high degree of cohesion and solidarity within the return communities" (1997, 62). He points to the high level of internal dissension within the return communities, particularly between the CCPPs and the various *sectores* (organized sectors) of women, young people, health promoters, and human rights activists formed in exile. For him the source of conflict stems from "the effects of political organization and awareness-raising (particularly amongst women) which occurred while the refugees were in refugee camps in Mexico, conflict over resources and differing attitudes to cooperation with the national government, the private sector and popular forces on the Guatemalan left" (61).

Change processes cause disruptions in relations of power. Agger (1994) talks about the identity conflict that women can experience when they leave their life in the private sphere and move out into political space, challenging male power. This move from the private to the public is a violation of boundaries. By moving out into the public sphere, women become visible, and visible women become dangerous women – both sexually and politically. This is particularly true for women who have undergone a process of transformation in exile. Guatemalan refugee women who organized in Mexico made the transition from the private to the public sphere. Women increasingly assumed positions of leadership within the refugee movement in Mexico, helping their community come to terms with the violence and trauma it had experienced and looking to the future as a time of growth and strength. On return, spaces where women were actively participating were challenged, sometimes violently. However, the transformation process is irreversible. Refugee women are an undeniable presence in the public sphere of the Guatemalan nation, which is precisely why many, both within and outside their communities, perceive them as threatening.

Mamá Maquín's Plan of Action for the Future emphasized the establishment of links with women in other communities who were not returnees. The challenge was how to go about this. As one of the strongest refugee organizations in Mexico, Mamá Maquín had a very clear focus on preparing women for return. Upon their return, however, new questions arose. What should Mamá Maquín do next? Should they remain an indigenous refugee women's organization? Should they open their membership to non-returnee women? What would their relationship with other women's organizations in Guatemala be? In the concluding section I consider an example of dialogues across boundaries and argue that further in-depth analysis of such initiatives is a necessary part of the search to understand the possibilities for new nation-building.

INTERACTIONS ACROSS BOUNDARIES

Tensions and differences were acknowledged between returnee and non-returnee women from the start of the return: the returned women "have been through a process. They have had the possibility for self-evaluation" (Crosby fieldnotes, 1994). The refugee women were seen as not having defined the nature of their presence upon return. What kinds of relationships do they want to establish? As Guatemala moves towards a post-peace accord era, what are the implications of the politics of negotiation between returnee and non-returnee women for the popular movement as it meets the challenges of difficult and uncertain times? In this final section I look at the National Women's Forum, which is an example of interactions between women across the boundaries that define Guatemalan civil society.

When the refugee return began, the Guatemalan popular movement was predominantly urban, *ladino*, and middle class.[6] The effect of years of militarized violence on the popular movement was very apparent: it was fragmented and polarized. As one female activist put it, "We are the result of so many years of disintegration" (Crosby fieldnotes 1994). This started to change as indigenous organizations, refugees, and women began to actively participate. An emerging identity of a women's movement is now challenging the gender divisions within organized civil society.

Within the Guatemalan popular movement, some women said they "have had to struggle for their own identity," identifying the trade union and popular movements as strong influences on women's self-definition (Crosby fieldnotes 1994). With respect to their participation in conflict resolution, the question many women asked was, "What is relevant to women's lives?" Another question frequently posed was, "What women are we talking about?" It is essential to consider the boundaries of "race," ethnicity, and class when considering women's participation. Those women who were involved in the popular movement tended to be *ladino*, although indigenous women also organized themselves (the National Coordinator of Guatemalan Widows – known as CONAVIGUA – is predominantly indigenous). Racial boundaries with respect to organizing are clearly maintained, although this was recognized as a problem that needed to be overcome.

The women's movement in Guatemala was still in its infancy in the mid-1990s; some women even claimed it did not exist. Only one organization, Tierra Viva (Living Earth), actually referred to itself as "feminist." There were, however, other women's organizations. Tierra Viva wished to be "a presence among many" and wanted women to organize to become autonomous. But Tierra Viva also argued for the development of various forms of alliances between women and within the popular movement more generally and for the need to look for "other types of possibilities" for civil society (Crosby fieldnotes 1994). This goal was very difficult given the context of social disintegration (for a more detailed discussion of women's organizing in Guatemala, see Blacklock in this volume). As one female member of the popular movement stated: "There is no respect for diversity, for the idea that others can have their own voices. The militarized identity of Guatemalan society has allowed few possibilities for socialization. It is very difficult to be a feminist in this kind of culture."

With the signing of the Agreement on Resettlement of the Populations Uprooted by the Armed Conflict in June 1994, a technical commission (CTEAR) was formed to oversee the implementation of the accord; it was comprised of two representatives from the government, two from the affected populations, and two from the international community (who would have a voice but no vote). The Consultative Assembly of the Uprooted Population (ACPD) was created to represent the uprooted populations and name members to the commission. The ACPD was comprised of many, but not all, of the organized uprooted population (the CCPP/Northwest did not become a member, for example).

The ACPD had a Coordinator of Uprooted Women, comprised of women's organizations from sectors such as the CPRs, widows, single mothers, the internally displaced, refugees, and returnees. According to one member, "the Coordinator is a space where we can speak about our situation and our needs to demand our rights as uprooted women, in general and within the framework of the peace accords" (quoted in *Reunion* 6, no. 3, spring 1998, 2). The Coordinator was an active participant in the National Women's Forum, which was created out of the peace accords with the objective of promoting "a broad, pluralistic, and representative body of women for permanent consultation and dialogue, taking into account the diversity in the country [and encouraging] national conciliation and reconciliation; equity between men and women; and the identification, incorporation, and participation of women's organizations." For uprooted women, the forum provided them with a space in which to "express ourselves and share the proposals we have elaborated," an opportunity they had not had within their own communities, or under the framework of the Accord on the Resettlement of the Population Groups Uprooted by the Armed Conflict.

The structure of the forum was designed to bring women together at the local, regional, and national levels. According to the ACPD Women's Coordinator, "for the first time in Guatemalan history, women from the various sectors of the women's movement – indigenous, uprooted, peasant, private sector, churches, political parties, and government and state bodies – are working and struggling together as women" (*Reunion* 6, no. 3, spring 1988, 3).

It is important to point out that the forum encountered problems and difficulties from its inception and continued to be a conflictive space. The national government was accused of trying to influence the composition of the forum, and then later on it was argued that URNG-affiliated women were dominating the space. Issues of representation and legitimacy were continuously debated, and one commentator went as far as calling the whole initiative a farce. However, as I have emphasized throughout this paper, challenging and crossing boundaries is difficult, and even dangerous. Change necessitates the disruption of power relations. Moreover, strategies of resistance are often neither coherent nor cohesive, particularly within a context where histories of violence and militarization have produced fragmentation and polarization. As Mohanty argues, "resistance inheres in the very gaps, fissures and silences of hegemonic narratives" (1997, 38). In exile, the refugees developed a contesting, imagined community, but such a community was neither homogenous nor harmonious. As Stepputat argues, "in order to analyse how armed conflict and reconciliation articulates with social organization and identity at the frontier, we may employ the notion of community as a heuristic devise for the identification of boundaries, identities, and political

194 Identity and Community

struggles in these contexts" (1997, 5). Neither should the capacity of still-dominant national narratives to challenge any threats be underestimated, as the military's massacre of eleven people in the refugee return community of Aurora 8 de octubre, Xamán, in 1995 violently demonstrated.

At the beginning of this chapter I argued that in the context of Guatemala's tragic history only a profound transformation of the social and political organization would create a real and lasting peace. To begin to understand the nature of such a transformation, it is important to ask "Who is challenging boundaries and initiating change?" The example I examined was the exile and return experience of Guatemalan refugees, women in particular. Now the question becomes "How are the internal boundaries of the nation being challenged?" Dialogues across the boundaries that encompass new, previously unimaginable, practices of cooperation and pay attention to "difference" as the expression of unequal power relations can result in an emerging alternative sense of ownership of the "nation." As refugee women argue, "We are Guatemalans, and we need to feel that we are a part of the Guatemalan nation" (Crosby fieldnotes 1994). The challenge is to search for ways of building on and strengthening this active and participatory sense of national belonging.

NOTES

1 This paper is based on field research undertaken in 1994 with the financial support of a CIDA Awards for Canadians (administered by the Canadian Bureau for International Education) and the Centre for Refugee Studies at York University. It was briefly updated in 1998 in the course of doctoral field research supported by the Social Sciences and Humanities Research Council of Canada (SSHRCC). I would like to thank numerous people in Guatemala and also David Morley, Liisa North, and Alan Simmons for their comments, advice, and suggestions.
2 Such documents came mainly from the Assembly of Civil Society, the Permanent Commissions, and Mamá Maquín.
3 The data in the remainder of this paper is drawn from field notes and observations, unless otherwise indicated. All translations are by the author.
4 Although the scope of this paper allows only for discussion of Mamá Maquín, three other refugee women's organizations also organized returns: Ixmucane (which participated in returns to northern Guatemala; Madre Tierra (returns to the southern area of Guatemala); and the Association of Guatemalan Dispersed Women Ixchel Flor de la

Esperanza (collective returns to southern Guatemala).
5 *From Refuge to Return: The Organizational Experiences of Refugee Women in Chiapas.*
6 A major omission in this paper is an examination of the indigenous movement, which has moved from strength to strength in post-peace-accord Guatemala and is providing some of the strongest contestations of national imagining.

11 Democratization and Popular Women's Organizations

CATHY BLACKLOCK

From the mid-1980s to the mid-1990s there was an upsurge in popular women's political organizing. At the conclusion of my field research in late 1993, there were approximately twenty such organizations located in Guatemala City, a growing number of poor women's neighbourhood associations in the marginal, shantytown areas of the city, and a significant number of women's organizations and collectives in the countryside.[1] Through the 1990s these women's organizations have taken on an increasingly significant role in civil society and the politics of the popular movement, yet there is relatively little information available about them.

The central premise of the discussion presented below is that democratization and the growth of women's organizations are integrally related. Democratization – understood as a two-phased process of repression and controlled political liberalization – has been fundamentally rooted in economic crisis and has affected women's lives in gender-specific ways. I argue that the overall impact has been the creation of the conditions for the potential politicization and mobilization of women – collectively and around issues affecting their gender identity. I also argue, however, that the ongoing and pervasive culture of fear in Guatemala has inhibited a grass-roots mobilization of this potential. The growth of women's organizations in the 1980s and 1990s has reflected, instead, the influence of several phenomena, such as the demonstration effect of other mothers' groups in Latin America, the international and regional impact of feminism, and the political strategy of the popular movement in contesting democratization. I argue that the combined effect of such forces has been the creation of a cadre of women leaders who have initiated the formation of women's organizations in a top-down manner. The chapter concludes with a brief overview of the political character of the popular women's political organizations.

DEMOCRATIZATION

The importance of economic crisis to the process of democratization in Guatemala is discussed in detail by other contributors to this volume. What I would like to emphasize are the social and political repercussions for women that have stemmed from the contradictions embedded in the superimposition of industrialization on the predominantly agrarian economy in Guatemala. In effect, the outcome of the economic crisis that came to a head in the late 1970s was severe social crisis. By this time, however, the Guatemalan military had developed into an extremely powerful institution with significant economic interests. Due to its inability to pursue a proactive strategy towards the economic crisis, the capitalist class capitulated in responding to the societal crisis rooted in the deteriorating economic situation by relying on the military to turn its repressive capacity on society in a pact of domination.

The extremity of the repression that ensued and its general consequences are discussed in detail in other contributions to this volume. It is important to note here, however, that the national-security strategy pursued by the military through the early 1980s had as its longer-term objective the political liberalization of Guatemala. By 1984 the military had begun implementation of the final phase of its counterinsurgency plan, which was the limited political liberalization, or "opening," signaled by the election of 1985. For the military, however, the necessary precondition for this political liberalization was the successful "pacification" of civil society through repression. Formal liberalization, packaged and marketed by the military as democratization, was always understood within the national-security doctrine framework, which declared politics to be an extension of war.

Bearing in mind the antecedent repression, it is, nonetheless, important to consider what opportunities for popular resistance and contestation may have been generated by the processes of democratization. My particular concern here is to evaluate the effects of this repression – democratization dynamic – on women.[2]

WOMEN'S CAREGIVING AND CARETAKING WORK

To evaluate the effects of repression it is useful to consider briefly the social construction of gender in Guatemala. Women have historically been deemed responsible for the work entailed in the reproduction of the family as a social unit. This convention has meant that the family has been the locus of the social construction of women's identity. In the gendering of women's identity in terms of the family are contained two general and related types of women's work: the caregiving work necessary to the maintenance of the social relations of the family and the caretaking work necessary to the physical maintenance of the family.

To understand the construction of women's gender roles and identity in Guatemala, I have employed the categories of caregiving and caretaking, rather than the more usual categories of reproductive and productive work, because the latter tend to be correlated with the private and public spheres, respectively. This is not meant to suggest that the reproductive/productive schema is unhelpful or unimportant for understanding women's roles. Rather, in choosing to distinguish two broadly different types of women's work – caregiving and caretaking – I emphasize two key points about the Guatemalan situation. One is the blurring of the distinction between reproductive and productive work – and hence, of the private and public spheres – that is emerging in the context of crisis and globalization. For in the case of Guatemala, women's responsibilities for maintaining the family – usually understood as reproductive work in the private sphere – have led to a large flow of women into the informal economy as they have found it necessary to generate more income in the family unit as a result of economic crisis and neoliberal policies. While this work may be understood within the framework of productive labour and the public sphere, this approach misses the crucial point that the women themselves understand this part of their work as integral to their roles in the family and in the private sphere.

The second point is that the categories of caregiving and caretaking work stress the significance of women's attitudes towards their work and their social roles. For as is discussed in greater detail below, the potential for women's politicization and mobilization was created through the impact that repression and economic crisis had on their *perception of and social relationship to* their work and their roles. This potential, then, arises from the sense that has emerged among women of the popular classes that both repression and economic crisis have negatively affected their lives by destabilizing their ability to perform their work. This is to say that the potential for women's politicization has been created through the ways in which women have interpreted the significance of, and concomitantly, attributed meaning to, the effects of repression and crisis on their lives.

DEMOCRATIZATION AND ITS IMPACT ON WOMEN

The period of repression had a specific impact on women above all because the violence perpetrated by the military in the late 1970s and early 1980s constituted an attack on the social relations of the family. As in many other Latin American countries, the widespread and arbitrary atrocities committed by the military in Guatemala left virtually no one untouched or untouchable. The atrocities were perpetrated in a seemingly arbitrary manner that went far beyond political reprisal to encompass an attack on people with virtually no involvement in politics. The repression succeeded in its goal of terrorizing the population into acquiescence. Importantly, however, the massive scale of violent repression also appeared to the majority of the population as inexplicable and unjustifiable. This societal perception led to a politicization of the violence and repression as political space opened through the political liberalization and created some scope for the expression of popular discontent.

The disappearance or murder of husbands, fathers, sons, and daughters also threatened and undermined the ability of women, who are predominantly responsible for the social relations of the family, to perform their caregiving and nurturance work in the maintenance of family relations. The lives of women as wives and mothers were drastically affected by events that they were unable to rationalize or justify. The impact was particularly marked for the women whose relatives disappeared during the repression, for the uncertainty of death prolonged their feelings of loss and grief and inhibited the restabilization of their attitudes towards their caregiving work. In this manner, then, the extreme violations of human rights became a concrete, lived issue around which women could potentially be politicized and mobilized.

The economic crisis underlying the process of democratization has also had particular repercussions for women's lives. In some ways these effects have been more complex, given the multifaceted nature of the economic crisis and the factors that have intersected with it, such as the violent repression, the policies of neoliberalism that ensued in the later 1980s, and extant patriarchal structures. In general, however, the socioeconomic effect of this crisis has been the severe impoverishment of the majority of the Guatemalan population. While the decline in the standard of living has had many societal repercussions, the family as a social unit has been particularly affected. For my purpose here, two general trends are worth highlighting. First, as prices have risen and real wages have declined, families have come to need more than one income. Furthermore, these economic pressures have also led to the disintegration of family units as increasing rates of alcoholism, domestic violence, and abandonment have taken their toll.

Women have been acutely affected by these trends. Both the increasing financial needs of the family and the disintegration of the family unit have contributed to a drastic increase in the work entailed in women's caretaking of the family. Indeed, the work of a great number of women as caretakers of the household has greatly expanded to encompass direct and frequently total responsibility for income generation and economic provision for the family. In families affected by abandonment, abuse, and alcoholism on the part of the husband, the women have effectively become single heads of households. In light of the growing necessity for multiple family incomes, this trend has meant that those who have fallen into the most extreme poverty have generally been women and children.

The stress experienced by women entailed in this amplification of their work and responsibilities has been further exacerbated by related dynamics. One result of the violence was that thousands of women were left widowed, another form of family disintegration that left even more women as single heads of households who were immediately forced to provide for the economic welfare of their families. This dynamic relation between economic crisis and repression had repercussions for other women in the family unit as well. Very frequently, older daughters came to be expected to contribute to the family income and were often sent off at a very young age to work as domestics in private homes, which again, obviously led to further dissolution of the social relations of the family.

The advent of a neoliberal approach to economic crisis in the latter half of the 1980s also exacerbated the effects on women. While the Guatemalan state has historically undertaken and supported extremely limited social welfare measures, some institutions and state policies did, nevertheless, provide the populace with some minimal social security, most of which was the legacy of the two democratically elected governments of the "ten years of spring" from 1944 to 1954. In the late 1980s even these limited institutions and policies came under attack.

The impact of all these factors has been intensified by structures of patriarchy in Guatemalan society that have only served to limit the ability of women to respond to the increased pressures and work. In Guatemala patriarchy has historically been culturally constructed and expressed in *machismo*, which has had many economic repercussions that have all contributed to effectively exclude women of the popular classes from most paths to economic advancement. Among the most notable has been the exclusion of women from education, which has resulted in a shockingly high level of illiteracy among women – particularly indigenous women – and a low level of socially and economically valued skills. The ability of women to improve their standard of living has been severely limited as a result: most women have been confined to the margins of the economy in highly exploitative and, frequently, physically dangerous work, such as street-vending and domestic work in the informal sector, jobs in the *maquiladoras* (assembly plants), prostitution, and so on, at a time when their financial responsibilities for the family have been increasing. Again, this economic circumscription of women's lives has served only to further exacerbate the trend toward the feminization of poverty.

To summarize briefly, the period of violent repression and the economic crisis underlying the process of democratization in Guatemala has destabilized the socially constructed gender roles and identity of most women in the popular classes. Because this impact has been overwhelmingly negative, it has generated a population of women with a *potential* for politicization. However, the very complexity of the dynamics involved has constrained women's ability to respond politically to the economic crisis and subsequent neoliberalism. In addition, the pervasive culture of terror has more generally functioned to inhibit political participation, even for the desperate relatives of victims of human rights abuses and the disappeared. Thus, despite the extreme impact of violence and economic crisis on women, the many factors constraining their lives prohibited them from mobilizing in a grass-roots manner to contest their deteriorating life conditions.

THE INFLUENCE OF INTERNATIONAL AND REGIONAL DYNAMICS ON THE PROCESS OF DEMOCRATIZATION

The potential created for the political mobilization of women may well have remained dormant if it had not been for the influence of other factors shaping the Guatemalan political environment, two of the most salient of which are here considered: the influence of the growing politicization of women in Latin America generally and the international and regional manifestations of feminism. The argument made below is that the upsurge in the formation of women's political organizations that began in the latter half of the 1980s must be understood as an historically specific process.

One phenomenon that had a demonstration effect in Guatemala was the growth of women's political organizing to protest the human rights violations perpetrated by military regimes in the 1970s and early 1980s (Alvarez 1990; Jaquette 1991; Jelin 1990). For example, the mothers' groups that formed in Argentina, Chile, and El Salvador to fight for those who had disappeared in the dirty wars quickly developed an international reputation for their human rights work. The new awareness of women's potential political contribution was reinforced by other regional political developments. For example, in several important respects, the Guatemalan situation paralleled that of Nicaragua where an armed insurgency also struggled against a right-wing regime. As a result, the promotion of women's political support for the revolutionary struggle by the FSLN (Sandinista National Liberation Front) in Nicaragua through the Association of Women in the National Situation (AMPRONAC) (which in 1980–81 became the Association of Nicaraguan Women Luisa Amanda Espinoza, or AMNLAE) was observed carefully by revolutionary leaders in Guatemala. Over time, the widespread participation of Nicaraguan women in AMNLAE had a demonstration effect on the popular movement in Guatemala by illustrating the potential role to be played by women's political organizations in a revolutionary movement.[3]

The demonstration effect was further galvanized by the growing influence of feminism in Guatemala. Indeed, various dimensions of feminism – at the level of ideas, embodied institutionally and legally, and expressed in political movements – all served to reinforce the growing awareness of women's potential contribution to the popular struggle. This growing influence reflected several related developments through the 1970s and 1980s, including the growth of an international women's movement and the work of the United Nations during the UN Decade for Women. Both of these forces helped to promote a growing international awareness of the specificity and importance of women's problems. In the field of international development, one concrete political outcome was an emerging policy prioritization of "women in development" on the part of both nongovernmental development organizations and state donor agencies. This nascent interest came to be politically symbolized in the elaboration and codification of the UN Convention against All Forms of Discrimination against Women.[4]

Underlying the emergence of the international women's movement was the development of national and regional women's movements. In Latin America the spread of feminism was simultaneously evidenced and promoted through the series of Latin America and Caribbean Feminist Encounters (*Encuentros Feministas*) that began in Bogota in 1981 (Miller 1991, 235).[5] Importantly, an increasing number of Central American women participated in these encounters, particularly in the one held in 1986 in Mexico.[6] Their participation heightened the exposure of Central American women to the growing force of Latin American feminism and generated a developing gender perspective on the political problems and issues they faced. Two related outcomes stemming from this gender politicization were that Central American women began to perceive and act on the need to develop a feminist position specific to their regional realities and they began to undertake joint action initiatives to address issues and problems of common concern. For example, in August 1989 Central American women organized their first Central American Women's Encounter (*Encuentro Centroamericano de Mujeres*), in which all five countries were represented. The purpose was to review and assess the Esquipulas II accords from a women's perspective. The women decided to form the Permanent Assembly of Central American Women for Peace (Asamblea Permanente de Mujeres Centroamericanas Por la Paz). The establishment of this assembly prompted the formation of the Coordinator of Women's Groups of Guatemala (COAMUGUA) in 1989. Its purpose was to strive to create political space in Guatemala for women's specific demands and to coordinate the participation and representation of Guatemalan women in the regional assembly.

Central American women more generally continued to recognize and address the specificity of their regional issues in subsequent Central American Encounters, which were held in Honduras in August 1991 and in Nicaragua in March 1992. Furthermore, Central American women undertook responsibility for organizing and hosting the Sixth Latin American Feminist Encounter, which was held in El Salvador in November 1993.

It is useful at this point to consider who, more specifically, were the women in Guatemala who came to be influenced by this growing influence of feminism. Within the popular classes they were women who were situated to be exposed to broader political developments like the growing impact of feminism, above all women who were able to attend the politically progressive and intellectually oriented environment of the University of San Carlos, which has historically been a site of radical political opposition grounded intellectually in

Marxism. In the late 1970s and into the 1980s, however, some women within San Carlos also came to be influenced by broader international and regional dynamics of feminism.

The importance of feminism at the level of ideas and as a political movement slowly gained ground in the university milieu in a number of ways. Some Guatemalan women associated with the university participated in the regional Feminist Encounters. The dissemination of feminists ideas also occurred as both academic and popular Latin American feminist literature gained a growing audience. These influences were further reinforced by resource support made available by international agencies operating in Guatemala, such as UNIFEM (UN Development Fund for Women). Reflecting their own policy mandates to promote women in development, these organizations began to encourage popular awareness of gender issues and offer support in the development of gender-analysis skills.

Reflecting this developing interest in feminism, some women faculty members and students began to work collectively to develop an analysis that incorporated both class and gender and, stemming from this analysis, to promote awareness of women's issues. This process occurred particularly within the faculty of social work and the discipline of sociology, where women faculty and women students are concentrated. An immediate result was the formation of women's study circles and feminist collectives or working groups and the increasing effort of women to challenge the class-dominated ideology of the powerful university students' movement and the control of this movement by male students. In the longer term, however, the extremely important outcome has been the formation of a cadre of relatively highly educated women possessing an analysis of class and gender who are politicized around women's issues as manifested in the Guatemalan context, who have budding leadership skills that would enable them to form women's organizations, and who share the political conviction that such organizations are necessary to make the fight for women's issues a priority.

The impact of these developments on intellectual trends within the university hence had an important effect on the shape of the popular movement: it led to the political organizing of women around women's issues, which occurred in several ways. For example, a number of the politicized and skilled women students very frequently came to work for development-oriented Guatemalan NGOs in order to fulfil the practicum requirements for their university degrees. Through this work they gained practical experience in organizing and community development. They also frequently became frustrated with the lack of gender analysis informing this work and the discrimination they experienced personally in their work. Their dissatisfaction often led them to become involved in the formation of women's organizations in which they would be free to control both the philosophical and practical aspects of their work.

As well, these ideas were often well received by women political activists, especially those in the trade union movement who were receiving similar stimulation from another direction at the same time. The union federations in Guatemala with ties to international unions were experiencing the trickle-down effect of the impact of feminism and the women's movement at the international level.[7] Consequently, the promotion of women's leadership was slowly being encouraged both ideologically and financially in some of the locals by union internationals. The result of these reinforcing influences was the generation of another body of women leaders within the popular movement. These women have been very active in forming women's committees within the union federations and various affiliated and autonomous unions.

More generally, the political strategy pursued by the popular movement in the context of political liberalization served to create an environment conducive to the formation of popular women's political organizations. In its effort to mobilize in the wake of the repression of the early 1980s, the popular movement struggled to force a wider opening of the limited political space that had been created by holding a presidential election. By demanding respect for rights and freedoms, as well as the institutions to safeguard them, the popular movement additionally worked to create space for the political participation of civil society. The period of political liberalization thus served to focus the attention of the popular movement on the need to expand political participation in order to contest democratization.

An environment conducive to politicizing, mobilizing, and organizing efforts was subsequently created. It was in this environment, then, that a handful of women leaders emerged and formed women's organizations that would undertake the work necessary to transform the potential for a widespread politicization of women into concrete mobilizing and organizing initiatives. The leadership skills and acumen of these women enabled them to access the international financing increasingly available for women's development initiatives and use such resources to establish women's organizations.

GENERAL CHARACTERISTICS OF WOMEN'S ORGANIZATIONS

The actual processes of the formation of the women's organizations have varied quite significantly, lending to each a distinct organizational character. Nevertheless, the organizations have several features in common.

One common feature is the *emergent nature* of the organizations, which reflects the process of formation. All the women's organizations have formed over time: often a period of several years passed between the initial inception of an organization and its actual public establishment. Thus, although there are official dates of establishment, it is important to recognize that the formation of these organizations has generally been a slow and ongoing process, most often because of the time involved in searching for and obtaining funding for the organizational initiatives imagined by the women leaders. On this point it must be recognized that without exception the women's organizations are financially dependent on international funding, which was often crucial to the actual establishment of them. The degree of funding and support that the organizations have secured varies considerably, and this generates tensions and rivalry among the organizations. Often the reasons for the support of specific organizations have more to do with dynamics in the North, rather than realities in Guatemala.

For example, Tierra Viva, the one explicitly feminist organization in Guatemala, has garnered significant support from various feminist organizations in the United States because it reflects their own feminist principles, priorities, and identity. Tierra Viva is, however, criticized in Guatemala for its middle-class politics – that is, feminist agenda – and for being out of touch with the realities of the *pobladora* – the women from the poor, marginalized sectors of the country.

The funding received by CONAVIGUA is also a source of tension between the women's organizations. Since the 1980s were also a time of burgeoning Northern consciousness about indigenous peoples worldwide, the identity of CONAVIGUA is doubly appealing to funders, in that it articulates the issues both of "women" and of "first peoples." Not surprisingly, CONAVIGUA has received tremendous international support. In California the Marano County solidarity organization focuses its work specifically on CONAVIGUA and sends American women with needed skills and expertise to support the organization for four-month stints. CONAVIGUA was also the focus of a huge solidarity campaign by women's organizations in Norway. This campaign raised enough money to buy a house in Guatemala City for the offices of CONAVIGUA. Having secure office accommodation is unprecedented among the women's organizations, most of which struggle to meet the rental payments on inadequate office space. Visiting the offices of CONAVIGUA is indeed an object lesson on this issue: it is completely outfitted with the latest high-technology office equipment, including a fax machine, an extensive computer network, a paper shredder, and so on, most of which the CONAVIGUA women themselves do not know how to use or care to do so (they hire a *ladina* woman office manager).

It is also important to recognize that a publicly declared date of establishment and naming of an organization does not mean that the women's organizations are generally solid, dense, and firmly entrenched. The organizations are, indeed, still very much in a state of flux – or in a process of becoming – in that organizational identity is evolving. This situation is indicated, for example, by the frequency with which objectives, mandates, and so forth, are redefined. It is important to note that, again, this common fluidity reflects the relationship between the Guatemalan women's organizations and the system of international funding and international donor agencies. In fact the fluidity of the organizations is provoked by their precarious financial situation and their chronic need to seek and secure international funding. This chronic financial instability makes both staffing and programming decisions very much contingent on successfully obtaining international funding; such success is often determined by the ability of the women's organizations to perceive funding priorities and translate them into project proposals.

A chronological analysis of promotional pamphlets and some material of the organizations reveals sometimes subtle and sometimes dramatic changes in organizational identity. These changes are frequently driven by the perceived demands of international funding agencies in developing funding applications and proposals. The women's organizations strive to describe what they want to do in the current language of the North. Whether it be WID, WAD, or GAD (Women in Development, Women and Development, or Gender and Development), "the building of civil society," the "deepening of democracy," or something else, the women's organizations must package their own ideas about what they want in a fashion that appeals to Northern funders. This absolutely essential strategy is recognized by the women's organizations, since they generally maintain themselves through project funding, skimming off such funds the bare minimum necessary to maintain the operations of the organizations.

Another related feature of the women's organizations is that their formation has been "top-down," which reflects the central role played by highly politicized and conscientized women leaders in the formation process. As a consequence, the process of formation has not emerged from a grass-roots base, which has had implications for the general structure of the organizations, and, in turn, for many other aspects of their functioning. They are not built on a mass-membership base but are, rather, comprised of very small nuclei of fairly exceptional women – exceptional both in their relatively high level of education and their visible leadership role in a *machista* society. This small, elite structure affects the ongoing organizational development process, the nature and structure of decision making, and the relationship between the organizations and the broader population of women in the popular classes.

The ongoing organizing process within each organization is driven and directed by this small cadre of women who feel they have ownership of, and responsibility for, the organizations that they have essentially created. Their organizational visions are highly influenced by the more general understanding in the popular movement of the need to develop participatory ability in the *pueblo* and by their practical work experience in promoting such participation through the use of popular-education strategies. Reflecting the vision of the women leaders, these organizations are focused primarily on building organizing capacity in a larger group of women at an intermediate level: their effort is not immediately directed at mass mobilization, a goal that is assessed as too advanced, given both the relative strength of the organizations and the need to build participation slowly in a society gripped by the culture of fear. The goal, then, is rather to build the capacity of an intermediate stratum of women to organize other women at the community level. Thus the work of these organizations is focused on developing the participatory abilities of women: this strategy has involved, above all, promoting women's self-esteem, as a first step in the process of women's politicization. Building on the experience of the popular movement, the women's organizations use a popular education approach in their work. By offering educational workshops and skills-training to *pobladoras*, the women's organizations create a learning environment conducive to women's self-development and valorization of women's political participation.

The organizational development of the women's organizations, then, is not about building a membership base. It is rather about developing and promoting women's participatory capacity, with the longer-term goal of fomenting further, independent women's organizational initiatives, whether within the shantytown communities, the church, the union, or elsewhere. From this it can be seen that the work of the women's organizations in building the capacity of women to participate politically is part of the broad political project of the popular movement to strengthen civil society.

At times, however, this effort to promote women's self-development and participatory capacity takes on a dimension of clientalism.

This is an important issue that warrants some discussion. The power relations embedded in the women's organization are complex. On the one hand, because of the way the organizations originated within the popular movement, the nuclei of women leaders who formed the women's organizations have generally continued to direct and control the organizations. Here, as in broader Guatemalan society, the model of decision-making and authority is hierarchical. Strong leaders make decisions autonomously and issue directives that are followed. Decision-making is not democratic but, rather, reflects the ideas of the leaders. For example, within the all-important process of generating funding, bare lip-service is paid to the idea of consultation with or input from the women who participate in the work and activities of the organization.

On the other hand, the organizations seek to encourage self-valorization in women, with the goal of enabling the independent exercise of agency, decision making, and, ultimately, further political organizing initiatives by women. So, while the projects designed to achieve this goal are determined and elaborated in a hierarchical manner, the projects themselves aim to foster in women proficiency in an opposite process.

Another characteristic the women's organizations share is the political posture of "double militancy" of the leaders. This reflects the history of their relationship to the popular movement, which is a movement dedicated to class struggle. The women who are now leaders of women's organizations were very frequently first politicized through their involvement as youth in a sector of the popular movement. In Guatemala the popular movement is built from various "sectors" of civil society that represent, for instance, the labour unions, the student movement, churches, nongovernmental organizations, indigenous peoples' organizations, human rights organizations, and so on. While these sectors have their own interests, they also together work towards the common goal of a class transformation of society.

For most of the women leaders, their first politicization through involvement in a "sector" remains extremely important to them, as does a deeply engrained belief in the overarching class-politics agenda of the popular movement. Thus, while the leaders of the women's organizations are newly politicized personally around the issue of gender, they have tended to incorporate this into their ongoing activism, assuming in the process a politics of "double militancy." One significant consequence of this tendency towards women's "double militancy" is that the growth of an autonomous women's movement has been inhibited in Guatemala. Rather, the leaders of women's organizations have employed their understanding of gender to address the issues of the *poblodora* in an effort to contribute to the class struggle of the popular movement.

CONCLUSION

The growth of popular women's political organizations in the 1980s and 1990s was not in any way a necessary or predictable outcome of democratization. It must, rather, be explained through a historical and empirical form of analysis that strives to illuminate the interplay of economic, political, and social dynamics in Guatemala and the contradictions contained within them. In particular, the analysis presented above has focused on exploring the impact on women of such contradictory dynamics. I have argued that in Guatemala economic crisis spawned democratization, that this process had gendered repercussions, and that these repercussions were articulated in women's politicization and organizing through the influence of feminism and the political orientation of the popular movement.

NOTES

1 This paper is based on field research for my doctoral dissertation completed between April 1992 and August 1993. I would like to thank the Social Sciences and Humanities Research Council of Canada (SSHRCC) for its support of this research through a Doctoral Fellowship and the International Development Research Centre (IDRC) for its support through a Young Canadian Researcher's Award.

   This paper is concerned with popular women's organizations and does not attempt to consider professional middle-class women's organizations, such as associations of women journalists, and so forth. While the Grupo Femenino Pro Mejoramiento Familiar (GRUFEPROMEFAM, Feminine Group for the Betterment of the Family), a women's organization related to the labour movement, was founded in 1986, it was between 1988 and 1992 that organizing really took off. In 1988 three women's organizations were formed: Tierra Viva (Living Earth), COMFUITAG (Women's Committee of the Labor Federation of Food and Allied Workers/International Union of Food and Allied Workers' Associations of Guatemala), and CONAVIGUA (National Coordination of Guatemalan Widows). In 1989 Grupo Guatemalteco de Mujeres (Guatemalan Women's Group) officially formed after a year of preliminary work. In 1991, four women's organizations formed: CENTRACAP (Centre for Domestic Workers), Niña Madre (Child Mothers), the women's unit of the NGO IDESAC (Institute for the Socio-Economic Development of

Central America), and, after two years of preliminary work, Mujer y Vida (Women and Life). In 1992 another four women's organizations were established: Comisión Nacional de Mujeres (National Women's Commission), the Women's Committee of UNSITRAGUA (Trade Union Unity of Guatemalan Workers), Mujer de Esperanza (Women of Hope), and FAMDEGUA (Guatemalan Families of the Detained and Disappeared). In addition, the following four groups were also formed (no dates are available): the women's unit of the NGO FUNDESCO, Colectivo de Estudios Femenistas (Feminist Studies Collective), Comité de Mujeres de Primero de Mayo (Women's Committee of the First of May Labor Federation), and Superandonos Juntas (Overcoming Together).

2 While there has always been some participation of women in the politics of the popular movement in Guatemala, it has usually been within the structure of male-dominated organizations. For a brief discussion of women's organizations from 1950 to 1980, see García and Gomáriz (1989, 205, 208). As they discuss, the few predecessors of the women's organizations of the 1980s and 1990s were the Alianza Feminina Guatemalteca (Guatemalan Feminine Alliance), which formed between 1944 and 1954, and the Union de Mujeres Guatemaltecas (Union of Guatemalan Women), which formed in 1975.

3 Criquillon (1995, 209–37) discusses in detail the development of a women's movement in Nicaragua and its relationship to the FSLN from the late 1970s to the early 1990s. See also Seitz (1992, 162–74).

4 For a discussion of the significance of the UN Decade for Women for the general growth of feminism in Latin America, see Miller (1991). For a concise statement regarding the early general position adopted by the UN towards women, see United Nations Office of Public Information (1978, ch. 5). The UN Convention against All Forms of Discrimination against Women was signed on 18 December 1979. Guatemala ratified the convention on 29 June 1982. Significantly, this convention is widely used in the popular-education work of the women's organizations to justify and legitimize their demands for women's rights.

5 The Encounters have been held as follows: 1981, Bogota; 1983, Lima; 1985, Santos (Sao Paulo); 1987, Taxco, Mexico; 1990, Argentina; 1993, San Salvador. For a discussion of these encounters in relation to the growth of feminism in Latin America, see Miller (1991, esp. chap. 7).

6 Given the extremely limited resources of most women's organizations, the ability to travel overland to the encounter in Mexico was a very important factor in encouraging the participation of Central American women generally, and Guatemalan women specifically, since Guatemala shares a border with Mexico and transportation is relatively good.

7 FESTRAS-UITA (Federación Sindical de Trabajadores de la Alimentacion, Afines, Servicios y Similares-Unión Internacional de Trabajadores de la

Alimentación y Afines [Union Federation of Food, Allied, and Service Workers-International Union of Food and Allied Worker's Associations]) is only one example in Guatemala of a union federation with international linkages. As its name implies, it is a member of the International Union of Food and Allied Worker's Associations, with headquarters in Geneva. The history of FESTRAS-UITA is complex. COFUITAG (Unión Internacional de Trabajadores de la Alimentación y Afines-UITA-Guatemala [International Union of Food and Allied Workers-UITA-Guatemala]) was formed in June 1986 and evolved into FESTRAS-UITA in 1991.

12 Guatemalan Refugees and Returnees: Place and Maya Identity

CATHERINE NOLIN HANLON

This chapter provides an overview of the patterns of displacement that took place between the early 1980s, the time of the initial exodus of Maya refugees from Guatemala to Mexico, and May 1995. It also examines contemporary avenues of refugee resettlement, with particular emphasis on choice of resettlement location. The vast majority of Guatemalan refugees in Mexico were Maya Indians who fled their homeland during a brutal counterinsurgency war in the early 1980s. Initial questions that stimulated my research into this refugee situation centred around issues of place and identity. Where had refugees fled from? Which regions of Guatemala were most affected by the violence? Where did refugees settle after they reached Mexico? How did life in exile affect Maya identity? Were people living in conditions somewhat similar to those they had lived in in Guatemala, or did they feel far removed from home, when they might be only a few metres across the border? Was there a strong connection with the land they had fled? What drove the refugees to return to a land as violent as the one they had fled? And where had those who had returned chosen to resettle? Was it a site of their choice, or had they been "redirected" to a destination of the military's choice? Who had controlled the geography of return?

Elsewhere I have provided compilations of the vast range of Guatemalan refugee statistics on which much of this discussion is based (Nolin Hanlon 1995). Every statistic for each month varies from source to source. But I do not wish these particularities to deter readers from seeing the broader picture.[1] When taken together, the refugee statistics I have compiled convey general trends in movement and settlement that help us discern three complex, fluid scenarios discussed in the first part of this chapter: flight, exile, and return.

The scenarios discussed in the first part allow the issues of place and identity to be explored in the second part. The phenomena of flight, exile, and return highlight the intimate connection between Maya peoples and ancestral land or land they have transformed by labour. Because this bond is strong enough to pull Maya peoples home to often precarious resettlement conditions, the primacy of place in the construction and representation of Maya identity is explored. At every stage in the process of flight, exile, and return, expressions and representations of Maya identity illuminate the complex web of cultural continuity and change. I contend that the meaning of "being Maya" differs between individuals in different times and different places and that a metamorphosis of identity is evident in accordance with two factors: with the shifting of the sites of representation from rural Guatemala to exile abroad, and with the passage of time.

REFUGEE SCENARIOS

Flight Maya peoples in highland Guatemala were the overwhelming majority of those who were forcefully and brutally displaced from their homes and communities during the counterinsurgency sweeps of the late 1970s and early 1980s (see, for example, AGIR 1988). Their flight was unorganized, massive, and unprecedented. While indigenous Guatemalans fled to a number of countries, the primary purpose here is to discuss the situation of Mayas who fled to the southern Mexican state of Chiapas and settled there in United Nations (UN) refugee camps. Though camp refugees constituted a small proportion of the larger Maya refugee population, this group has been chosen as the focus of study because data are more readily available for them than for dispersed and officially "unrecognized" refugees.

The majority of refugees hailed principally from the Guatemalan departments of Huehuetenango, El Quiché, El Petén, and San Marcos in northwest Guatemala (COMAR 1985, 13). Geographically, Huehuetenango and El Quiché were dominated by *indígenas*, indigenous people who made up a clear majority of the population (approximately 90 to 99 percent in the rural areas). The extent and intensity of the use of force varied over time and space. The military coup of 1954 was followed by more than four decades of brutal repression, culminating in civil war and the forced migration of Maya peoples into Mexico. Key to understanding this violent conflict, which forcefully displaced well over 200,000 Guatemalans – mostly Maya – out of the country, is the fact that the Guatemalan state was never able to incorporate its indigenous population into an "imagined national community" (Stepputat 1994, 13; Crosby, this volume). The question of land ownership has always been tied to the displacement, exploitation, and massacre of Guatemala's indigenous peoples, events that are forever lodged in the collective memory of Maya peoples.

By 1980 the human rights situation within Guatemala was of considerable international concern, but much worse was to follow. Between 1980 and 1984 the Guatemalan army destroyed, by its own count, 440 villages, most of them Maya communities (Wright 1993b; Smith-Ayala 1991). The Guatemalan government's scorched-earth policy (or counterinsurgency activity, in their terminology) drove one million Guatemalans from their homes. The overwhelming evidence derived from early surveys of assisted refugees in Mexico (Americas Watch 1984; Aguayo 1984; Hagan 1987) and research conducted by Manz (1988a,b) and reported by the United Nations Research Institute for Social Development (UNRISD 1987) and the Washington Office on Latin America (WOLA 1989), as well as the contributors to a special issue of *Refuge* (1994), is that the place of origin of Maya refugees consistently corresponded to the highland regions of Guatemala where military operations increased in the early 1980s. The plight of these refugees, therefore, can be interpreted as a response to political, not economic, factors.

For the most part, Maya refugees fled from either their ancestral lands – land held within family circles, generation upon generation, high in the mountains of Huehuetenango and El Quiché – or from "frontier" areas they had colonized up to thirty years earlier. In order to appear to be dealing with the land distribution crisis of the 1960s and 1970s, the Guatemalan government promoted a number of colonization programmes that sought to resettle people in sparsely settled regions of the country, such as the Petén and the north of Huehuetenango, Alta Verapaz, and El Quiché.[2] In the 1960s the area known as the Ixcán, a lowland rainforest that extends from the Ixcán River to the Chixoy River, was perceived as suitable land for settlement (see map). The colonized areas, therefore, may be considered land transformed by labour – land gained during the grand colonization schemes of the 1960s and 1970s in lowland regions near the Mexican border. It was from ancestral land and land transformed by labour that survivors of the back-country massacres vanished across the border.

Settlements of the Ixcán region, 1993

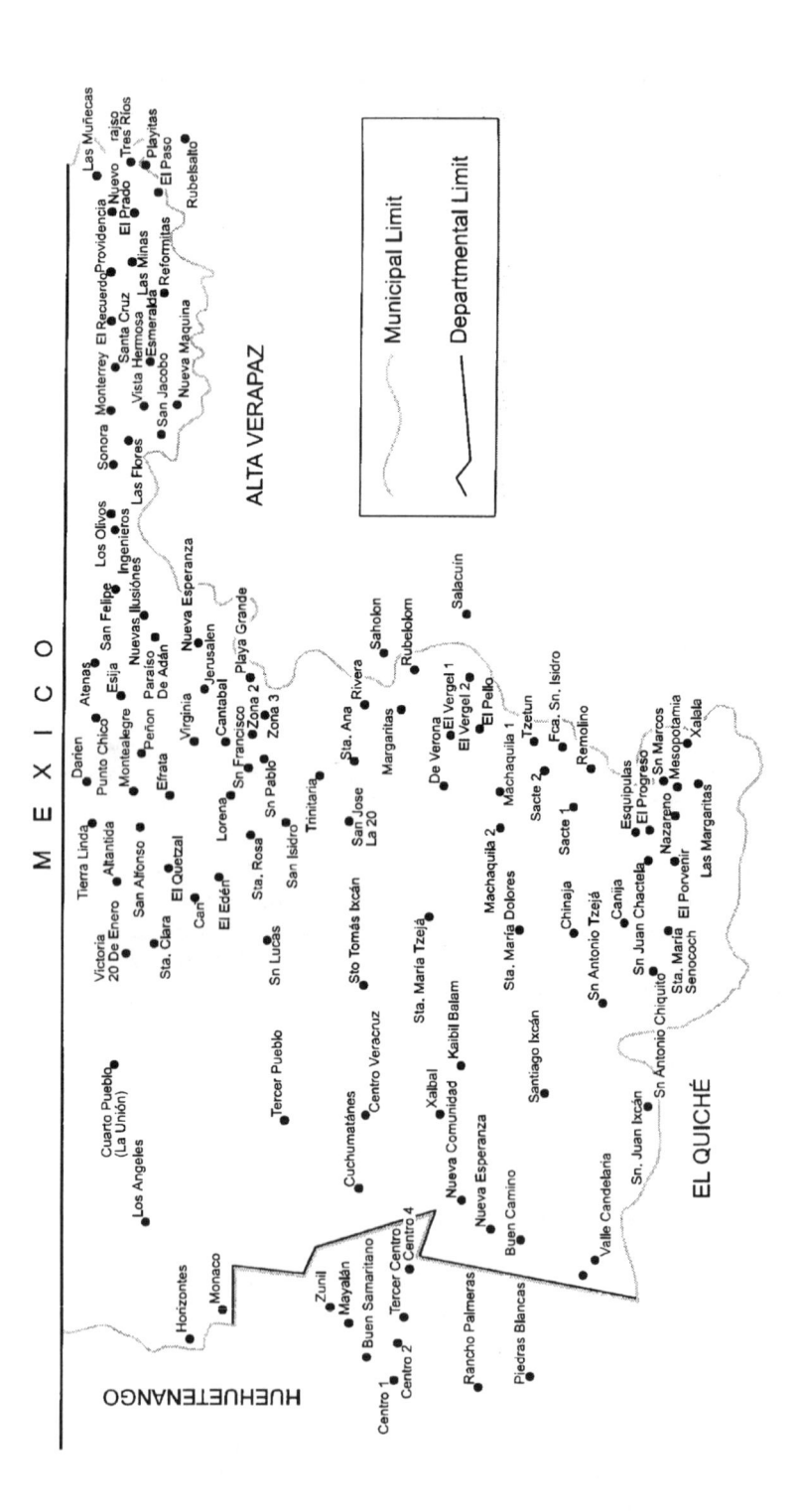

Source: COINDE (Consejo de Instituciones de Desarrollo), using data from PRODERE (Development Program for Displaced Pesons, Refugees, and Returnees in Central America).

The brutal counterinsurgency programme focussed its activities in the western highlands and adjacent lowland areas that were predominately Maya life spaces. No region was harder hit by the counterinsurgency activities in 1981 and 1982 than the Ixcán. Manz (1988a, 127) and others identify the Ixcán as the region from which most refugees fled. For many southern Mexico was the logical geographical and historically rooted solution to their need for asylum. Due to the nature of the forced migrations, the specifics of place of origin in Guatemala and place of exile in Mexico are, unfortunately, unavailable. Nevertheless, the geographical dimension of the decision to flee to Mexico should not be downplayed. For the Maya along the frontier edge of El Quiché and Huehuetenango, exile in Mexico was the logical geographical response to state terror.[3]

It is difficult, if not impossible, to reconstruct the exact route taken at an exact time by the refugees from Guatemala to their settlements in Mexico (Salvadó 1988, 18). The routes were usually complex, since many refugees did not take a direct path from their place of origin to their place of settlement in southern Mexico. Additionally, even when testimonials had been gathered by human rights organizations, names and specific places of origin were concealed for security purposes. This procedure was vital for the safety of the refugees and for family and community members who remained in Guatemala. Consequently, direct links could not always be made between place of origin and place of exile. Generally, though, there was a significant increase in the number of Guatemalan refugees in 1982 and 1983, with regular movement into Chiapas well into 1984. The Institute of International Relations and Peace Research (IRIPAZ 1992, 3) cites a 1984 report of the Mexican Commission for Aid to Refugees (COMAR) that disclosed that 85.4 percent of the refugees originated from the department of 10 ten percent from El Quiché, and 4.1 per cent from El Petén. For the most part, refugees arrived as individuals and families in southern Chiapas from departments in northwestern Guatemala. Likewise, survivors from the Ixcán and El Petén cooperatives and the department of Alta Verapaz found refuge as whole communities in camps in the Lacandón rainforest.

Exile Many Guatemalan Mayas who were violently displaced from their ancestral lands and lands transformed by labour seized the geographical option of exodus across the frontier to Mexico. Life in exile for the refugees in Mexico changed over time and space, as conditions varied from camp to camp and support for their plight was met with diverse reactions. In addition to surviving deprivation, malnutrition, mistreatment, and military attacks, the Maya refugees also formed a united group in order to negotiate the inhospitable political terrain of their return.

By 1983 it had become clear to all parties involved – refugees, international workers, and governmental agencies – that the problems of Guatemalans in refugee camps in Chiapas would not come to a rapid conclusion, as had been anticipated. Though the initial mass migration was over, small numbers of people were still spilling across the border. With individuals continuing to leave their land, safe return to the Guatemalan countryside could not be guaranteed. As a result, the refugees agreed to wait for conditions to improve before their return. COMAR and the United Nations High Commissioner for Refugees (UNHCR) suggested a plan that called for the establishment of refugee camps in the Mexican states of Campeche and Quintana Roo, located in the Yucatán peninsula (see map). These initiatives finally led the Mexican government to announce on 30 April 1984 that it intended to relocate the refugee populations living in the Lacandón rainforest camps. This meant another uprooting for the Guatemalan refugees – but this time with the protection of the Mexican government and the presence of the UNHCR and "with a sure and certain hope for the future" (COMAR 1985, 12).

Resistance to resettlement plans was vigorous and almost unanimous. Geographical and cultural concerns were central to the opposition to removal from the camps (Manz 1988a, 152). Relocation from the familiar landscape and environment of Chiapas to camps even further removed from their homelands was unacceptable for many. Refugees had often been crossing back into Guatemala to check their lands and harvest food for those in the camps. This would no longer be possible. As well, the refugees knew that they would be losing touch with their Mexican hosts, families, and friends when they were transferred hundreds of kilometres to a distant life in the Yucatán.

Between May and August 1984, approximately 12,500 Guatemalan refugees were resettled in transit centres in Hecelchacan, Campeche, and then moved to permanent settlements in Pich (later named Quetzal-Edzná) and Canasayab, a more sparsely populated zone in the state of Campeche (UNHCR 1984a, 12). These transfers, though protested by many refugees, continued throughout the year. By the end of 1984, 17,006 refugees had been relocated to the states of Campeche and Quintana Roo from twenty-six camps in Chiapas (COMAR 1985, 14).

In March 1984, as negotiations were underway for the removal of refugees from the border lands of Chiapas to the Yucatán, the Guatemalan government presented a plan for the repatriation of approximately 30,000 refugees to their place of origin (UNHCR 1984b, 37).

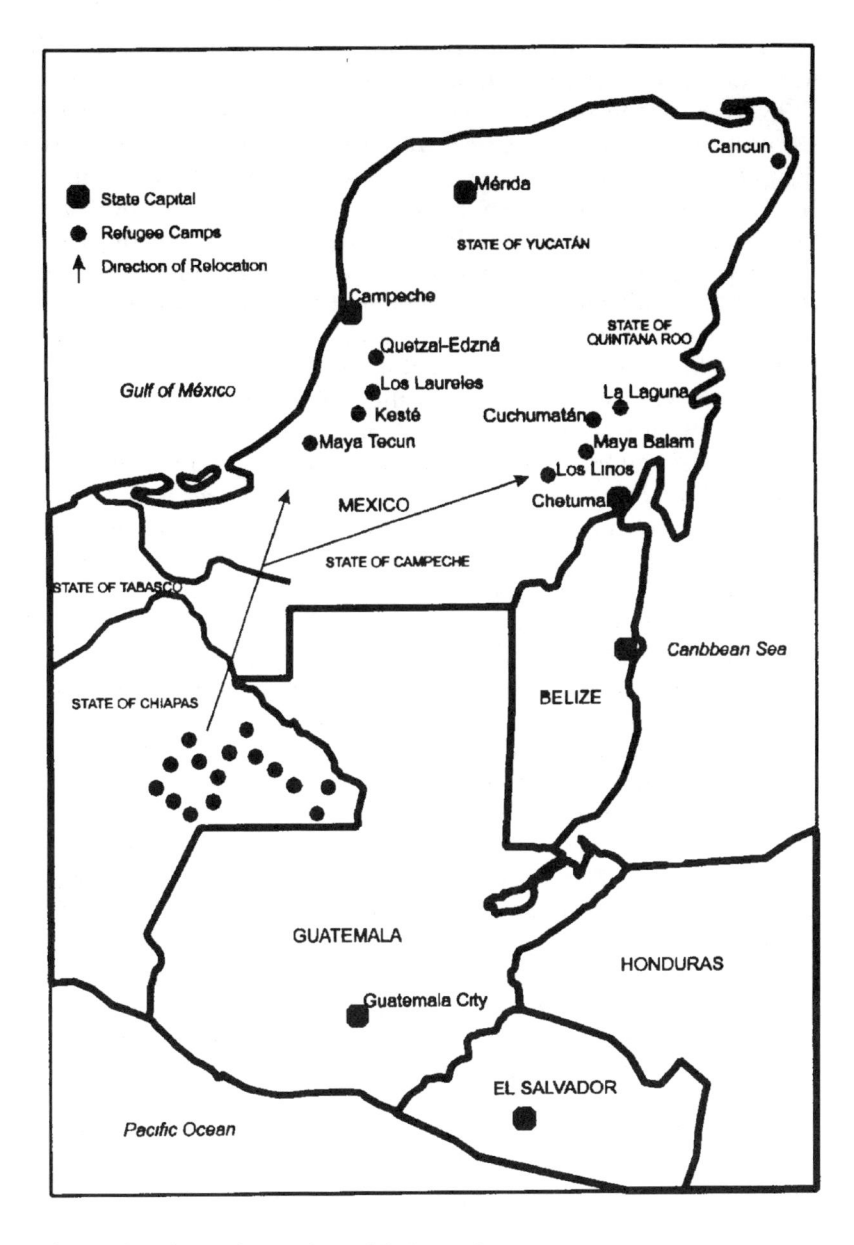

Refugee relocation to Campeche and Quintana Roo
Source: Adapted from UNHCR: GUATE PL/ 2304, 1993, and *Refugee Magazine* (UNHCR), March 1989, 23.

The Guatemalan government continued to promote the process of "voluntary repatriation" well into 1985. Taking office in January 1986, President Vinicio Cerezo, like former President General Ríos Montt, extended an invitation to refugees "to return to their native villages or any other place of their choice in Guatemala" (UNHCR 1986, 5). But UNHCR documents (1986) indicate that according to the Guatemalan media, *all* returnees had, in fact, been placed in "development centers" after crossing the border, rather than experiencing the anticipated freedom.[4] What of President Cerezo's invitation? This would not be the last time that the Guatemalan government would misrepresent its intentions and activities to the international community and the refugees themselves.

As will be discussed in the next section, the contradictory and highly questionable position of the Guatemalan government fueled the urgency with which refugees organized themselves in Mexico to negotiate their rights. By being or becoming politically savvy and politically active, the refugees made substantial progress in their bid to return home as a recognized civilian population ready to participate in the democratic process of building a new Guatemala. Still, obstacles continued to block the majority of refugee requests for collective and organized returns to areas of their choice.

Return For the vast majority of Maya refugees living in UN camps in southern Mexico, life in exile had always been considered temporary. Two strategies for return predominated within the camps: individual voluntary repatriation and negotiated collective return.

Research into the return of Guatemalan refugees makes a clear distinction between "repatriation" and "collective return" (Stepputat 1994; see also the introduction to *Refuge* 1994). Repatriation, it is argued, connotes something that is done *to* the refugees by their governments and international organizations, with minimal input from the refugees themselves. This process regularly played out as the simple transport of refugees to their place of origin. But the UNHCR favoured voluntary repatriation as the desired outcome of any refugee crisis and published widely on the concept.[5] As a solution to life in exile, voluntary repatriation was the chosen option for a small, though significant, number of Guatemalan refugees.

For those refugees who were not satisfied with the process of voluntary repatriation and who felt their exile was not only a personal struggle but a highly charged political struggle, something more self-directed was required. And so, in addition to the concept of repatriation (*la repatriación*), the refugees developed the concept of collective return (*el retorno*): a collective, voluntary, and organized return to

221 Place and Maya Identity

Guatemala. No longer would the process be strictly directed *at* the refugees; they were now intimately bound into the decision-making negotiations. With their participation in the negotiations, the refugees were actively seeking to return home under very different conditions from those they had fled. Just as the refugees had been transformed by their experience in exile, so too might the returnees effect a transformation of Guatemalan society.

In order for the refugees in Mexico to return to Guatemala under their own initiative, rather than solely under the direction of external agencies, they organized themselves in 1987 into the representative negotiating entities that have been discussed earlier in this volume, the Permanent Commissions of Guatemalan Refugees in Mexico (CCPP). It was not until October 1991, however, when the Guatemalan Refugee Agency (CEAR) signed a joint statement with the CCPP that the latter were acknowledged as an official negotiating body concerned with organizing gradual returns in 1992. In October 1992, after four years of negotiation and six years after President Cerezo's invitation to return, the Basic Accord for Repatriation was signed by the Guatemalan government and the CCPP. In the accord the refugees' six conditions for return were confirmed and validated, thus laying the foundation for all future returns to be "collective and organized" by the refugees themselves.

The organization of the CCPP in Mexico can be seen as a major turning point for the Maya community in exile. No longer were the communities to be pushed into unsafe and uncertain individual repatriation with little or no input into the decision about their return destination site. With the accords of 8 October 1992 signed between the CCPP and the Guatemalan government, the refugees would have direct influence on their future. Individual repatriations continued, though in fewer numbers than the repatriations of those who returned collectively through the CCPPs.

All the successful return groups chose their destination site – according to the Basic Accord of 8 October 1992, this choice is a right of the returnees. This accord did not mean that there was no longer interference from the military or government, however. When the lists of organized potential return groups were examined in relation to the list of successful return groups, various manipulations were evident. Why did so few return? Many groups wanting to return to their lands located within areas considered "conflict zones" or in areas where the military or large landowners did not want them to relocate faced indefinite negotiations. Obstacles such as denial of land credits and denial of access to former lands blatantly violated the agreements between the CCPP, CEAR, and the Guatemalan government.

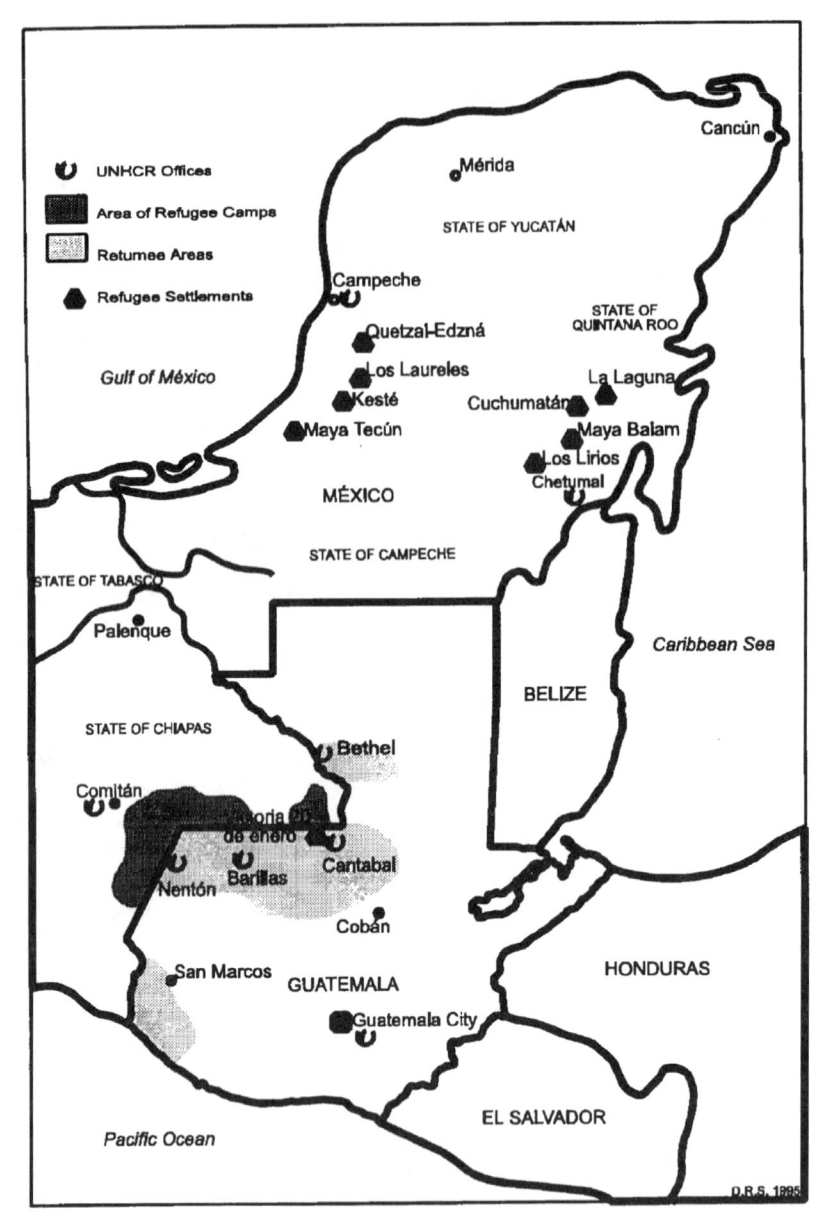

Location of refugee camps/settlements and returnee areas
Source: Adapted from UNHCR: GUATE PL/2304, 1993, and *Refugee Magazine* (UNHCR), March 1989, 23.

The map illustrates the general spatial distribution of Maya refugees in Mexico and returnees in Guatemala. A number of sources, from the UNHCR, CEAR, and COMAR to various non-governmental organizations (NGOs) and church-based groups have been consulted in order to piece together the fragmented puzzle of the geography of the collective returns of Maya refugees to Guatemala. It would appear that two-thirds of the returnees returned to their lands, either ancestral lands or lands transformed by labour, while the rest chose to go elsewhere.[6]

As requested by the UNHCR and COMAR, the refugees organized for a collective return to permanent sites. But the sites chosen by the refugees for settlement in Guatemala tended to be in politically volatile areas, which made safe return and settlement uncertain. These were, in fact, the very areas from which they had fled. And so the UNHCR, COMAR, and the Instancia Mediadora (IM) insisted that refugees wait in Mexico until lands in these regions were secured with titles, those living on the lands compensated and removed, and all paperwork finalized. This arrangement allowed the Guatemalan military and large landowners – who did not want to see the return of the very people they had driven from the country years before – to create obstacles to the return process. Consequently, the pace of the returns was slow due to the two main stumbling blocks of land negotiations and provision of credits for purchasing land.

Do patterns emerge with respect to the geography of the thirteen confirmed, organized, and collective returns? When the details of the migration from Mexico to Guatemala are examined, many relevant points can be made. To begin with, there were approximately 13,200 official returnees to Guatemala between January 1993 and May 1995. Two groups with a total of 3,773 individuals returned in 1993, approximately 4,700 individuals participated in five returns in 1994, and six groups composed of close to 4,800 people returned in the months between January and May 1995. What was the geographical variation of departures and destination sites? Generally, 60 percent of returnees originated from the camps of the Yucatán (40 percent from Quintana Roo; 20 percent from Campeche), while 40 percent of returnees departed from camps in Chiapas.

Table 4 illustrates the pull of the Ixcán cooperative lands for both collective returns and individual voluntary repatriations. A clear picture emerges of the Ixcán region as the most favoured return destination from camps in all three Mexican states. The highest absolute numbers departed from Quintana Roo (approximately 4,471), but the highest percentage left from Campeche (75 percent). Alta Verapaz was another important destination, receiving returnees from

Table 4
Destination of Collective Returns, 1993–95

Huehuetenango	Percentage of Total	Individuals
Ixcán	58	7,731
Alta Verapaz	23	3,080
El Petén	8	1,121
Huehuetenango	8	1,000
Escuintla	3	375

all three Mexican states. As with the returnees going to the Ixcán, many refugees from Alta Verapaz had fled to the large Lacandón rainforest camps that were eventually relocated to Campeche and Quintana Roo in 1984. It was logical that their return would take place from these different regions in Mexico.

The sole return to the department of El Petén originated from Campeche and Quintana Roo, since either the refugees had fled directly to Campeche from the Petén in the early 1980s or they had been part of the relocation programme of 1984. In contrast to this, the vast majority of participants in the only successful return to Huehuetenango were from Chiapas. These refugees had settled further west around Comalapa and therefore avoided relocation. In this way, a return to lands close to their own in Guatemala was manageable.

Incidents in the Ixcán and Alta Verapaz have brought into sharp focus the criticisms long voiced by the CCPP, NGOs, and international observers of the Guatemalan government's lack of political will to fulfil its obligations to the return process.[7] Problems of financing and access to land stalled attempts of organized groups wanting to return to their desired destinations. By controlling both the credit agencies and the land agencies, the Guatemalan government had the leverage to control refugee land purchases and therefore the return destination of the returnees. Pressured by the military and economic elites opposed to the return, the government closely controlled the geography of the returns. For example, the Inter-Church Committee on Human Rights in Latin America states in an unpublished draft report (ICCHRLA 1995, 35) that the Guatemalan Association of Agriculturalists (AGA) "has made an internal agreement to not sell any lands to refugees in the south of the country." This type of activity was reinforced by military opposition and carried out with military intimidation of returnees.

The military's grand plan in this epic struggle over land, it seemed, was to pit *campesino* against *campesino*, government-resettled Mayas against Maya returnees, and people who stayed during the violence against people who fled to Mexico. As events in the Zona Reyna revealed, this plan was highly effective. The support offered by most local populations for the returnees was subsequently jeopardized as Raul Martinéz and his organization threatened the entire return process in their bid to control the lands of the Zona Reyna.

PLACE AND MAYA IDENTITY

What happens to our sense of place, to our sense of identity when we are violently uprooted from a home we never imagined we would have to leave? Why, once forcefully displaced, do some of us hold on to a memory of a home we may never see again? What is it that causes some people to return home and others to stay away, even when certain guarantees for their safety are acknowledged? What bonds tie people to the land of their birth, a bond that lives on even in the darkest days of exile and draws them back despite unchanged and uncertain conditions? What connections between land and life, between people and place, may be discerned in the three stages of flight, exile, and return? These questions have fueled considerable discussion about the Guatemalan refugees in Mexico. Though a definitive answer to these questions may be elusive, the questions themselves provide a starting point in the exploration of place and Maya identity.

The Maya and their way of life have been under attack for almost five hundred years, and yet something continues to be understood as "Maya." Armed with such recognized categories of analysis as race, class, and gender, researchers are finding that there is much about Maya identity that complicates its description and representation. In addition to the internal negotiations of identity within Maya culture, external forces have ceaselessly confronted the Maya with their own constructions of "Indianness." In other words, Maya identity is both individually constructed and externally challenged, an outcome of self-affirmation and the affirmation of others.

Adding to the complexity, Mayas have migrated throughout the continent. Rural Guatemala is no longer a single, homogeneous domain of Maya culture, if indeed it ever was (Lovell 1995). Due to historical circumstances, a rich tapestry of Maya self-expression is evident from Central America and Mexico to the United States and Canada, where individuals and communities sustain a Maya identity. Consequently, Maya identity must be seen as a product of some combination of continuities and transformations, resistance and oppression, present conditions and historical realities, community belonging and migrant disorientation. Analyses of various expressions and representations of Maya identity illuminate the complex web of cultural continuity and change.

The central argument here is that the meaning of "being Maya" differs between individuals in different times and different places. There can be no definitive statement of its meaning, for it is individually constructed and externally contested in the broader society. Rather, the meaning and acknowledgment of this identity shifts on a continuum of acceptance – being Maya in one's home community must be different from being Maya in a site of refuge. I would suggest that in the writings of Maya individuals, whether they take the form of autobiography, testimonial, fiction, storytelling, or informant correspondence, a metamorphosis of identity is evident in relation to two factors: the shifting of the sites of representation from rural to urban Guatemala, to migration or exile abroad; and the passage of time.

Place and Identity Harvey (1993, 55) claims that "no social group can be truly unitary in the sense of having members who hold to singular identities." Therefore, any survey of individual and group identity will be best understood as the exploration of contested categories consisting of heterogeneously constructed subjects who internalize "otherness" by virtue of their relations to the world (Harvey 1993). Identity is always an incomplete process – a process rather than an outcome. Any individual's identity is a composite of forces such as gender, class, religion, and ethnicity (Edwards 1991; Buijs 1993; Mohanty 1991), all of which have the potential to divide and unite in ways that evolve over time and space.

Bondi (1993, 98) argues that "the emphasis on *where* – on position, on location – is allowing the question of identity to be thought of in different ways." Geography is often overlooked when considering the elements of identity, but for geographers the importance of place and location is of utmost concern. A focus on both place and identity allows attention to be given to "the crucible in which experiences are contested, a contest that is fundamentally cultural in an active sense" (Watts 1988, 32).

Various conceptual definitions of place have been brought forward in debates in cultural theory about identity, since the terminology of space, location, positionality, and place figures prominently in literature (cf. hooks 1981; Morrison 1987). It should be noted that theories of identity and location derived from cultural studies and literary studies often centre on the themes of cultural belonging, of home and exile, of urban experiences (cf. Carter, Donald, and Squires 1993), yet also suggest that place no longer matters, that the luxury of locating identities is no longer viable in our changing world. Clearly, for many peoples, especially those exiled or displaced from their homelands, places no longer provide *straightforward* support to their identities. But this should not indicate that places no longer provide *any* support for identity formation. Instead it can be argued that as people shift their places in the world, so too will the impact and influence of places on identities.

Place can be regarded as that segment of space that an individual or group inscribes with special meaning, value, and intentions (McKean Parmenter 1994). Throughout this section, I suggest that as the *sites* of representation of Maya identity shift, so too, will the meaning of Maya identity shift along the contoured ideological terrain of acceptance by both Mayas and non-Mayas. As the 1990s unfold, the Maya are rapidly becoming one of the most dispersed indigenous societies in the Americas. Exile or migration allows for numerous external forces that influence cultural change and reinforce certain essentials of the culture.

Identity acquires durability and permanence according to the stories we tell ourselves and others about our history. It is with this idea in mind that Harvey (1993, 63) develops the concept of "situated knowledge" – the construction of our identities and our world based on our specific location, our "place." Each Maya life can be read as an individual biography, created of heterogeneous experiences, factors, and particularities, and therefore, an influence of "situatedness" permeates each identity. Santiago Atitlán, Guatemala City, Chiapas, Indiantown – the representation of Maya identity, both at the individual and group level, must be penetrated by what is outside them. Clifford (1986) explains this phenomenon with his theory of "traveling cultures"; others invoke the varying "ethnoscape" of Maya identity (Hesse 1993). Rather than being a testament to a form of environmental determinism, these references to terminologies of place are a recognition of circumstance and its impact. This association between place or circumstance and identity is reinforced by the analysis of Hawkins (1984, 7) when he states: "Since many Indians speak Spanish and adopt *Ladino* material culture, the best description of an Indian is one who identifies himself or herself and is identified by others as being Indian."

Hawkins' definition, I would suggest, is critical to understanding what "being Maya" means. While his description of being Indian may sound ambiguous, in reality it remains far from arbitrary precisely because it must be recognized and affirmed by others, not simply self-asserted (Watanabe 1995, 14). It then follows that someone from Lake Atitlán or from Guatemala City can still express his or her Mayaness, for this definition clearly allows for the possibility that

Maya individuals and communities may change their circumstances (that is, their locations or place) yet still remain Maya.

The experience of exile must certainly be a considered dimension in the description of Maya identity as it is conveyed by Menchú (1984). This utilization of the memory of past experience in order to construct a textualized identity is not without problematic constraints, but it may also lead to a magnified and more forceful testimony of an identity that is in the process of growing and developing new layers. Most significantly, this powerful use of memory is evident in the writing of migrant Maya. Life-stories, whether oral or written, of individuals and communities in the process of migration or exile most often develop an association with the concept of "imaginary homelands" (Rushdie 1991) – the creation of a "remembered Guatemala" that all can reminisce about while away from home. As the community of Maya people becomes more differentiated, the challenge becomes one of continued redefinition of Mayaness to preserve what is essential (Farriss 1983) while allowing for the added dimension of migrant or refugee experience. Undoubtedly, a metamorphosis of Maya identity can be expected as members of the group shift from a place of "belonging" (that is, the home community in Guatemala) to a place of refuge or migration (Stepputat 1994).

Since Maya identity is so strongly connected with the community (most Mayas, when questioned about their identity, will often relate the answer to their place of birth, by saying, "I am San Migueleño," rather than "I am Mayan"), what will the future hold for the Maya outside Guatemala? Maya from many different communities, in addition to non-Maya individuals, are now sharing a "home." What will be the common ground for cultural survival? Can there be a collective Maya identity (Stepputat 1994) sustained through this transition? Perhaps Maya individuals in exile are creating an imagined community based on collective memory and a collectively constructed sense of Mayaness (Anderson 1983; Stepputat 1994) that fits itself at some point along the continuum of acceptance (see also Torres' contribution to this volume).

To address this concern, I now return to the findings outlined in the first part of this chapter regarding the repatriation and collective return processes of Guatemalan refugees from Mexico. This exploration will reflect the point that Hall makes about identity: "That every identity is placed, is positioned in a culture, a language, a history. Every statement comes from somewhere, from somebody in particular" (in Bottomley 1992, 132).

Maya Place and Identity Many researchers lean towards an historical view of ethnicity (Field 1994, 237) and away from an overemphasis on fixed ethnic markers. For too long, terms had been employed for the Maya that in no way corresponded with their self-identity and consciousness. When we listen to the voices of the Maya, to their myths and legends, to their worldviews, to their reflections on exile, a picture emerges that reveals clearly the strong association of traditional identity with a *municipio* (township) or a certain village (Tax 1963; Smith 1990; Wilson 1993; Watanabe 1984, 1995; Hanks 1990).

As the first ethnographer to fix the *municipio* as the proper site of Maya identity, Tax (1963) conveyed Maya worldviews as an articulation of Maya perceptions of themselves and their existence as a community. This same connection between individual and community is expressed by Smith (1990) when she emphasizes that Maya identity is rooted in place rather than in a general sense of "Indian." Wilson (1993) articulates this relationship with the term "anchored communities" to illuminate the cornerstone of community identities, which is location, the local geography. Watanabe's doctoral thesis, entitled "We Who Are Here" reinforces this theory (1984, 12): "The *municipio* represents a holistic community that is at once part of a larger regional and historical context as well as a meaningful social reality for the individuals living within it ... Indian ethnic identity in Guatemala relates directly to the nature and meaning of this community."

Hanks (1990) provides insight into the relationship between ethnic identity and community with a minutely detailed linguistic ethnography of Maya and their lived space. He explores the complex relationship the Maya have with the earth, revealing the Maya worldview that holds that, regardless of its configuration, every kind of space has a *yùumil* (lord, owner) to whom it belongs. This bond links space and place to sets of responsibilities among owners of different ranks and kinds. These spaces range from the cosmos, whose "lord" is God, to the smallest parcel of land transformed by labour (388), which one can call *tinwiknal* (my place). Hanks further argues that it is a matter of common sense for most adult Maya that they all have relatively fixed positions from which they move habitually, yet they remain anchored to them and return there.

I would argue that conceptualizations of Maya identity should go beyond simple sentiments about land and livelihood or romantic statements about land and life. The Maya word *naabl* (way of being) involves abiding attachment to the place first settled by local ancestors and the immediate "condition" of one's blood and its effects on how one behaves. Through this association with the blood, *naabl* "conventionally internalizes in each individual connectedness to ancestral place" (Watanabe 1984, 190). But economic circumstances have led to movement away from ancestral lands. One must therefore ask, How is a sense of Mayaness maintained in places of new settlement? And, related to this, are returnees from Mexico choosing to return to these newly settled lands or to their ancestral lands? Do they have a choice?

Agnew (1993, 269) maintains that "cultural worlds are grounded geographically in the experience of place." His statement is most forcefully illustrated by Maya connections with birthplace, ancestral lands, and new lands transformed by labour. Place of origin shapes Maya identity, yet with the shifting of place and time, identity does not fall apart. It is revitalized and reshaped in a metamorphosis of meaning. As Watanabe (1984) suggests, Maya distinctiveness appears not to depend so much on the retention of *what* is Indian as it does on precisely *who* is an Indian in the social sense of belonging to a community where other Indians live. Identity becomes not so much a question of outward as of inward expression.

If this concept is extended outside of the traditional boundaries of Maya culture in Guatemala to the population of exile in Mexico, then as long as something grounds exiles and refugees in a sense of Mayaness, location would not be a constraint. New layers of experience do not require the annihilation of the base or foundation of place-informed identity. Even though their place and homes can be denied *physically* by forced displacement, they still continue to resonate throughout the "imaginations" (Carter, Donald, and Squires 1993) of displaced Maya communities and inform the decision-making process for return. As the community in exile planned, organized, and demanded safe return to Guatemala, they were in the process of cultural restructuring (Wilson 1993). Maya identities and communities were not and could not be what they had been. Experiences away from home, a life of uncertainty, and refugee settlement with people from various communities and linguistic groups must have influenced expressions of Maya identity. It must always be remembered that culture is dynamic, not static; even if the violence of the early 1980s had not occurred, these communities would have inevitably changed on their own, albeit for very different reasons.

Conditions in the refugee camps of Chiapas, Campeche, and Quintana Roo created new communities of association. Over a decade, common exodus produced strong bonds through the development of return organization committees and representatives. One can extrapolate from the information provided in the first part of this chapter that the refugee associations, to some extent, provided "imagined communities" for a common return to Guatemala.

The initial Maya displacement was mainly into the Mexican state of Chiapas, which had a social and physical environment relatively similar to the regions where massive flight from Guatemala originated. On the other hand, the subsequent shift of thousands of refugees from UN camps in Chiapas to new settlements in Campeche and Quintana Roo forced the Maya into a setting markedly different from highland Guatemala. This second forced disconnection from a familiar landscape was too much for many: some refugees left the camps to blend in with surrounding communities, others vanished, and still others demanded immediate coordination of returns to Guatemala. Communiqués and reports from the CCPPs described the subjective experience in exile, stressing "outsidedness" from both Guatemalan and Mexican life and differentiating it from the "insidedness" of home.

Yi-Fu Tuan (1980, 3–8) distinguishes between the concepts of "rootedness" and a "sense of place"; the distinction relates nicely to the phenomena of exile and displacement. Mayas in exile repeatedly alluded to their sense of rootedness, of insidedness, of belonging while in Guatemala; they articulated, in relation to a homeland, their sense of place that is a "self-consciously constructed attachment to local environment ... which requires distance between self and place" while in Mexico. Guatemala became a lived or remembered or imagined place for those who survived the violence. These variations in perception created real problems as refugees returned to lands in Guatemala from which some people had never fled and that, in some cases, new people claimed as their own, to lands on which the army resettled displaced peoples, and to lands set aside as nationally protected parks (see Egan's chapter in this volume).

Refugees from "conflict zones" such as the Ixcán frequently were not allowed to return to their original communities but instead were routed to temporary or permanent camps or "model hamlets" (Earle 1991, 797). These settlements were planned, operated, and supervised by the army, with severe restrictions against movement, assembly, occupation, and sometimes even the practice of religion. In the early years of repatriation, the desire to leave Mexico seems to have been a stronger motivating factor than the desire to return to a specific location. Research by Manz (1988a) indicates that for those who *did* return to their homes, a general state of low-intensity violence permeated their existence, since often the violence tended to single out returnees.

As was suggested previously, displacement blurred the boundaries of the experiential/home community. Birthplace could no longer be seen as a straightforward pillar of identity for the Maya, though it was a most vital component of identity. But seasonal labour, migration, colonization schemes, and forced displacement influenced and reshaped this relationship with birthplace. Therefore, an understanding of Maya identity does not depend on whether refugees did or did not return to their ancestral lands and home communities. Of greater importance is the fact that they never ceased to hold on to the memory of land that is "part of their being," part of what makes them Maya. This land, then, would include newly settled lands in the Ixcán and Petén, most notably revealed in the case of those who left their ancestral land and homes in Huehuetenango for the Ixcán colonization programmes of the 1960s and 1970s. The desire to return to these lands illustrated the connection to land transformed by labour, to "their place" (Hanks 1990).

The return process is about the future that the Maya wish to create for themselves within the confines of a minority-ruled country. I would argue that the Maya have not returned in order to resurrect the communities they left behind. The return process is about their future, about the re-creation of Maya life with some combination of traditional life-ways and the dimensions of change that occurred with the refugee experience. The patterns of return illustrate a desire to move back to Guatemalan soil, either to ancestral lands or to lands transformed by labour, with some families choosing to follow members of their exile community to new locations. A new shift in strategy seemed to coincide with the 1994–95 instability in Chiapas and subsequent pressure from Mexican officials on the Guatemalan government to bring an end to this horrific chapter in their history. Subsequently, the CCPP undertook more forceful measures in order to ensure that all who wished to return to Guatemala could do so. At the same time the Guatemalan government set up obstacles at every turn to slow the process down. The CCPP felt they no longer had the luxury of negotiation for specific parcels of land for each group. Consequently, many groups suggested a return to temporary sites in Guatemala as a precaution against an irrevocable breakdown in negotiations for safe, collective return.

The fate of the return process was bound to the broader peace negotiations between the Guatemalan government and rebel forces. Smith (1990, 279) has suggested that the primary goal for the Maya appeared to be "the creation of a new and stronger general Maya identity" in order to provide a unified front to negotiate indigenous rights and claims to place in what the URNG (1994) statement on indigenous rights calls "the Guatemala of the Future ... a pluricultural, multilingual nation." The fragmentation and diversity of Maya culture that has seen them through the centuries is no longer a source of strength (Lovell 1992, 59–60). Cultural-survival strategies based on political, spatial, and linguistic differences among the Maya are now converging on some level. Though there is no refugee voice to speak for all in exile, coordination on certain issues may be essential to a successful future in negotiations of land claims and other indigenous rights. Cultural diversity must be recognized and maintained, but unity as a political voice seems a necessary compromise for comprehensive, wide-ranging, substantive change for indigenous peoples in Guatemala.

CONCLUSION

With the theoretical considerations of place and Maya identity at the forefront, this chapter has sought to examine the patterns of Maya displacement from Guatemala to Mexico and contemporary avenues of refugee resettlement. Though refugee statistics are often contradictory, a general picture has emerged of two-thirds of returnees having negotiated for a return either to their place of origin or to land they have transformed by labour. In light of the political situation of Guatemala in the years 1993 to 1995, return to these two categories of land often meant resettlement to zones of continued conflict. Through discussion of the intimate connection the Maya, including returning refugees, have with the local geography of their home community in addition to land on which they have worked, I have attempted to explore the bonds that tie people to a place, the bonds that draw the Maya back to Guatemala despite unchanged and uncertain conditions. For the returning refugees, identity as Mayas has been transformed by experiences in exile and many have returned collectively in order to continue that process of change.

NOTES

1 For insight into the problems with refugee statistics from the perspective of the UNHCR, see UNHCR (1993a, 145–7). For statistical problems specific to the Guatemalan refugee situation, see Hagan (1987).
2 The participants in these colonization schemes were principally indigenous peoples of the groups Mam (from Todos Santos, Huehuetenango), Q'anjob'al, K'iche', and Q'eqchi'. See AGIR (1988, 28).
3 Peoples of the areas more central to the highlands, such as southern Quiché, Sololá, Baja Verapaz, and Chimaltenango, did not have this "geographical" option of flight to a neighbouring country. Here many people were trapped and caught by the military or had to flee to the mountains, the coast, or the capital.
4 "Development centres" and "model villages" were created by the Guatemalan military as centres for re-education and de-programming of

the civilian population, which was viewed as the base of support for the guerrilla movement. In these centres, the civilian population was given the chance at a "new life" under the supervision of the military.

5 For an overview of the UNHCR position on the changing nature of voluntary repatriations (that is, repatriations to less than safe conditions, as in areas with continuing civil wars), see UNHCR (1993b, 103–20); see also UNHCR (1985, 5; 1988, 7).

6 The choice of those settling in new areas in Guatemala upon their return was influenced by such factors as the loss of everything and everyone to the violence of the 1980s and the desire to start over in a new area. Others felt more compelled to remain with the communities formed in exile.

7 The cautious satisfaction felt regarding the pace and conditions of the returns from September 1994 to March 1995 was shattered after the collective return to the Ixcán of 19 April 1995. Most transfers were carried out without incident, except for the returnees attempting resettlement in San Juan Ixcán and San Antonio Tzejá. Reports and urgent actions of human rights and solidarity groups such as NISGUA, NCOORD, ICCHRLA, and Amnesty International revealed the crisis situation in the Ixcán. The government's willingness to allow the Civil Defense Patrol (PAC) led by Raul Martínez and his organization, Association Pro-Legalization of Lands/Zona Reyna, to block the return of approximately fifty-eight returnee families – to intimidate them, to threaten their human rights, and to place in jeopardy the agreements of the return – was serious and disconcerting. Raul Martínez continued his intimidation of the returnees through June 1995 and took five international accompaniers hostage on 28 June 1995. This action threatened not only future returns to Zona Reyna but the entire return process itself. If an individual or group opposed to the return of refugees could manipulate the government with violent and illegal actions, then there was cause for serious concern about the safety and security offered by the Guatemalan government. See NISGUA (1995); NCOORD (1995b, c). The Alta Verapaz region was the site of the Xamán massacre of October 1995. The citizens of Xamán, a returned refugee community, were about to celebrate the first anniversary of their return to Guatemala when military personnel opened fire on the returnees.

PART FIVE

NGO Networks and Governmental Assistance

13 Theorizing Accompaniment

BARRY LEVITT

The agreement signed on 8 October 1992 between the government of Guatemala and the Permanent Commissions of Guatemalan Refugees in Mexico (CCPP) was a breakthrough in many ways. For the refugees in question, it signified a renewed hope that their exile, which for some has lasted for over a decade, might one day end. For other Guatemalans, particularly those involved in popular movements, it symbolized a crack in the armour of one of the world's most repressive states.

For the international community and the multitude of nongovernmental organizations (NGOs) around the world engaged in various forms of solidarity with the peoples of Guatemala, the agreement represented something truly novel as well. The security of refugees, in refuge and upon return to their countries of origin, had previously been considered largely the domain of the United Nations, specifically the UN High Commissioner for Refugees (UNHCR), and of the individual governments involved. In the case of Guatemalan refugees, a consortium of several foreign embassies and two international NGOs (Grupo Internacional de Apoyo al Retorno, or GRICAR) had also been involved in refugee issues. In the agreement of 8 October, however, something quite different was stipulated. In section 3, subsection A, the signatories agreed that "accompaniment during the return is understood to include the physical presence of the Human Rights Ombudsman [of Guatemala], the UNHCR and GRICAR, in keeping with each of their mandates, as well as of international governmental and non-governmental organizations, national and foreign religious or lay organizations, and renowned individuals, during the period of transfer, resettlement and reintegration of the returnees" (translated in *Special Document* of *Central America Report* 19, 1992). Thus, an officially sanctioned mandate was created for private individuals and NGOs to play a role in the refugee return process.

In response to this opening, a number of NGOs that had previously been involved in Guatemalan refugee issues launched programs to provide accompaniment for the return process. Foreign citizens, as long as they had letters of support from a foreign NGO or a Guatemalan NGO, could participate.[1]

What exactly is "accompaniment"? The term connotes something more substantive than "human rights observer." Although ostensibly neutral and noninterventionist, accompaniment is nonetheless a practice that is done for or with a *person* or a *group*; it is not just a process. In this case, for example, the United Nations would be observing the return, whereas accompaniers would be accompanying the *returnees*. The essential idea of accompaniment is that foreign citizens use their "power" as foreigners in an attempt to safeguard the security of individuals or groups at risk of harassment or persecution by their own state or an agent thereof. Based on the training materials of some accompaniment NGOs, the statement can be made that there is also an element of mediation and conflict de-escalation, as well as longer-term goals of education and transsocietal solidarity.

In the Guatemalan context, accompaniment NGOs were not limited to the physical returns themselves. As stated in the accords, the returnees had the right to accompaniment during their "resettlement," with no time limit stipulated. The CCPPs also requested accompaniers for land survey teams, work brigades, delegations, and any other prereturn ventures. Furthermore, not all accompaniment NGOs limited themselves to working under the rubric of the agreement of 8 October. Many organizations also worked with Communities of Population in Resistance (CPRs) and other internally displaced groups with whom the government had not signed any agreements. What is perhaps the original transnational accompaniment NGO, Peace Brigades International (PBI), had been accompanying an array of popular organizations in Guatemala and elsewhere for over a decade.

It is my belief that this practice of accompaniment is an important innovation in transnational and transsocietal relations, particularly in terms of the power afforded to individuals and nonstate actors. While there is nothing new about solidarity activists from the North going to the South, the institutional context in which accompaniers serve renders this form of accompaniment rather unique. By institutional context, I am referring to the organizational structures of the NGOs and their relationships with each other, with the government, and with the returnees.

There is a paucity of well-developed theoretical literature in the social sciences on NGOs in general and on this relatively new organizational form in particular. In this paper I will attempt to address this deficiency by evaluating some ideas and theories that relate to the practice of accompaniment. I will begin with an extremely cursory depiction of the accompaniment organizations that existed in 1995, their policies, and their practices. I will then evaluate three possible models for understanding these NGOs. One approach, drawn from the literature of neo-Marxist international relations theory, suggests that their practices have the potential to transform structures of power radically. Another approach, offering an assortment of concrete criticisms, portrays these NGOs in a very negative light, arguing that they are ineffectual at best and dangerous at worst. A third approach, based upon the relatively scarce literature on theories concerning development-promotion NGOs, represents a "middle ground" between the two. Accompaniment NGOs, in fact, may embody many of the same virtues and be subject to many of the same limitations that characterize their development-oriented counterparts. As such, I will suggest that this third approach is most appropriate for the conceptualization of accompaniment NGOs, although the more optimistic and pessimistic approaches do shed light on certain important issues.

Before engaging in this evaluation, I will pose one final question: why might it be important to locate the practice of accompaniment theoretically? I believe that it is in the long-term interests of these organizations and the Guatemalan groups with whom they work to think about, and question, the wider implications of their work. The day-to-day pragmatic problem-solving with which these NGOs are occupied can potentially limit their capacity to step back and examine themselves. While a theoretical discussion of accompaniment may be the luxury of academia, I nevertheless hope that it will be useful.

SUMMARY DESCRIPTION OF ACCOMPANIMENT ORGANIZATIONS

Although many of the international accompaniment organizations in Guatemala were fairly similar in their structure and policies, certain key differences did exist. In this section I will compare and contrast a number of the accompaniment organizations working in Guatemala in the mid-1990s. In doing so, my goal is not to depict these groups in great detail. Rather, I hope to impart a general sense of what accompaniers were doing and how they did it, in order to facilitate the theoretical discussion that follows. To this end, I will briefly describe several of these NGOs by broadly answering two sets of questions.

First, what is the degree of infrastructural sophistication and internal cohesion within the organization in question? Is it truly a coherent organization, or is it more of a placement agency for individuals? Is it tied to NGOs in the home country? Does it have a coordination mechanism, such as permanent staff or volunteers in the region, or a central liaison in the home country? Is the organization fairly consistent in its presence in Guatemala? What kind of training do accompaniers receive? How prepared are the accompaniers in terms of their fluency in Spanish and knowledge of the Guatemalan context? What is expected of individual accompaniers upon return to their home country?

Second, what kind of work do the accompaniers perform while in Guatemala? Does the organization attempt to adhere to principles of nonintervention, or are accompaniers expected to do more than observe, record, and communicate information, that is, to undertake "development work"? If accompaniers are allowed or expected to be more than observers, what guidelines or restrictions exist?

Peace Brigades International PBI was the oldest and most institutionally experienced accompaniment organization working in Guatemala. As a global NGO, it had projects in Sri Lanka, Colombia, and Haiti, as well as in First Nations communities in Canada. Accompaniers originated from many different countries, although almost all were from the North. The international coordinating body of the Central America project was located in Toronto.

In Guatemala, PBI responded to the accompaniment requests of many different popular organizations, including those representing refugees and displaced persons. As a rule, the PBI team responded to a request from returnees only in cases of dire need, however, since most other accompaniment NGOs worked specifically and exclusively with returnees and the internally displaced, whereas PBI covered a broader spectrum of organizations (for example, human rights agencies and labour unions).

Infrastructurally, PBI was highly sophisticated. It maintained a permanent residence in Guatemala City and a consistent corps of long-term accompaniers, most of whom stayed for twelve months or more. The accompaniment team conducted coordination and decision making on a nonhierarchical, consensus basis. Predeparture selection and training of accompaniers took place over a week-long, intensive session; for those selected, further preparation in the North and orientation in Guatemala was provided. PBI had a well-developed international communications network to transmit information regarding the political situation in general and, in cases of emergency, threats to accompaniers or to the Guatemalans they were accompanying. Although accompaniers were not formally representatives of NGOs or sponsoring communities in their home country, upon return to the North they were expected to do public education work or training assistance for PBI.

While working in Guatemala, accompaniers were expected to adhere strictly to PBI's noninterventionist policies. They were not to get involved in the groups they accompanied or engage in any significant work beyond observing, chronicling, and reporting events. Individual accompaniers generally did not spend more than two weeks on any one assignment; in fact, most assignments were for one day or less and took place in and around Guatemala City.

Project Accompaniment (PA) – Canada PA-Canada had a presence in the region that predated the initial return to the Ixcán in 1993; even before the signing of the accords, a number of the individuals who formed PA were working with the refugees in Mexico. It, too, had a very sophisticated infrastructure for coordination and communication, although one that was slightly more hierarchical than PBI's infrastructure. Two paid staff members funded by CUSO (formerly Canadian University Service Overseas) served as Southern coordinators, assisted by part-time and volunteer coordinators in Guatemala and, in the past, Mexico. Coordination at the national and regional levels also took place in Canada, although this structure was in a state of transition. Selection and training consisted of a six-day intensive session in Canada and, for those selected, a one-week orientation in Mexico and Guatemala.

PA responded only to requests from the CCPP and the Association of Dispersed Refugees of Guatemala (ARDIGUA), the signatories of government accords. Accompaniers were expected to follow a policy of nonintervention, although possible exceptions could be made, provided that accompaniers contributed to a project of the refugees or of another NGO, rather than initiating a new one. The minimum commitment from volunteers was six weeks, but the average stay was approximately three months.

PA had been active in the NGO community in Canada and was a member of the Central America Monitoring Group (CAMG), a consortium of NGOs. Furthermore, individual PA volunteers had to be linked to a support group in Canada, although there was a great deal of leeway about the types of organizations that could fulfil this requirement. Upon return, accompaniers were expected to perform educational and solidarity work with their supporting organization and for broader constituencies.

Proyecto Acompañamiento-Austria/HOLACOM-Netherlands Organizations with structures and policies fairly similar to PA included Proyecto Acompañamiento–Austria, and the Dutch Project for the Accompaniment of the Uprooted Population, or HOLACOM-Netherlands. One difference, in the case of PA-Austria, was that accompaniers were not required to be linked to an organization in Austria, nor were they required to do work upon return to their country. Nonetheless, many fulfilled the former requirement, and most fulfilled the latter. Also, PA-Austria was a very new organization in 1995, and as such had not stationed a long-term volunteer coordinator in Guatemala. HOLACOM and PA-Austria also differed significantly from PA-Canada in that they did work with CPRs and other internally displaced groups.

Guatemala Accompaniment Project (GAP)-USA GAP was a creation of the National Coordinating Office on Refugees and the Displaced of Guatemala (NCOORD), a Chicago-based NGO. As of the autumn of 1995, the program was in the planning phase. For comparative purposes, the salient feature of this program was that, unlike all other then operating accompaniment NGOs, GAP actually required its participants to do significant "development" work while in Guatemala. Participants were required to implement a project of their own design while living continuously in one community. This requirement held only for long-term accompaniers, that is, accompaniers staying for one year; GAP also allowed for medium-term accompaniment, that is, accompaniment of three to twelve months, which would not involve any technical work.

Cadena para un Retorno Acompañado (CAREA)-Germany The distinguishing features of CAREA were its relative lack of infrastructure and the fact that it did not require accompaniers' linkages to organizations in Germany. Its informal methods of ensuring organizational continuity appeared to function well, however. A permanent presence of six accompaniers was maintained, and incoming groups were given orientation by outgoing groups. Furthermore, although accompaniers did not represent NGOs in the home country, CAREA itself was very much integrated into the network of solidarity organizations in Germany and the European Community.

Foro Internacional–Denmark The Danish organization Foro Internacional (FI) was unique among accompaniment NGOs in that its participants were eligible for a government-run unemployment benefits program. As a result, FI usually maintained the single largest group of international accompaniers in Guatemala. FI had a relatively low level of infrastructure, however; there was no coordinating mechanism in Guatemala. Furthermore, since the Danish government and the organization's office in Denmark did not explicitly stipulate the nature of the work to be performed and had little power to enforce restrictions on accompaniers, it was difficult to ascertain the policies and practices of FI, since it lacked the consistency of other NGOs. Problems involving the knowledge and language skills of Danish accompaniers were reported in the past, although training and selection in Denmark, a two-day process, were later systematized and made somewhat more rigorous.

To understand the dynamics of accompaniment in Guatemala fully, one must also examine the mechanisms of coordination among these NGOs. Primarily, this interaction was taking the form of monthly meetings in Guatemala City. These forums were open to all accompaniers, including those who were unaffiliated, or *sueltos*. In general, each organization would have a few, not all, of its members present; however, coordinators of organizations, for those that had them, usually attended. At these meetings the NGOs attempted to ensure that the distribution of accompaniers in communities and on planned refugee delegations was adequate and that foreseeable requests would be satisfied. The meetings were also a forum to voice suggestions and complaints.

Each month a different theme was explored by those in attendance; meetings were co-chaired on a rotating basis by two or three people who were responsible for presenting the theme for discussion and also for inviting various members of Guatemalan NGOs and international organizations when their participation was deemed necessary. Other activities of the forum included several efforts to purchase paid advertising space in Guatemala City newspapers, to publicize the accompaniers' presence, and, especially, to put visible pressure on the government to remove obstacles to refugee returns and to comply with the accords that it had signed. Although the forum had no real power to coordinate or discipline accompaniers, tentative discussions were taking place among some NGOs concerning the centralization of certain aspects of decision-making power in a more formalized future version of these gatherings.

The other site of coordination was a post in Veracruz, Ixcán. The person who occupied this voluntary (and largely self-appointed) position was charged with ensuring an adequate and continuous accompaniers' presence in all the return communities in the Ixcán region. An informal rule was that each community would be assigned a minimum of two international accompaniers. Beyond keeping track of accompaniers' whereabouts and serving as a clearing house for communications, it was unclear what power this coordinator exercised. In one case, the Ixcán coordinator received a complaint about an accompanier from a community and disciplined her by forbidding her to continue working in the region.

Overall, then, there was a certain order to the practice of accompaniment, despite the disparate and sometimes anarchic nature of the organizations in question.

Now that I have depicted a representative sample of accompaniment NGOs and the manner in which they interacted, I will examine three possible theoretical approaches and tentatively evaluate their usefulness in understanding these organizations and their work.

THEORIZING ACCOMPANIMENT

I begin this section with a brief caveat. There are surely a multitude of different ways to conceptualize the practice of accompaniment. I have chosen to examine frameworks with which I am familiar, not necessarily ones that are most useful, although some of my ideas have emerged from discussions with accompaniers and representatives of Guatemalan refugee organizations. I do not believe that any one of the models that I propose takes account of all aspects of the phenomenon, nor do I think that any one framework can explain accompaniment in its entirety. The theoretical lens through which one views accompaniment is largely a matter of emphasis; it depends on which organizations and which aspects of accompaniment in practice one chooses to examine. Thus, my elaboration of three different models is done not to find the "right" one but instead to take an initial step towards understanding a relatively new organizational form and to illustrate its most salient features.

Accompaniment as Counterhegemonic Transnational Social Movement

According to the transnational social-movement approach, accompaniment NGOs are examples of institutions that, by their existence and practice, work to change the structures of international and intersocietal relations. This approach is strongly informed by the ideas and writings of Antonio Gramsci.

Among the significant insights that Gramsci brought to the social sciences was his conception of states and civil society. For Gramsci, the power of states stems not only from the formal organizations of "politics," such as parties, the military/police, bureaucracies, and the like. Rather, the direct domination exercised by these institutions is complemented by the coercive and indirect power of civil society. Via this state-society complex, dominant social forces can exercise hegemony over subordinate groups by presenting political projects as embodying "common-sense" principles and universal interests, rather than narrow and particular interests. As Gramsci perceived it, "The general notion of State includes elements which need to be referred back to the notion of civil society (in the sense that one might say that State = political society + civil society, in other words hegemony protected by the armour of coercion)" (1971, 263). Furthermore, Gramsci believed that in countries with strong political societies and weak civil societies (such as prerevolutionary Russia), the most appropriate strategy for social change was a "war of movement," in the style of a military campaign. He also recognized, however, that in a country with a relatively strong civil society (such as Italy in the era in which he lived), a different strategy was required, since significant power relations existed not only in political society but in civil society as well. In such countries, Gramsci called for a "war of position," in which power is gained by means of strategically situating one's forces within society. In a war of position, civil society becomes an important site of struggle.

Gramsci conceived his political philosophies in the context of the nation-state and wrote almost nothing that pertained directly to international relations. Later scholars, however, have employed the Gramscian conception of hegemony on a transnational scale. In particular, Robert Cox has been credited with initiating the neo-Gramscian approach to the global political economy. According to Cox, structures of power may be examined in light of three interrelated and mutually affective or interactive categories of forces or "potentials." These are material capabilities, ideas, and institutions. Simply defined, "material capabilities" refers to the ability to produce and destroy. Ideas, as a category of forces, include both shared or coincidental notions of social relations and, as well, collective images of social order that may differ among groups within a given historical context. Institutions, then, are conceived of as amalgams of ideas and material power, although institutions also take on their own historical significance (Cox 1986). Hegemony, as defined by Cox, refers to the relative "fit" or convergence among these three categories of forces.

How may we view the concepts of hegemony and counterhegemony at the global level? Using the neo-Gramscian approach, Stephen Gill has suggested that a new global hegemony is supplanting the structures of world order in which nation-states in general, and the United States in particular, were the dominant social forces. The dominant social forces in this emerging hegemonic world order are those of a "transnational capitalist class." Globalization and deregulation of finance and production in a "free-market" system are ideas that are held to be virtuous within this order. In Northern societies, Gill observes a "new constitutionalism" that reduces democratic control over the economy by shielding its key aspects from public accountability (1992). These changes are reflected in the institutions that have gained primacy in this new world order: international financial institutions such as the International Monetary Fund (IMF) and the World Bank, the General Agreement on Tariffs and Trade (GATT), the finance ministries of various states, and the like. In this emerging system, a counterhegemonic struggle would necessarily involve alternatives to neoliberalism, structural adjustment policies, globalization of production, and the universalization of market capitalism. Moreover, such a struggle would require the formation of linkages among similarly struggling groups, linkages that cross and transcend national borders.

In what ways might this model be appropriate to an analysis of accompaniment NGOs in Guatemala? Accompaniers, for the most part, are not acting merely as individuals but as representatives of concerned communities, grassroots organizations, or progressive social movements in their home countries. While they are accompanying, Northerners very concretely facilitate base-level communication across societies, and they can help mobilize resources (although usually nonmaterial resources) in their home countries to assist the returnees' organizations. Most accompaniers are required to engage in some form of educational or solidarity work upon return to the North. Furthermore, accompaniers are in Guatemala at the request of organizations that are themselves linked horizontally to other popular movements in Guatemala. While the refugee return emerges from a specific political context, the issue of displaced persons in general is extremely important among the country's popular movements. On its face, it appears that accompaniment may well be a concrete form of transnational counterhegemonic struggle. Although weak in material power, accompaniment NGOs have a great capacity in the realm of ideas and institutions: providing an alternate source of information and forging nonelite transnational links among societies.

These points notwithstanding, there are ample grounds for arguing that this paradigm is not, in fact, useful in understanding and theorizing accompaniment. Is the national-societal context of contemporary Guatemala a case of a strong civil society or a case of a strong state with a weak civil society? Without assigning any inherent virtues to civil society over the state, it is nonetheless unclear whether or not, in Gramscian terms, social change in Guatemala requires a war of movement or a war of position. One could argue that the role of accompaniers is to protect and support the strengthening of civil society in general and popular movements in particular. Accompaniment is mostly limited to organizations of returning refugees, however, which are perhaps not representative of popular movements in that the force of international institutions is also supporting the return and resettlement. In other words, accompaniers are only complementing a political project of the hegemonic institutions of world order, broadly defined.

This is not to suggest that the just resettlement of displaced Guatemalans is not a site of political struggle. In the national context of Guatemala, the organization of marginal groups is considered threatening to the existing structures of power and to the groups that benefit from and wield this power. The organization of returnees, in particular, is politically charged because it evokes Guatemala's lengthy and brutal counterinsurgency campaigns.

Yet in the global context, the returnees and the accompaniers are operating within a framework not only sanctioned but also enforced by hegemonic institutions of the Guatemalan state and the international system. Accompaniment NGOs, and indeed the returns themselves, have involved the integral participation of a multitude of UN agencies, the Guatemalan state apparatus, foreign governments, and foreign embassies.

Moreover, the issue of displaced persons in Guatemala is only peripherally tied to the emerging world order foreseen by Gill. While it is true, for example, that the returnees have expressed concern over the increased commercialization of agriculture, their main struggles thus far have pertained almost exclusively to land acquisition and physical return. As well, while Guatemalan society is surely affected by changes in world order, the nature of social control at the national and local levels is extremely complex and is not reducible to shifts in world order. While the trends noted by Gill may be visible in the Guatemalan context, they are not the major issues that frame the struggle of the returnees or of many other popular movements in Guatemala. These organizations are more concerned with justice and democratization at the national level; although many are engaged in struggles over land and production, few frame their struggles in ways that respond to contemporary transformations in world order. The most salient structures of power facing marginal groups in Guatemala predate the current trends by decades, perhaps centuries.

Even if one were to accept the dubious argument that the Guatemalan NGOs in question were struggling against global hegemonic forces, applying the neo-Gramscian approach in this case remains fraught with difficulties. First, unlike some transnational solidarity organizations, accompaniment NGOs do not link similarly located groups in Northern and Southern societies. Thus, the transnational alliance may not exist except in the vaguest terms. Furthermore, one could argue that accompaniment organizations do not forge transsocietal linkages at all. Lasting linkages may well be more rhetorical than concrete. An individual accompanier may raise some awareness of Guatemalan social issues in her/his community, but these organizational linkages may not endure beyond this increased awareness, with the exception of organizations already committed to solidarity with Guatemalans or refugees. In other words, after the slides have been shown and the lectures have been given, few lasting ties may have been created. Thus it would seem misplaced to equate the practices of accompaniment NGOs with the formation of a transnational, counterhegemonic alliance.

The "Cynical Views"

Another set of frameworks for thinking about these organizations includes a myriad of pragmatic critiques of accompaniment, in theory and in practice. In an attempt to address a large number of these critiques with expedience, I will loosely group them under three broad headings: accompaniment as misplaced goodwill, as paternalism/imperialism, and as adventure tourism.

Accompaniment as Misplaced Goodwill One stream of criticism holds that the support of accompaniment NGOs for one specific constituency, that is, refugees or displaced persons, is arbitrary at best and dangerous at worst. It is unlikely that returning refugees are the least empowered people in Guatemala; many have benefited, in a sense, from the experience of refuge, in terms of enhanced political awareness, better health care, and education.

Anthropologist David Stoll (1994) has taken this line of argument one step further. He has argued that in cases of conflict over land between returned refugees and other Guatemalan groups, accompaniers and the international community unfairly tip the balance in favour of the returnees. Furthermore, he has accused accompaniers of taking an overly simplistic stance, reducing each conflict to "the army versus the people," when historical realities can be far more complex, particularly in a country with a notoriously arcane land titling system, legacies of armed conflict, and large-scale internal migration.

While there are truths embedded in such arguments, I would suggest that it is this line of critique that is misplaced. The reasons for accompanying returnees, as opposed to other groups, are several. The most significant of these is the request of the refugees for international accompaniment, which is ensconced in the accords that they signed with the government. Some NGOs, notably PBI, do indeed accompany other popular organizations; however, most accompaniment NGOs felt, even at the peak of their volunteer recruitment, that they were spread too thinly just by covering communities of returnees. As more returns were realized, lack of resources could have become even more of a problem.

I share David Stoll's belief that Guatemalan communities that oppose certain resettlements cannot be dismissed as mere pawns of the military. Still, the perceived significance of the refugee returns for the peace and democratization processes has suggested that by supporting returnees, accompaniers have been benefiting a larger constituency than the returnees alone. Ultimately, the Guatemalan state may be held accountable for the political and social morass that has been largely its creation, although the conflict has manifested itself mainly among competing groups of peasants.

Lastly, accompaniment NGOs have become becoming increasingly alert to the effects of their presence on intrasocietal conflicts. For example, as of spring 1995, PBI was no longer providing accompaniment in the hotly contested land dispute at Los Cimientos, Chajul, since the presence of foreign accompaniers appeared to aggravate, rather than ameliorate, that complicated dispute.

Accompaniment as Paternalism/Imperialism Another line of argument holds that accompaniment, despite its noninterventionist rhetoric, is nonetheless a pretext for Northern interference in Guatemalan society and in the South in general. Very few accompaniers are from Southern countries, by heritage or residence. The power of accompaniers to function as they do stems largely from their foreign passports. Furthermore, accompaniment is a short-term, unsustainable solution to a long-term problem of human rights violations. As well, by their very presence, these foreigners are skewing political and social systems.

Again, while there is some value to these criticisms, I find them, on the whole, misplaced. In an ideal world, perhaps each society and every individual and group within it could be free from external contacts and constraints, although this seems highly improbable. Since the elite level of contemporary Guatemalan society has enjoyed a great deal of support, both active and structural, from external social forces, it would seem unfair to criticize accompaniers or the Guatemalan NGOs that requested their presence on the grounds that they interfere with an internal political process. Furthermore, while accompaniment is perhaps a short-term solution, its rationale is that it helps to carve out political space for organizations to function safely and effectively, both immediately and, one hopes, in the future.

Accompaniment as Adventure Tourism A third line of critique maintains that accompaniers are generally not motivated by solidarity; instead they are thrill seekers who have found a vehicle to engage in tourism with overtones of adventure and righteousness. Not all accompaniers act on behalf of NGOs; at any given time there are a number of *sueltos*, or unaffiliated accompaniers, at work. Usually they are backpacking tourists who hear about accompaniment projects and either show up in a community expecting to be welcomed or petition a Guatemalan NGO for a letter of support so that they can be "official." In the mid-1990s, summertime in Guatemala brought a glut of self-selected accompaniers.

While it is always difficult to discern individuals' personal motivations for political action, I would disagree with the above argument as a convincing condemnation of accompaniment as a practice. Most official, or affiliated, accompaniers have at least some training, and most organizations are fairly stringent regarding the personality, knowledge level, and language skills of prospective personnel. I would agree that the presence of unaffiliated accompaniers poses a problem for the practice as a whole. My sampling of official accompaniers and organizational personnel, however, suggested a great deal of antipathy towards *sueltos*. While many untrained accompaniers do their work very well, it is also the case that many official accompaniers have experienced problems with *sueltos*. It was the opinion of the majority of my informants that this problem could only be solved by the returnees' organizations. In fact, in times of perceived need, such as a large return, the returnees' organizations have not only allowed but also requested *sueltos*.

To sum up, it is apparent that accompaniment as a practice has been subjected to a wide range of criticism. Accompaniers have been alternately labelled as naïve do-gooders, paternalistic meddlers, or exploitative adventure tourists. While there are aspects of these arguments that merit attention, I find them, on the whole, unconvincing.

Accompaniment as Progressive Development Assistance

A third way of conceptualizing accompaniment NGOs is as a form, albeit novel, of North-South development assistance. Although the focus of activity is not the redistribution of material resources, accompaniment nonetheless fits the paradigm of aid.

According to the typology of NGOs proposed by David Korten in *Getting to the Twenty-First Century*, certain important changes have occurred within development organizations over the past fifty years. These changes are portrayed by Korten as "generations" of organizational style. While the emergence of each successive generation is chronologically ordered, it is clearly not the case that one organizational form is neatly superseded by another. These characteristics exist simultaneously, not only among NGOs in a specific time and place but also within individual organizations.

According to Korten, the *first generation* of NGOs emerged from the efforts of governments and civil societies to rebuild Europe after the Second World War. The NGOs of this era were concerned with providing food, medicine, and other supplies to those less fortunate, first in Europe, then in the South. Aid was conceived as short-term assistance targeted at individuals or families, as a way of alleviating neediness, or lack of sufficient material goods.

When it became apparent to some that this model of aid addresses symptoms rather than causes of poverty, a *second generation* of NGOs emerged. The focus of their strategy was long-term, and emphasized community development and self-help, with the NGO serving to mobilize material, technical, and human resources. Empowerment of aid recipients, rather than the creation of dependencies, was valued. By forming so-called partnerships with Southern organizations, Northern NGOs acted on the assumption that the potential for development, as defined by the North, was present everywhere, but needed to be mobilized by an external agent.

For many Northern NGOs that adopted this strategy, and for their Southern "partners," these principles seemed difficult to actualize, however. The constraints posed by policies and power structures at various levels reduced self-help efforts to thinly veiled assistance, with dependence on outside resources continuing to pose a problem. Thus, a *third generation* strategy emerged that focused on creating an institutional and policy setting that facilitates, rather than constrains, the struggles of Southern peoples. Nonetheless, in this third generation strategy, the impetus for development assistance has continued to come from the North. Programs are valued for their "participatory" quality, but the Southern NGOs are still confined to the role of aid recipients.

Korten further asserts that a *fourth generation* of NGOs is in its nascent stages. The strategy of these NGOs is based on a vision of social movements as the central actors in a development process that goes beyond simple economic growth to encompass issues such as human rights, gender, and the environment. Northern NGOs serve primarily as lobbyists and educators, providing services and solidarity to the peoples' movements that they support; NGOs do not "artificially" create such movements.

In Korten's idealized framework, accompaniment strongly resembles a fourth generation strategy. In the accompaniment mode, NGOs do provide assistance in the form of foreign observers, but they do not generally provide material aid. Furthermore, most accompaniment NGOs engage in activism and popular education in their home countries and require individual participants to contribute in this way. As for a conception of development assistance that involves more than economic growth, the very purpose of accompaniment is to reduce the potential for human rights abuse. While the goal of noninterventionism would ostensibly prevent accompaniers from actively working on issues such as gender or the environment unless requested to do so, these issue areas are being addressed by the Guatemalan organizations themselves, at least at the level of rhetoric, and often beyond.

Using a broader definition of accompaniment, another scholar has also contributed to defining and locating this organizational form. Laura Macdonald (1991) has posited four categories of relationships between Northern and Southern NGOs representing a spectrum of relative levels of interventionism. At the extreme end of this spectrum, Macdonald locates practices such as the use of U.S.-based NGOs by the U.S. Agency for International Development (USAID) to support its counterinsurgency strategies in Honduras, El Salvador, and Guatemala. Less blatantly interventionist, but with power nonetheless concentrated in the North, are relations of *paternalism*, in which Northern funding agencies or NGOs exercise a great deal of control over their Southern partner NGOs. In some cases, a paternalistic approach leads Northern organizations actually to create a local group in the South. A third type of NGO relationship, in Macdonald's typology, is that of *laissez-faire*. This term characterizes an arm's length relationship in which cash flows and progress reports are the only significant interactions between Northern and Southern organizations.

Macdonald also sees the emergence of a fourth type of relationship, which she calls *accompaniment*. "This relationship is based upon respect for control by the local agency and an attempt to provide non-monetary forms of support for the struggles of local groups and a deeper form of commitment to the processes of social change in the Third World. Forms of support may include training in key areas, brigades and exchanges, and human rights advocacy. Another important element is political advocacy work within the agency's own country in order to promote social change in their home countries and support for processes of change in the Third World" (1991, 70). This description, in my opinion, accurately depicts the specific practice of accompaniment that is the subject of this paper.

Other aspects of accompaniment in practice also suggest that it is appropriate to conceive of it as a form of development assistance. First, as mentioned earlier, at least one accompaniment NGO actually does provide concrete forms of development assistance. Second, several of the accompaniment organizations examined herein have strong linkages with more traditional types of development NGOs, both in their origins and in their current administration. Third, in matters of resources and legitimation, accompaniment and development NGOs have similar types of relationships with states and societies. They conduct fundraising campaigns and solicit the support of churches and state development agencies; many count on the backing of their country's embassies in the South. Thus, I would argue for a theory of accompaniment NGOs based on existing conceptualizations of other types of NGOs, particularly those involved in international development.

CONCLUSIONS

Having broadly depicted the organizational structures and policies of accompaniment NGOs in Guatemala, I suggested three possible frameworks for theorizing about them. The first, based on a neo-Gramscian approach to global social change, I found to be overly optimistic about the capacity of these NGOs to struggle for change at the transnational level. The second, based on an assortment of specific criticisms of accompaniment in theory and in practice, I found to be excessively cynical and pessimistic. The third approach, based on theories of development NGOs, appears to be the most appropriate of the three.

Like development NGOs, accompaniment organizations can adopt more or less interventionist strategies, choose policy approaches that accord more or less respect to the people whom they aspire to support, and put greater or lesser effort into the formation of transnational alliances for social change. Thus, I believe that much depends upon the organizations themselves, how conscious they are of the implications of their presence and their policies, and how much they can learn from each other and from the histories of other NGOS.

NOTES

1 My work is largely based on field experience in Guatemala in 1995 as a volunteer of Project Accompaniment, and on interviews conducted with one person each (they prefer to remain anonymous) from the UNHCR (2 June 1995) and the PBI (4 June 1995); with Jonathan Moller and Melanie Boesger of NCOORD (1 June 1995); Renata Sova, coordinator of Proyecto Acompañamiento-Austria (26 May 1995); the Coordinator of HOLACOM (25 May 1995); Guido Zemp, Ixcán Coordinator of COSAR-Switzerland; Ursula Baumgartner (also of COSAR); and Daniel Sicher of CAREA (29 April 1995).

14 Canadian Foreign Aid as Support for Human Rights and Democratization in Guatemala

VIVIANA PATRONI AND JIM GRONAU

Since the late 1980s, the principal stated goals of Canada's development assistance program in Guatemala have been to contribute to the peace process and to consolidate democracy. The Canadian International Development Agency (CIDA) chose to do this by dedicating the greater proportion of its funding to strengthening rural community development in indigenous areas. Thus, since 1990 most Canadian bilateral aid to the country has been delivered through CIDA's program in Support to Local Development Projects (PADEL), which is designed to enhance both the economic prospects of the communities it has supported and to assist in the consolidation of democracy.

Here, we first deal with the enormous challenges that peace building and democratization face in Guatemala, by briefly describing critical aspects of the country's recent political and socioeconomic evolution (in the first two sections). We then turn to the criteria upon which our evaluation of the PADEL program is based (the third section), including our understanding of the proper role for international aid in a country like Guatemala, which is characterized by the systematic and violent marginalization of broad sectors of the population. In the next sections those criteria are used to develop a description and evaluation of PADEL community development projects. In the conclusion we draw attention to contradictions between Canada's stated foreign-aid policy priorities in Guatemala and the concrete realities of PADEL.

In addition to secondary sources, this chapter is based on interviews in Canada and field research in Guatemala conducted under the sponsorship of Canada-Americas Policy Alternatives (CAPA), which has published a longer version of this work. The authors visited PADEL projects and conducted interviews with personnel from nongovernmental organizations (NGOs) and other groups in the summer of 1994. Important changes have occurred in the country since then. Nevertheless, an evaluation of the PADEL program up to that date is relevant for understanding how foreign assistance might contribute to promoting movement toward peace and democracy, social conditions that are essential to the return of refugees. The evaluation is also relevant for identifying future ways to assist poor communities that have suffered displacement and have had to endure a difficult process of reconstruction.

THE TORTURED PATH OF DEMOCRATIZATION

As the peace negotiations progressed, several accords encompassing human, economic, and social rights were reached. The agreements, however, generally fell short of responding to deeply felt popular demands for justice and an end to impunity. Meanwhile the United Nations, in its role of mediating and monitoring the accords, encountered obstruction by government officials and opposition from the military, particularly with respect to MINUGUA's mandate to investigate human rights abuses (Jonas 1996, 6). While UN verification played a positive role in signaling the international community's commitment to a peace settlement, its effects, as of mid-1996, were still limited: systematic human rights abuses and impunity continued to prevail (see Stephen Baranyi's report in this volume on UN involvement).

Although negotiations were expected to end the civil war by late 1996, the conditions that gave rise to the armed conflict had actually deteriorated. Politically, postwar Guatemala will be characterized by a complex set of old and new demands that must be answered if lasting peace is to be achieved. That these demands will be met is far from certain, given the weakness of civic and popular organizations and the intransigence of the privileged.

When, in 1986, the military handed formal power to an elected civilian president, Vinicio Arévalo Cerezo, the scorched-earth stage of the counterinsurgency strategy had been completed. The army's massive killing and depopulation of the countryside and its more selective violence in the cities had left the insurgent Guatemalan National Revolutionary Unity (URNG) considerably weakened. Most nonviolent groups that had advocated major reforms were nearly wiped out. The 1986 move to democracy was consequently limited to elections conducted in less than satisfactory conditions. Ultimately, the only real improvements Cerezo's administration was able to cite were a decline in the number of massacres and an increase in foreign aid.[1]

There was little improvement after the election of Cerezo's successor, Jorge Serrano Elías, in 1991. Social and economic conditions continued to deteriorate, while the human rights situation hardly improved. Real political power remained in the hands of the military, and Serrano's democratic credentials were even sparser than Cerezo's. Thus, when his May 1993 attempt to assume dictatorial powers failed and human rights ombudsman Ramiro de León Carpio assumed the presidency, optimism about positive change ran high.

During his tenure as ombudsman, de León Carpio had spoken out frequently and unhesitatingly against the Serrano government's human rights practices and especially against the army and its Civil Defense Patrols (PACs) (Kennedy Cuomo et al. 1993). It was not long, however, before de León Carpio caved in to military pressure. Optimism faded once again in the face of the army's continuing stranglehold on the country's political life and an increase in human rights violations.[2]

Still, Guatemala's volatile political process acquired new dimensions in 1994 that made it distinct from the experience of previous decades. Particularly relevant for our analysis were, first, the increasing participation of broad organized sectors of Guatemalan society in the peace process (see Fonseca's contribution to this volume); and second, the participation in the November 1995 general elections of a center-left coalition of several popular and indigenous organizations, the New Guatemalan Democratic Front (FDNG). While the FDNG won only six seats in Congress, these victories were important in a country where politics has been dominated by parties of the right and political dissent has consistently met with repression.

INEQUALITY AND UNDERDEVELOPMENT

Contemporary advocates of "trickle-down" economics insist that the best way to raise living standards is to increase economic growth rates. Guatemala's sustained economic growth during the 1960s and most of the 1970s proved to be no antidote to poverty and inequality (Feres and León 1990, 143). Indeed, the outstanding result of post-1950 export-oriented agricultural growth was increasingly concentrated land ownership: during the period when peace negotiations were getting underway, 2 percent of landowners controlled 65 percent of arable land (Barry 1992, 40). In contrast, 548,000 peasant families had holdings averaging only three acres. According to official estimates, 62 percent of Guatemalans lived in poverty – 57 percent in the urban areas and 86 in the countryside. Extreme poverty affected 34 percent of the population; in the rural areas, it reached 72 percent (Palencia 1994, 40).

The most recent phase of the popular uprising, dating from the late 1970s, and the brutal response it elicited worsened the living conditions of most Guatemalans. From the mid-1980s forward, the economic impact of social conflict was compounded by the neoliberal stabilization and restructuring measures adopted under pressure from international financial institutions (IFIS) and donor governments, including Canada: the burden of those policies fell on the backs of the Guatemalan poor. As a report commissioned by the United Nations Development Program (UNDP) noted about El Salvador's comparable situation, proponents of neoliberal restructuring have been unwilling to subordinate or alter their economic policy prescriptions concerning market development and the downsizing of the state to respond to the social reform requirements of building long-term peace (Boyce 1995, 2067).

Unless economic policy responded fully to the demands arising from the peace process, however, neither mechanism was likely to operate successfully. In other words, a constructive resolution of the violent political struggles that have characterized Guatemala's contemporary history will have to be based on a strategy to overcome the socioeconomic exclusion of the majority of people. Progress in that direction, in turn, is not conceivable unless institutions are built that effectively dispute the exclusionary nature of Guatemala's political system.

CRITERIA FOR EVALUATING CANADIAN AID TO GUATEMALA

Our premise is that attempts to build sustainable peace will not succeed without action to address directly the conditions described above. A corollary is that in Guatemala development assistance can contribute to the peace process only to the extent that it facilitates the organization of the politically and economically marginalized to satisfy their needs and aspirations.

If support for grassroots projects is the tool chosen to strengthen the political and economic position of the marginalized – which is the case of PADEL – then these community-based undertakings must be developed with two goals in mind.[3] One is the transformation of community projects into vehicles that enable the people involved to learn how to organize themselves during all stages of the project's conception, implementation, and evaluation. Foreign aid then provides ways to make community goals into a viable project through the provision of financial and technical resources.

Enhanced organizational capacity and confidence is only part of the answer, however. Support for community projects must also help in breaking down the political and economic isolation of many of Guatemala's community groups and organizations. One of the most negative results of political repression and its resulting culture of fear has been the atomization of grassroots initiatives. For this reason, the other objective of foreign aid for community-based development must be the creation of channels of communication and collaboration, first of all among the funded communities and then also among those communities and other local, regional, and national organizations. This kind of networking is pivotal for organizing the demands of marginalized sectors for new and reformed development patterns that permit progress toward long-lasting peace.

It follows from the above that Guatemala's NGOs and other intermediate organizations have a critical role to play. Several key functions have generally been ascribed to NGO intervention and participation in community-based development projects. NGOs can be very effective in enhancing communication among beneficiaries of different projects or community groups, and they can be optimal channels for the diffusion of new technology, helping to adapt it to the community's needs and to accelerate the process of learning. Equally important, NGOs and intermediate organizations can speed up the processes of breaking down the isolation of many communities and helping them to link up with other groups that face similar problems. This last function has important political implications, since the linkages created among small and otherwise isolated community groups can enhance their capacity to organize effectively.

This is not to say, however, that the relationships between NGOs and local communities are always unproblematic. Paternalism figures prominently among the capital sins of NGOs involved in development work. The only antidote against paternalistic reliance on external or ready-made solutions is the active participation of the community itself in all aspects of project conception, implementation, and evaluation. It goes without saying that this can be a slow process; moreover, very special circumstances are required for participation to be entirely meaningful and genuine (Macdonald 1995).

It is equally relevant to consider the different overall political approaches of various NGOs with respect to development and to their relations with local groups. There are a very large number of NGOs in Guatemala; estimates are as high as seven to eight hundred (Garst 1993, 83). Obviously, all these NGOs do not share the same commitments to social equity, grassroots participation, and political transformation. It is still possible, however, to identify without major difficulties those NGOs and coordinating bodies that have unambiguously supported the popular sectors in their search for a viable pattern of development and democratization based on respect for the full complement of social, economic, political, and cultural human rights.

THE SUPPORT TO LOCAL DEVELOPMENT PROJECTS PROGRAM (PADEL)

PADEL became effective in March 1990 through an assistance agreement signed by CIDA and SEGEPLAN, the Guatemalan government's development agency. The Canadian government stipulated that funds would not be disbursed through the Guatemalan government. Instead, both governments agreed to appoint SOCODEVI (Societé de Coopération pour le Développement International), a Canadian NGO, as the implementing agency. SOCODEVI had financed projects of its own in Guatemala since 1986, mostly in the cooperative movement.

PADEL's stated objective was to support small community-based projects by reinforcing communities' organizational and developmental capacities. Until the approval of a Democratic Development Fund (DDF) in 1994, Canada did not have any special program in Guatemala to finance human rights and democratization projects as such. Thus, PADEL also financed several initiatives not strictly related to productive activities. PADEL has supported four main types of projects:

1 Revenue-generating projects. These mostly rural projects were aimed to improve agricultural production and facilitate the marketing of agricultural products and the purchase of inputs; assistance was also provided for the establishment of small commercial enterprises and the production of handicrafts.
2 Training and technical assistance. This aspect of the program became increasingly important, particularly the training of community administrative personnel involved in the projects and of employees in organizations that provided technical consulting to community groups. Some groups also received training directly related to productive activities.

3 Economic and social infrastructure at the community level. This kind of support was aimed to help the general functioning of community projects. Assistance under this category included construction of community buildings, water-supply facilities, and so on. Projects related to public health, education, and environmental protection were also included in this category.
4 Initiatives related to human rights. This encompassed, primarily, the construction of a human rights library, financial support for a centre providing for street children's legal needs, and a public information campaign on human rights. This area of assistance, which later became part of the DDF mandate, will not be discussed here. (See table 5 below for a sectoral breakdown of projects.)

By March 1994, a total of 114 projects had been approved. In some cases PADEL supported more than one phase of a project. Beneficiaries – characterized by varying degrees of internal organizational coherence and capacity – included community groups, cooperatives, development committees, Guatemalan NGOs, and international NGOs.

OBSERVATIONS AND EVALUATION

Below, we will focus on the PADEL-supported "productive" projects that aimed to assist mostly indigenous communities by supporting their economic activities or by providing technical or managerial training related to those activities. We will also deal briefly with "municipal training" (included in table 6 under "others") because of the implications of such training for promoting democratization.[4] A large portion of PADEL financing was concentrated in areas where the majority of the population had suffered displacement in the early 1980s. Although the communities of internally displaced were in great need of assistance, they had attracted much less international attention than returning refugees (interview with Canadian Ambassador James Fox, head of political section José Herran-Lima, and CIDA officer Martha ter Kuile, Guatemala City, 27 June 1994.) Consequently, PADEL decided to focus its programming on widows, orphans, and the displaced (CIDA 1992, 2).

The discussion is organized with reference to PADEL's key choices regarding project implementation, that is, decisions concerning direct work with communities, limitation of funding to two years, control over goal definition and evaluation, interest charged on rotating funds, and attention given to market access.

Table 5
Distribution of CIDA-Financed Projects, by Sector, 31 March 1994

Sector	Amount Approved (Can$)	Percentage of total
Training	803,455	11.23
Public health	468,532	6.55
Environment	203,000	2.84
Agriculture	3,262,188	45.60
Construction	377,637	5.28
Community organizing	414,345	5.79
Commerce (crafts)	450,349	6.29
Services	258,061	3.61
Women	345,390	4.83
Human rights	571,950	7.99
Total	7,154,907	

Source: PADEL, Rapport Trimestriel, 31 March 1994.
Note: A total of 114 projects were approved. Percentages may not add up to 100 due to rounding.

Table 6
Distribution of CIDA-Financed Projects, by Type of Organization, 31 March 1994

Type of Organization	Amount Approved (Can$)	Percentage of total
Community groups	834,913	11.67
Cooperatives	2,606,922	36.44
Development cmt	895,747	12.52
Guatemalan NGOs	2,148,443	30.03
International NGOs	363,232	5.08
Others	350,650	4.90
Total	7,154,907	

Source: PADEL, Rapport Trimestriel, 31 March 1994.
Note: A total of 114 projects were approved. Percentages may not add up to 100 due to rounding. In addition, the amouns disbursed to the organizations listed sum to slightly more ($7,199,897) than the total amount shown in the original source as having been disbursed ($7,154,907).

Direct Work with Communities PADEL decided to work directly with communities, that is, to avoid funding projects through intermediary organizations. This decision did not mean that NGOs were excluded. In several cases they were direct beneficiaries of projects. Nevertheless, PADEL emphasized increasing community group autonomy vis-à-vis intermediate organizations. Thus, for instance, if an NGO was to be involved in a project by providing training, it was the community itself that contracted the NGO's services and established the terms of the relationship through a formal agreement.

According to PADEL officials, direct funding of community-based groups aimed to provide an alternative to the often paternalistic relationship established between intermediate organizations and the community groups they sought to assist (SOCODEVI n.d., 5–6). The decision was also based on the obviously sound idea that eliminating administrative intermediaries maximizes the funds available for the project. In addition, because Guatemalan NGOs, as community organizers, were systematically targeted by the army in its counterinsurgency campaigns, it was clear that association with them could carry some political risks.

While we recognize that all these arguments favour direct work with communities, we are convinced that PADEL's decision to avoid a closer working relationship with NGOs and intermediate organizations was misguided with reference to its goals of providing support for democratization and strengthening the peace process.

First, the decision was based on a simplistic understanding of the factors that sustain paternalism in community-based development projects. In Guatemala, as elsewhere in Latin America, the goodwill of outside private sources has become an increasingly critical variable in the survival of communities. This dependence is primarily the result of cutbacks to already deficient public services made by states in order to satisfy the strictures of neoliberal adjustment programs imposed by IFIs and donors like Canada (Vilas 1996b). Consequently, the fact that communities had the power to decide whether or not they would contract services from intermediate organizations did not necessarily mean that they escaped paternalism. It seems to us that the possibility of fostering nonpaternalistic relationships with organizations and institutions outside the community can acquire real meaning only when community groups have increased their collective capacity to influence state decision makers to enact policies that begin to deal with outrageously deficient public services and widespread poverty.

Second, we need to question whether this decision acted as an obstacle to the formulation of demands at a broader regional level. Collaboration with NGOs familiar with the larger national scene could have broadened the perspectives of small and isolated communities. Such communities often concentrate almost exclusively on their particular economic circumstances and lack the resources to develop an analysis that would allow them to make sense of the broader regional economic and political frameworks within which their project must function (interview with Edgar Vasquez of the Consejo de Instituciones de Desarrollo (COINDE), Guatemala City, 7 July 1994).

Thus the representative of one Guatemalan NGO stated that "little projects," by themselves, cannot be effective instruments of change; instead, support is needed for the organizing that is the sine qua non for achieving basic changes in the country's socioeconomic structures. Another NGO spokesperson explained that his group's prime objective was to gain land rights for landless peasants, a goal that the NGO saw as thoroughly political, absolutely essential to dealing with rural poverty, and achievable only through unity (interviews with NGO members of the Coordinadora de ONGs del Occidente, Quetzaltenango, Guatemala, 15 July 1994).

Despite its desire to contribute to peace and democratization processes in Guatemala, PADEL's approach to community development therefore failed to contribute significantly to the achievement of those objectives. A more open attitude toward joint work with recognized, progressive Guatemalan NGOs could have prevented some of these major shortcomings. At the same time, more PADEL funding for intermediary organizations would have provided NGOs with some protective legitimacy, so fundamental to their growth and development in the context of continued human rights abuses.

Limitation of Funding To prevent communities from becoming dependent on an externally sponsored program, project funding was not expected to extend beyond a two-year period. While this limitation might have been an incentive for communities to learn to rely on their own resources, this PADEL decision entailed other important consequences for the projects' workings.

First, PADEL would only choose projects that were likely to have a rapid and visible short-term impact in a community. Positive short-term impacts may not be sustainable, however, without the development of mechanisms for a longer process of involvement in, and support for, community attempts to solve urgent economic and social problems.

Second, the most serious shortcoming of the two-year limit was the stress it placed on communities because of the expectation that they would undergo often dramatic changes in a short period of time. This was particularly the case among community groups with rudimentary levels of organization. The stress was compounded by the fact that communities were expected to plan productive activities with reference to new economic criteria with which they were not necessarily familiar.

Third, although some relationships were to be maintained between PADEL and the recipient communities after projects were completed, they were not sufficient to provide access to the resources that communities needed to continue with their new productive activities successfully.

Control over Goal Definition and Evaluation Guatemalans familiar with PADEL projects raised fundamental questions concerning the program's goal setting and evaluation procedures. Two key concerns were voiced: there was a divorce between ambitious project goals and the actual economic constraints that communities faced, and there were potentially negative effects on recipient communities from such overly ambitious goals on recipient communities. As we have noted, significant change was expected during the period of project implementation. This, of course, need not have been a major problem in itself, but when the program was inflexible, serious negative consequences for the community followed.

For instance, when recipients do not clearly understand a project's goals and methods, the danger arises that they might accept the conditions for financing simply in response to the need to obtain funding. The definition and redefinition of project objectives may simply become adjustment to rules established by an external actor rather than a learning process for a community. There was evidence to suggest that this had happened with some PADEL projects.

Similar problems emerged from evaluation mechanisms, with particularly serious consequences for communities that failed to reach preestablished targets. On some occasions, when evaluations were negative, PADEL withheld funds, a measure that produced major frictions within the beneficiary group. For some community members, such punitive measures simply represented another instance of control by outside forces. The overall impact in these cases was the creation of divisions among project participants; no nonhierarchical instrument was offered to refine objectives with the full participation and understanding of project members. These flaws in the methodology used to determine the parameters within which the projects had to advance also reflected PADEL's only partial understanding of the history, culture, and problems of beneficiary communities.[5]

Interest Charged on Rotating Funds Canadian funding of small community projects had two major components. One was a grant to provide technical training to the community; the other was a grant to create a fund for the provision of credit. PADEL considered it extremely important that the interest charged on loans corresponded to the actual rate of interest a commercial loan would bear. The reason behind this decision was intended to familiarize beneficiary communities both with the workings of financial markets and with the calculation of alternative costs involved in the planning of production.

Clearly, the availability of Canadian funds implied a net gain for all groups, since very few of them could have access to bank loans, and many had had no alternative to borrowing from local money lenders, who charged extremely high interest rates. The fact that the loans had to be repaid with real interest rates of more than 10 percent per year, however, meant that only commercially oriented projects could qualify for credit. Whatever activity a group financed through the loan had to produce sufficient profit to cover the costs incurred by borrowing. This requirement turned out to be extremely difficult for communities barely at subsistence levels or without stable access to markets. If what was sought was to familiarize project participants with the process of economic decision making, then the same objective could have been achieved even with lower interest rates. Other development NGOs in Guatemala, for instance, charged very low real interest rates of approximately 2 to 3 percent per year. PADEL's approach bespeaks a lack of understanding of feasible short-term economic goals for marginalized communities barely emerging from the displacement, violence, and trauma of the civil war.

Attention Given to Market Access In the case of agricultural produce, the most important impediment to profitability was the small size of the parcels worked by the peasants. Most of their land was dedicated to the cultivation of corn, the single most important component of the peasant family's diet. Because the market price of corn was low, projects sought to diversify production in order to increase the communities' economic potential. Problems emerged from very high levels of market uncertainty (including sharp price fluctuations) and the highly disadvantaged position of peasant producers within existing market structures.

This difficulty was certainly not restricted to PADEL: it was the core of the dilemma faced by most rural development projects and most small peasant producers everywhere in Guatemala and, indeed, in Central America and beyond. Nevertheless, PADEL did not attempt to assist communities in finding and developing alternative markets and institutional arrangements for independent small producers. A probably more worrying concern was that PADEL did not appear to have a clear analysis of the potential dangers involved in production for export markets.[6]

Several NGOs interviewed for the study pointed out that, beyond the elaboration of appropriate institutional arrangements that might permit peasant communities to profit from production for external markets, the articulation of domestic markets remains a critical issue for Guatemala. They argued that foreign aid could play a critical role in key areas such as reduction of transportation costs, support to develop quality-control systems, and technical aid to create basic marketing infrastructure.[7]

With regard to the municipal projects funded by PADEL, it should be noted that when Guatemala's government decentralizes its public sector – another aspect of neoliberal adjustment – municipal governments will become increasingly important in the lives of small towns and rural communities. Thus PADEL-supported projects to train the staff of some small municipalities certainly responded to an important need.

The first phase of these training projects, which began in February 1992, encompassed a total of six municipalities in the department of Huehuetenango, one of the places most severely affected by the counterinsurgency campaigns of the early 1980s. In July 1992 the project was extended to another twelve municipalities because extra funding became available through changes in the exchange rate (interview at Fundacion Centroamericana de Desarrollo, or FUNCEDE, Guatemala City, 1 July 1994). So in 1994, eighteen municipalities were participating in a second phase.

The projects involved the training of municipal staff (with about six staff, on average, per municipality) through workshops on various local government jobs (treasurer, secretary, and so on). The goal was to increase the technical capacity of the municipalities to program and administer long-term development projects.

Any evaluation of the municipal training projects must consider two points: first, the gap the project was intended to fill and, second, the projects' viability given the political realities in Guatemala. Regarding the first point, the projects attempted to provide municipal governments with some concrete administrative tools in order to better fulfil their role in the advancement of programs to overcome the most serious constraints deriving from isolation and lack of resources. Very importantly, grassroots organizations were given an opportunity to have input into the elaboration of these development programs. Consequently, in the course of these projects, some grassroots organizations were able to articulate effectively their own programs for municipal action and successfully contest local elections (interview at Servicios Jurídicos y Sociales, or SERJUS, Guatemala City, 12 July 1994). PADEL support proved critical in allowing them to develop concrete plans of action for their regions.

Despite the serious material limitations that PADEL could not surmount by itself, work at this level of government was of great importance. Several persons from various Guatemalan NGOs agreed that the training of municipal staff was important and may become even more important if the national government's commitment to provide municipalities with greater fiscal resources becomes a reality.

The achievements of the project's first stage, however, were not entirely positive when it came to consolidating local committees at the grassroots level (FUNCEDE n.d., 3). This was not surprising in a country where political and military control at the local level was one of the traditional underpinnings of the system of domination. Precisely for this reason, increased community participation in the definition of local government tasks is where most observers agreed that the emphasis should be placed.

This leads us to the second evaluation point – the program's political feasibility. Since the program was bound to create conflicts with traditional powerholders, the projects' longer-term viability has depended on the overall direction of political change. Increasing democratic participation in local government may induce dramatic shifts in the configuration of power. In concrete terms, increasing grassroots participation has meant challenging corruption and the power of traditional parties, as well as of the military.[8]

CONCLUSIONS

In an attempted evaluation of Canada's contribution to the tortuous peace and democratization processes in Guatemala, several other issues need exploration.

First of all, there is a tension between the actual delivery of CIDA assistance programs and the notion of human rights presented in the agency's documents, where these rights are identified as an indivisible set of political, social, cultural, and economic rights (CIDA 1994, 26). The Canadian assistance program in Guatemala has not succeeded in integrating all these aspects. Problems do not arise just from the problematic viability of small community projects as development alternatives and as contributions to peace and democracy. The key issue relates to macroeconomic policy: is progress toward peace, democracy, and respect for human rights congruent with the process of neoliberal economic restructuring that Guatemala is undergoing and that Canada endorses?

In fact, the neoliberal consensus has come under question as a consequence of the precarious growth outcomes of more than a decade of adjustment and the rapidly increasing rates of poverty and social inequality. Thus, a recent World Bank report on Latin America identified the failure to reduce poverty and to lessen inequality as major obstacles to sustaining its favoured adjustment policies (Burki and Edwards 1995, 15). The authors of the report cited the need for increased growth rates and for more effective social programs to attend to the needs of the poorest sectors and also called for action in areas such as land reform, other forms of asset redistribution, and redevelopment of the state's capacity to take a leading role in the modernization process (17–18). Such action is particularly necessary in a country like Guatemala where extreme inequalities were at the root of the conflicts that ravaged the country over the past decades.[9]

Second, and related to the above, if Canada (and other donors) intend to contribute, as PADEL did, to a more fluid participation of assisted communities in national and international markets, then the extremely unequal distribution of the assets and wealth of Guatemala's economic actors has to be squarely faced. Clearly the problem for peasant communities and marginalized populations was not about integration to capitalist markets but instead about substantial improvements in the conditions under which they entered into market relations (Hewitt de Alcantara 1993).

Markets tend to generate economic concentration and inequality. The problem that CIDA and other donors have not addressed is what kind of assistance to grassroots economic initiatives might guarantee market participation on a more equitable basis. In our opinion, progress in that direction implies assistance programs that increase the capacity of project beneficiaries to influence the economic policy-making process.

Third, and also related to the previous points, is the question of local NGO involvement. Major defects in the conception and implementation of PADEL projects could have been avoided through the more active participation of NGOs. The areas where cooperation was needed that were identified by Guatemalan NGOs, in this respect, were the elaboration of terms of reference for assistance programs and a more active liaison between implementing agencies and community-based groups. Guatemalan NGOs could also have provided critical expertise in connecting community initiatives with broader development alternatives that linked various communities.

Finally, if Canada and other countries seek to have an impact on democratization and peace building, then strengthening organization within civil society is essential. Thus the arm's-length relation of PADEL with local NGOs was counterproductive. There is no denying that NGO participation in development in Guatemala carries major political risks, but those risks must be assumed if the goal is progress toward democratization and long-term peace. Today such a choice can be made in the context of the May 1996 accord on socioeconomic and agrarian issues signed by the government and the URNG. The accord recognized the need to increase popular participation in the planning of development, to improve the access of the poor to social services and employment, to enlarge the fiscal and technical capabilities of the state, and to improve the distribution of land. The implementation of these reforms, however, will require the recognition of popular demands embodied in political forces as yet not formally represented in Congress. Creating the conditions for such a political outcome will be the real test of the final peace agreement.

NOTES

1 During the presidency of Efrain Ríos Montt (March 1982–August 1983), 10,566 Guatemalans were killed in massacres and 2,796 in extrajudicial executions. During the Cerezo administration (January 1986–December 1990), the number killed in massacres was far lower, but extrajudicial executions numbered 2,025 (Comisión de Derechos Humanos de Guatemala 1991, 34–5, 89–91).

2 The human rights situation accounts for part of the decline in optimism. During the first half of 1993, when Serrano was in power, there were 70 extrajudicial executions, 229 assassinations, and 5 cases of torture. In the second half of the year, with de León as president, there were 178 extrajudicial executions, 198 assassinations, and 13 cases of torture (Oficina de Derechos Humanos del Arzobispado de Guatemala 1994, 297, 299, and 307).

3 The criteria are based on those elaborated by Kowalchuck and North (1994) and in the works included in Miller (1992).

4 In addition to municipal training, the "others" category includes initiatives in the area of human rights and projects not related directly to productive activities.

5 For a detailed analysis of the acute economic, social, and political hardships facing internally and externally displaced communities upon their

return, see *Donde esta el futuro? Procesos de reintegracion en comunidades de retornados* (AVANCSO 1992).

6   The risks connected to export markets were emphasized by several of the NGOs interviewed for the evaluation. A number of analysts have presented overviews of the drawbacks of nontraditional agro-export promotion, e.g., Thrupp (1994) and Green (1995), esp. 130–53.
7   For an analysis of the importance of articulating regional and domestic markets as a part of a strategy to improve social conditions and promote peace, see the study on Peru prepared by Rosemary Thorp for the Inter-American Development Bank (IDB 1995).
8   Rigoberta Menchú, the K'iche' Maya woman who won the Nobel Peace Prize in 1992, signals the importance local politics (Menchú 1996).
9   The report does not question neoliberal adjustment policies as such. Its recommendations are directed toward making those policies politically sustainable over the long run.

15 Concluding Reflections: Refugee Return, National Transformation, and Neoliberal Restructuring

LIISA L. NORTH AND
ALAN B. SIMMONS

In this concluding chapter we, as editors of the volume and coordinators of the workshops that brought the authors together for the exchange of ideas, provide some reflections on the principal conclusions that can be derived from this body of work. The chapter is organized into three sections. We begin with a review of general conclusions on the nature and context of Guatemalan refugee return and the sociopolitical forces affecting national transformation, by which, it bears reiteration, we mean movement toward greater democracy, respect for human rights, and social justice. This review is followed by an examination of specific findings on the impact of the refugee return. We conclude with some comments on likely future developments and issues that have both theoretical and practical policy implications. Although our reflections focus on Guatemala and the contributions of the works included in this volume, we also occasionally point out contrasts and similarities with parallel processes in other Central American countries and draw on some recent publications – especially Clark Taylor's detailed study of a return community (1998) – that provide additional confirmation for the basic arguments developed in this volume.

The evidence in the volume does not permit a simple resolution of our underlying doubts concerning the evolving balance between regressive and progressive forces in Guatemala. However, it does permit us to examine these forces in greater detail and to identify how they shaped the refugee return and its transformative potential. In the following, we first draw attention to conclusions that find wide support in relatively coherent evidence from the volume considered as a whole.

THE NATURE AND CONTEXT OF THE RETURN

Our specific research objective was to analyze Guatemalan refugee return as a limited but strategic vantage point for better understanding the prospects for peace, democracy, and development in Guatemala. We also hoped that a clearer understanding of the Guatemalan case might be useful in efforts to address similar issues in other countries that are struggling to overcome the legacies of antidemocratic political systems and civil war. This said, the broad thrust of evidence in the book allows us to identify the distinctive features of the Guatemalan case vis-à-vis that country's Central American neighbours.

Unique Features of the Guatemalan Refugee Return

The volume has drawn attention to the unusual return process in which the Guatemalan refugees were directly involved in negotiating the conditions of their collective and self-led resettlement. This return emerged from a distinctive political-cultural context, civil war, and refugee-flight pattern. The refugees came overwhelmingly from the indigenous Maya regions that suffered the massacres of 1981–83. They also shared strong historical and cultural ties to their specific places of origin. Speaking little or no Spanish, most settled close to Guatemala in neighbouring countries and did not possess the information, skills, or inclination (to begin with at least) for integrating into the urban centres of their host countries. Many retained their desire to return home even after many years of exile, as Torres' and Nolin Hanlon's contributions (chapters 9 and 12) relate.

In the camps in Mexico the refugees began to develop contacts and skills for initiating political discussions with the government of Guatemala. Although the government (with the military) established its own repatriation program, the refugees involved in promoting a self-organized collective return did not participate in it. Rather, they held off going back until after they had successfully negotiated an accord, signed in 1992, that covered the conditions for their return. These conditions included access to land, security guarantees, the right to international accompaniment, and a waiver of the obligation to serve in the militarized Civil Self-Defense Patrols (PACs) to which all rural men were subject (see Levitt, chapter 13, on international accompaniment).

The 1992 accord was a remarkable achievement in light of the historic exclusion of the Maya from effective citizenship and the fact that from the "army's perspective they had been 'infected' by contact with the guerrillas, human rights training, and by successful experience in organizing [in Mexico]. They could not be counted on to fit the army's control system" (Taylor 1998, 3). Indeed, the return negotiations and the accord – like other conflict resolution processes in Central America in the 1990s – would not have been possible without strong backing from international actors, the United Nations in particular. Among many other initiatives, the international community legitimized indigenous struggles by conferring the 1992 Nobel Peace Prize on Maya activist Rigoberta Menchú: she had documented the pervasive racism of Guatemalan society and the terrors of military repression in her autobiography.

The Guatemalan refugee exodus and return reveal significant contrasts and parallels with another Central American case, El Salvador. In large part, the refugee flight from El Salvador in the 1980s also involved rural people. Unlike the Guatemalans, however, they were people who had been integrated or assimilated into the national Spanish-speaking culture and, as a result, were able to insert themselves quite quickly into international urban as well as rural labour markets in Mexico and in those regions of the United States where previous immigration from Cuba, Puerto Rico, Mexico, and other Latin American and Caribbean nations had established large Spanish-speaking communities. Salvadoran refugees dispersed more widely and were less deeply committed to returning home. Nevertheless, Salvadorans in refugee camps across the border in Honduras did seek a negotiated collective return, as did groups among the half million internally displaced within El Salvador. Precise comparisons with the return and resettlement of Guatemalans are not possible, but certain significant similarities stand out. Some of the internally displaced Salvadorans were resettled under official state and military aegis; the process was much like what took place in Guatemala. Others were resettled and given assistance by nongovernmental organizations (NGOs). Still others found the leadership for resettlement within their own communities.

A comparison of the developmental outcomes in the three types of resettlement communities in El Salvador showed that the participatory process led by the displaced themselves was the most successful, while the state-administered return was the least successful (Edwards and Tovar Siebentritt 1991). This finding raises important policy-relevant questions for future research in both countries. Were the initial successes of the participatory process in El Salvador sustained over the following years? Have the self-led returns in Guatemala, overall, been more successful than government- and military-organized resettlements in reconstituting economically and socially viable communities? Beyond the question of participation, what other elements – such as access to land, credit, and markets – distinguish successful return communities? To what extent are "success stories" replicable?

Another unique aspect of the context of Guatemalan refugee return arose from the participation of civil society in the peace negotiation process, as Fonseca (chapter 4) relates. In January 1994 – about one year after the first highly publicized return – the Guatemalan government and the Guatemalan National Revolutionary Unity (URNG) signed a framework agreement for the conduct of negotiations. It included the establishment of an Assembly of Civil Society (ASC) that was mandated to discuss and make proposals on the substantive issues under discussion by the negotiation teams of the government and the URNG. The assembly was composed of representatives of ten social sectors and, although the returnees were not included among them, the displaced populations were included. Thus, in contrast to El Salvador, where civil society could only "watch" the peace negotiations, the return in Guatemala took place in a context of rising social mobilization and effervescence in which various sectors that overlapped with the returnees – for example, the organizations of the displaced, indigenous peoples, and women – were indirect but formally recognized participants in the negotiation process.

Finally, in most circumstances it is the exodus of refugees that receives wide publicity, and return remains invisible. In Guatemala it was the other way around. The Guatemalan army successfully cordoned off the rural areas during its savage rampage of the early 1980s, and the massive exodus of indigenous refugees remained largely hidden from the eyes of the nation and the world. By contrast, the return was highly visible: the first bus-loads of people who reentered were greeted by Nobel Laureate Rigoberta Menchú at the frontier, they were accompanied by international observers, and they made "a grand-tour" through Guatemala's major cities on their way back to a resettlement community that was actually close to the Mexican border. The refugees wanted to "clarify publicly" what had happened to them and to plant a "kind of seed" in everyone's mind (returnee quoted by Taylor 1998, 46).

These unique features generated optimism concerning the impact of returnees on national transformation. However, the return also took place within a political-economic context whose oppressive features remained largely intact.

Historical-Institutional Legacy

A second broad conclusion concerns the devastating impact of Guatemala's antidemocratic institutions and its thirty-six-year-long civil war on the refugee return and the possibilities of national transformation.[1] These institutions (discussed more fully in the introduction to this volume and in various chapters) include social, economic, legal, and political arrangements that were sustained by military force and systemic reliance on coercion to extract labour from indigenous communities.

The broad features of the historical legacy are common to Central America as a whole (with the partial exception of Costa Rica), and they emerged out of the constitution of coffee and banana export economies during the Liberal revolutions of the second half of the nineteenth century. The region's countries developed political-economic structures that depended on external capital yet received only modest reinvestment of profits from abroad; established very large export sectors that generated few backward and forward linkages to the national economy, so that internal markets remained weak; depended on large amounts of unskilled low-wage labour and, hence, invested little in education and health; manifested extreme concentration of all types of productive assets (access to land, finance, technology, and so on) (Furtado 1970, 47–9, 100–4). Most of the population was excluded from the benefits of the economic growth that did take place, while class, ethnic, and gender disparities were reinforced, since the organization of the export economies, which included the dispossession and privatization of indigenous community lands, favoured local elites, foreign investors, men, and *ladinos* (the word for non-indians in Central America) (Samper 1993, 66–7, 85, 94). Since socio-political order was maintained by force, with the exception of Costa Rica, periodic rebellion and its violent repression characterized these nations. Guatemala eventually became the most militarized of the region's countries.

The pervasiveness and depth of military control emerged, in turn, out of a particularly oppressive political-economic and cultural order. Although all Central American countries exhibit high degrees of inequality in access to land (Weeks 1985, 112), in Guatemala land concentration was exceptionally acute in the leading coffee sector, giving rise to a particularly powerful and politically conservative "coffee elite" that "controlled more land and people and had a tighter hold on the people than did any other coffee elite in Central America. Its power rested on the captive allegiance of its serfs and the armed force at its command" (Paige 1997, 75). The concentration of political and economic power in the hands of that elite was coupled to a racially based social stratification system. The poor and landless in Guatemala are overwhelmingly indigenous peoples who live apart in their communities and migrate seasonally to harvests in the export production zones, whereas the rural populations of the neighbouring countries are, in their great majority, *ladinos.* Landlessness, poverty, and oppressive gender relations characterize the Central American region, but the virulence of racism and the enormity of social class inequalities reach extreme manifestations in Guatemala, as several chapters in the volume make clear.

The refugee flight from Guatemala in the 1980s was the consequence of a racist and tragically vicious bloodbath that, in the Cold War context of the time, was presented as a necessary counter-insurgency campaign. The vast majority of casualties were unarmed indigenous civilians who were targeted in genocidal attacks that, according to many scholars, were aimed to destroy an increasingly autonomous indigenous cooperative movement that had been gaining ground since the 1960s (see, for example, Davis 1983). Or, in other words, they point out that army massacres began before the expansion of the guerrilla forces that formed the URNG. The Recovery of Historical Memory Project (REMHI) of the Guatemalan Archbishop's Human Rights Office, in four carefully researched volumes, has presented documentation on 422 massacres (more than 90 percent of them carried out by the military; with the remainder perpetrated by guerrilla forces and unknown parties) and analyzed the searing impacts of the violence on individuals, families, and communities (1998, 34–8).

A major question that is addressed from different perspectives in various chapters concerns the implications of refugee return for this legacy of racism, inequality, and violence that involves the denial of all human rights – political, social, cultural, and economic. Evidence from the works presented in this volume points to the ways in which Guatemalan indigenous refugees abroad developed more complex identities with transformative potential. They continued to see themselves as members of their own specific regional-linguistic communities, but they also began to see themselves as members of a broader Maya population. In the refugee camps in Mexico, of necessity, they adopted Spanish as a new language for communication among themselves and with their hosts. To organize their well-being and security and to work for a return, they established contacts with international agencies and developed skills for collective action.

Since women became key actors in the refugee communities, as Torres and Crosby document (chapters 9 and 10), the development of organizational skills and shifts in identity also fundamentally affected their gender roles and race- and gender-linked aspects of identity. Terms used by indigenous Guatemalan refugee women to identify themselves became more varied by context (that is, depending on where they were and to whom they were speaking) and included, at least when dealing with foreigners, the adoption of a Guatemalan identity, something that would have been far less likely previously, given their historical self-view as K'iche', Q'anjob'al, Mam, Q'eqchi', and so on, oppressed by the Guatemalan state.

These cultural transformations in the refugee camps, while more dramatic and defined than those that were taking place among nonrefugee indigenous people in Guatemala, nevertheless paralleled shifts in indigenous identity and political movements within the country. Moreover, new ways of thinking – among those who fled and those who remained – emerged in good part from the interaction of indigenous leaders with national and international humanitarian and development institutions. While the seeds and potential for greater recognition of indigenous people and their rights were evident among the returnees and among indigenous leaders, the racist legacy of Guatemalan society remained very much in place. The fact that members of the elite who still countenance (in Piero Gleijeses' words) "the occasional need to kill an Indian" to assure subservience no longer kill with the same frequency as in the past is not necessarily a reflection of diminished racism. Rather, the evidence suggests that those who might be tempted to kill must take into account greater risks now that an internationally monitored human rights regime has been put in place. (The origin and limitations of that regime are discussed below, with reference to neoliberalism.)

In sum, the political-military system in Guatemala, while changing in the face of internal and external pressures, continued to function in an authoritarian and threatening manner to exert a brake on transformation. The evidence provided by this volume in this regard is overwhelming. Moreover, the political transformations of the 1990s were evolving in a highly unfavourable economic policy context.

Neoliberal Restructuring

The overall direction of economic policy and political change in Guatemala, as elsewhere in Central and South America since the early to mid 1980s, has respected the tenets of neoliberalism. This doctrine, now global in scope, rejects a developmental role for the state and insists on reliance on market forces for the allocation of resources in society. Neoliberal economic policies in Latin America, also known as structural adjustment policies (SAPs), have been implemented under pressure from the major donor countries (the United States in particular), powerful international financial institutions (IFIs) like the International Monetary Fund (IMF) and the World Bank, as well as the World Trade Organization (WTO). Specific policies include the liberalization of trade and finance, the privatization of state enterprises and public services, the deregulation of labour markets, and the downsizing of the state in general. The doctrine's prescriptive framework is strongly supported by the large multinational corporations, and it overwhelmingly favours the rights and mobility of capital over the rights and mobility of labour.

While often ignored, neoliberalism is also, somewhat paradoxically, associated with a commitment to civil and political rights and the maintenance of electoral democracy. These are supported not only as values in themselves but also to reduce the costs of (armed, coercive) social control and to create a climate in which international business and trade can be carried out without disruption and fear of arbitrary state action, on the one hand, or revolution, on the other. Egregious human rights abuses, after all, do not ensure a secure investment climate.

The evidence from the studies assembled in the volume fully confirms our initial concerns (see the introductory chapter) about the implications of neoliberalism for refugee return and national transformation. The evidence also supports conclusions that go beyond our broad initial concerns and provides the basis for a more detailed conceptualization of neoliberal institutions and the mechanisms through which they operate in Guatemala. The general conclusion is that neoliberalism plays a complex and often ambiguous or contradictory role. It supports some aspects of democratic transformation while at the same time supporting changes that limit democracy and sustain (or even increase) socioeconomic inequality, thereby incubating the potential for a return to violent repression and armed resistance.

While the economic prescriptions of neoliberalism tend to favour the views and interests of antidemocratic elites, the limited but real commitment to human rights and democracy has a more ambiguous impact: human rights and democratic practices are advanced in the direction sought by Guatemala's progressive forces, but advance is also limited. Evidence for the ambiguous and contradictory impact of neoliberalism on refugee return and national transformation may be found in various places in this volume. The following interrelated points address some well-supported themes.

280 Journeys of Fear

The New Dance of Rhetoric and Practice Monumental contradictions between political rhetoric and practice in Guatemala were characteristic of previous epochs of repressive rule. As noted in the introduction to this volume, the reforms of the "democratic spring" of 1944-54 were rolled back in the following years: political parties were dissolved, labour legislation was rescinded, peasant farmers who had benefited from land reform were evicted, and generalized political repression became the norm. Incredibly, these measures were reframed by the Guatemalan state and its international supporters (principally the United States) as reforms intended to promote peaceful development and to liberate Guatemala from communist tyranny (see Handy 1994, 192-207). Later, in the 1980s, press-ganged villagers and the strategic hamlets into which displaced populations were herded became "civil patrols," "model villages," and "development poles."

The rise of neoliberalism since the transition to electoral democracy in Guatemala in 1986 has been accompanied by a more complex pattern of contradictions between political rhetoric and actual state policies. The gap between rhetoric and practice has narrowed in some areas and increased in others; overall, it has taken on a new, but still dangerous, slant. The narrowing is evident in the tangible, albeit limited, improvements in respect for human rights and democratic practices that are documented throughout the volume. Governments are now elected (although only a minority of citizens vote); peace is promoted by accords that give political status to the URNG; and human rights have been better protected through the support and vigilance of the UN peace-building mission (MINUGUA), surveillance by national and international NGOs, and the monitoring of the UN Commission on Human Rights until mid-1998.[2]

Wide and growing gaps are evident in other areas, particularly with regard to social justice and socioeconomic inequality. Neoliberal rhetoric promises that increased foreign investment and trade expansion will lead to economic growth that will benefit all; that structural adjustment policies (SAPs) will make the state more efficient and the public more self-reliant. However, the outcomes to date have been very different. Various chapters document the continuing insecurity of the landless , the poor , and women in particular (Blacklock, chapter 11), a fact reflected in the increased migration for economic reasons documented by Castillo (chapter 8). These unhappy trends create an extremely weak basis for sustaining the limited democratic and human rights gains.[3]

The gap between what has been promised and what has been delivered leads the Guatemalan government to engage in ongoing efforts to control resistance and block further democratization and the reforms, such as land redistribution, that could emerge from broader democracy. Part of this control effort relies on the standard rhetorical tools of politicians: state officials and their international supporters reframe what is happening to make it appear progressive. The other part involves continuing reliance on institutions of coercive control and repression that inhibit political organization. The two control measures overlap when the military continues to threaten and intimidate but stops short of massacres and widespread killings so as not to tarnish the image of a progressive state.

In summary, in neoliberal Guatemala, the state promotes limited democratic practices so that it can present itself to the world as a democratic state. It also promotes a minimum human rights regime so that it can say that it is a modern, legitimate state, worthy of entering into international trade agreements. At the same time, state officials continue to use threats and intimidation to block more thorough-going democratic and human rights reform. The combination of rhetorical reframing and coercion in the context of enormous unresolved problems of social justice, inequality, and democratic participation creates a tense and potentially volatile situation.

Minimalist Human Rights and Democracy As noted, within the prevailing neoliberal approach, democracy and human rights are defined in narrow terms as pertaining only to the political and civil realms. Moreover, within those realms, both democracy and human rights are conceived in terms of a "minimum" or a "just sufficient" amount to provide the necessary guarantees for the smoother functioning of the global trade system, which, of course, presupposes a system of politically stable nation states with enough legal and regulatory powers to guarantee the security of international investment, private property, patent rights, and the like. In a parallel fashion, the heavy (and expensive) military control of dissent in developing countries that prevailed during the Cold War has given way to efforts to bring about control through increasing attention to the legitimization of political systems. Consequently, democracy is promoted, but for the most part only with regard to its most basic expression as "one person, one vote." Although political assassinations – which continue to take place – are now condemned, co-optation (by elites and international investors) of politicians and political parties, before and after elections, is ignored.

Markets That Cannot Redistribute Wealth: Land and Employment The roots of extreme elite opposition to land reform are made clear by de Villa and Lovell (chapter 3). But elite opposition was not the only reason why land reform was rejected out of hand by government representatives involved in the peace negotiations. In accord with neoliberal ideology, for the IFIS and other international organizations land reform is simply not a priority in an economy where market forces (including land sales and purchases) are assumed to lead to the optimally efficient allocation of resources that maximizes production and welfare.

Moreover, SAPs and the associated roll-back of state responsibility created a poor environment for any new program like land reform that could be carried out only by establishing institutions to sort out land ownership, decide on criteria for redistributing land, and administer the actual redistribution. In fact, as Egan and Nolin Hanlon document (chapters 6 and 12), the Guatemalan government did not even honour the 1992 Refugee Return Accord's commitment to purchase lands for returnees. As evidence in this volume shows, the actual purchase and distribution of land has been marked by delays, foot-dragging, and unfulfilled promises arising from cut-backs in state programs and lack of funding for land purchases due to insufficient government revenue; the refusal of local landowners to sell to returnees; and the lack of coherent state leadership. The state allowed, and the military even encouraged, conflicts among returnees, those who had been settled by the army on their former lands, demobilized soldiers seeking land for settlement, and so on. As Nolin Hanlon states, the situation is characterized by ongoing "low intensity violence." Similarly, a National Coordinator of Indigenous Peasants (CONIC) leader was led to state that the peace-accord-mandated measures on land simply added up to "yet another hoax practised on the Guatemalan people" (*Reunion* 3, no. 3, January–March 1997, 6). Such perceptions bode ill for efforts to promote peace and development.

No doubt certain sectors of Guatemalan society have benefited from international capital flows and trade expansion, even though the economy as a whole remains weak and at the mercy of fickle international markets and investments seeking fast returns. Sectors that have expanded in recent years include textile production and light-assembly manufacturing, much of which is in "free-trade zones." While the new foreign investment has helped to generate economic growth and has created many urban jobs, especially for young women, it has not had a visible impact on reducing very high urban unemployment levels that are fed by rural-to-urban migration and even higher levels of rural unemployment. Of the 90,000 young people who enter the labour market every year, only 10 percent find work in the formal sector of the economy (Sistema de las Naciones Unidas 1998, 4). Nor has the new investment had a positive impact on overall wage rates. One apparent reason for this is that Guatemala and other Central American nations continue to export in global competition with other low-wage export economies.

In fact, foreign corporations are already pushing into the areas where refugees have returned to exploit petroleum and timber resources, as well as cheap labour. Our fears concerning the potentially devastating human and environmental impacts of opening up of the return regions to this type of investment are echoed in Taylor's richly detailed analysis of the return of Guatemalan refugees to the village of Santa María Tzejá in the Ixcaán (1998, 113–15 and 131–3).

Demilitarization, Democracy, and Peace Although none of the chapters in the volume deal exclusively with Guatemala's armed forces, all, in one way or another, necessarily address their power. As Fonseca demonstrates (chapter 4), the slow pace of the peace negotiations can be attributed largely to military resistance. Thus it is not surprising that, while state spending on social programs was cut back, the military's budget remained sacrosanct. Demilitarization – like much else in Guatemala – appears to exist in rhetoric only. The evolution of the size of the country's army is revealing. In 1986, when the civilian Cerezo assumed power, the army had 30,000 soldiers, *more* than it had during the height of the massacres in the early 1980s and about three times as many as it had in 1975. With the advent of electoral democracy, and even as peace negotiations advanced, the army continued to grow. By 1996, when the guerrilla forces were reduced to operating in small pockets and the civil war was ending, there were some 42,000 soldiers (IISS various years). Moreover, in addition to its own TV station, during the 1960s and 1970s the military had acquired major economic power in its own right through its Pension Institute and the Banco del Ejército (Brenes and Casas 1998, 43–76; see also Aguilera Peralta 1989, 20–6).

The standard assumption among those promoting peace was that as armed challenges to state authority receded, the army would begin to scale back. Such an assumption is also consistent with the broad objectives of SAPs, namely, to cut back state expenditures. Yet, the evidence to date indicates that little has changed. The army still had 38,500 men in uniform in 1997 (almost four times its

1975 size), and its budget remained at the high levels of the pre-accord era. It remained to be seen whether or not the one-third reduction in the budget and in the size of the military mandated by the Accord on Strengthening Civil Power and the Role of the Army in a Democratic Society (September 1996) would really be carried out. In any case, even if the reductions take place (and the army claims that they are taking place), Guatemala's ground forces will remain larger (at about 25,000 men) than they were in 1975 (at roughly 10,000).[4]

While these figures are perturbing, it must also be recognized that the process of democratization and negotiation opened up political spaces for the social movements that eventually obtained the formal dissolution of the misnamed Civil Self-Defense Patrols in the last-negotiated accords that ended the civil war in December 1996. The PACs formed a key component of the system of military control that the army had established in the countryside, where the majority of the Guatemalan population still resides. Two organizations composed largely of indigenous women – the Coordinator of Guatemalan Widows (CONAVIGUA) and the Mutual Support Group (GAM), discussed by several volume contributors – played a leading role in the campaign to begin the demilitarization of rural communities that the dissolution of PACs makes legally possible. The letter of the law, however, will not be easy to carry out (see, for example, North 1998).

The Self-Limiting Nature of Development Aid and International Monitoring in the Neoliberal Context An important focus in aid programs that operate within the neoliberal framework consists of support for local-community development, micro-banking, poor peoples entrepreneurship, and other similar initiatives. Canadian aid to Guatemala, as discussed by Patroni and Gronau (chapter 14), illustrates the trend, which is not without merit. Grass-roots-based development projects can facilitate local organization for expanding democratic spaces, in addition to improving the material conditions of life. Nevertheless, in Guatemala as elsewhere, these programs function at odds with structural adjustment policies (SAPs) that privatize services (making them inaccessible to the poor), deregulate labour markets (leading to wage reductions), and the like. Paradoxically, those policies are encouraged by the same aid-donor nations that finance community development programs. In this way, the contradiction between neoliberal macroeconomic policy and development aid (to empower local communities and promote social progress) remains hidden and largely unaddressed.

The same contradiction can be found between UN peace-monitoring and peace-promotion programs and the SAPs prescribed by the IMF in Central America, a contradiction identified by Alvaro de Soto (the principal UN mediator of the Salvadoran peace accords) and Graciana del Castillo (then economic advisor to the UN secretary general). They described post-peace-accord El Salvador as a patient on the operating table "with the left and the right sides of his body separated by a curtain and unrelated surgery being performed on each side" (quoted by Boyce and Pastor 1997, 295). Subsequently, a comprehensive set of studies commissioned by the United Nations Development Program (UNDP) on the compatibility of SAPs and peace building in El Salvador concluded that "*unless the peace process is allowed to reshape economic policy, both will fail*" (287, emphasis in the original). As Baranyi (chapter 5) indicates, MINUGUA and even the IFIs took note of the UNDP study's recommendations on El Salvador. Nevertheless, at the time that Patroni and Gronau completed research for their chapter, there was no indication of deviation from the prevailing economic orthodoxy on the part of the Canadian International Development Agency (CIDA).

In short, peace processes oriented toward the promotion of democracy and the resolution of the problems that had caused civil wars were advanced with international assistance for a very broad range of initiatives. They included assistance to grass-roots organizations and creative educational programs on conflict resolution sponsored by the Unit for the Promotion of Democracy (UPD) of the Organization of American States (OAS). But the SAPs on which IFIs and major donors conditioned assistance – policies that denied a developmental and redistributive role for the state – were skewing the balance of power further in favour of the powerful elite economic groups organized into the Chamber of Agricultural, Commercial, Industrial, and Financial Associations (CACIF). And that concentration of power, of course, lay at the root of underdevelopment, political violence, and militarization in Guatemala and Central America: that is, with the exception of Costa Rica, both states and markets had functioned within power relations that had led to the promotion of the short-run interests of consolidated national private groups and foreign investors rather than the long-run interests of the society as a whole

Environmental and Gender Double-Talk The list of policy areas that are affected in contradictory ways by neoliberal prescriptions is extensive. Evidence in this volume addresses their two-sided impact on the environment and women (see chapters 6 and 11 by Egan and Blacklock, respectively). These are fields where progressive international movements have been active for many years. Both environmental sustainability and gender equity are now deeply entrenched in the rhetoric of development-aid programs and the peace and development efforts of international agencies. Typical of this trend, proposals to the Canadian International Development Agency (CIDA) must clearly state how the project will contribute to protecting the environment and improving women's status, regardless of the substantive focus of activity. Yet neoliberalism also promotes privatization and state-downsizing, which limit government support to programs in all areas, including environmental protection and the education and equitable incorporation of women in society.

The results of these contradictory elements are evident in Guatemala. The Maya Biosphere is an important environmental protection undertaking, but it is subject to widespread corruption and abuses that allow private firms to log for profit within the Biosphere, while landless peasants who once farmed there, as Egan relates (chapter 6), are prohibited from returning. International agencies and NGOs have also supported women's development organizations in Guatemala, but these organizations are still debilitated by the limited involvement of poor women, especially at the level of leadership and in rural areas. Meanwhile, the earlier-mentioned assembly and light-manufacturing operations in Guatemala's free-trade zones are providing new employment opportunities for women, but in jobs that, as Blacklock found (chapter 11), seemingly reinforce traditional gender, class, and racial stereotypes and in enterprises that repress all attempts to organize the work force.

Contradictory Tendencies with Respect to International Migration A central feature of neoliberalism is its insistence on the freedom and mobility of capital and trade goods, combined with its indifference, neglect, and opposition to the rights and mobility of labour. In a global economy operating under neoliberal principles, capital moves freely from one country to another, but workers who seek jobs in other countries find their path increasingly restricted and controlled.

Furthermore, wealthy nations encourage only those kinds of migratory movements that will increase their own wealth, without regard for issues of social justice. Specifically, they favour the permanent immigration of highly skilled and wealthy individuals from any place in the world, including poor countries. They also admit seasonal-visa workers for low-paid agricultural jobs but establish controls to ensure that they return home and do not generate any social costs (for health, schooling) for the host nation. And they also favour international treaties that allow their own managers and professionals to travel and work in countries where multinational corporations set up branch plants. Correspondingly, the wealthy nations are increasingly hostile to undocumented migration and asylum seekers, although the economic and political pressures favouring emigration from small, poor countries remain very high (Simmons 1995, 1997a). These general policy directions are evident in the recent evolution of U.S. and Canadian immigration policies and in the way in which the North American Free Trade Agreement (NAFTA) deals with international migration (Simmons 1996).

Guatemala is affected in various ways by the international migration regime built into the neoliberal global political economy. As Castillo (chapter 8) points out, rural and urban households reveal an increasing reliance on labour circulation within the nation and internationally for income and household survival. Because legal flows of migrants are subject to more and more restrictions, interpersonal and underground linkages that channel the recruitment and employment of undocumented workers in wealthy nations, particularly the United Sates, have been reinforced. So too have migrant links to other sub-rosa activities, such as smuggling and the international drug trade. In a perverse fashion, the core values of the neoliberal system wind up supporting undocumented migration and even criminal organization. Those values promote "entrepreneurship" and "self-reliance" at all levels – among migrant workers, their families, and those employers in receiving countries who profit from employing cheap, undocumented migrant labourers.

Peace without Social Development? The powerful advocates of neoliberal policies in the World Bank, the IMF, the WTO, transnational corporations, and donor nations assume that sustainable economic growth, social improvement, and political stability will follow from the adoption of the "new" economic policies based on neoliberal doctrines. But, in fact, as Michael Pettis, a business school professor, has pointed out, those policies of liberalization, privatization, and export promotion have been tried in the past – they "are not at all new and ... historically they have not led to sustainable economic growth" in Latin America (1996, 6). Indeed, there are many parallels between contemporary neoliberalism and the old liberalism of Central America's late-nineteenth-century export-economy consolidation era – that is, reliance on export production, cheap labour, and foreign investment.

Beyond the question of economic growth per se, as the above-cited UNDP report on El Salvador makes clear, there are many good reasons for believing that the economic problems of Guatemala and other Central American countries cannot be solved without first, or at least simultaneously, addressing problems of equity, social development, and democratization in order to build the peace required for sustainable economic growth. It bears noting that it was unresolved social equity and development problems and the associated patterns of coercive social and political control that led to civil wars in El Salvador, Nicaragua, and Guatemala.

The links between choice of economic policy, social equity, and possibilities of democratization cannot be ignored. As René Poitevin points out (chapter 2) "neo-liberalism's prescriptions drain politics of all meaning and goals, since all struggles for power will be in vain, given the disappearance of the state as a centre of power or as an instrument of change." Party politics and elections make little sense if the critical policy choices are taken out of the public realm and left in the hands of private national and international organizations. In this situation, it is not surprising that voter turnout manifested a tendency to drop in Guatemala even as elections became more open.

RETURNEES AND THEIR LIVES IN GUATEMALA

The evidence reported in this volume concerning the impact of returnees on their home communities or places of resettlement is preliminary. Fieldwork on the chapters that deal with the question was carried out mostly in 1995–96, when the return process had been underway for only a few years and the refugees were at an early stage of resettlement. Thus our comments take the form of hypotheses and questions regarding the future, as much as they point to the findings of our contributors. Overall, it appears that the refugees, despite their transformative goals and new perspectives and skills, had a limited impact on home communities during the years immediately following their return. Their modest contribution to change may be largely explained by the fact that resistance to deeper transformation has been overwhelming in Guatemala. Antidemocratic, racist elites and the military remained powerful, and they remained opposed to the distributive reforms and more profound expansion of human rights and democracy sought by the returnees and others.

As Taylor puts it in the study, mentioned above, of the return to Santa María Tzejá in the Ixcán, the military's first line of defense was to keep people ignorant of the provisions of the return and other accords; the second was to "generate sufficient fear among the population to prevent those who had some knowledge of human rights from pursuing those rights"; and the third was to "demonize, divide, and demoralize ... [the returning refugees] who had both knowledge of human rights and the will to demand their rights." If none of that worked, then violence was the last resort (1998, 146). Army propaganda and control in the rural areas had been effective." People said they were told that the refugees were 'bad people' whose heads had been filled with foreign ideas. Those who stayed were told not to get involved with refugee organizations, with the threat if they did they would be inviting the return of the violence of 1982" (148).

To be sure, the forces of neoliberalism have led to certain improvements in human rights and democracy, but, as argued, these improvements have been supported up to a "low ceiling" or minimum set of standards that leaves plenty of room for the use of coercive force and intimidation. Foreign development assistance channeled to local communities has undoubtedly benefited returnees and others in those localities where such programs exist, but at the same time, such assistance has done little to reverse the damaging impacts of adjustment policies that limit opportunities for rural and poor workers. Each "brake" on transformation that arises from traditional elites or from the ambiguous and half-hearted support for change associated with neoliberal practices serves to limit the transformative potential of the refugee return. In this context, the transformative political project of the refugees has fared poorly, and their overall impact in the regions where they have settled has been far less than they would have hoped, although some success stories also exist.

Moreover, the resettlement process itself contains elements that have further limited the impact of the returnees. First of all, their life project was always linked to a return to the land and to the re-formation of indigenous communities. In a national context where small farmers continue to be squeezed out by lack of land, inadequate credit, and poor prices, the back-to-the-land project runs against the continuing drift of rural people to urban areas and into international migration channels. Small rural producers in Guatemala are continuing to be pushed out to the cities and to other countries. As the evidence on this process indicates, many of the war-displaced, as well as other migrants, live very poorly in city slums (see Gellert, chapter 7). The fact that urban poverty is preferred is just an indication of the much greater poverty, lack of opportunity, and in many cases, continued repression in their home communities.

Second, based on evidence presented by Gellert and Castillo (chapters 7 and 8), small farm families in Guatemala are increasingly dependent for survival on circulation to seasonal jobs in export agriculture within Guatemala, Mexico, and the United States. According to some observers, "almost all Maya communities have members who have emigrated abroad" (COPMAGUA 1997, 30). One fears that the returnees or at least some of their children, with their broader understanding of the external world and their new skills, will become caught up in the same kind of labour circulation or become dependent for income on the petroleum and timber companies and the urban assembly industries, or *maquilas*, that are moving, or planning moves, into El Petén and Ixcán. If so, the returnees' transformative project may shift from regenerating traditional rural Maya communities toward a future oriented to external opportunity and individual (rather than collective) well-being and mobility, as has happened in other Guatemalan villages (Popkin 1997, 13–17; Rodríguez 1997, 21–3).

Third, the political project of the returnees contains a mix of elements, including some rather conservative ones. For example, the goals for recreating their former communities are a conservative element that overlaps only in part with broader social transformations. It overlaps with the quest for human rights, democracy, and government services (roads, health care, schools) that will allow them to participate in the national economy and gain increased political representation within the nation. But it does not necessarily overlap with changing gender roles. Women returnees find that the leadership and participation that they enjoyed in refugee camps in Mexico, as described by Torres (chapter 9), are not necessarily welcomed or expected in the return communities in Guatemala, where traditional leaders and men seek to reassert their authority.

The divisions generated by these and other sources of contention among the returnees themselves and in the returnees' relations with the people who remained in Guatemala, under the military's control in the PACs, have generated havoc in some of the return communities (Crosby, chapter 10; Taylor 1998, 94–6 and passim). Those divisions have, of course, been fomented by the military and its allies, but they were also a consequence of lack of preparation on the part of most returnees for dealing with the social, political, and cultural conditions created by more than a decade of military control and propaganda in the areas of return and resettlement (Taylor 1998, 147–52, 189–97).

Finally, Taylor singles out a source of problems that is not addressed in our work, that is, dependency on foreign donors. In effect, "the refugees had become habitual receivers" in the camps in Mexico. A UNHCR worker pointed out to Taylor that projects in the Mexican camps that were heavily funded by the European Community "did not take into account the conditions refugees would face on their return." An employee of Habitat, an NGO, described her experience with the returnees, in contrast with her experience with those who had stayed, in the following terms: "They come with the full security that everyone is awaiting their arrival to help them. So it is very hard to work with this group of people that is so accustomed to receiving everything ... This group is very different from the people who stayed here. Many times the latter group show more disposition to work, and when they want something, they help themselves and do it" (quoted by Taylor 1988, 118).

However, the overall picture is not entirely bleak. Some return communities – like Santa María Tzejá – have been quite successful and have had positive impacts in neighboring areas; women's organizations have helped resolve conflicts that have arisen between returning refugees and those who had settled on the lands the returnees had previously occupied; and seeds of change were planted with the visibility of the return and the terms of the 1992 accord. Thus, despite the many factors that limit the impact of returnees on national transformation, the potential for such contributions remains evident. Crosby (chapter 10) makes this point by drawing attention to ongoing efforts by various groups, particularly those representing indigenous interests, to develop supportive networks among themselves and with returnees in order to achieve common goals. In a similar vein, Egan expresses the hope that return communities, while a small part of rural Guatemala, might spark a "resurgent rural development movement, similar to the one that flourished prior to the repression of the 1980s." Greater positive impacts may be realized if appropriate support programs are established.

THE FUTURE: PRIORITY ISSUES AND POLICY OPTIONS

In this final section, we summarize and comment on the policy-relevant conclusions suggested by the evidence in this volume. The general questions are, first, what future roles could progressive international actors play with respect to the settlement of refugees (and other displaced people)? Second, how could programs be designed to support a more profound national transformation? Third, what steps can the returnees and other prodemocratic actors in Guatemala take to advance such transformation?

The questions, as posed, place the burden for future transformative change on those who most seek it, namely, progressive national and international actors. Baranyi (chapter 5) argues that the traditional elite and antidemocratic elements in the military who oppose such changes must in the end "compromise" and pay their share of taxes, abide by the law, organize economic activities that do not require coercive repression of wage demands, and so on. Moving antidemocratic elites toward such compromises will not be easy. It will require careful, deliberate, and concerted efforts on the part of those seeking transformation. Steps suggested by our collective research include those outlined below. We list the steps separately for each of several classes of actors. However, success will depend on coordination of efforts and strategies by all involved.

International Organizations and Donor-Country Agencies

The important role of international actors in supporting progressive efforts among refugees and others who seek transformation is strongly confirmed in various chapters of this volume. At the same time, two closely related concerns regarding the future role of international actors are singled out. One is the fear that setting only minimal standards for human rights and democracy in the context of the "trade not aid" neoliberal regime will force international peace and development promotion agencies, first, to water down their programs in Guatemala and, then, to withdraw prematurely at a moment when their presence is still badly needed. The other is the worry that international agencies and NGOs will fail to recognize the need to develop new ways of working in Guatemala that advance beyond what was done in the past. New ways of working are required to rectify the limitations of previous efforts and to address new realities. These concerns lead to various recommendations for different classes of international actors.

Among the *international organizations*, MINUGUA – the UN human rights and peace verification mission in Guatemala – and the UNDP have been and continue to be critically important progressive actors in Guatemala. Maintaining the positive thrust of their efforts will require hard work on the part of these agencies and their donor government and non-governmental supporters. The priorities involve maintaining the independence and rigour of MINUGUA's verification procedures, expanding the latter to effectively cover the Accord on the Rights and Identity of Indigenous Peoples and the Accord on Socioeconomic Aspects and the Agrarian Situation, and clarifying and strengthening the division of labour between the different MINUGUA units (see Baranyi, chapter 5).

Given that the impact of peace and development efforts to date has been less than was hoped for, new strategies need to be formulated and pursued. For example, the principal recommendation of the earlier-cited UNDP study on the Salvadoran peace process is equally relevant for Gautemala. Its authors advocate the abandonment of current "adjustment conditionalities" that make major foreign assistance depend on the implementation of neoliberal SAPs, and they argue for their replacement by "peace conditionalities" that would make assistance dependent on the full implementation of all aspects of peace accords (Boyce et al., "Executive Summary of Principal Findings"). The study points out that the single-minded pursuit of economic growth objectives will undercut the possibilities of achieving long-term peace and that renewed conflict will, in turn, undercut the possibilities of economic growth. The thrust of that conclusion is scarcely new to progressive critics of trends in development aid, and it is shared by the contributors to this volume.

Of course, neither MINUGUA nor the UNDP nor the United Nations acting on its own can ensure major changes in international development assistance policies. That would require the concerted efforts of all *principal donor nations* involved in supporting the implementation of the peace accords in Guatemala and a change of heart at the IMF, to which those donors belong. Thus the obstacles to policy change at the international level are as daunting, if not more daunting, than in Guatemala. Nevertheless, we hope that the evidence presented here will provide support for arguments in favour of rebalancing the priorities and strategies. Such a rebalancing will not take place unless human rights groups, civic movements, independent development-promotion organizations, and others in the donor countries engage in informed advocacy to change their governments' foreign and international-trade policies, along with their voting patterns in the IMF, the World Bank, and multilateral organizations in general. Together with the abandonment of SAPs, among the specific recommendations for advocacy could be the establishment of an internationally financed land reform fund.[5]

The *non-governmental organizations* of donor countries receive mixed reviews from the contributors to this volume. On the one hand, NGOs are perceived to have played a very positive role, closely linked to the work of progressive international agencies in local community development, in refugee resettlement, and with refugee women's organizations. Levitt (chapter 13) describes how accompaniment of returnees on reentry and resettlement in Guatemala was carried out professionally and responsibly and how accompaniment programs responded to the returnees' needs for security. On the other hand, several chapters affirm that paternalism is widespread in the relationship between the hundreds of foreign NGOs working in Guatemala and their local counterparts. The result, Poitevin argues, is that foreign NGOs have taken over tasks that should be undertaken by Guatemalan nongovernmental and civil society organizations (chapter 2). More careful studies of the impact of NGOs on the capacity of Guatemalan organizations are required. In the interim, the following recommendations are worthy of careful consideration.

The tendency of many NGOs to carry out directly activities that local people can perform better must end. The role of the donor-country NGOs, according to Levitt, should shift to become one of "lobbyists and educators, providing services and solidarity to the people's movements that they support" and not one of "artificially [creating] new services and organizations" that do not have a base in Guatemalan society. This role would correspond to a new and welcome stage in the relationship between foreign and national NGOs.

While development activities at the local level must remain a priority, the importance of human rights as a precondition (or at least a simultaneously linked condition) for development cannot be overstressed. NGOs have been particularly important in providing support for human rights work in the past, and this work should continue to be a privileged area of concentration in the future. Specific activities could include work not only with returnees but with the even larger numbers of displaced persons (Castillo, chapter 8), marginalized rural-urban migrants (Gellert, chapter 7), and Central American and Guatemalan organizations that have been established to work specifically with such groups (see the section on policies related to migrants and the displaced, below).

National NGOs and Local Communities

Political decentralization is, fortuitously, an area of common concern among neoliberals – in the Guatemalan government and in powerful multilateral organizations – and NGOs that focus on promoting local participation to deepen democracy and improve respect for human rights. This suggests that local NGOs (and their foreign supporters) should pay particular attention to links with and support to municipal governments, since state social and development programs are increasingly becoming the responsibility of governments operating at the local level (Magnusson 1994).

The returnees, Maya peoples in general, and NGOs working with both, as Levitt suggests, need to work out a strategic vision of their future. Progress in this direction has taken place. There is a rising awareness among returnees and the Maya that they must construct a collective project that transcends their specific regional linguistic communities. Such a collective project would need to take into account transformations in the international system, the implications of rural and urban development for their life-styles, and the changing identities of Guatemalan indigenous youth who, as Poitevin points out, speak their native language and simultaneously adopt English as the lingua franca for dealing with the wider world. This will be an enormous task requiring the support of all those outside the indigenous community who are committed to social justice and development in Guatemala. Various chapters in this volume show how the multifaceted identity of returnee women – indigenous and *ladino* – could provide a rich base for building a new strategic vision. Parallel trends are emerging more generally among the Maya and bode well for efforts to develop new images of their future and place in a transformed nation.

Migration and Migrant-Related Initiatives

Parts of several chapters draw attention to the importance of migrants and migration processes in the process of national transformation. What policies might strengthen progressive outcomes from different kinds of migration? This is a relatively new question on the policy agenda in Guatemala. Hence, the observations and recommendations presented below are rather speculative, and they are offered simply to draw attention to some policy and research questions.

Internal Migration and Transformation The circulation of labour (mostly female) from small towns and rural areas to *maquilas* has become important in Guatemala, as both Gellert and Blacklock observe (chapters 7 and 11). However, the transformative potential of these movements is ambiguous. As noted previously, *maquila* jobs and incomes may promote new identities and aspirations among women, yet this work is structured within existing class inequalities, racial and gender discriminations, and often violent opposition to labour rights by employers. Little is known about the effects of the *maquila* experience on the women, the husbands and children who in some cases accompany them to the city, and their families in home communities. Most likely, those effects are contradictory, both strengthening traditional roles and expanding images of alternative futures.

"Forced Migration" alongside Resettlement While returnees and former soldiers were "re-settled," the transformative impacts of other patterns of migration that arise from the civil wars and the neoliberal international order are worrisome. This has been noted recently by the Central American Regional Association on Forced Migration (ARMIF), a coalition of NGOs working toward regional transformation.[6] ARMIF uses "forced migration" to refer to people pushed out of their home communities by lack of opportunities. That phenomenon, the association argues, is not only prevalent but on the rise throughout the region. It emerges from a punishing combination of circumstantial causes and structural factors: included among the former are efforts by hundreds of thousands of war-displaced people to return to their homes or find alternative places to settle; the demobilization of former soldiers who are also seeking places to settle; and, in the case of Guatemala, the return of large numbers of refugees from Mexico. The structural causes include, most importantly, the high concentration of land and other assets among large export producers and the neoliberal economic model that does not address high levels of unemployment.

Central America's forced migrants face dismal options. Their movements and settlement in new locations could have transformative potential were they to find places with stable work and educational opportunities, but they seldom do. When they seek to take up residence on or near export plantations, the plantation owners demand (and receive) military assistance to evict them. Those who take up residence in urban slums may also find that old economic, racial, and other barriers remain firmly in place.

In the case of Guatemala, the war-displaced and the forced migrants are overwhelmingly of Maya origin. Many find themselves in urban slums, isolated from home communities. What might be done to help them settle successfully into urban life? Changes in identity will depend on the kinds of communities migrants create in the cities. Will these be ethnic enclaves? Or will they be ethnically mixed, Spanish-speaking communities with broader Maya or Guatemalan identities? How will such formations affect efforts toward transformation? Will migrants to cities be able to retain links to home communities and develop links to national Maya organizations? With enormous levels of population displacement taking place in rural areas, home communities have been eroded, while incorporation into social organizations in the new places of residence is held back by the culture of fear. Meanwhile, both in the cities and the countryside continued violence now also takes the form of explosive levels of criminal activity to which villagers (possibly incited by military-linked provocateurs) have responded with lynchings. All this clearly carries tremendous potential for generating disorganization rather than progressive national transformation.

Clearly, however, the plight of forced migrants has attracted local, regional, and international attention, and it has generated collaboration between old and new progressive institutions and concerned scholars (see CONGCOOP/CAM 1997; *Acción Concertada* 6, no. 19, 1997).

International Migration and Transformation The circulation and migration of Central Americans to jobs and residence in other countries may generate considerable potential for national transformation. However, as noted, these international movements are subject to increasing restrictions by receiving nations. Hypotheses concerning migration impacts on social transformation and development in Central America, where little research has been done on these questions, can be informed by more extensive studies conducted in Mexico. New research needs to distinguish more carefully between the impacts arising from different kinds of migration in different origin countries and communities, among different social classes of migrants, and at different points in the historical evolution of policies and other circumstances governing international migration. The following questions and hypotheses touch on these dimensions.

It is generally agreed that migrants' remittances provide substantial income support for families and funding for community development that fill in or compensate for the lack of such mechanisms in the neoliberal model. According to a Guatemalan government spokesperson, there are one and a half million Guatemalans (documented and undocumented) in the United States, and in 1995 they sent $U.S.416.5 million to relatives and communities back home (Pensabenne 1997, 8). What are the implications of the tightening of immigration controls in receiving nations for income transfers and local investment projects? Research on the economic impacts of international migration conducted in Mexico and other countries in the hemisphere (El Salvador and the Dominican Republic, for example) provides a plausible but still uncertain basis for developing hypotheses relevant to Guatemala: uncertain because different studies have come to very different conclusions, suggesting that context plays a very important role in determining the outcomes of international migration.

Some studies have found that out-migration leads to decline in the economic circumstances of origin communities: the most-skilled workers leave; if they return, it is to live off remittances rather than to work or invest; young people lose interest in schooling, seeking instead manual work abroad as a faster and easier option; local production falls when workers are not available, and so on. Other studies have found the opposite effect: migrant remittances raise living standards; migrants return with skills and savings for local investment; the inflow of income stimulates local commerce, construction, and even manufacturing, and so on (see Massey et al. 1994; Simmons 1997b).

One possible interpretation of the mixed findings is that migration outcomes depend on the context – that is, they vary from one region and social class to another. Wealthier families (with land or businesses) tend to use migration as way of generating capital for investment and expanding holdings. Wealthier communities with more buoyant economies tend to provide opportunities for investment that attract migrant remittances and entrepreneurship. In contrast, poorer families and families in poorer communities with few possibilities for profitable investment in land or small business use migrant earnings mostly for subsistence. Unfortunately, the poor rural communities of Guatemala where so many refugees and circulating migrants originate are more likely to fit the latter pattern. It may also be that it is the poorest rural communities that are most negatively affected by neoliberal SAPs.

Overall, the evidence available on migrant support for community development and increasing levels of remittances to Guatemala and other Central American countries is very impressive. It is often forgotten that the remittances may also hide the money-laundering activities of drug traffickers and that the links between migrant and home communities also involve criminal networks. As one of the foremost scholars of Central American militarism points out, "refugee migration during the 1980s established links between Central America and United States street gangs such as the infamous Crips and Bloods. Most significant in – but by no means confined to – El Salvador, these links involve not only narcotics but smuggling stolen vehicles from the United States, arms trafficking, bringing illegal immigrants into the United States ... document falsification, prostitution, and money laundering" (Millet 1995, 72).

International Solidarity and Transformation It appears that the neoliberal international order creates a situation in which the observation of human rights, at least in third-world countries, is less and less dependent on official intergovernmental agencies and more dependent on the emergence of international NGOs and the internationalization of civil society. This is what the downsizing of states and the increasing power of international capital appear to augur. Nations and corporations wish to be relieved of the costs and the tax burden of monitoring and sanctioning states that do not protect civil and economic rights. International capital would likely be particularly favourable to turning human rights monitoring over to civil society if the resulting human rights regime would therefore be weak, except in certain extreme cases that capital found threatening.

To what degree can solidarity across borders respond to this situation? What about the power of public opinion and national and international NGOs in the emerging context? Could it turn out to be more effective than might be expected, in part due to the forces of globalization? Whereas in the course of capitalist development in the advanced industrialized countries people turned to state institutions for rights protection, in societies like Guatemala people have always relied on nonstate institutions – both old (churches, unions, community associations) and new (the press and, most recently, networking via e-mail and fax) – for rights protection.

To what degree can the migrant communities in the advanced capitalist countries respond to human rights and developmental crises in their home societies? Research on this question is at a very early stage of development. Some recent work on the social and political dimensions of "transnational communities" – such as Dominicans in New York (Basch et al. 1994) and Mexicans in California (for example, Goldring 1996) – indicate that they may have a major role to play in political processes, gender relations, and local development initiatives in home countries, building schools, churches, and playgrounds and sponsoring cultural activities, for example. The impacts are mediated by the maintenance of strong links between origin and migrant communities through frequent visits, expatriate contributions to political activities at home, and expatriate donations to community development programs.

In sum, our review points to a number of policy-relevant proposals and to promising avenues for exploring the transformative potential of international migration. New social linkages, identities, and transformative potentials are emerging within a changing international system. These provide a promising terrain for progressive actors and researchers alike.

NOTES

1 The scorched-earth campaign of the early 1980s was only the most gruesome aspect of a civil war that dated back to 1960.
2 For a critical analysis of the withdrawal of the UNCHR from Guatemala and the very worrisome human rights situation in the country, see *Alerta* 1998, no. 1–2, 3, 6–7.
3 According to Amnesty International's 1997 report (published June 1998), Guatemala shares with El Salvador and Honduras the sad distinction of being one of the countries "with the worst human rights records in Central America." In 1998, "[t]he United Nations Verification Mission in Guatemala ... reported that 120 lynchings – described as "social cleansing" – had taken place since March 1996, mainly in rural areas. The Chief Prosecutor's Office launched investigations in only 24 cases" (*Tico Times*, 10 July 1998).
4 The editors would like to thank Marshall Beier for reviewing the yearly issues of *The Military Balance* from 1975 to 1998, where the figures cited are reported.
5 This suggestion is derived from the work of Irma Adelman (1988, 493–507).
6 See the special issue of *Acción Concertada* on forced migration (6, no. 19, 1997). This is the publication of the Cencertación Centroamericana de Organismos de Desarrollo (Central American Association of Development Organizations).

APPENDIX

Acronyms

ACPD Asamblea Consultiva de la Población Desplazada (Consultative Assembly of the Uprooted Population)
AGA Asociación Guatemalteca de Agricultores (Guatemalan Association of Agricultural Producers)
AMNLAE Asociación de Mujeres Nicaraguenses Luisa Amanda Espinoza (Association of Nicaraguan Women Luisa Amanda Espinoza)
AMPRONAC Asociación de Mujeres ante la Problemática Nacional (Association of Women in the National Situation)
ARDIGUA Asociación de Refugiados Dispersos de Guatemala (Association of Dispersed Refugees of Guatemala)
ARMIF Asociación Regional para las Migraciones Forzadas (Central American Regional Association on Forced Migration
ASC Asamblea de la Sociedad Civil (Assembly of Civil Society)
AVANSCO Asociación para el Avance de las Ciencias Sociales en Guatemala (Association for the Advancement of Social Sciences in Guatemala)
CACIF Comité Coordinador de Asociaciones Agrícolas, Comerciales, Industriales y Financieras (Chamber of Agricultural, Commercial, Industrial, and Financial Associations)
CACM Central American Common Market
CAMG Central America Monitoring Group
CAPA Canada-Americas Policy Alternatives
CAREA Cadena para un Retorno Acompañado – Germany (Network for an Accompanied Return – Germany)

CCPP Comisiones Permanentes de Representantes de los Refugiados Guatemaltecos en México (Permanent Commissions of Guatemalan Refugees in Mexico)
CDHG Comisión de Derechos Humanos de Guatemala (Guatemalan Human Rights Commission)
CEAR Comisión Especial para la Atención de Repatriados or Comisión Nacional para la Atención de Repatriados, Refugiados y Desplazados (Guatemalan Refugee Agency)
CEIDEC Centro de Estudios Integrados de Desarrollo Comunal (Centre for Integrated Studies on Communal Development)
CERJ Consejo de Comunidades Etnicas Runujel Junam (Runujel Junam Council of Ethnic Communities)
CERLAC Centre for Research on Latin America and the Caribbean
CIA Central Intelligence Agency of the United States
CIC Coordinator of Civil Institutions for Participation and Information in the Peace Process
CIDA Canadian International Development Agency
CIFCA Copenhagen Initiative for Central America
CIREFCA Conferencia Internacional sobre Refugiados en Centro América (International Conference on Central American Refugees)
CNDH Comisión Nacional de Derechos Humanos/México (National Commission of Human Rights/Mexico)
CNR Comisión Nacional de Reconciliación (National Reconciliation Commission)
COAMUGUA Coordinadora de Agrupaciones de Mujeres de Guatemala (Coordinator of Women's Groups of Guatemala)
COCADI Coordinadora Cakchiquel de Desarrollo Integral (Cakchiquel Integral Development Coordinator)
COCIPAZ Coordinadora Civil para la Paz (Civil Coordinator for Peace)
COINDE Consejo de Instituciones de Desarrollo (Council of Development Institutions)
COMADEP Comision Méxicana para Ayuda de los Desplacedos (Commission to Aid the Displaced)
COMAR Comisión Mexicana de Atención a Refugiados (Mexican Commission for Aid to Refugees)
COMG Consejo de Organizaciones Mayas de Guatemala (Council of Guatemalan Maya Organizations)
CONAGRO Comisión Nacional Agrícola (National Agricultural Council)
CONAP Consejo Nacional de Areas Protegidas (National Council of Protected Areas)

Acronyms

CONAVIGUA	Coordinadora Nacional de Viudas de Guatemala (National Coordinator of Guatemalan Widows)
CONGCOOP	Coordinación de Organizaciones y Cooperativas (Coordinator of Nongovernmental Organizations and Cooperatives)
CONIC	Coordinadora Nacional de Indígenas Campesinos (National Coordinator of Indigenous Peasants)
COPMAGUA	Coordinadora de Organizaciones del Pueblo Maya de Guatemala or Coordinadora de Organizaciones del Pueblo Maya de Guatemala Saq'bichil (Coordinator of the Organizations of the Maya People of Guatemala)
CPRS	Comunidades de Población en Resistencia (Communities of Population in Resistance)
CRS	Centre for Refugee Studies, York University
CSC	Coordinadora de Sectores Civiles (Coordinator of Civil Sectors)
CTEAR	Comisión Técnica del Acuerdo Para el Reasentaniento (Technical Commisison of the Accord for Resettlement)
CUC	Comité de Unidad Campesina (Peasant Unity Committee)
CUSO	Canadian University Services Overseas
CVDC	Voluntary Civil-Defence Patrols, or PACS
DDF	Democratic Development Fund
DPA	Department of Political Affairs of the United Nations
EAP	Economically Active Population
EGP	Ejército Guerrillero de los Pobres (Guerilla Army of the Poor)
EU	European Union
FAO	United Nations Food and Agriculture Organization
FAR	Fuerzas Armadas Rebeldes (Rebel Armed Forces)
FDNG	Frente Democrático para una Nueva Guatemala (Democratic Front for a New Guatemala)
FEDECOAG	Federación de Cooperativas Agrícolas de Guatemala (Federation of Guatemalan Agricultural Cooperatives)
FLACSO	Facultad Latinoamericana de Ciencias Sociales (Latin American Faculty of Social Sciences)
FMLN	Frente Farabundo Martí de Liberación Nacional (Farabundo Marti National Liberation Front)
FONAPAZ	Fondo para la Paz (Fund for Peace)
FONATIERRA	Fondo Nacional de Tierra (National Fund for Land)
FSLN	Frente Sandinista de Liberación Nacional (Sandinista National Liberation Front)
FTN	Franja Transversal del Norte (Northern Transverse Strip)

FUNCEDE — Fundación Centroamericana de Desarrollo (Central American Development Foundation)
FUNDAPAZD — Fundación para la Paz, Democracia y el Desarrollo (Foundation for Peace, Democracy and Development)
FYDEP — Empresa Nacional para la Promoción y Desarrollo Económico del Petén (National Enterprise for the Promotion and Economic Development of the Petén)
GAD — Gender and Development
GAM — Grupo de Apoyo Mutuo (Mutual Support Group)
GAP-USA — Guatemala Accompaniment Project – United States
GATT — General Agreement on Tarrifs and Trade.
GDN — Gran Diálogo Nacional (Great National Dialogue)
GRICAR — Grupo Internacional de Apoyo al Retorno (International Group of Support for the Return)
HOLACOM — Proyecto Holandés de Acompañamiento a la Población Desarragaida (Dutch Project for the Accompaniment of the Uprooted Population)
IDB — Inter-American Development Bank
ICCHRLA — Inter-Church Commitee on Human Rights in Latin America
IDB — Inter-American Development Bank
IFIS — international financial institutions
ILO — International Labor Organization
IM — Instancia Mediadora (Mediation Group)
IMF — International Monetary Fund
INC — Instancia Nacional de Consenso (National Organization for Consensus)
INE — Instituto Nacional de Estadistica (National Statistical Institute)
INGOS — international nongovernmental organizations
INTA — Instituto Nacional de Transformación Agrícola (National Institute for Agrarian Transformation)
IRIPAZ — Instituto de Relaciones Internacionales y de Investigaciones para la Paz (Institute of International Relations and Peace Research)
LAWG — Latin America Working Group
MICIVIH — UN Civilian Mission in Haiti
MINUGUA — Misión de las Naciones Unidas en Guatemala (United Nations Mission in Guatemala)
NAFTA — North American Free Trade Agreement
NCOORD — National Coordinating Office on Refugees and the Displaced of Guatemala/USA
NGOS — nongovernmental organizations
OAS — Organization of American States

ODHA Oficina de Derechos Humanos del Arzobispado (Archbishop's Human Rights Office)
PA-Canada Project Accompaniment-Canada
PACS Patrullas de Autodefensa Civil (Civil Self-Defence Patrols, Civil Patrols, or Voluntary Civil Self-Defense Committees)
PADEL Projets d'Appui au Développement Local (Program of Support to Local Development Projects, of CIDA)
PBI Peace Brigades International
PDH Procuraduría de los Derechos Humanos (Office of the Human Rights Counsel)
PGT Partido Guatemalteco del Trabajo (Guatemalan Workers Party)
REMHI Proyecto de Recuperación de la Memoria Histórica (Recovery of Historical Memory Project)
SAPS structural adjustment policies
SEGEPLAN Secretaría General de Planificación (General Planning Secretariat, Government of Guatemala)
SERJUS Servicios Jurídicos y Sociales (Legal and Social Services)
SOCODEVI Societé de Cooperación pour le Developpement International
UASP Unidad de Unión y Acción Popular (Unity of Union and Popular Action)
UNAGRO Unión Nacional Agrícola (National Agricultural Union)
UNDP United Nations Development Program
UNHCR United Nations High Commissioner for Refugees
UNHRC United Nations Human Rights Commission
UNIFEM United Nations Development Fund for Women
UPD Unit for the Promotion of Democracy of the Organization of American States
URNG Unión Revolucionaria Nacional Guatemalteca (Guatemalan National Revolutionary Unity)
USAID United States Agency for International Development
WAD Women and Development
WID Women in Development
WOLA Washington Office on Latin America
WTO World Trade Organization

Bibliography

NEWSPAPERS AND PERIODICALS

Acción Concertada. San Salvador: Órgano de la Concertación Centroamericana de Organismos de Desarrollo (Central American Association of Development Organizations).
Alerta. Toronto: Inter-Church Committeee on Human Rights in Latin America (ICCHRLA).
Cerigua. Guatemala: Centro Exterior de Reportes Informativos sobre Guatemala (CERIGUA).
La Hora. Guatemala City daily.
La Nación (Costa Rica), as reprinted in *Central America NewsPak.* Albuquerque, NM: Human Rights Documentation Exchange.
Libertas. Montreal: Newsletter of the International Centre for Human Rights and Democratic Development (ICHRDD).
Miami Herald, as reprinted in *Central America NewsPak.*
Prensa Libre. Guatemala City daily.
Reunion. Guatemala: CONGCOOP.
Tico Times, as reprinted in *Central America NewsPak.*

BOOKS, ARTICLES, AND OTHER REFERENCES

Adams, Richard. 1991. Strategies of Ethnic Survival in Central America. In *Nation-States and Indians in Latin America.* Edited by Greg Urban and Joel Sherzer. Austin, TX: University of Texas Press.

Adelman, Irma. 1988. A Poverty-Focused Approach to Development Policy. In *The Political Economy of Development and Underdevelopment*. 4th ed. Edited by Charles K. Wilber. New York: Random House.

Afkhami, Mahnaz. 1994. *Women in Exile*. Charlottesville, VA, and London: The University of Virginia Press.

Agger, Inger. 1994. *The Blue Room*. London and New Jersey: Zed Books.

AGIR (Association Guatemala Information/Recherche). 1988. El nuevo éxodo de los mayas. *Trace*, no. 13.

Agnew, John. 1993. Representing Space: Space, Scale and Culture in Social Sciences. In *Place/Culture/Representation*. Edited by James Duncan and David Ley. New York and London: Routledge.

Aguayo, Sergio. 1984. *El exodo centroamericano: Consecuencias de un conflicto*. Mexico City, Mexico, n.p.

Aguilera Peralta, Gabriel. 1988. The Hidden War: Guatemala's Counterinsurgency Campaign. In *Central America: Regional Dynamics and U.S. Policy in the 1980s*. Edited by Nora Hamilton et al. Boulder, CO, San Francisco, and Oxford: Westview Press.

- 1989. *El fusil y el olivo. La cuestión militar en Centroamérica*. San José, Costa Rica: FLACSO and Editorial DEI.

- 1994. *Los temas sustantivos en las propuestas de paz*. Debate, no. 24. FLACSO-Guatemala.

- 1995a. Gobernabilidad, democracia y elecciones en Guatemala. Paper presented at Nineteenth International Congress of the Latin American Studies Association, Washington, DC, September.

- 1995b. Guatemala: El proceso y los acuerdos de paz 1991–1995. Unpublished paper.

Aguilera Peralta, Gabriel, and Karen Ponciano. 1994. El espejo sin reflejo: la negociación de paz en 1993. *Debate*, no. 23. FLACSO-Guatemala.

Aldana, Carlos. 1996. Análisis del Acuerdo Global de Derechos Humanos. *Debate*, no. 34. Guatemala City, Guatemala: FLACSO-Guatemala.

Alvarado Constenla, Luis. 1983. *El proceso de urbanización en Guatemala*. Guatemala: Centro de Estudios Urbanos y Regionales, Universidad de San Carlos de Guatemala.

- 1984. *El desarrollo capitalista de Guatemala y la cuestión urbana*. Guatemala: Centro de Estudios Urbanos y Regionales, Universidad de San Carlos de Guatemala.

- 1988. El proceso de urbanización en Guatemala. *GEOISTMO* 2, no. 2.

Alvarez, Sonia E. 1990. *Engendering Democracy in Brazil: Women's Movements in Transition Politics*. Princeton, NJ: Princeton University Press.

Americas Watch Committee. 1984. *Guatemalan Refugees in Mexico, 1980–1984*. New York: Americas Watch.

- 1986. *Civil Patrols in Guatemala*. New York: Americas Watch. August.

Amnesty International. 1998. Urgent Network (electronic bulletin). May 7.

Anderson, Benedict. 1983. *Imagined Communities: Reflections on the Origin and Spread of Nationalism.* London and New York: Verso.
Anderson, John. 1996. Power in Guatemala Shifts to Civilians, *Guardian Weekly*, 15 December.
Anderson, Perry. 1979. *Lineages of the Absolutist State.* London and New York: Verso.
APROFAM. 1994. *Guatemala: Datos básicos.* Guatemala City, Guatemala: Asociación Pro-Bienestar de la Familia de Guatemala.
Arbour, Frances. 1994. The Voices of Women: A New Force Shaping the Guatemalan Return. *Refuge: Canada's Periodical on Refugees* 13, no. 10.
Arias, Arturo. 1990. Changing Indian Identity: Guatemala's Violent Transition to Modernity. In *Guatemalan Indians and the State, 1540–1988.* Edited by Carol A. Smith. Austin, TX: University of Texas Press.
Asamblea de la Sociedad Civil. Various years. Internal documents. Guatemala City, Guatemala: Asamblea de la Sociedad Civil.
AVANCSO (Asociación para el Avance de las Ciencias Sociales en Guatemala). 1990. Política institucional hacia el desplazado interno en Guatemala. *Cuadernos de Investigación.* No. 6. Guatemala City, Guatemala: AVANCSO.
– 1991. "Vonós a la Capital" Estudio sobre la emigración rural en Guatemala. *Cuardenos de Investigación.* No. 7. Guatemala City, Guatemala: AVANCSO.
– 1992. *¿Donde está el futuro? Procesos de reintegración en comunidades de retornados.* Cuadernos de Investigación. No. 8. Guatemala City, Guatemala: AVANCSO.
– 1997. La ciudad y los desplazados por la violencia. *Debate,* no. 15. Guatemala: FLACSO-Guatemala.
Bakhtin, M. M. 1981. *The Dialogic Imagination.* Austin, TX: University of Texas Press.
Banco Mundial. 1995. *Informe anual 1995.* Washington, DC: Banco Mundial.
Baranyi, Stephen. 1995. *The Challenge in Guatemala: Verifying Human Rights, Strengthening National Institutions and Enhancing an Integrated Approach to Peace.* London: Centre for the Study of Global Governance, London School of Economics.
– 1996. MINUGUA, la ONU y el proceso de paz guatemalteco. *Debate,* no. 33. FLACSO-Guatemala.
Barry, Tom. 1992. *Inside Guatemala.* Alburquerque, NM: The Inter-Hemispheric Education Resource Center.
Basch, Linda, Nina Glick Schiller, and Cristina Szanton Blanc. 1994. *Nations Unbound. Transnational Projects, Postcolonial Predicaments, and Deterritorialized Nation States.* Luxembourg: Gordon and Breach Science.
Basic Accord for Repatriation. 1992. 8 October.
Bastos, Santiago, and Manuela Camus. n.d. *Quebrando el silencio: Organiza-*

ciones del Pueblo Maya y sus demandas (1986–1992). Guatemala City, Guatemala: FLACSO.
– 1994. *Sombras de una batalla. Los desplazados por la violencia en la ciudad de Guatemala.* Guatemala City, Guatemala: FLACSO.
– 1995. *Abriendo caminos: Las organizaciones mayas desde el Nobel hasta el Acuerdo de Derechos Indígenas.* Guatemala City, Guatemala: FLACSO.
Bernstein, Jacob. 1995. Fear of Attacks by Army Drives Farmers into Jungle. *Dallas Morning News*, 19 March.
Bertrand, Michel. 1987. *Terre et société coloniale: Les communautés Maya-Quiché de la region de Rabinal du XVIe au XXIe siècle*. Mexico City, Mexico: Centre d'Etudes Mexicaines et Centroamericaines.
Bhabha, Homi K. 1994. *The Location of Culture*. New York and London: Routledge.
Bilsborrow, R., and Martha Georas. 1992. *Rural Population Dynamics and Agricultural Development: Issues and Consequences Observed in Latin America*. Ithaca, NY: Cornell University, Institute for Food, Agriculture and Development.
Bilsborrow, R., and P.F. DeLargy. 1991. Land Use, Migration and Natural Resources Deterioration in the Third World: The cases of Guatemala and Sudan. *Population and Development Review*. Supplement to vol. 16.
Birdsall, Nancy, and Richard Sabot. 1994. Inequality as a Constraint on Growth in Latin America. *Development Policy* 3, no. 3.
Bondi, Liz. 1993. Locating Identity Politics. In *Place and the Politics of Identity*. Edited by Michael Keith and Steven Pile. New York and London: Routledge.
Bongaarts, John. 1982. The Fertility Inhibiting Effects of the Intermediate Fertility Variables. *Studies in Family Planning* 13, no. 6/7.
Bottomley, Gillian. 1992. *From Another Place: Migration and the Politics of Culture*. Cambridge: Cambridge University Press.
Boutros-Ghali, Boutros. 1995. *United Nations Mission for the Verification of Human Rights and of Compliance with the Commitments of the Comprehensive Agreement on Human Rights in Guatemala. Report of the Secretary-General.* A/49/955. New York, 11 August.
Boyce, James K. 1995. Adjustment toward Peace: An Introduction. *World Development* 23, no. 12.
Boyce, James K., and Manuel Pastor Jr. 1997. Macroeconomic Policy and Peace Building in El Salvador. In *Rebuilding Societies after Civil War: Critical Roles for International Assistance*. Edited by Krishna Kumar. Boulder, CO, and London: Lynne Rienner Publishers.
Boyce, James, et. al. 1995. *Adjustment towards Peace: Economic Policy and Post-War Reconstruction in El Salvador*. San Salvador: UNDP.
Brenes, Arnoldo, and Kevin Casas. 1998. *Soldiers as Businessmen: The Economic Activities of Central America's Militaries*. San José, Costa Rica: Arias

Foundation for Peace and Human Progress and Swiss Agency for Development and Cooperation.
Brunner, José Joaquín. 1992. *América Latina, cultura y modernidad.* Mexico City, Mexico: Grijalbo.
Buijs, Georgina. 1993. *Migrant Women: Crossing Boundaries and Changing Identities.* New York: St Martin's Press.
Burki, Shahid Javed, and Sebastian Edwards. 1995. *Latin America after Mexico: Quickening the Pace.* Washington, DC: The World Bank.
Burns, Allen F. 1993. *Maya in Exile: Guatemalans in Florida.* Philadelphia, PA: Temple University Press.
Burns, E. Bradford. 1986. *Eadweard Muybridge in Guatemala, 1875: The Photographer as Social Recorder.* Berkeley, Los Angeles, and London: University of California Press.
Bustamante, Jorge. 1995. Immigration from Mexico and the Devaluation of the Peso: The Unveiling of a Myth. Paper presented at the Nineteenth International Congress of the Latin American Studies Association, Washington, DC, September.
Butler, Judith. 1992. Contingent Foundations. In *Feminists Theorize the Political.* Edited by Judith Butler and Joan Scott. New York and London: Routledge.
Cambranes, Julio C. 1985. *Café y campesinos en Guatemala, 1853–1897.* Guatemala City, Guatemala: Editorial Universitaria.
Campos Carr, Irene. 1990. Women's Voices Grow Stronger: Politics and Feminism in Latin America. *NWSA Journal* 2, no. 3.
Carmack, Robert M. 1983. Spanish-Indian Relations in Highland Guatemala, 1800–1944. In *Spaniards and Indians in Southeastern Mesoamerica: Essays on the History of Ethnic Relations.* Edited by Murdo J. MacLeod and Robert Wasserstrom. Lincoln, NE, and London: University of Nebraska Press.
- 1995. *Rebels of Highland Guatemala: The Quiché-Mayas of Momostenango.* Norman, OK, and London: University of Oklahoma Press.
- ed. 1988. *Harvest of Violence: The Maya Indians and the Guatemalan Crisis.* Norman, OK, and London: University of Oklahoma Press.
Carter, Erica, James Donald, and Judith Squires. 1993. *Space and Place: Theories of Identity and Location.* London: Lawrence and Wishart.
Castillo, Manuel Angel. 1990. Contexto regional y migraciones a la frontera sur de México. In *Seminario de información y análisis sobre trabajo migratorio y transfronterizo, e indocumentados.* Tapachula, Mexico: Senado de la Republica-LIV Legislatura.
- 1993. Migraciones de indígenas guatemaltecos a la frontera sur de México. Guatemala: Centro de Estudios Urbanos y Regionales. CEUR. Universidad de San Carlos. Bulletin no. 18.
- 1994a. A Preliminary Analysis of Emigration Determinants in Mexico,

Central America, Northern South America and the Caribbean. *International Migration* 32, no. 2.
- 1994b. Chiapas: Escenario de conflicto y refugio. *Demos Carta Demográfica Sobre México*, no. 7.
- 1995a. Migration, Development and Peace in Central America. In *International Migration, Refugee Flows and Human Rights in North America: The Impact of Free Trade and Restructuring.* Edited by Alan Simmons. Staten Island, NY: Centre for Migration Studies.
- 1995b. Immigration in Mexico: A Policy Brief. In *Central American Migration to Mexico and the United States: A Post-NAFTA Prognosis.* PEW Monograph Series no. 1. Washington, DC: Hemispheric Migration Project, Center for Intercultural Education and Development (CIED), Georgetown University. November.
- 1996. *Tipos y volúmenes de la inmigración en la frontera sur de México.* Mexico City, Mexico: Comisión Binacional para el Estudio de las Migraciones. August.
- 1997. Gobernabilidad, paz y desarrollo regional. *Diálogo.* Electronic Bulletin, no. 9 (October). FLACSO-Guatemala.

Castillo, Manuel Angel, and James Hathaway. 1996. Temporary Protection. *Refuge: Canada's Periodical on Refugees* 15, no. 1.

Castillo, Manuel Angel, and Silvia Irene Palma. 1991. Los transmigrantes centroamericanos en su ruta hacia el norte. Paper presented at Conferencia Preparatoria para la Conferencia Internacional sobre Integración Económica, Políticas Migratorias y Derechos Humanos en América del Norte. Mexico, DF: CEDDU, Colegio de México. Mimeographed, 15 November.
- 1992. *Proyecto de investigatión sobre caracteristicas y efectos de las migraciones internacionales en communidades Guatemaltecas – informe del prediagnóstico.* Guatemala City, Guatemala: Alianza para el Desarrollo Juvenil Comunitario. Mimeographed, November.
- 1994. *International Emigration in Central America: A Survey of Trends and Impacts.* Mexico City, Mexico: IOM/UNFPA, Project Emigration Dynamics in Developing Countries. Mimeographed.
- 1996. *La emigración internacional en Centroamérica: Una revisión de tendencias e impactos.* Guatemala City: FLACSO.

Castillo, Manuel Angel, and Fabienne Venet. 1996. Inmigración y políticas migratorias en México. Foro sobre migración regional: Mexico, Centroamérica y Estados Unidos. Mexico, DF 9 March. Mimeographed.

CCPP (Comisiones Permanentes de Representantes de los Refugiados Guatemaltecos en Mexico). 1993. *Acuerdos para nuestro retorno a guatemala.* Guatemala City, Guatemala: CCPP.
- 1994. What Are Our Aims. *The Return to Guatemala: International Bulletin of the Permanent Commissions of Guatemalan Refugees in Mexico-Northern Branch.* No. 1. April–May.

- 1995. *Declaración de Tikal.* Guatemala City, Guatemala, 6 April.
CEIDEC (Centro de Estudios Integrados para el Desarrollo Comunal). 1990. *Guatemala, Polos de Desarollo: El caso de la deestructuracíon de las comunidades indígenas.* Vol. 3. Mexico: Centro de Estudios Integrados de Desarrollo Comunal/Editorial Praxis.
Centro de Estudios de Guatemala. 1994. *La democracia de las armas: Gobiernos civiles y poder militar.* Guatemala City, Guatemala: Centro de Estudios de Guatemala.
CEPAL (Comisión Económica para América Latina). 1980a. *Centroamérica: Evolución económica desde la posguerra.* Mexico City, Mexico: CEPAL/MEX/ODE/34.
- 1980b. *Notas sobre el trasfondo histórico del desarrollo centroamericano.* Mexico City, Mexico: CEPAL/MEX/ODE/35.
- 1991a. *Remesas y economía familiar en El Salvador, Guatemala y Nicaragua.* México: Naciones Unidas, Doc. LC/MEX/L15.
- 1991b. *Guatemala: remesas internacionales y economía familiar.* Mexico: Naciones Unidas, Doc. LC/MEX.R.251/Rev. 1.
- 1992. *Guatemala: Evolución económica durante 1992.* Mimeographed. Mexico City, Mexico: CEPAL.
CEPAL/FNUAP/CELADE (Comisión Económica para América Latina, Fondo de Naciones Unidas para Actividades en Población, Centro Latinoamericano de Demografía). 1993. Población, equidad y transformación productiva. Paper presented at Conferencia Regional Latinoamericana y del Caribe sobre Población y Desarrollo. Mexico City, Mexico. April–May.
Chackiel J., and S. Schkolnik. 1997. Latin America: Less Advanced Groups in Demographic Transition. *Proceedings of the 1997 International Population Conference.* Liège, Belgium: IUSSP.
Chinchilla, Norma, and Nora Hamilton. 1996. *Recuerdos de la patria, definiciones del presente: Percepciones de parte de los inmigrantes centroamericanos en los Estados Unidos.* Los Angeles: California State University, University of Southern California.
CHRLA (Centre for Human Rights Legal Action). 1993a. *In Situ Report on the First Collective Return of Refugees to Guatemala: January-February 1993.* Washington, DC: CHRLA.
- 1993b. *On-Site Report on the First Collective Return of Refugees to Guatemala, Comunidad Victoria 20 de enero, Ixcán: March-April 1993.* Washington, DC: CHRLA.
CIDA (Canadian International Development Agency). 1992. *Support to Local Development Projects (PADEL), Guatemala, 432/15586–Terms of Reference for a Mid-Term Evaluation.* November 4.
- 1994. *Draft CIDA Policy on Human Rights, Democratization and Good Governance and Related Background Documents.* Ottawa: CIDA.
Clegg, Harry. 1996. Guatemala's War Grinding Down. *San Francisco Chronicle,* 14 May.

Cleland J., and G. Rodriguez. 1988. The Effect of Parental Education on Marital Fertility in Developing Countries. *Population Studies Occasional Papers*. No 3. London: London School of Economics.

Clifford, James. 1986. Partial Truths. In *Writing Culture: The Poetics and Politics of Ethnography*. Edited by J. Clifford and G. Marcus. Berkeley, Los Angeles, and London: University of California Press.

CNDH (Comisión Nacional de Derechos Humanos de México). 1995. *Informe sobre violaciones a los derechos humanos de los inmigrantes: Frontera Sur*. Mexico City, Mexico: CNDH.

COCADI (Coordinadora Cakchiquel de Desarrollo Integral), ed. 1989. *Cultura maya y políticas de desarrollo*. Chimaltenango, Guatemala: Ediciones COCADI.

COINAP-UNICEF. 1997. *Estudio cuantitativo de las áreas urbano marginales del Area Metropolitana de Guatemala*. Guatemala: Comisión Interinstitucional para la Atención a las Areas Precarias Urbanas-Fondo de las Naciones Unidas para la Infancia. Preliminary document.

Cojtí Cuxil, Demetrio. 1989. Problemas de "la identidad nacional" guatemalteca. In *Cultura maya y políticas de desarrollo*. Edited by COCADI. Chimaltenango, Guatemala: Ediciones COCADI.

– 1996. Estudio evaluativo del cumplimiento del acuerdo sobre identidad y derechos de los pueblos indígenas. *Debate*, no. 34. FLACSO-Guatemala.

Colchester, Marcus. 1991. Guatemala: The Clamour for Land and the Fate of the Forests. *The Ecologist* 21, no. 4.

COMAR (Comisión Mexicana para la Ayuda a los Refugiados). 1985. *Refugiados guatemaltecos*. México, DF: COMAR.

COMG (Consejo de Organizaciones Mayas de Guatemala). 1995. *Construyendo un futuro para nuestro pasado: derechos del pueblo maya y el proceso de paz*. Guatemala City, Guatemala: Editoral Cholsamaj.

Comisión de Derechos Humanos de Guatemala. 1991. *1981–1991: 10 años de impunidad*. Mexico City, Mexico: Comisión de Derechos Humanos de Guatemala.

CONGCOOP/CAM (Coordinación de Organizaciones y Cooperativas/Centro Arquidiocesano de Atención al Migrante). 1997. *El impacto de las migraciones de guatemaltecos al exterior, reflexiones y datos iniciales (Memoria de un Taller)*. Guatemala City, Guatemala: CONGCOOP/CAM.

Convención sobre Asilo. 1928. Sexta Conferencia Internacional, La Habana. 20 February.

Convención sobre Asilo Diplomático. 1954. Décima Conferencia Interamericana, Caracas, 28 March.

Convención sobre Asilo Territorial. 1954. Décima Conferencia Interamericana, Caracas, 28 March.

Convención sobre Asilo Político. 1933. Septima Conferencia Internacional Americana, Montevideo, 26 December.

COPMAGUA (Coordinadora de Organizaciones del Pueblo Maya de Guatemala Saq'bichil). 1997. Migraciones Mayas al exterior. In *El impacto de las migraciones de guatemaltecos al exterior, reflexiones y datos iniciales (Memoria de un Taller)*. Edited by CONGCOOP/CAM. Guatemala: CONGCOOP/CAM.

Cox, Robert. 1986. Social Forces, States, and World Order. In *Neorealism and its Critics*. Edited by Robert O. Keohane. New York: Columbia University Press.

Criquillon, A. 1995. The Nicaraguan Women's Movement: Feminist Reflections from Within. In *The New Politics of Survival: Grassroots Movements in Central America*. Edited by Minor Sinclair. New York: The Ecumenical Program on Central America and the Caribbean (EPICA) and Monthly Review Press.

CSUCA, and Programa Centroamericano de Ciencias Sociales. 1984. Declaración de Cartagena sobre los Refugiados. Coloquio sobre protección internacional de los refugiados en América Central, México y Panamá: Problemas jurídicos y humanitarios. Cartagena, Colombia, 22 November.

– 1978 a. *Estructura agraria, dinámica de población y desarrollo capitalista en Centroamérica*. San José, Costa Rica: EDUCA.

– 1978 b. *Estructura demográfica y migraciones internas en Centroamérica*. San José, Costa Rica: EDUCA.

Davis, Shelton H. 1983. State Violence and Agrarian Crisis in Guatemala: the Roots of the Indian-Peasant Rebellion. In *Trouble in Our Backyard: Central America and the United States in the Eighties*. Edited by Martin Diskin. New York: Pantheon Books.

– 1988. Introduction: Sowing the Seeds of Violence. In *Harvest of Violence: the Maya Indians and the Guatemalan Crisis*. Edited by Robert M. Carmack. Norman, OK, and London: University of Oklahoma Press.

de Soto, Alvaro, and Graciana del Castillo. 1994. Obstacles to Peacebuilding. *Foreign Policy*, no. 94.

– 1995. Implementation of Comprehensive Peace Agreements: Staying the Course in El Salvador. *Global Governance* 1, no. 2.

Dennis, Phillip, Gary Elbow, and Peter Heller. 1988. Development under Fire: The Playa Grande Colonization Project in Guatemala. *Human Organization* 47, no. 1.

Díaz-Polanco, Héctor. 1992. Indian Communities and the Quincentenary. *Latin American Perspectives* 19, no. 3.

Dunkerley, James. 1988. *Power in the Isthmus: A Political History of Central America*. New York and London: Verso.

Earle, Duncan M. 1988. Mayas Aiding Mayas: Guatemalan Refugees in Chiapas, Mexico. In *Harvest of Violence: The Maya Indians and the Guatemalan Crisis*. Edited by Robert M. Carmack. Norman, OK, and London: University of Oklahoma Press.

- 1991. Measuring the Maya Disconnection: Violence and Development in Guatemala. *American Ethnologist* 18, no. 4.
Early, John D. 1982. *The Structure and Evolution of a Peasant System: The Guatemalan Case.* Boca Raton, FL: University Presses of Florida.
Eckstein, Susan. 1989. *Power and Protest in Latin America.* Berkeley, Los Angeles, and London: University of California Press.
Edwards, Beatrice, and Gretta Tovar Siebentritt. 1991. *Places of Origin: The Repopulation of Rural El Salvador.* Boulder, CO and London: Lynne Rienner Publishers.
Edwards, Louise. 1991. Voices from a Silent Refuge. *NACLA Report on the Americas* 25, no. 1.
Egan, Brian, and Alan Simmons. 1994. Refugees and the Prospects for Peace and Development in Central America. *Refuge. Canada's Periodical on Refugees* 13, no. 10.
Enloe, Cynthia. 1993. *The Morning After: Sexual Politics at the End of the Cold War.* Berkeley, Los Angeles, and London: University of California Press.
European Commission. 1995. *Strategy for Medium-Term Aid to Guatemala.* Brussels: European Commission.
- 1996. *Strategy for Medium-Term Aid to Guatemala.* Brussels: European Commission.
Falla, Ricardo. 1992. *Masacres de la selva: Ixcán, Guatemala (1975–1982).* Guatemala City, Guatemala: Editorial Universitaria.
- 1994. *Massacres in the Jungle: Ixcán, Guatemala, 1975–1982.* Boulder, CO: Westview Press.
Farriss, Nancy M. 1983. Indians in colonial Yucatán: Three perspectives. *Spaniards and Indians in Southeastern Mesoamérica: Essays in the History of Ethnic Relations.* Edited by Murdo MacLeod and Robert Wasserstrom. Lincoln, NE: University of Nebraska Press.
FEDECOAG (Federación de Cooperativas Agrícolas de Guatemala). 1993. *Las relaciones de poder en las zonas del retorno en El Petén.* Guatemala City, Guatemala: FEDECOAG.
Fei, John.C.H., and Gustav Ranis. 1964. *Development of the Labor Surplus Economy: Theory and Policy.* Homewood, IL: Irwin.
Feres, Juan Carlos, and Arturo León. 1990. The Magnitude of Poverty in Latin America. *CEPAL Review*, no. 41.
Field, Les. 1994. Who Are the Indians? Reconceptualizing Indigenous Identity, Resistance, and the Role of Social Science in Latin America. *Latin American Research Review* 29, no. 3.
Figueroa Ibarra, Carlos. 1976. *El proletariado rural en el agro guatemalteco.* Mexico, DF: UNAM, Facultad de Ciencias Políticas y Sociales, Thesis.
Fix, Michael, Jeffrey S. Passel, Maria E. Enchautegui, and Wendy Zimmerman. 1994. *Immigration and Immigrants. Setting the Record Straight.* Washington, DC: The Urban Institute.
FLACSO, SEGEPLAN, and SAFLAC. 1992. *El proceso de ajuste estructural y sus*

efectos sobre la población vulnerable. Guatemala City, Guatemala: FLACSO, SEGEPLAN, and SAFLAC. Mimeographed.

Flores, Margarita. 1996. Equidad y transformación productiva: Requisitos para el desarrollo sostenible en Guatemala. Paper presented at Seminario Internacional: Los Retos de la Paz y Desarrollo en Guatemala. Guatemala City, Guatemala: FLACSO-Guatemala, August.

Franco, Leonardo. 1996. Evaluación de la tarea de verificación de la Misión de las Naciones Unidas de Verificación de los Derechos Humanos en Guatemala-MINUGUA. *Debate* no. 33. FLACSO-Guatemala.

Frelick, Bill. 1991. *Entre la espada y la pared: la odisea de Centroamericanos atravesando México*. Washington, DC: U.S. Commitee for Refugees.

– 1995. North America–Country Report. *1995 World Refugee Survey*. Edited by U.S. Commitee for Refugees. Washington, DC: Immigration and Refugee Services of America.

– 1996. Toward the Reformulation of International Refugee Law–Symposium Report. *Refuge. Canada's Periodical on Refugees* 15, no. 1.

FUNCEDE (Fundación Centroamericana de Desarrollo). n.d. *Limitaciones y obstáculos, Región Huista*. Mimeographed.

Fundación Myrna Mack. 1995. *Coyuntura Guatemalteca: Noviembre 1995*. Electronic communication from fmmack@nicarao.apc.org, through the Human Rights Network. 2 November.

FUNDAPAZD (Fundación para la Paz, Democracia y el Desarrollo). 1994. *Documentos de la Asamblea de la Sociedad Civil-ASC. May–October*. Guatemala City, Guatemala: FUNDAPAZD.

Furtado, Celso. 1970. *Economic Development of Latin America: Historical Background and Contemporary Problems*. Cambridge: Cambridge University Press.

Gálvez, Victor. 1995. Gobernabilidad precaria y demandas populares. In *La gobernabilidad en Centroamérica*. Vol. 2. Guatemala: FLACSO-Guatemala.

Gálvez Borrel, Victor, et al. 1997. *¿Qué sociedad queremos? Una mirada desde el movimiento y las organizaciones mayas*. Guatemala: FLACSO.

García, Ana Isabel, and Enrique Gomáriz. 1989. *Mujeres centroamericanas: efectos del conflicto*. Vol. 2. San José, Costa Rica: FLACSO.

García Canclini, Nestor. 1995. *Culturas híbridas: estrategias para entrar y salir de la Modernidad*. Mexico City, Mexico: Grijalbo.

García, Carlos Ochoa. 1996. Refugees and the Guatemala Peace Process. In *International Migration, Refugee Flows and Human Rights in North America*. Edited by Alan Simmons. New York: Center for Migration Studies.

Garst, Rachel. 1993. *FIS y FONAPAZ en Guatemala: ¿una nueva relación Ong-Estado?* Guatemala City, Guatemala: COINDE.

Garzaro Andrino, Mónica Edith. 1998. *Racismo y acuerdo sobre identidad y derechos de los pueblos indígenas en Guatemala*. Thesis. Universidad de San Carlos, Escuela de Ciencia Política, Guatemala.

Gellert, Gisela. 1992. Desarrollo de la estructura espacial en la Ciudad de

Guatemala desde su fundación hasta la revolución de 1944. In *Ciudad de Guatemala. Dos estudios sobre su evolución urbana (1524–1950)*. Edited by Gisela Gellert and J.C. Pinto Soria. Guatemala: Universidad de San Carlos de Guatemala.

- 1995. *Ciudad de Guatemala: Factores determinantes en su desarrollo urbano (desde la fundación hasta la actualidad)*. Guatemala City, Guatemala: FLACSO.
- 1997a. *El Impacto de la migración centroamericana en comunidades de orígen de El Salvador y Guatemala. El caso de Guatemala: Transformaciones sociopolíticas a causa de la migración a Estados Unidos en comunidades seleccionadas del Altiplano Occidental.* Guatemala City, Guatemala: FLACSO.
- 1997b. Principales cambios en la dinámica de la población. In *Evaluación de la Sostenibilidad en Guatemala*. Edited by FLACSO-WWF. Guatemala City, Guatemala: FLACSO.

General Statistical Office (Government of Guatemala), CELADE (UN-Latin American Demographic Centre), and CIDA (Canadian International Development Agency). 1985. *Guatemala: Population Estimates and Projections, 1950–2025.* Guatemala City, Guatemala: General Statistical Office-CELADE-CIDA.

Gill, Stephen. 1992. Economic Globalization and the Internationalization of Authority. *Geoforum* 23, no. 3.

Gleijeses, Piero. 1988. *Politics and Culture in Guatemala.* Ann Arbor, MI: Center for Political Studies, Institute for Social Research, University of Michigan.

- 1991. *Shattered Hope: The Guatemalan Revolution and the United States, 1944–1954.* Princeton, NJ: Princeton University Press.

Gobierno de la República de Guatemala. 1982. *Plan Nacional de Seguridad y Desarrollo.* Guatemala City, Guatemala: Centro de Estudios Militares.

Goldring, Luin. 1996. Blurring Borders: Constructing Transnational Community in the Process of Mexico-U.S. Migration. *Research in Community Sociology*, no. 6.

Gorostiaga, Xabier, and Peter Marchetti. 1988. The Central American Economy: Conflict and Crisis. In *Central America: Regional Dynamics and U.S. Policy in the 1980s.* Edited by Nora Hamilton et al. Boulder, CO, San Francisco, and Oxford: Westview Press.

Gramsci, Antonio. 1971. *Selections from the Prison Notebooks.* New York: International Publishers.

Green, Duncan. 1995. *Silent Revolution.* London: Cassell.

Green, Linda. 1994. Fear as a Way of Life. *Cultural Anthropology* 9, no. 2.

Griffin, Keith. 1989. *Alternative Strategies for Economic Development.* London: MacMillan, in association with OECD Development Centre.

Grupo de Apoyo a Refugiados Guatemaltecos. 1983a. *Informe de un genocidio: Los refugiados Guatemaltecos.* Mexico City, Mexico: Ediciones de la Paz.

- 1983b. *Los refugiados guatemaltecos y la contrainsurgencia.* Mexico City, Mexico: Ediciones de la Paz.
Habermas, Jürgen. 1995. *Moral Consciousness and Communicative Action.* Cambridge: MIT Press.
Hagan, Jacqueline M. 1987. *The Politics of Numbers: Central American Migration during a Period of Crisis, 1978–1985.* MA thesis, University of Texas, Austin.
- 1994. *Deciding to be Legal: A Maya Community in Houston.* Philadelphia, PA: Temple University Press.
Handy, Jim. 1984. *Gift of the Devil: A History of Guatemala.* Toronto: Between the Lines Press.
- 1994. *Revolution in the Countryside: Rural Conflict and Agrarian Reform in Guatemala 1944–1954.* Chapel Hill, NC: University of North Carolina Press.
Hanks, William F. 1990. *Referential Practice: Language and Lived Space among the Maya.* Chicago and London: University of Chicago Press.
Harvey, David. 1993. Class Relations, Social Justice and the Politics of Difference. *Place and the Politics of Identity.* Edited by Michael Keith and Steven Pile. New York and London: Routledge.
Hawkins, John. 1984. *Inverse Images: The Meaning of Culture, Ethnicity and the Family in Postcolonial Guatemala.* Albuquerque, NM: University of New Mexico Press.
Hesse, Barnor. 1993. Black to Front and Black Again. *Place and the Politics of Identity.* Edited by Michael Keith and Steven Pile. New York and London: Routledge.
Hewitt de Alcantara, Cynthia. 1993. *Real Markets: Social and Political Issues of Food Policy Reform.* London: Frank Cass.
Hill, Robert M. II, and John Monaghan. 1987. *Continuities in Highland Maya Social Organization: Ethnohistory in Sacapulas, Guatemala.* Philadelphia: University of Pennsylvania Press.
hooks, bell. 1981. *Ain't I a Woman: Black Women and Feminism.* Boston: South End Press.
Human Rights Watch/Americas. 1996. *Guatemala, Return to Violence: Refugees, Civil Patrollers, and Impunity.* Vol. 8, no 1(b), 18 January. Washington, DC.
Hunter, Alan. 1995. Los nuevos movimientos sociales y la revolución. *Nueva Sociedad.* No. 136. Caracas, Venezuela.
ICCHRLA (Inter-Church Committee on Human Rights in Latin America). 1995. *Draft Report on Guatemala.* July. Mimeographed.
IDB (Interamerican Development Bank), Social Policy Agenda Group. 1995. *Challenges for Peace: Towards Sustainable Social Development in Peru.* Washington, DC: IDB.
Ignatius, Sara. 1993. *An Assessment of the Asylum Process of the Immigration and*

Naturalization Service. Cambridge, MA: National Asylum Study Project, Harvard Law School, Immigration and Refugee Program.
IISS (International Institute of Strategic Studies). 1975 to 1998. *The Military Balance.* London and Oxford: International Institute of Strategic Studies (to 1995/96), and Oxford University Press (1995/96 onward).
INE. 1989. *Guatemala, población urbana y rural estimada por departamento y municipios, 1985–90.* Guatemala City, Guatemala: Instituto Nacional de Estadística. 1996. *X Censo Nacional de Poblacíon y V de Habitación. República de Guatemala.* Guatemala City: Instituto Nacional de Estadística.
INE-FNUAP (Instituto Nacional de Estadística, and Fondo de Población de las Naciones Unidas). 1991. *Perfil de la pobreza en Guatemala.* Vol. 5, *Informes Estadísticos.* Guatemala: Instituto Nacional de Estadística.
Inforpress Centroamericana. 1995. *Compendio del proceso de paz I: Guatemala 1986–1994.* Guatemala City, Guatemala: Inforpress.
INM (Instituto Nacional de Migración). 1996. *Estadística Migratoria,* Vol. 2, no. 6. Mexico, DF: Secretaría de Gobernación. June.
INS U.S.(Immigration and Naturalization Service, United States). Annual and monthly reports. Washington, DC: U.S. Government Printing Office.
IRIPAZ (Instituto de Relaciones Internacionales y de Investigaciones para la Paz). 1991. *Cronologías de los procesos de paz: Guatemala y El Salvador.* Guatemala City, Guatemala: IRIPAZ.
– 1992. Vetoes and Obstacles for Return: The Role of the Refugees in the Actual Guatemalan Peace Process. Paper presented at Conference on Migration, Human Rights and Economic Integration. Toronto: Centre for Research on Latin America and the Caribbean (CERLAC), York University.
Jaquette, Jane S. 1991. *The Women's Movement in Latin America: Feminism and the Transition to Democracy.* Boulder, CO, San Francisco, and Oxford: Westview Press.
Jelin, Elizabeth. 1990. *Women and Social Change in Latin America.* London: UNRISD/Zed Books.
Joba, Dorothy J. 1984. Santiago de los Caballeros, 1604–1626: Society and Economy in Colonial Guatemala. PHD diss., University of Connecticut.
Jonas, Susanne. 1991. *The Battle for Guatemala: Rebels, Death Squads, and U.S. Power.* Boulder, CO: Westview Press.
– 1995. Transnational Realities and Anti-Immigrant State Policies: Issues Raised by the Experiences of Central American Immigrants and Refugees in a Trinational Region. *Estudios Internacionales* 6, no. 11.
– 1996. Between Two Worlds: The UN in Guatemala. Paper presented at conference, Peacemaking and Democratization in the Hemisphere: Multilateral Approaches, April, at the North-South Center, University of Miami.
Jones, Chester L. 1940. *Guatemala: Past and Present.* Minneapolis, MN: University of Minnesota Press.

Jones, Jeffrey. 1990. *Colonization and the Environment: Land Settlement Projects in Central America.* Tokyo: United Nations University Press.

Keen, Benjamin, and Mark Wasserman. 1984. *A Short History of Latin America.* Boston: Houghton Mifflin Company.

Kennedy Cuomo, Kerry, Helen Merkling, and Nan Richardson. 1993. *Persecution by Proxy: The Civil Patrols in Guatemala.* New York: The Robert F. Kennedy Memorial Center for Human Rights.

King, Arden R. 1974. *Cobán and the Verapaz: History and Cultural Process in Northern Guatemala.* New Orleans: Tulane University Press.

Korten, David. 1990. *Getting to the Twenty-First Century: Voluntary Action and the Global Agenda.* West Hartford, CT: Kumarian Press.

Kowalchuk, Lisa, and Liisa North. 1994. *Canadian Development Assistance in El Salvador: A Contribution to Peace-Building?* Toronto: CAPA occasional paper.

Kramer, Wendy. 1994. *Encomienda Politics in Colonial Guatemala, 1524–1544: Dividing the Spoils.* Boulder, CO, San Francisco and Oxford: Westview Press.

Kramer, Wendy, W. George Lovell, and Christopher H. Lutz. 1990. Fire in the Mountains: Juan de Espinar and the Indians of Huehuetenango, 1525–1560. In *Columbian Consequences.* Vol. 3. Edited by David H. Thomas. Washington, DC: Smithsonian Institution Press.

Krishna, Anirudh, and Roland Bunch. 1997. Farmer-to-Farmer Experimentation and Extension: Integral Rural Development for Smallholders in Guatemala. In *Reasons for Hope. Instructive Experiences in Rural Development.* Edited by Anirudth Krishna, Norman Uphoff, and Milton Eastman. West Hartford, CT: Kumarian Press.

Krznaric, Roman. 1997. Guatemalan Returnees and the Dilemma of Political Mobilization. *Journal of Refugee Studies* 10, no. 1.

Larrea, Carlos. 1996. Economic Liberalization and Labour Market Trends in Latin America: What Hope for the Poor? Paper presented at conference, Reducing Poverty in Latin America and the Caribbean: Challenges for the New Millenium. Toronto, FOCAL and SID/University of Toronto.

Lewis, W. Arthur. 1954. Economic Development with Unlimited Supplies of Labour. *The Manchester School of Economic and Social Studies* 22, no. 2.

López Rivera, Oscar A. 1997. *De la agonía a la esperanza cautiva.* Guatemala City: Pastoral de la Movilidad Humana, Conferencia Episcopal de Guatemala.

Lovell, W. George. 1985. From Conquest to Counter-Insurgency. *Cultural Survival Quarterly* 9, no. 2.

– 1990. Maya Survival in Ixil Country, Guatemala. *Cultural Survival Quarterly* 14, no. 4.

– 1992. *Conquest and Survival in Colonial Guatemala: A Historical Geography of the Cuchumatán Highlands, 1500–1821.* Revised edition. Montreal and Kingston: McGill-Queen's University Press.

- 1993. Epidemias y despoblación en Guatemala, 1519–1632. In *Historia general de Guatemala*. Vol. 2. Edited by Jorge Luján Muñoz. Guatemala City, Guatemala: Fundación para la Cultura y el Desarollo.
- 1995. *A Beauty That Hurts: Life and Death in Guatemala*. Toronto: Between the Lines.

Lovell, W. George, and Christopher H. Lutz. 1994. Conquest and Population: Maya Demography in Historical Perspective. *Latin American Research Review* 29, no. 2.

Lovell, W. George, and William R. Swezey. 1990. Indian Migration and Community Formation: An Analysis of *Congregación* in Colonial Guatemala. In *Migration in Colonial Spanish America*. Edited by David J. Robinson. Cambridge: Cambridge University Press.

Luján Muñoz, Jorge. 1988. *Agricultura, mercado y sociedad en el Corregimiento del Valle de Guatemala, 1670–80*. Guatemala City, Guatemala: Editorial Universitaria.
- 1993. Balance. In *Historia general de Guatemala*, Vol. 2. Edited by Jorge Luján Muñoz. Guatemala: Fundación para la Cultura y el Desarollo.
- 1994. Balance. In *Historia general de Guatemala*, Vol. 3. Edited by Jorge Luján Muñoz. Guatemala City, Guatemala: Fundación para la Cultura y el Desarollo.

Lungo, Mario, and Manuel Angel Castillo. 1996. *Estudio "Acciones para la integración social de Centroamérica." Componente Migraciones*. Guatemala: Consejo de Integración Social Centroamericano-Fondo de las Naciones Unidas para la Infancia (UNICEF).

Lutz, Christopher H. 1994. *Santiago de Guatemala, 1541–1773: City, Caste, and the Colonial Experience*. Norman, OK, and London: University of Oklahoma Press.

Lutz, Christopher H., and W. George Lovell. 1990. Core and Periphery in Colonial Guatemala. *Guatemalan Indians and the State, 1540 to 1988*. Edited by Carol A. Smith. Austin, TX: University of Texas Press.

Lykes, M.B. 1993. Human Rights and Mental Health among Latin American Women in Situations of State Sponsored Violence. *Psychology of Women Quarterly* 17, no. 4.

Macdonald, Laura. 1991. Supporting Civil Society: Nongovernmental Assistance to Costa Rica and Nicaragua. PHD diss., York University.
- 1995. A Mixed Blessing. The NGO Boom in Latin America. *NACLA Report on the Americas* 28, no. 5.

MacFarlane, Neil S., and Thomas G. Weiss. 1994. The United Nations, Regional Organisations and Human Security: Building Theory in Central America. *Third World Quarterly* 15, no. 2.

MacLeod, Murdo J. 1973. *Spanish Central America: A Socioeconomic History, 1520–1720*. Berkeley, Los Angeles, and London: University of California Press.

Magnusson, Warren. 1994. Dissidence and Insurgency: Municipal Foreign Policy in the 1980s. In *Artful Practices*. Edited by Henri Lustiger-Thaler and Daniel Salée. Montreal: Black Rose.

Mama Maquín. 1994. *De refugiadas a retornadas: Memorial de experiencias organizativas de las mujeres refugiadas en Chiapas*. Mexico City, Mexico: Mama Maquín and CIAM.

Manz, Beatriz. 1988a. *Refugees of a Hidden War: The Aftermath of Counter-insurgency in Guatemala*. Albany, NY: State University of New York Press.

– 1988b. *Repatriation and Reintegration: An Arduous Process in Guatemala*. Washington, DC: Centre for Immigration Policy and Refugee Assistance (CIPRA), Georgetown University.

– 1994. Exodus, Resistance, and Readjustments in the Aftermath of Massacres. Epilogue to Ricardo Falla, *Massacres in the Jungle: Ixcán, Guatemala, 1975–1982*. Boulder, CO, San Francisco, and Oxford: Westview.

Massey, Douglas S., Joaquin Arango, Grame Hugo, Ali Kouaci, Adela Pellegrino, and J. Edward Taylor. 1994. An Evaluation of International Migration Theory: The North American Case. *Population and Development Review* 20, no. 4.

McCarthy, Thomas A. 1978. *The Critical Theory of Jürgen Habermas*. Cambridge, MA: MIT Press.

McCleary, Rachel. 1996. Guatemala: Expectations for Peace. *Current History* 95, no. 598.

McClintock, Anne. 1991. "No Longer in a Future Heaven": Women and Nationalism in South Africa. *Transition*, no. 51.

– 1993. Gender, Nationalism and the Family. *Feminist Review*, no. 44.

McCreery, David J. 1994. *Rural Guatemala, 1760–1940*. Stanford: Stanford University Press.

McKean Parmenter, Barbara. 1994. *Giving Voice to Stones: Place and Identity in Palestinian Literature*. Austin, TX: University of Texas Press.

Menchú, Rigoberta. 1984. *I, Rigoberta Menchú, An Indian Woman in Guatemala*. London and New York: Verso.

– 1993. Introduction to *Guatemalan Women Speak*, by Margaret Hooks. Washington, DC: EPICA.

– 1996. Interview with Rigoberta Menchú Tum. *NACLA Report on the Americas*, 29, no. 6.

Michel, James H. 1996. *Development Co-operation: Efforts and Policies of the Members of the Development Assistance Committee. DAC 1995 Report*. Paris: Organisation for Economic Cooperation and Development (OECD).

Millan Valenzuela, René. De la difícil relación entre estado y sociedad. *Perfiles Latinoamericanos* 4, no. 4. FLACSO-Mexico.

Miller, Francesca. 1991. *Latin American Women and the Search for Social Justice*. Hanover, NH, and London: University Press of New England.

Miller, Robert, ed. 1992. *Aid as Peacemaker.* Ottawa: Carleton University Press.
Millet, Richard L. 1995. An End to Militarism? Democracy and the Armed Forces in Central America. *Current History* 94, no. 589.
MINUGUA (Misión de las Naciones Unidas para Guatemala). 1995. *Third Report of the Director of the United Nations Mission for the Verification of Human Rights and of Compliance with the Commitments of the Comprehensive Agreement on Human Rights.* A/50/482, 12 October.
– 1996. *Cuarto informe del Director de la Misión de las Naciones Unidas de Verificación de Derechos Humanos y del Cumplimiento de los Compromisos del Acuerdo Global sobre Derechos Humanos en Guatemala.* A/50/878. 24 March.
Mohanty, Chandra Talpade. 1991. Cartographies of Struggle: Third World Women and the Politics of Feminism. In *Third World Women and the Politics of Feminism.* Edited by Chandra T. Mohanty, et al. Bloomington, IN, and Indianapolis: Indiana University Press.
– 1997. Women Workers and Capitalist Scripts: Ideologies of Domination, Common Interests, and the Politics of Solidarity. *Feminist Geneologies, Colonial Legacies, Democratic Futures.* Edited by Jaqui Alexander and Chandra Talpade Mohanty. London and New York: Routledge.
Mohanty, Chandra Talpade, et al., eds. 1991. *Third World Women and the Politics of Feminism.* Bloomington, IN, and Indianapolis: Indiana University Press.
Molina Mejía, Raúl. 1995. Demilitarization of Guatemalan State and Society. Paper presented at the Nineteenth International Congress of the Latin American Studies Association, Washington, DC, September.
Molyneux, Maxine. 1985. Mobilization without Emancipation? Women's Interests, State and Revolution in Nicaragua. *New Social Movements and the State in Latin America.* Edited by David Slater. Amsterdam: CEDLA.
Monteforte Toledo, Mario. 1997. *La frontera móvil.* Mexico, DF: UNAM and Guatemala: Naciones Unidas & Ministerio de Cultura y Deportes.
Moore, Henrietta. 1988. *Feminism and Anthropology.* Cambridge: Polity Press.
Morrison, Toni. 1987. *Beloved: A Novel.* New York: Knopf.
Mosquera Aguilar, Antonio. 1990. *Los Trabajadores Guatemaltecos en México. Consideraciones sobre la corriente migratoria de trabajadores guatemaltecos estacionales a Chiapas, México.* Guatemala: Editorial Tiempos Modernos.
MUNI. 1986. *Informe de investigación sobre Servicios y Recursos de Asentamientos en estado de pobreza del Área Metropolitana, para Factibilidad de Atención del Programa de Alimentos por Trabajo.* Guatemala City: Municipalidad de Guatemala.
Nash, June. 1982. Implications of Technological Change for Household-Level and Rural Development. In *Technological Change and Rural Development.* Edited by P.M. Weil and J. Eltereich. Newark, DE: University of Delaware Press.
– 1995. The Reassertion of Indigenous Identity: Mayan Responses to State Intervention in Chiapas. *Latin American Research Review* 30, no. 3.

NCOORD. 1995a. Could It Be That This Is Really the "Year of the Returns"? *NCOORD Newsletter* 3, no. 3.
— 1995b. Two *U.S. Citizens Held Hostage in the Guatemala*. 29 June.
— 1995c. *Urgent Action: Hostages in the Zona Reyna*. 30 June.
Nelson, D. M. 1996. Maya Hackers and the Cyberspatialized Nation-State: Modernity, Ethnostalgia, and a Lizard Queen in Guatemala. *Cultural Anthropology* 1, no. 3.
Nicholson, Linda. 1990. *Feminism/Postmodernism*. New York and London: Routledge.
NISGUA. 1995. *Rapid Response Alert: Crisis in the Return to Zona Reyna*. 14 June.
Nolin Hanlon, Catherine L. 1995. *Flight, Exile and Return: Place and Identity among Guatemalan Maya Refugees*. MA thesis, Queen's University.
North, Liisa L. 1998. Reflections on Democratization and Demilitarization in Central America. *Studies in Political Economy*, no. 55.
North, Liisa, Yasmine Shamsie, and George Wright. 1995. *A Report on Reforming the Organization of American States to Support Democratization in the Hemisphere: A Canadian Perspective*. Toronto: Centre for Research on Latin America and the Caribbean (CERLAC), York University, with the Canadian Foundation for the Americas (FOCAL).
O'Dogherty, Laura. n.d.. *Centroamericanos en la Ciudad de México. Desarraigados y en el silencio*. Mexico City, Mexico: Academia Mexicana de Derechos Humanos.
Oficina de Derechos Humanos del Arzobispado de Guatemala. 1994. *Informe Anual 1993*. Guatemala City, Guatemala: Oficina de Derechos Humanos del Arzobispado de Guatemala.
Ordóñez M., César. 1990. Migraciones de trabajadores guatemaltecos y crecimiento económico en el Soconusco, Chiapas. *International Migration* 28, no. 1.
— 1993. *Eslabones de frontera. Un análisis sobre aspectos del desarrollo agrícola y migración de fuerza de trabajo en regiones fronterizas de Chiapas y Guatemala*. Tuxtla Gutiérrez, Mexico: Universidad Autónoma de Chiapas.
Ordoñez Yaquián, Tito. 1995. *Escenarios, esquemas de desarrollo y políticas macroeconómicas*. Second edition. Guatemala City, Guatemala: FLACSO.
PADEL. 1994. *Rapport Trimestriel*. Hull: CIDA. March.
Padilla, Luis Alberto. 1995. La negociación bajo el signo de las mediaciones interna y externa. *Estudios Internacionales* 6, no. 11.
Paige, Jeffery M. 1997. *Coffee and Power: Revolution and the Rise of Democracy in Central America*. Cambridge: Harvard University Press.
Palencia, Tania. 1994. *Proyecto de Apoyo a la Democracia y a los Derechos de la Persona en Guatemala*. Guatemala City, Guatemala: CECI.
Passerini, Luisa. 1992. *Memory and Totalitarianism: International Yearbook of Oral History and Life Stories*. Oxford: Oxford University Press.
Patai, Daphne. 1988. *Brazilian Women Speak: Contemporary Life Histories*. New Brunswick, NJ: Rutgers University Press.

Pensabenne, Gloria. 1997. Situación actual de las políticas gubernamentales en relación a las migraciones. In *El impacto de las migraciones de guatemaltecos al exterior, reflexiones y datos iniciales (Memoria de un Taller)*. Edited by CONGCOOP/CAM. Guatemala City, Guatemala: CONGCOOP/CAM.

Pérez Sainz, Juan Pablo, Manuela Camus, and Santiago Bastos. 1992. ... *todito, todito es trabajo. Indígenas y empleo en Ciudad de Guatemala*. Guatemala: FLACSO-Guatemala/Serviprensa Centroamericana.

Pettis, Michael. 1996. The Liquidity Trap: Latin America's Free Market Past. *Foreign Affairs* 75, no. 6.

Piel, Jean. 1989. *Sajcabajá: Muerte y resurrección de un pueblo de Guatemala 1500–1970*. Guatemala City, Guatemala: Seminario de Integración Social.

Pinto Soria, Julio César. 1989. Apuntes históricos sobre la estructura agraria y asentamiento en la Capitanía General de Guatemala. In *Estudios sobre la Guatemala Colonial*. Edited by Stephen W. Webre. South Woodstock, VT, and La Antigua, Guatemala: Plumsock Mesoamerican Studies and Centro de Investigaciones Regionales de Mesoamérica.

Poitevin, René. 1993. Guatemala: La crisis de la democracia. Dudas y esperanzas en los golpes de estado de 1993. *Debate*, no. 21. FLACSO-Guatemala

Popkin, Eric. 1997. Santa Eulalia, Huehuetenango: resultados de un estudio. In *El impacto de las migraciones de Guatemaltecos al exterior, reflexiones y datos iniciales (Memoria de un Taller)*. Edited by CONGCOOP/CAM. Guatemala City, Guatemala: CONGCOOP/CAM.

PHD (Procuraduría de los Derechos Humanos de Guatemala). 1996. *Los Derechos Humanos en Guatemala, 1995*. Guatemala: Procuraduría de los Derechos Humanos de Guatemala.

PRISMA (1995). *El Salvador: Dinámica de la degradación ambiental*. San Salvador: Programa Salvadoreño de Investigación sobre Desarrollo y Medio Ambiente.

Pronunciamiento de los Sectores Civiles. 1992. Guatemala. 11 June.

Quiñonez, Juan. 1996. Análisis del Acuerdo de Reasentamiento de las Poblaciones Desarraigadas por el Conflicto Armado Interno. *Debate*, no. 34. Guatemala: FLACSO.

Radcliffe, Sarah A., and Sallie Westwood. 1993. *"VIVA": Women and Popular Protest in Latin America*. New York and London: Routledge.

Reding, Andrew. 1997. *Democracy and Human Rights in Guatemala*. New York: World Policy Institute, New School for Social Research.

Refuge, Canada's Periodical on Refugees. 1994. Special Issue on Central America, 13, no. 10.

REMHI (Proyecto Interdiocesano de Recuperación de la Memoria Histórica de la Oficina de Derechos Humanos del Arzobispado de Guatemala). 4

Vols. 1998. *Nunca Más.* Guatemala: Oficina de Derechos Humanos del Arzobispado de Guatemala.

Rivera Cusicanqui, Silvia. 1986. *Oprimidos pero no vencidos: Luchas del campesinado Aymara y Quechua de Bolivia, 1900–1980.* Geneva: UNRISD.

Roberts, Lisa. 1998. Women Struggle for Voice and Vote. *Proyecto A*, no. 3. July.

Rodríguez, Antonieta. 1997. Chapas, Nueva Santa Rosa. In *El impacto de las migraciones de Guatemaltecos al exterior, reflexiones y datos iniciales (Memoria de un Taller).* Edited by CONGCOOP/CAM. Guatemala City, Guatemala: CONGCOOP/CAM.

Rojas Bolaños, Y. 1995. La gobernabilidad: Su validez como categoría analítica. In *Gobernabilidad y Democracia en Centroamérica.* Vol. 2. Guatemala City, Guatemala: FLACSO.

Rushdie, Salman. 1991. *Imaginary Homelands: Essays and Criticisms 1981–1991.* London: Granta Books.

Ruthrauff, John. 1996. *A Case Study: Influencing Consultative Group Meetings of the World Bank. Guatemala.* Silver Spring, MD: Center for Democratic Education.

Said, Edward. 1984. The Mind of Winter: Reflections on Life in Exile. *Harpers* 269, no. 1612, September.

Salvadó, Luis Raúl. 1988. *The Other Refugees: A Study of Nonrecognized Guatemalan Refugees in Chiapas, Mexico.* Washington, DC: Hemispheric Migration Project, Center for Inmigration Policy and Refugee Assistance, Georgetown University.

Samper, Mario. 1993. Café, trabajo y sociedad en Centroamérica, 1870–1930. *Las repúblicas agroexportadoras, 1870–1945. Historia general de Centroamérica*, Vol. 4. Edited by Víctor Hugo Acuña Ortega. San José, Costa Rica: FLACSO.

Sandoval Villeda, Leopoldo. 1997. Tenencia de la tierra, conflictos agrarios y acuerdos de paz. *Diálogo.* Electronic Bulletin, 8 August. FLACSO-Guatemala.

Schild, Veronica. 1991. Recasting "Popular" Movements: Gender and Political Learning in the Neighbourhood Organizations in Chile. Paper presented at CEDLA/CERLAC Joint Workshop. Amsterdam: CEDLA.

Schirmer, Jennifer. 1993. Seeking Truth and the Gendering of Consciousness. In *"VIVA": Women and Popular Protest in Latin America.* Edited by Sarah Radcliffe and Sallie Westwood. New York and London: Routledge.

Schlesinger, Stephen, and Stephen Kinzer. 1982. *Bitter Fruit: The Untold Story of the American Coup in Guatemala.* Garden City, NY: Doubleday

Schmid, Lester James. 1967. The Role of Migratory Labor in the Economic Development of Guatemala. PHD diss., University of Wisconsin.

Schwartz, Norman. 1990. *Forest Society: A Social History of Petén, Guatemala.* Philadelphia, PA: University of Pennsylvania Press.

Secretariado de la ONU. 1996. Comunicado del portavoz del Secratario General sobre el proceso de paz en Guatemala. New York. 6 May.

Seitz, Barbara J. 1992. From Home to Street: Women and Revolution in Nicaragua. In *Women Transforming Politics: Worldwide Strategies for Empowerment.* Edited by Jill M. Bystydzienski. Bloomington, IN, and Indianapolis: Indiana University Press.

SEGEPLAN/GTZ (Secretaría General del Consejo Nacional de Planificación Económica, Misión Técnica Alemana). 1995. *Lineamientos para una estrategia de ordenamiento territorial.* Guatemala: SEGEPLAN, Dirección de Planificación Regional-GTZ, Programa Las Verapaces.

SEGEPLAN-UNICEF. 1993. *Caracterización de las Areas Precarias en la Ciudad de Guatemala.* Guatemala City, Guatemala: Criterio, consultores en urbanismo, planificación y arquitectura.

Sherman, William L. 1979. *Forced Native Labor in Sixteenth-Century Central America.* Lincoln, NE, and London: University of Nebraska Press.

Schöultz, Lars. 1988. Guatemala: Social Change and Political Conflict. In *Trouble in Our Backyard: Central America and the United States in the Eighties.* Edited by Martin Diskin. New York: Pantheon.

Siebert, Renate. 1996. Women and the Mafia: Power of Silence and Memory. In *International Yearbook of Oral History and Life Stories.* Vol. 6 of *Gender and Memory.* Edited by Selma Leydesdorff, Luisa Passerini, and Paul Thompson. Oxford: Oxford University Press.

Simmons, Alan. 1995. *Economic Globalization and Immigration Policy: Canada Compared to Europe.* Paper presented at conference, Organizing Diversity: Migration Policy and Practice, Canada and Europe, at Bergen Dal, Netherlands, 8–12 November.

– 1997a. Economic Integration and Designer Immigrants: Canadian Policy in the 1990s. In *Transnational Realities and Nation States: Trends in International Migration and Immigration Policy in the Americas.* Edited by Max Castro. Miami, FL: North-South Center Press, University of Miami.

– 1997b. International Migration and the Transformation of the Americas: Impacts on Migrant Sending Countries in the Late 20th Century. Paper presented at the Twenty-third General Conference of the International Union for the Scientific Study of Population. Beijing. October.

– ed 1996. *International Migration, Refugee Flows and Human Rights in North America: The Impact of Free Trade and Restructuring.* Staten Island, NY: Center for Migration Studies.

Sistema de las Naciones Unidas en Guatemala. 1998. *Guatemala: Los contrastes del desarrollo humano.* Guatemala City, Guatemala: Naciones Unidas.

Smith, Carol A. 1978. Beyond Dependency Theory: National and Regional Patterns of Underdevelopment in Guatemala. *American Ethnologist* 5, no. 3.

- 1984. Local History in Global Context: Social and Economic Transitions in Western Guatemala. *Comparative Studies in Society and History* 26, no. 2.
- ed. 1990. *Guatemalan Indians and the State, 1540 to 1988.* Austin, TX: University of Texas Press.

Smith-Ayala, Emily. 1991. *The Grandaughters of Ixmucane: Guatemalan Women Speak.* Toronto: Women's Press.

Smith, Sidonie. 1990. Constructing Truths in Lying Mouths: Truthtelling in Women's Autobiography. *Studies in the Literary Imagination* no 23.

Solarcs, Jorge, ed. 1993. *Estado y nación: Las demandas de los grupos étnicos en Guatemala.* Guatemala: FLACSO.

Sollis, Peter. 1996a. Binding the Wounds: Multilateral Humanitarianism, Peace and Democracy in Central America. Paper presented at conference, Peacemaking and Democratization in the Hemisphere: Multilateral Approaches, the North-South Center, University of Miami, April.
- 1996b. Partners in Development? The state, NGOs, and the UN in Central America. In *NGOs, the UN and Global Governance.* Edited by Thomas G. Weiss and Leon Gordenker. Boulder, CO, and London: Lynne Rienner Publishers.

SOCOVEDI. n.d. . *Rapport d'interprétation du mandat.* Mimeographed.

Special Document. 1992. *Central America Report* 19, no 41.

Spivak, Gayatri Chakravorty. 1992. Women in Difference: Mahasweta Devi's "Douloti the Bountiful." In *Nationalisms and Sexualities.* Edited by Andrew Parker et al . New York and London: Routledge.

Stepputat, Finn. 1994. The Imagined Return Community of Guatemalan Refugees. *Refuge. Canada's Periodical on Refugees* 13, no. 10.
- 1997. Post-War Guatemala: Encounters at the Frontier of the Modern State. *Livelihood, Identity and Instability: Papers from an International Workshop.*

Stewart, Katheleen. 1996. *A Place on the Side of the Road.* Princeton, NJ: Princeton University Press.

Stoll, David. 1990. "The Land No Longer Gives": Land Reform in Nebaj, Guatemala. *Cultural Survival Quarterly* 14, no. 4.
- 1993. *Between Two Armies in the Ixil Towns of Guatemala.* New York: Columbia University Press.
- 1994. Guatemala: Solidarity Activists Head for Trouble. Unpublished paper.

Stupps, P.W., and R.E. Bilsborrow. 1989. The Effects of Population Growth on Agriculture in Guatemala. Paper presented at Annual Meeting of the Population Association of America, Baltimore. 29 March–1 April.

Tax, Sol. 1963. *Penny Capitalism: A Guatemalan Indian Economy.* Chicago: University of Chicago Press.

Taylor, Clark. 1998. *Return of Guatemala's Refugees: Reweaving the Torn.* Philadelphia, PA: Temple University Press.

Thrupp, Lori Ann. 1994. New Harvest, Old Problems: Feeding the Global Supermarket. *NACLA Report on the Americas* 28, no. 3.

Tololyan, Khachig. 1991. The Nation-State and Its Others. *Diaspora* 1, no. 1.

Trudeau, Robert H. 1993. *Guatemalan Politics: The Popular Struggle for Democracy.* Boulder, CO, and London: Lynne Rienner Publishers.

Tsing, Anna Lowenhaupt. 1993. *In the Realm of the Diamond Queen.* Princeton, NJ: Princeton University Press.

Tuan, Yi-Fu. 1980. Rootedness versus Sense of Place. *Landscape* 24, no. 1.

United Nations. 1994. *Report of the International Conference on Population and Development.* Document A/Conf. 171/13. New York: United Nations.

UNDP (United Nations Development Program). 1991. *Human Development Report 1991.* New York and Oxford: Oxford University Press.

– 1994. *Human Development Report 1994.* New York and Oxford: Oxford University Press.

– 1996. *Human Development Report 1996.* New York and Oxford: Oxford University Press.

– 1997. *Human Development Report 1997.* New York and Oxford: Oxford University Press.

UN-ECLAC (United Nations Economic Commission for Latin America and the Caribbean), Mexico Office. 1984. The Crisis in Central America: Its Origins, Scope and Consequences. *CEPAL Review,* no. 22.

UNHCR (United Nations High Commission on Refugees). 1984a. *Refugees Magazine,* no. 10, October.

– 1984b. *Refugees Magazine,* no. 3, March.

– 1985. Promoting Voluntary Repatriation. *Refugees Magazine,* no. 21, September.

– 1986. *Refugees Magazine,* no. 31, July.

– 1988. Voluntary Repatriation. *Refugees Magazine,* no. 54, June.

– 1993a. *Acuerdo Entre la CEAR, CCPP y ACNUR.* 1993.

– 1993b. *Voluntary Repatriation of Guatemalans from Mexico.*

– 1993c. *The State of the World's Refugees: The Challenge of Protection.* London: Penguin Books.

– 1993d. Going Home: Voluntary Repatriation. In *The State of the World's Refugees: The Challenge of Protection.* London: Penguin Books.

– 1996. Assistance to Guatemala in the Field of Human Rights. Session 52. E/CN.4/1996/L.81. April.

United Nations Office of Public Information. 1978. *The United Nations and Human Rights.* New York: United Nations.

UNRISD (United Nations Research Institute for Social Development). 1987. *Social and Cultural Conditions and Prospects of Guatemalan Refugees in Mexico.* New York: UNRISD.

Urban, Greg, and Joel Sherzer, eds. 1991. *Nation-States and Indians in Latin America.* Austin, TX: University of Texas Press.

URNG (Unidad Revolucionaria Nacional Guatemalteca), General Command. 1994. *The Guatemala of the Future Will be a Pluricultural, Multilingual Nation, with National Unity Declaration by the URNG General Command.* Guatemala: Unidad Revolucionaria Nacional Guatemalteca (URNG), General Command.

USAID. 1982. *Land and Labour in Guatemala: An Assessment.* Washington, DC: United States Agency for International Development.

U.S. Committee for Refugees. 1995. *1995–World Refugee Survey.* Washington, DC: Immigration and Refugee Services of America.

Velásquez Carrera, Eduardo Antonio. 1989. *Desenvolvimiento capitalista, crescimento uirbano e urbanizaçao na Guatemala, 1940–1984.* Sao Paulo: Faculdade de Economia e Administraçao, Universidade de Sao Paulo.

– 1993. Algunos Aspectos de la Discusión Sobre la Periodización Histórica del Desarrollo Económico-Social y Urbano-Regional de Guatemala. In *Economía Urbana y Periodización Histórica de Guatemala. Dos Estudios.* Edited by Eduardo Antonio Velasquez Carrera and Oscar Guillermo Pelaez Almengor. Guatemala City, Guatemala: Universidad de San Carlos de Guatemala, Centro de Estudios Urbanos y Regionales.

Vertiente Norte. 1994. The Return to Guatemala. International Bulletin of the Permanent Commissions of Guatemalan Refugees in Mexico. October–November.

Vilas, Carlos M. 1996a. Prospects for Democratisation in a Post-Revolutionary Setting: Central America. *Jounal of Latin American Studies* 28, no. 2.

– 1996b. Neoliberal Social Policy: Managing Poverty (Somehow). *NACLA Report on the Americas* 29, no. 6.

Vlach, Norita. 1992. *The Quetzal in Flight: Guatemalan Refugee Families in the United States.* Westport, CT: Praeger Publishers.

Warren, Kay B. 1998. Indigenous Movements as a Challenge to the Unified Social Movements Paradigm for Guatemala. In *Cultures of Politics, Politics of Cultures: Re-visioning Latin American Social Movements.* Edited by Sonia E. Alvarez, Evelina Dagnino, and Arturo Escobar. Boulder, CO: Westview Press.

Warren, Robert. 1993. *Estimates of the Resident Illegal Alien Population: October 1992.* Washington, DC: Immigration and Naturalization Service (INS). August.

Watanabe, John M. 1984. "We Who Are Here": The Cultural Conventions of Ethnic Identity in a Guatemalan Indian Village, 1937–1980. PHD diss., Harvard University.

– 1995. Unimagining the Maya: Anthropologists, Others, and the Inescapable Hubris of Authorship. *Bulletin of Latin American Research* 14, no. 1.

Watts, Michael. 1988. Struggles Over Land, Struggles Over Meaning: Some Thoughts on Naming, Peasant Resistance and the Politics of Place. In *A*

Ground for Common Search. Edited by R. Golledge, H. Couclelis, and P. Gould. Goleta, CA: Santa Barbara Geographical Press.

Weeks, John. 1985. *The Economies of Central America.* New York: Holmes and Meier.

Weffort, Francisco. 1994. *¿Cual Democracia?* San José, Costa Rica: FLACSO.

Weiss Fagen, Patricia. 1993. Peace in Central America: Transition for the Uprooted. *World Refugee Survey.* Washington, DC: U.S. Committee for Refugees.

Whetten, Nathan L. 1961. *Guatemala: The Land and the People.* New Haven, CT: Yale University Press.

Wilkinson, Daniel. 1995–96. "Democracy" Comes to Guatemala. *World Policy Journal* 12, no. 4.

Williams, Robert G. 1994. *States and Social Evolution: Coffee and the Rise of National Governments in Central America.* Chapel Hill, NC, and London: University of North Carolina Press.

Wilson, Richard. 1993. Anchored Communities: Identity and History of the Maya-Q'eqchi. *Man* 28, no.1.

Wing, H.E. 1988. *USAID/Guatemala Agriculture Sector Development Strategy, 1988–1992.* Washington, DC: Office of Rural Development, report no. 25, U.S. Agency for International Development.

WOLA (Washington Office on Latin America). 1989. *Uncertain Return: Refugees and Reconciliation in Guatemala.* Washington, DC: WOLA.

– 1996. Funding for MINUGUA and MICIVIH Human Rights Missions. Washington, DC: WOLA. Mimeographed.

Woodward, Ralph L. Jr. 1993. *Rafael Carrera and the Emergence of the Republic of Guatemala, 1821–1871.* Athens, GA, and London: University of Georgia Press.

World Bank. 1995. Closing statement by Mr Edilberto L. Segura, Chairman. Guatemala Informal Donors Meeting. Paris: World Bank, 21 June.

Wright, Ronald. 1993a. "The Death List People." In *Home and Away.* Toronto: Alfred A. Knopf.

– 1993b. *Stolen Continents: The "New World" through Indian Eyes.* Toronto: Penguin Books.

Yaschine Arroyo, Iliana. 1995. *Un hecho sin precedentes: Las negociaciones y el acuerdo para el retorno entre el gobierno de Guatemala y los refugiados guatemaltecos en Mexico.* Thesis, Centro de Estudios Internacionales, El Colegio de Mexico.

Zetter, Roger. 1988. Refugees and Refugee Studies–A Label and an Agenda. *Journal of Refugee Studies* 1, no. 1.

Zolberg, Aristide R., Astri Suhrke, and Sergio Aguayo. 1989. *Escape from Violence.* New York: Oxford University Press.

Zurayk, Huda, Nabil Younis, and Hind Khattab. 1994. Rethinking Family Planning Policy in the Light of Reproductive Health Research. *International Social Science Journal* 46 (September).

Contributors

STEPHEN BARANYI is a senior program officer at the Internatoinal Development Research Centre (IDRC). He has worked for the Department of Foreign Affairs and International Trade, the Canadian International Development Agency, and with several European NGOs. Baranyi has published articles and monographs on the role of NGOs, the United Nations, the OAS, the European Union, and the Canadian government in the promotion of human rights and peace.

CATHY BLACKLOCK is assistant professor of political science at Huron College, University of Western Ontario, and a research associate of the Centre for Research on Latin America and the Caribbean (CERLAC) at York University. She recently co-edited the spring 1998 issue of *Social Politics*, titled "Citizenship: Latin American Perspectives," and co-authored an article on human rights for the same issue. She is engaged in research on women's organizations, human rights and democratization in Latin America.

MANUEL ANGEL CASTILLO is a professor and researcher at the Centro de Estudios Demográficos y de Desarrollo Urbano at El Colegio de México, Mexico City, where he also completed his MA in 1988. He has published numerous works on migration, development, and peace issues in Guatemala and Central America, on migration policies in receiving countries, and on international migration in general. Castillo has also taught in several Mexican and

Guatemalan academic institutions; has worked as a consultant for Mexican government agencies and international organizations; and is a member of several nongovernmental organizations, including Sin Fronteras.

ALISON CROSBY is a doctoral candidate in the Department of Sociology at York University. She is currently engaged in field work in Guatemala for her doctoral dissertation on women's organizing across boundaries in the post-peace accord nation, funded by a Social Sciences and Humanities Research Council of Canada (SSHRCC) Doctoral Fellowship. Before completing her MA in Environmental Studies in 1995, also at York University, she worked with refugee and women's organizations in Mexico and El Salvador during 1992–93. Crosby is a graduate fellow of the Centre for Research on Latin America and the Caribbean (CERLAC) at York University and a member of the Women in Conflict Zones Network, an international group of feminist academics and activists working in war-torn societies.

BRIAN EGAN is a self-employed researcher and writer, based in Victoria, BC, and a board member of the Victoria International Development Education Association (VIDEA). He completed his MA in environmental studies at York University in 1995, where he focused on the political ecology of deforestation and conservation in northern Guatemala. Egan has worked with a variety of environmental and development organizations, including Project Accompaniment, a Canadian NGO that provides accompaniment to Guatemalan refugees returning from Mexico.

MARCO FONSECA is a doctoral candidate in the graduate program in social and political thought at York University. He has been a lecturer in Latin American Studies and Spanish at Middlesex University in London, England (1996–98), and more recently a lecturer in international political economy at Wilfred Laurier University (1999). He has published articles on the transformation of the public sphere and the peace process in Guatemala. Fonseca also served as a research consultant for the Guatemalan segment of the documentary *Voices of Change*, which premiered at the Fourth UN Conference on Women in China in 1995 and at the Toronto International Film Festival in the same year.

GISELA GELLERT has been a researcher at the Latin American Faculty of Social Sciences in Guatemala (FLACSO-Guatemala) and the coordinator of its area in urban studies since 1992. She received her advanced degree in human geography from the Martin Luther University in Halle/Wittenberg, Germany. Since 1978, Gellert has been involved in a broad range of research and teaching activities in Guatemala and has published widely on various themes in urban geography, population, environment, sustainable development, the prevention and mitigation of disasters, and, most recently, migration.

JIM GRONAU was contracted by Canadian University Services Overseas (CUSO) in 1993 to work in Guatemala with the coordinator of Nongovernmental Organizations and Cooperatives (CONGCOOP), an umbrella organization with twenty-nine institutional members. He is currently the coordinator of the Communications Program of the CONGCOOP – which produces two publications, *Reunion* (available electronically at http:/www.rds.org.gt/congcoop, in English) and *Reencuentro* (available at the same site and also in printed format, in Spanish); he is also a regular contributor to *Americas Update*, a Canadian quarterly. Gronau completed his MA in the graduate program in social and political thought at York University in 1990.

BARRY LEVITT is a PHD candidate in political science at the University of North Carolina at Chapel Hill. He received his MA in political science from York University in 1995. In 1994 he was an observer of the Mexican elections, and in 1995 he volunteered for Project Accompaniment to observe refugee returns in Mexico and Guatemala. Levitt has written on environmental and land-tenure issues in Guatemala and is currently conducting research on political parties in Peru.

W. GEORGE LOVELL is professor of geography at Queen's University, Kingston, Ontario. A frequent visitor to Guatemala over the past twenty-five years, he has published widely on the country's history and culture, especially the role played by Maya peoples in shaping the Guatemalan past. Among his books are *Conquest and Survival in Colonial Guatemala* (1992) and *A Beauty That Hurts: Life and Death in Guatemala* (1995).

CATHERINE NOLIN HANLON is a doctoral candidate in the Department of Geography at Queen's University, Kingston, Ontario, where she received her MA in 1995. Her MA research focused on the Guatemalan refugee return, a topic on which she co-authored an article with W. George Lovell. She is currently engaged in PHD dissertation field work in Canada on Guatemala. "Passage Landscapes: The Maya Diaspora and the Struggle of an Emergent Guatemalan Community in Toronto, Canada," explores the interconnected issues of community, place, identity, transnational migration, and remittance commitment. Nolin Hanlon is also a member of the Project Accompaniment network in Canada.

LIISA L. NORTH is a professor in the Department of Political Science at York University and a fellow of York's Centre for Research on Latin America and the Caribbean (CERLAC). She is the author of works on the origin of El Salvador's civil war and on Canadian foreign policy with regard to the Central American conflicts and peace processes. She has published monographs and articles on democratization, party politics, civil-military relations, development policies, and grass-roots-based economic enterprises in Latin America and on UN peace promotion and monitoring efforts in Central America.

VIVIANA PATRONI is assistant professor of political science at Wilfrid Laurier University and a fellow of the Centre for Research on Latin America and the Caribbean (CERLAC) at York University. She completed her doctoral degree in the graduate program in social and political thought at York University in 1994. Patroni participated as an international observer in the Mexican elections of 1997 and is currently engaged in research on labour and private sector issues in Mexico and Argentina.

RENÉ POITEVIN is director of the Guatemala branch of the Latin American Faculty of Social Sciences (FLACSO-Guatemala). He received his doctoral degree in political sociology from the René Descartes University and the Ecole des Hautes Etudes en Ciences Sociales in Paris, France, in 1974. He has published widely on many aspects of Guatemalan politics, society, and development processes.

ALAN B. SIMMONS is associate professor of sociology and a fellow of the Centre for Research on Latin America and the Caribbean (CERLAC) at York University. He is author of numerous publications on migration and development issues, refugee movements, and international migration in Latin America and the Caribbean, and on Canadian immigration policy. His most recent book is an edited volume, *International Migration, Refugee Flows and Human Rights in North America: The Impact of Free Trade and Restructuring* (1996).

M. GABRIELA TORRES is working on her doctoral degree in Anthropology at York University. She completed her MA in anthropology at the Latin American Faculty of Social Sciences in Quito, Ecuador (FLACSO-Ecuador). As a community development worker in Vancouver, BC, she attended to the needs of Latin American youth in their process of integration into Canadian society.

GONZALO DE VILLA, before becoming president of the Rafael Landívar University in Guatemala, was dean of political and social sciences and a member of the Directive Council at the same University. He completed his MA in the graduate program in social and political thought at York University in 1988. De Villa was founding member, researcher, and president of the governing board of the Association for the Advancement of Social Sciences in Guatemala (AVANCSO), where he was also involved in variety of research projects on internal migration patterns in Guatemala.